SOCIAL WELFARE IN CANADA
Understanding Income Security

Education is the most powerful weapon which you can use to change the world.

— Nelson Mandela

SOCIAL WELFARE IN CANADA

Understanding Income Security

STEVEN HICK

Carleton University

THOMPSON EDUCATIONAL PUBLISHING, INC.
Toronto

Information on how to obtain copies of this book is available at:

Website:	www.thompsonbooks.com
E-mail:	publisher@thompsonbooks.com
Telephone:	(416) 766-2763
Fax:	(416) 766-0398

National Library of Canada Cataloguing in Publication

Hick, Steven F.
    Social welfare in Canada : understanding income security / Steven F. Hick.
Includes bibliographical references and index.

ISBN 1-55077-139-6

1. Social security—Canada—Textbooks. 2. Income maintenance programs—Canada—Textbooks. I. Title.

HV105.H5 2004   362.5'82'0971   C2004-900712-2

Copy Editing: Elizabeth Phinney
Proofreading: Colborne Communications
Photo Research: Jane Affleck
Cover Design: Elan Designs

Every reasonable effort has been made to acquire permission for copyrighted materials used in this book and to acknowledge such permissions accurately. Any errors or omissions called to the publisher's attention will be corrected in future printings.

We acknowledge the support of the Government of Canada through the Book Publishing Industry Development Program for our publishing activities. We also acknowledge the support of the Government of Ontario through the Ontario Media Development Corporation Book Initiative.

Printed in Canada.
1 2 3 4 5   08 07 06 05 04

Contents

Acknowledgments

Like the earlier volume *Social Work in Canada: An Introduction*, this book owes a debt of gratitude to Allan Moscovitch for his early guidance. A special thanks is owed to the graduate students that provided feedback and ideas, including Cheryl Parsons, Amy McGee, Kate Belcher, Teresa Raposo, Monica Reinvall, Carole Bourque and Erin Brown. They improved the book tremendously. Monica and Amy, in particular, were instrumental in helping me liven up the more detailed sections.

The real work for this book takes place in the classroom as students engage in dialogue, become energized about a social issue or ask astute questions. I am always encouraged and motivated by my students to write textbooks. Their zest for learning, insightful questions and promise for the future inspire me to spend hours and hours tapping away at my computer keyboard. A sincere thank you to my classes of 2002/03 and 2003/04 for using a draft version of this book as their text, and providing invaluable advice through questions and discussion. I cannot count the number of times that a student asked for clarification on some section of the book, which would spur me to dash home and write a paragraph. Finally, I would like to thank my Human Rights Practice and Civil Society class of 2003. I was reading their papers while editing this book, and several ideas and margin quotes were derived from their work.

I am grateful for the comments from the three anonymous reviewers that took the time to wade through a very early draft of this book. Their comments gave me direction and pointed out several areas that needed elaboration. My family – Vaida, my partner, Justin, my son, and Kristina, my daughter – provided numerous ideas that contributed directly to my writing. Finally, my whitewater kayaking friends that I met through the Ottawa paddling club Coureurs de Bois need to be recognized for their input. Conversations while floating down rivers provided me with invaluable insight into how "ordinary Canadians" will identify with (or not) and grasp my ideas.

Forestry workers in the western Newfoundland community of Deer Lake protest the massive cuts to the Unemployment Insurance programs in front of the Revenue Canada Taxation Centre in St. John's, 1996 (CP PHOTO/*St. John's Evening Telegram*/Joe Gibbons).

Preface

This books fills a need for a text that provides a general idea of the multiplicity of perspectives on social welfare while at the same time giving a fairly detailed overview of the many programs that exist. It is intended for students who are relatively new to social policy analysis, social work and other human service disciplines who need a broad survey of the field. It is also appropriate for students in public administration, social work, economics, political science or sociology who may not be familiar with the various welfare programs.

The content of the book is divided into two parts. The first part (Chapters 1-7) introduces the theory and approaches to social welfare. Chapter 1 introduces the basic concepts and sets the context. Chapter 2 surveys the origins and emergence of income security. Chapter 3 unravels the assortment of theories and approaches that underlie much of the discussion of Canadian income security. Chapters 4 to 7 each take a different angle in looking at the issues: Chapter 4 focuses on the labour market and employment; Chapter 5 examines the impacts of globalization on social welfare and the potential of human rights; Chapter 6 looks at women's issues in relation to welfare services; and Chapter 7 examines poverty and inequality. Both the beginner and the veteran social policy analyst or practitioner needs to understand the multiplicity of perspectives on these issues.

The remaining chapters (Chapters 8-11) present how specific income security programs are organized, how they operate and some of the debate around social welfare reform. Chapter 8 focuses on Employment Insurance and Workers' Compensation; Chapter 9, on Social Assistance or Welfare; Chapter 10, on families and children's benefits; and Chapter 11, on programs for the elderly and retired.

This book does not presume that there is one best theory or approach for analyzing social policy and income security programs. Indeed, there is no single unified theory that students can take away and apply to Canadian social policy and programs in every instance. This book challenges readers to look at the multiple perspectives and then to examine each and every policy and program in context and in detail before arriving at a recommended course of action.

Steven Hick
Carleton University

Seniors protest on Parliament Hill against the government's de-indexing of Old-Age Pensions, Ottawa, June 19, 1985. The current system may be strained over the next 35 years by the doubling of the percentage of persons aged 65 and over (CP PHOTO/Fred Chartrand).

1

Introducing Social Welfare

What This Book Is About

Social welfare is a defining feature of Canadian society. The social services and income security programs available to citizens, provided or funded by the various levels of government, affect nearly every Canadian at some point in his or her life. Indeed, in view of its scope and importance, it is perhaps a little surprising that few citizens are aware of the components of the system, the history of social welfare provision in Canada, or the current issues and concerns surrounding it.

Income security programs are at the centre of the welfare state in Canada. These programs do much more than protect the poor from destitution; income security programs are used by all sectors of society. Over the course of our lives, almost everyone benefits from Canada's income security system. Some people retire and draw retirement benefits, some become incapacitated and draw on income support benefits, while others may become unemployed and require Employment Insurance (EI). In short, income security programs provide social protection for all Canadians, if and when they need it.

"The untrammeled intensification of laissez-faire capitalism and the spread of market values into all areas of life, is endangering our open and democratic society."

— billionaire financier George Soros in "The Capitalist Threat," Atlantic Monthly, Volume 279, No. 2, February 1997.

Unfortunately, our "social safety net," as it has come to be called, has been seriously eroded in recent years. The causes are many and varied, but this has happened so quietly that some staunch defenders have termed this process a form of "social policy by stealth." All the more reason, then, for citizens to be aware of the history of social welfare in our country and the current threats that it faces.

This textbook examines the role of income security in our society and economy, and reviews the current state of affairs. It will enable you to become familiar with the income security concepts and issues in Canada today.

SOCIAL WELFARE: WHAT'S IN A DEFINITION?

The term "social welfare" has numerous usages, but we often see four basic themes:

1. Social welfare as a philosophical concept – an abstract set of principles to enable society to seek solutions to social problems.

2. Social welfare as a product – the legislated documents that prescribe how income security and social services are to be carried out.

3. Social welfare as a process – a series of changes that is never fully developed due to shifting contexts.

4. Social welfare as a framework for action – both a product and a process.

In fact, social welfare is all of these. Social welfare provides solutions to problems, but also pertains to the quality of life and social well-being. It is therefore intertwined with politics, economics and culture.

TWO COMPONENTS OF SOCIAL WELFARE

- Income security: financial or material assistance provided to increase the income or other resources of individuals and families.

- Social services: personal or community services provided to help individuals and families to improve their social well-being.

THE CANADIAN WELFARE SYSTEM

The **social welfare system** consists of a combination of income security programs and social services. Although it is not always easy to distinguish between an income security provision and a social service, there is a difference.

Income security provides monetary or other material benefits to supplement income or maintain minimum income levels (e.g., Employment Insurance, Social Assistance, Old Age Security and Workers' Compensation). Members of our society need a stable income to survive. If everyone could meet his or her income needs through wages from employment, investment income or inheritance, the need for income security programs would be drastically reduced or eliminated. Without income security programs, Canadians would be much more financially vulnerable.

Social services (personal or community services), on the other hand, help people improve their well-being by providing non-monetary aid to persons in need. Offered by social workers, services include probation, addiction treatment, youth drop-in centres, parent-child resource centres, child care facilities, child protection services, shelters for abused women and counselling. (The field of social services is addressed in a companion textbook entitled *Social Work in Canada: An Introduction.*)

Income security programs and social services are provided to citizens through social policies. Social policies are the overall rules and regulations, laws and other administrative directives that set the framework and objectives for state social welfare activity. The government and specific social programs develop the policies (e.g., the Canada/Quebec Pension Plan). Social programs are specific initiatives that implement and follow social welfare policies.

• The Welfare State

Taken together, the range of programs and services available to Canadian citizens is commonly referred to as the welfare state. The term came about after World War II when what was known as the "warfare" state was refocused on the daily welfare of people. A **welfare state** is a system in which the state protects the health and well-being of its citizens, especially those in social and financial need. The key functions of the welfare state are: (1) using state power to achieve desired goals (powers include government, bureaucracy, the judiciary and political parties); (2) altering the normal operation of the private marketplace and (3) using grants, taxes, pensions, social services and minimum-income programs such as welfare and social insurance.

The basic purpose of Canada's social welfare system is straightforward: to help people through difficult times until they can rebuild their lives. The system helps people face a variety of contingencies or difficulties, such as retirement, unemployment, loss of income, disability, illness, violence, homelessness, addiction, racism, warfare, death, separation, divorce, ageing of family members and responsibilities associated with additional children. These contingencies can be grouped into three interrelated categories: (1) contingencies that threaten economic survival, (2) contingencies that threaten the integrity of the person and (3) contingencies that affect the family.

In Canadian society, income from employment is by far the largest source of income for survival. To help individuals and families face contingencies that affect their income, the Canadian governments at various levels provide a wide range of income security programs, and these are the subject of this volume.

TAX EXPENDITURES AS SOCIAL WELFARE

Textbook treatments of income security in Canada often miss the tax expenditure side of the public system. The principal function of the tax system is to raise the revenues necessary to fund government expenditures. However, the tax system is also an instrument of policy that serves to advance a wide range of economic, social, environmental, cultural and other public policy objectives.

Tax expenditures are foregone tax revenues resulting from special exemptions, deductions, rate reductions, rebates, credits and deferrals that reduce the amount of tax that would otherwise be payable. Tax expenditures include deductions for pension and Registered Retirement Savings Plan (RRSP) contributions, credits for charitable donations and benefits for families with children. Tax expenditures are often designed to encourage certain kinds of activities, or to serve other objectives, such as providing assistance to lower-income or elderly Canadians. While this is not often thought of as income security, it can dramatically affect the income of Canadians. By not collecting taxes from those who have a taxable income, an individual's income is effectively increased.

The use of tax expenditures for income security purposes is increasing in Canada. The Canada Child Tax Benefit (CCTB) is an example of an income security program that uses the tax system to distribute income, rather than using an expenditure benefit system. The main benefits of this approach are: (1) the programs do not bring the stigma of collecting welfare benefits, as the money is redistributed anonymously; (2) eligibility is determined on the basis of income as reported on the income tax return, rather than through an intrusive needs test; (3) tax-based income-tested programs are less costly to administer, as they use an already existing administrative structure (the tax system) and do not require the hiring of social workers to implement a needs test; and (4) the programs have a low profile and therefore may be more secure and less likely to be cut for political reasons.

Tax expenditure-based income security programs do not only benefit low-income Canadians. The programs have an appeal for higher-income Canadians who appreciate the low profile and non-stigmatizing nature of this type of income security. For instance, it is estimated that the CCTB will provide $8.4 billion in benefits to low-income people in 2004. The RRSP program, with both RRSP deductions for contributions and non-taxation of RRSP investment income, provided $16 billion in benefits to higher-income Canadians in 2002.

HOW TO PRODUCE WELFARE

A variety of mechanisms can be used to address social welfare needs:

- Markets (purchased welfare)
- Families (reciprocity of kin)
- Voluntary associations (private solidarity)
- Governments (solidarity among citizens)

Welfare programs help people through difficult times (photo courtesy of Dick Hemingway).

ANALYZING SOCIAL WELFARE PROBLEMS

It is common to feel overwhelmed when confronted with the prospect of analyzing a social welfare problem. Many students see social problems as too complicated with no clear solutions, and related subjects, such as economics and sociology, can be somewhat abstract and perplexing. Social problems are indeed usually very complex, but a systematic analysis can provide extensive insights and lead to solutions.

For the purposes of this textbook, we will define a **social problem** as a situation that is incompatible with some standard or norm held by a significant number of people in society, who agree that action is needed to alter the situation. In many cases this standard is already expressed in human rights codes or social policy legislation. Armed with a basic knowledge of social issues and how society works, it is possible to analyze social problems and point to possible solutions.

Consider the social problem of homelessness. If you ask a group of Canadians to think of a list of all the factors that cause or contribute to homelessness, you would end up with a long and varied list. The factors that arise from the discussion can be categorized according to internal factors and external factors. Internal factors refer to aspects that are personal or internal to the individual. External factors exist in society, and are of a policy, systemic or structural nature.

Once the list is completed, the group could discuss how each factor plays out in the particular context, and discuss possible solutions. Certain solutions may be emphasized over others. Often, a group will emphasize solutions to the individual factors, as they are frequently easier to address. In relation to homelessness, for example, which is often associated with alcohol or drug adduction, individual counselling may seem like a practical solution, since a wholesale change in the federal and provincial government's policy in relation to providing low-cost housing may seem daunting. Certainly, a comprehensive program of affordable housing will have a much larger impact in the long run on homelessness than a particular counselling activity with an individual who is homeless. Often it is necessary to address the internal and external factors simultaneously.

Below is a typical list of factors that are likely to contribute to homelessness; some could be said to be individual problems whereas some pertain more to the way our society operates.

External Factors
- Low income/unemployment/economic recession
- Lack of affordable housing/low vacancy rates
- Discrimination
- Low rates of Social Assistance
- Lack of social support systems/cutbacks in welfare
- Lack of educational opportunities

Internal Factors
- Mental illness
- Alcohol and drug addictions
- Disabilities, physical and mental
- Lack of job skills
- Laziness
- Family trouble

When analyzing social problems, external factors are those influences that are located in the wider society, and are systemic or structural. Internal factors, on the other hand, refer to things more personal to the individual and the immediate situation.

THE PROVISION OF SOCIAL WELFARE

Government participation in income security varies widely: the government provides cash benefits for disabilities, old age, survivors of the death of a spouse, occupational injuries and illness, sickness, families and unemployment. However, the direct government cash benefits do not reflect the entire spectrum of income security expenditures. There are several different methods of categorizing the social welfare available to Canadians. Before we explore the public welfare categories, note the distinction between public programs and private programs.

Public welfare takes place at the three levels of government: the federal or national government, the provincial and territorial governments and the regional and municipal governments. The various levels of government fund and deliver monetary benefit programs. The government also enforces employment-related policies and legislation, such as labour standards and minimum wage legislation, as well as policies that affect the quantity and distribution of employment and employment equity programs. These policies and legislation can affect the income of Canadians, and therefore can be considered a part of our income security framework.

Private welfare can be non-profit or for-profit, and provides "in-kind" benefits to those lacking income. In-kind benefits include such things as food, emergency shelter and other bare necessities. By law, organizations that provide these benefits are often registered, and rules and regulations govern their activities. Typically, these agencies are incorporated as non-profit corporations and receive funds from government and private sources. These agencies rarely charge money, given that they generally provide services to the destitute. Consider the Salvation Army. They receive their principal funding from individual donations, and they also receive funds to support their community activities from different levels of government. They are registered as non-profit organizations, and their boards of directors are composed of private citizens who are elected annually.

Income security is provided by for-profit organizations in certain areas, such as retirement pensions, dental and optical plans and private long-term disability insurance. These for-profit companies provide insurance, but their purpose is to generate a profit for the owner of the organization. Some countries, such as Norway, the Netherlands and Denmark, have substantial mandatory employer-paid income security programs. Canada does not.

The government is still the largest supplier of income security. However, with government cutbacks in recent years, more and more sources of income security protection are being provided by **non-profit and for-profit welfare agencies**. Food banks and emergency shelters are increasingly helping people with low incomes, while people with more material means are turning to private pensions and insurance programs to ensure their economic security in the future. All three organizations – public, private non-profit and commercial – are part of the income security system in Canada today.

Volunteers at the Daily Bread Food Bank in Toronto, 1991 (CP PHOTO/Edward Regan).

• Four Types of Programs

Public income security programs fall into the following four broad categories:

- **Social insurance**. These are programs that follow the insurance principle of shared risk. People contribute to insurance plans with the understanding that not everyone will need to access the benefits. Insurance-based programs are generally linked to employment. All workers contribute, and only those who contribute become eligible for benefits, should the need arise. Employment Insurance, Workers' Compensation and the Canada/Quebec Pension Plan are social insurance programs.

- **Minimum income**. These are programs that provide monetary assistance to those with no other source of income. They are primarily geared towards those deemed to be living in poverty, and the quantity of assistance tends to be determined by the minimum amount necessary to meet basic needs. Social Assistance, also called welfare or workfare, is a minimum income program.

- **Demogrants.** These are universal flat-rate payments made to individuals or households on the sole basis of demographic characteristics, such as number of children or age, rather than on the basis of proven need (as in minimum income programs) or contributions (as in social insurance programs). The Old Age Security (OAS) paid to all persons aged 65 and over was a universal program before a clawback was implemented. Now it is considered an income supplementation program. The former 1944 Family Allowance program, benefitting all families with children under the age of 18, was Canada's first widespread universal program.

- **Income supplementation**. These are programs that, as the name suggests, supplement income that is obtained elsewhere, whether through paid employment or through other income security programs. They are not intended to be the primary source of income. These programs may have a broad entitlement, in that they may be available to everyone within a very broad category, or they may be targeted to those most in need. The National Child Benefit Supplement (NCBS) and the Guaranteed Income Supplement (GIS) are income supplementation programs.

APPROACHES TO SOCIAL WELFARE

People differ in their views about income security and how to provide social protection to individual citizens and eliminate poverty, but the idea of providing income security to citizens in need is no longer a controversial one in Canada. Major disputes do arise, however, in determining which groups are in need and to what extent they need state assistance. Different approaches to social welfare are represented in these disputes. At the most basic level, two approaches to social welfare are discussed: these are the residual view and the institutional view.

"You're all on the wrong floor, try the basement" (National Archives of Canada/ C140612).

In the **residual view**, social welfare is a limited, temporary response to human need, implemented only when all else fails. It is based on the premise that there are two natural ways through which an individual's needs are met: through the family and the market economy. The residual model is based on the idea that government should play a limited role in the distribution of social welfare. The state should only step in when these normal sources of support fail, and individuals are unable to help themselves. Residual social welfare is highly targeted to those most in need. Additionally, residual social welfare tends to provide benefits at a low level in order to discourage use and make social welfare appear undesirable. Canadian public social welfare programs, from early history to the Depression of the 1930s, can be characterized as residual in nature. In the past two decades, we have moved back to this view.

In the **institutional view**, social welfare is a necessary public response that helps people attain a reasonable standard of life and health. Within this view, it is accepted that people cannot always meet all of their needs through family and work. Therefore, in a complex industrial society, it is legitimate to help people through a set of publicly funded and organized systems of programs and institutions. The institutional model attempts to even out, rather than promote, economic stratification or status differences. The period after World War II saw the beginning of the rise of the institutional view.

There are additional and more complex ways to distinguish between approaches to social welfare. (See Chapter 3 for an in-depth examination of how people differ on what to do about income security.) These varied approaches to social welfare capture the political controversy and economic debate surrounding social welfare today. It is useful to think about and understand the different approaches and theories, because each conveys a different sense of what social welfare is and how extensive it should be.

TORONTO HOMELESSNESS: A NATIONAL DISASTER

Toronto City Council has declared homelessness a national disaster. Little has changed since the mayor released a report entitled *Taking Responsibility for Homelessness: An Action Plan for Toronto.* The annual *Toronto Report Card on Homelessness* documents the current state of homelessness to enable us to develop responses. People who are homeless include people who

- live on the street,
- stay in emergency shelters,
- spend most of their income on rent or live in overcrowded conditions and
- are at serious risk of becoming homeless.

To read the entire report on-line, go to: http://www.city.toronto.on.ca/homelessness

PUBLIC INCOME SECURITY PROGRAMS

Canada's income security programs are in the newspaper headlines on a daily basis, and the effectiveness and affordability of such programs are frequent topics of discussion. The emphasis is often on the need to cut spending and to reduce the deficit, but the host of benefits that these programs bring to families, society and the economy are rarely mentioned. Nevertheless, many Canadians rely on the following income security programs to bring some economic stability to their lives, without which they would not be able to regroup and again be able to participate fully in society.

- **Employment Insurance (EI).** This federally administered program, originally called Unemployment Insurance (UI), dates back to 1940. Since then, UI has undergone numerous changes, including its name change to Employment Insurance. EI provides a level of income replacement to workers who are temporarily unemployed and meet strict eligibility conditions. Sickness, maternity and parental benefits are included in this program. Also included in EI are benefits for those whose livelihood depends on the fishing industry. Claimants are eligible for a range of re-skills development programs. EI is paid for through employer and employee contributions. Recently, the program has become restricted, providing coverage for fewer and fewer workers.

- **Workers' Compensation.** Workers' Compensation programs provide provincially administered benefits and are designed to protect individuals against income loss due to workplace injury or disease. Employers fund the programs. In return for participation in the provincial programs, workers waive their rights to sue their employers in the case of a work-related injury or disease. The first Workers' Compensation program was instituted in Ontario in 1914. This was the first social insurance type of program in Canada.

- **Social Assistance or Welfare.** Social Assistance programs have their roots in early municipal and provincial relief programs that were designed to provide minimal support to the deserving poor or those deemed unable to work because of age or infirmity. Gradually expanded to include those in need but without resources, Social Assistance has remained a residual program of last resort for those with no other source of income or savings. Social Assistance programs, also called welfare or workfare, have remained a provincial responsibility with some funding coming from the federal government. The provinces are free to design their own programs and set the level of benefits. In some provinces, "employable" recipients must participate in work placements. This is known as workfare.

- **Canada Child Tax Benefit (CCTB)/National Child Benefit Supplement (NCBS).** There is a long history in Canada of providing benefits to families with children. Some of these benefits have been and continue to be delivered through the tax system in the form of tax credits and exemptions, and others have been direct cash transfers. In 1944, a universal benefit called the Family Allowance was instituted, and this benefit went to all families with children, regardless of income. Over time, this benefit became targeted towards middle- and low-income families. In 1993, this benefit was eliminated completely. The Canada Child Tax Benefit includes two aspects: the CCTB basic benefit and the National Child Benefit Supplement. The CCTB provides a tax credit to those who qualify, based on an income test, as low- and middle-income families with children. Currently, up to 80 percent of families receive some portion of the CCTB. Some low-income families are eligible for an additional benefit – the NCBS. An interesting aspect of this federal benefit is that provinces are allowed to claw back the benefit from families on Social Assistance. All provinces take all or part of the benefit away from Social Assistance families, except for Newfoundland and New Brunswick. With the monies taken, the provinces are expected to reinvest in programs to help alleviate child poverty and its effects.

- **Canada/Quebec Pension Plan (C/QPP).** The Canada/Quebec Pension Plan is a national contributory and earnings-related pension program introduced in 1966. It provides benefits in the case of retirement, death and long-term disability. Employees and employers jointly finance the CPP and QPP, with current contributions supporting current beneficiaries. In this sense, the plan is a pay-as-you-go system. Any funds not paid out are invested for the purpose of creating a larger reserve fund. The plan consists of Retirement, Disability and Survivor's and Orphan's Death Benefits. Eligibility for this benefit begins at 60 years of age, with maximum benefits paid out after age 65. The pension is earnings-related, so there is a maximum amount for which claimants are eligible. It should also be noted that periods of low earnings, because of caring for young children, illness, unemployment or retraining, are considered exempt from the calculation. This provision is particularly significant for women, who often take time out of the labour force to provide caregiving.

- **Disability.** Severe and prolonged disability resulting in the inability to participate in the labour force qualifies one for a disability pension. This pension consists of both an earnings-related portion and a basic flat-rate portion, which is unrelated to the earnings one had while employed. Recipients may also qualify for supplemental child benefits if there are dependants. People with disabilities may be eligible to receive benefits through provincial Social Assistance programs, Workers' Compensation, the Canada/Quebec Pension Plan, and, in some cases, through the Veterans Disability Pension. Because there is no reason to assume that persons with disabilities are unable to work, eligibility is based upon a determination of their ability to work and the severity of the disability. Tax credits and exemptions play an important income security role for people with disabilities.

Maude Barlow of the Council of Canadians, 1996 (CP PHOTO/T. Hanson).

- **Survivor and Death Benefits**. In the case of a contributor's death, surviving family members may be eligible for benefits. These benefits are intended to provide support to both the surviving spouse and children.

- **Old Age Security (OAS); Guaranteed Income Supplement (GIS); Spouse's Allowance (SPA).** Between 1952 and 1989, all elderly Canadians received a universal monthly benefit called Old Age Security – an income security program financed and administered by the federal government. Prior to 1952, this benefit was targeted to the very low-income elderly population. Since 1989, the benefit has again become targeted, with only those who qualify because of low or modest income being eligible for benefits. OAS benefits are quite low in relation to the cost of living. Without another source of income upon retirement, such as C/QPP or Registered Retirement Savings Plans (RRSPs), many seniors would still live in poverty. To further assist those who do not have access to these programs, there are two related programs, the Guaranteed Income Supplement (GIS) and the Spouse's Allowance (SPA). The SPA is now called the Allowance. These benefits supplement the OAS for the low-income elderly. From 1966 until today, the GIS has provided a politically popular add-on to the OAS for those pensioners with little or no other income.

- **Veterans Disability Pension**. Income security programs for veterans specifically recognize the service of war veterans. A Veterans Disability Pension is available to those who apply to Veterans Affairs Canada, provided they have a service-related permanent disability resulting from an injury or disease. Income and assets are not considered as eligibility criteria; the benefit is based solely on the extent of the disability and the fact that it is military service-related. As is the case with disability benefits, what constitutes a disability and its extent is not always easily determined or agreed upon by all interested parties.

- **Occupational Benefits**. In addition to publicly administered benefits, private benefit plans also exist. These plans may be directly tied to one's workplace and include both retirement plans and other insurance-based benefits such as dental and drug plans, or they may be savings plans with tax-supported provisions, such as Registered Retirement Savings Plans (RRSPs). While individuals save and invest this money for future use, the government foregoes the collection of tax on this saved money. The lost revenue not collected by government amounts to billions of dollars per year.

GOVERNMENT SPENDING ON INCOME SECURITY

The expenditure for government-funded income security benefits covers just over one-quarter of government expenditures at all levels of government. Statistics Canada figures for 2001-02 show that the total expenditure for all levels of government on income security programs

Table 1.1: Selected Tax Expenditures (billions of $)

	2002	2003	2004
Employee stock options	575	585	595
Spousal credit	1,260	1,300	1,350
Equivalent-to-spouse credit	500	510	525
Canada Child Tax Benefit (CCTB)	7,870	8,050	8,405
RRSP deduction for contributions	7,395	7,930	8,360
Non-taxation of RRSP investment income	6,055	7,095	7,645
Non-taxation of lottery and gambling winnings	6,085	6,135	6,185

Source: Finance Canada, *Tax Expenditures and Evaluations* (2002). Retrieved from:
http://www.fin.gc.ca/toce/2002/taxexp02_e.html on October 26, 2002.

was $113 billion out of the total government expenditure of $430 billion
(or 26 percent of the total). In their publications, the government refers
to this expenditure as a social security expenditure, which refers to what
we are calling income security. Compare this figure to the expenditures
on health at $76.9 billion, and education at $64.1 billion. Clearly, the
various levels of government in Canada spend a considerable amount
on income security.

These figures only include direct government spending on pensions
and benefits for the elderly, Employment Insurance, Social Assistance,
child benefits and Workers' Compensation. The figure does not include
mandatory private social benefits provided by employers, voluntary private social benefits provided by charities or tax breaks for social
purposes.

A more detailed breakdown of statistics for 2002 shows that the largest expenditure of income security funding went to pensions and benefits for the elderly. Canada/Quebec Pension Plan spending totalled
$20.4 billion and the Old Age Security expenditure was $25 billion, for a
total of $51.4 billion (or 45 percent of the total of income security spend-
ing) (Health Canada 2002, 23). Our demographic trends show that the
elderly population in Canada will increase in the years ahead, which will
no doubt increase government income security expenditures.

At first glance, these big numbers may suggest that Canada is a rather
generous welfare state, but, in fact, the numbers are much lower than
those in most other developed countries. A 1995 ranking of income
security expenditures for countries in the Organization for Economic
Co-operation and Development (OECD) places Canada tenth among
twelve countries, outranking only the United States and Australia
(Adema 1999, 32). We fall behind even more if compared to the more
generous social welfare regimes. Our social expenditure of 11.4 percent
of GDP hardly compares with 22.9 percent of GDP for Finland and 21.4
percent of GDP for Denmark and Sweden (ibid., 15).

Total government revenue from taxation for all levels of government was $351 billion in 1996-97. In his book *Social Policy in Canada*, University of Toronto professor Ernie Lightman sheds light on the tax revenue sources of the Canadian government. The data reveals that corporations pay a relatively minimal 7.6 percent share of total taxes paid. Taxes paid through personal income taxes account for 32 percent, and sales taxes account for 19.8 percent (2003, 170-171). In short, individual Canadians are picking up a large share of the taxation tab.

Revenue Canada reports that Canadians with a taxable income between $30,000 and $40,000 paid 15 percent of their earnings in income tax in 1996. To determine if this is too high, compare the amount of taxes Canadians pay as a percentage of GDP with that of other countries. In Canada, the equivalent of 35.1 percent of GDP is paid in taxes to all levels of government. According to OECD data from 1994, this percentage of GDP is in the low range when compared to other developed countries. The majority of countries have higher tax loads, including Denmark (49.9 percent of GDP), Finland (46.7 percent of GDP) and Norway (41.3 percent of GDP).

DEBATING WELFARE

The amount of taxes we pay is invariably an issue in political debates about income security expenditures and government spending in general. Often, the discussions misleadingly portray us as the most over-taxed population in the industrialized world. Politicians are focusing on the tax burden to gain favour with concerned Canadians. They imply that Canadians are overtaxed, and argue that a decrease in taxes will make consumers consume more and investors invest more. The economy will grow, and this will result in more jobs and prosperity – or so the argument goes. The premise of this argument is questionable. Canadians are not taxed more than residents of most other industrialized countries, and a reduction in taxes does not automatically affect the economy in some magical way.

Another argument is that taxes stifle economic growth. Again, evidence from the OECD shows that Canada's economic growth rate was lower than that of the higher tax-load countries, so there seems to be more to stimulating economic growth than just lowering taxes. Moreover, some studies suggest that public spending on programs such as income security can have a greater impact on economic growth than tax cuts, because part of the tax cut will flow into savings and an increase in imports.

It is important to keep in mind that the role of taxation policy in redistributing wealth and fostering economic growth underlies many social welfare policy debates. However, the currently prevailing view that tax cuts will automatically lead to economic growth, which is held not so much by social work practitioners on the frontlines as by governments, economists and policymakers – is a highly oversimplified one.

"No, sonny, I ain't a corporate welfare bum — now beat it!" (Shane/National Archives/145005).

• The Beneficiaries of Income Security

As previously mentioned, most Canadians will draw benefits from the income security system at some time in their lives. We can divide the population into groups of 20 percent, or quintiles. According to their total income we see that, in 1980, the poorest quintile of the population received 46.5 percent of their income from government income security programs. This number increased to 59 percent in 1996. In 1980 the middle quintile of income earners received 6.9 percent of their income from government income security programs, up to 12.8 percent in 1996. Income security programs are key factors in shaping income distribution in Canada. These cash benefits are an important source of income for at least 60 percent of the population, and have become even more so since 1980. They also provide some benefits for the other 40 percent of the population.

In other words, all sectors of Canadian society benefit from income security programs, although different programs affect different sectors of society and different income groups. The Child Tax Benefit is spread across all income categories. Social Assistance is directed towards those who live in poverty with little other income, so it is of benefit to the lowest-income earners. Other programs, such as pension plans and Employment Insurance, provide social insurance funded through individual contributions. Since benefit levels are generally proportionate to earnings, middle-income households usually receive more from these programs than do low-income households.

SELECTIVE AND UNIVERSAL PROGRAMS

When designing income security programs, a key distinction is made as to whether they are universal or selective.

Universal programs are available to everyone in a specific category (such as people aged 65 and over and children), on the same terms and as a right of citizenship. The idea is that all persons are equally eligible to receive program benefits, regardless of income and financial situation.

Selective programs target benefits at those who are found to be in need or eligible, based on a means test (sometimes called an income test) or a needs test. A means test determines eligibility based on the income of the prospective recipient. The benefit is reduced according to income level, and there is always a level at which no benefit is granted. A needs test determines eligibility based on the income and the need of the prospective recipient. Eligibility criteria define need, which is then compared to the prospective recipient's life situation.

In the post-war era, universal programs were seen as a way to build national solidarity. More recently, they have been viewed as too expensive and have all but disappeared. The foremost objection to universal programs is their cost. Giving a benefit to everyone, regardless of income, means that even the wealthy get a benefit. On the other side of the issue, universal programs are less expensive to administer, as government workers are not required to scrutinize each person's situation. Selective programs are often viewed as more efficient and less costly, as the government provides benefits only to those most in need. However, identifying eligible recipients using means or needs tests can be administratively complex and costly and take money out of the system that could be directed towards benefits. In some cases, the higher administrative costs are being partially avoided by using the tax system as a method of determining eligibility and dispensing benefits. Increasingly, social policy experts are seeing that some selective programs are necessary for tackling poverty and inequality.

Universal program supporters maintain that universal income security promotes a sense of citizenship, solidarity and nationhood. They claim that selective programs for the needy tend to be punitive and stigmatizing, are more susceptible to cutbacks and lack necessary mass public support. If services are only for the poor, then they are likely to be poor services. Finally, many believe that universal income security programs can fulfill various economic functions, such as economic stabilization, prevention, investment in human resources and development of the labour force.

Over the years, Canada has had a mix of selective and universal programs. Governments have moved away from a focus on citizenship rights and inclusion, to an anti-poverty strategy geared towards promoting attachment to the labour force.

While some programs include aspects of universality, there are no income security programs remaining that can be exactly defined as universal. Health care and education are examples of universal service programs, but they are not income security programs. In the past, there were a number of universal income security programs available to Canadians. Family Allowance, which was available from 1944 to 1993, is the most commonly cited example. All families with a child under the age of 18 were entitled to a financial benefit. Because of the progressive tax system, wealthier people paid much of that back through taxation, but it was nevertheless an acknowledgment of citizenship entitlement and the importance and cost of raising children. In 1993, the Family Allowance was redesigned to become a targeted program, the National Child Benefit, now available to low- and middle-income families.

All of Canada's other income security programs offer selective entitlements. Most have complex selection criteria based on income, work history or the willingness to find a job. Employment Insurance is based on an insurance principle with eligibility tied to employment and income levels. Everyone within the broad category of "employee" pays into the program, and in this sense it is comprehensive, but a strict set of criteria determines who is eligible to receive benefits. The level of benefits depends on the earnings and contributions one has made. In recent years, eligibility for Employment Insurance has become more restrictive.

Other selective programs are based solely on how much money one has and whether this meets one's needs. To be eligible for Social Assistance or Ontario Works (as it is referred to in Ontario), one must pass through a means test, proving that income and assets fall below a certain specified maximum level. In provinces with workfare, such as Ontario and Alberta, applicants must also comply with an employment or train-ing placement. The benefit is then calculated by a social worker. Those wishing to access these programs must complete forms and possibly have an interview with a social worker in order to prove that they are in need and do not have the means to meets their needs. The National Child Benefit is another example of selective programming. If family income falls below a specified level, benefits are paid through the tax system.

CANADIAN FEDERALISM AND INCOME SECURITY

Canadian federalism has always influenced income security policy in Canada. **Federalism** is a system of government in which a number of smaller states (in this case, provinces and territories) join to form a larger political entity while still retaining a measure of political power.

When Canada was formed in 1867, social welfare was largely a pri-vate responsibility of the individual, family and church. The *British North America Act* (1867) said little about jurisdiction over income security or social services. The terms, in fact, did not even exist at the time. This omission caused Canada nothing short of political misery as it attempted to determine which level of government had the legislative jurisdiction to fund and deliver income security programs. Political wrangling, infor-mal side-deals between the federal government and the provinces and non-stop constitutional amendments formed the basis for our income security system. Throughout this process, income security slowly emerged as an area of federal authority. The provinces, on the other hand, largely prevailed in the delivery of social services. The Constitu-tion Act of 1982 did not change these arrangements.

The provision of social welfare by local and provincial levels of gov-ernment is consistent with the *Constitution Act* of 1982, which gave the provinces the responsibility for social services and income security, rather than the federal government. An important point to note is that, while the provinces were given this responsibility in general, the federal government retained its responsibilities for Aboriginal people, as defined by the *Indian Act*. The provision of social welfare to Aboriginal people is, therefore, somewhat different than for the rest of the population.

• Reforms to the Social Welfare System

Prior to 1996, federal government contributions to Social Assistance and social services had been funded through the **Canada Assistance Plan (CAP)**, established in 1966. One of the most significant changes to Canada's social welfare system arose with the introduction of the **Canada Health and Social Transfer (CHST)** in 1996. Federal govern-ment contributions to health care services and post-secondary education had been funded through Established Programs Financing (EPF) since 1977. Both CAP and EPF were replaced with the CHST. In its first two years, CHST paid the provinces $7 billion less than they would have received under CAP/EPF.

Anne McLellan following social union talks in Halifax, 1999 (CP PHOTO/Andrew Vaughan).

CAP was a 50/50 cost-shared program. Therefore, the federal government shared 50 percent of the cost of eligible Social Assistance and social services spending with the provinces. With CAP, federal transfers rose as provincial social welfare expenditures increased. CAP provided an economic stabilizing function. Federal transfers increased in economic recessions, thereby stimulating the economy through social spending. Conversely, CHST is a fixed per-capita or per-person amount based on the population of the province. Hence, federal transfers are not connected to either the needs of the people or the state of the economy. Many believe that it is the economic stabilizing effect of social spending that has prevented a depression-style drop-off in the Canadian economy since the Great Depression of 1930, and that with CHST this stabilizing effect is greatly reduced.

The national standards as set out in CAP are almost absent in CHST. CAP stipulated that the provinces must establish eligibility for Social Assistance based on need as determined by a means test, make services available for all those eligible regardless of when they established residency in the province, establish an appeals procedure and require no community service or other work (also known as workfare) in return for social benefits. The regulations associated with CAP were removed except for the ban on residency requirements, and funding regulations associated with Medicare were retained. Many policy analysts fear that, with the removal of national standards, provinces will establish very different benefit levels and eligibility criteria.

Another recent welfare reform is the **Social Union Framework Agreement (SUFA) of 1999** between the Government of Canada and the provinces and territories, with the exception of Quebec. According to the federal government, the social union initiative is the umbrella under which governments will concentrate their efforts to renew and modernize Canadian social policy. The objective of SUFA is to reform and renew Canada's system of social services and to reassure Canadians that their pan-Canadian social programs are strong and secure. So far, several welfare initiatives have been established under this framework, such as the National Child Benefit, the National Children's Agenda for child care and employability services for persons with disabilities.

The social union was largely a result of disapproval on the part of provincial governments over the unilateral cancellation of CAP and its replacement with CHST. The provinces wanted to be notified of and participate in formulating any future funding changes. They wanted the federal government to agree that, if it initiated any new social programs, even ones for which it paid the total costs, any province could opt out and take the cash instead with virtually no strings attached. The province would only be required to spend the money in the same general area as the national plan. The provinces also made it clear that they wanted more future influence over the federal government's actions when stepping into provincial jurisdictions.

While most social commentators have applauded SUFA's potential for collaborative positive change, there have been criticisms. Perhaps the most common concerns are the lack of inclusion of Aboriginal governments and the lack of a role for municipal governments. The latter is seen a a serious omission as municipal governments are increasingly responsible for implementing and partially funding SUFA-related social programs.

GLOBALIZATION AND SOCIAL WELFARE

Canada does not exist apart from the rest of the world. This is especially true as the era of globalization increasingly takes hold.

Economic globalization is the growing integration of international markets for goods, services and finance. It is the latest expression of market liberalism and the latest stage in the development of advanced capitalist economies. This globalization includes the expansion of free trade and investment, the expansion of trade in goods and services between countries, the geographical expansion and increase in power of transnational corporations (TNCs) and the use of agreements between nations and international bodies such as the World Trade Organization (WTO) to protect the rights of TNCs.

Globalization generally means that national and local governments increasingly tend to have less freedom to act on behalf of their citizens, especially on big economic and social questions of the day. In view of this, in the future, income security provision aimed at creating greater equality of income and opportunity among individuals will likely become intertwined with the issue of global human rights. Indeed, what might be called global social welfare (a concern with justice, social regulation, social provision and redistribution between nations) is already a part of the activities of various supranational organizations or international governmental organizations, such as the United Nations. The fight to gain and maintain global human rights in the face of economic globalization is, in many respects, today's epic struggle. Advocacy for equality within and between nations is an integral part of social welfare.

The economic pressures of globalization will continue to have a direct effect on income security policy and practice in this country. In many nations, especially poorer ones, economic restructuring and cutbacks to social programs have been imposed by international agencies, such as the World Bank and the International Monetary Fund, in the form of so-called "structural adjustment" (see Chapter 5 for details). The Canadian government is not immune to these pressures and adjusts its own income security programs to meet the new economic order and battle with other nations to be the most "investor friendly."

Unfortunately, the impact of globalization on Canada's income security programs at this point is being felt mainly by the most disadvantaged in our society, and they are also the ones who are least able to fight back. Cutbacks and strict eligibility criteria mean that many are often left without even the bare necessities. The rise in the number of people who are homeless, the growing number of food banks and the persistence of child poverty are signs of this. But, it is not only the very poor that suffer. The middle class is increasingly finding that high-paying jobs are moving offshore to corporate tax havens or export processing zones.

Critics say "globalization" means more profits for big business (National Archives of Canada/C145063).

REFERENCES

* Adema, W. 1999. *Net Social Expenditure*, Organization for Economic Co-operation and Development. Occasional Papers no. 39.

* Health Canada. 2002. Canada's Aging Population (prepared for the Second World Assembly on Ageing, a conference organized by the UN, held from April 8 to 12, 2002).

* Lightman, Ernie. 2003. *Social Policy in Canada*. Don Mills, Ontario: Oxford University Press.

Income security increasingly affects them as well, insofar as welfare cutbacks will mean that ordinary working Canadians may not be able to depend on the traditional social protection offered by such programs as Employment Insurance and Old Age Security.

CONCLUSION

The multi-faceted area known as social welfare includes two major components: income security (or programs that provide financial or material assistance) and social services (which provide personal and community services to help people improve their well-being). This text deals with income security, but this should not negate the importance of understanding social services and the work that social workers do. (A companion book entitled *Social Work in Canada: An Introduction* examines this other aspect of social welfare.)

Most citizens of Canada will face social or economic difficulties at some point in their lives. In an ideal world, income security allows all citizens to share the risk of events such as poverty, unemployment, disability and old age. Income security also helps to regulate and stabilize our economic and social system by putting money into the hands of consumers, which in turn stimulates the economy.

Canadians disagree about whether income security programs should be extended and strengthened, or whether they should be reduced. At the root of the debate are political ideologies, economic theories and basic notions about the role of income security in our society. Meanwhile, as the debate continues, federal, provincial and municipal governments have continued to make social spending cuts and our social welfare system has been more closely aligned with those of countries that have eroded their welfare systems to a bare minimum.

This is not the only course open to us. Other countries in Europe, notably Denmark and Finland, have continued to support and even expand their social welfare commitments, and continue to have good productivity and economic growth. As we look ahead, we must decide which direction we want to take as a society.

CHAPTER 1: INTRODUCING SOCIAL WELFARE

Discussion Questions

1. What are the main components of the social welfare system in Canada?
2. Define and compare the following terms: (1) social policy and social program and (2) public welfare and private welfare.
3. What is meant by the "residual" and "institutional" approaches to welfare?
4. What is the division of responsibilities between the federal and provincial governments, and what are the major changes brought about by the CHST of 1996 and the SUFA of 1999?

Websites

- **Social Work Glossary**
  http://www.socialpolicy.ca

  This site contains Steven Hick's personal collection of definitions of over 600 social welfare terms. It also includes links to publications and on-line course materials.

- **Canadian Council on Social Development (CCSD)**
  http://www.ccsd.ca

  CCSD is one of Canada's most authoritative voices promoting better social and economic security for all Canadians. A national, self-supporting, non-profit organization, the CCSD's main product is information and its main activity is research. It focuses on concerns such as income security, employment, poverty, child welfare, pensions and government social policies. Check out the Internet launch pad for a variety of excellent links.

- **Canadian Social Research Links**
  http://www.canadiansocialresearch.net

  This is Gilles Seguin's virtual resource centre for Canadian social program information. His purpose in creating and maintaining this site is to provide a comprehensive, current and balanced collection of links to Canadian social program information for those who formulate Canadian social policies and for those who study and critique them.

- **Social Union**
  http://www.socialunion.gc.ca

  The federal government's Social Union website has information about child benefits, the National Children's Agenda and disability benefits.

- **International Council on Social Welfare (ICSW)**
  http://www.icsw.org

  Founded in Paris in 1928, the ICSW is a non-governmental organization that now represents organizations in more than 50 countries. ICSW and their members are active in the areas of social development, social welfare and social justice. This includes issues such as food and nutrition, welfare and health services, social security, education and housing. It also includes many issues relating to economic development, human rights and community participation.

Key Concepts

- Social welfare system
- Income security
- Social services
- Welfare state
- Tax expenditures
- Social problem
- Public welfare
- Private welfare
- Non-profit and for-profit welfare agencies
- Social insurance
- Minimum income
- Demogrants
- Income supplementation
- Residual view
- Institutional view
- Universal programs
- Selective programs
- Federalism
- Canada Assistance Plan (CAP)
- Canada Health and Social Transfer (CHST)
- Social Union Framework Agreement
- Economic globalization

A Knights of Labour procession on King Street in Hamilton, Ontario, c. 1885. The Knights of Labour organized mass unionism in the main Ontario centres during this period in Canadian history (W. Farmer/National Archives of Canada/PA-103086).

2
The History of Social Welfare

Emergence and Decline of the Welfare State

Income security in Canada was created in the twentieth century and became an important social and economic tool after World War II. Early colonial practices in Canada mirrored the laws and ideas in England and France. This colonial inheritance brought distinctions between the "deserving" and "undeserving" poor and the belief that public assistance should be demeaning and punishing. These are ideas that still find their way into social welfare practices today.

———

A number of key historic events influenced the path of development of our public income security programs. Among these are confederation, industrialization, two world wars, the Great Depression, urbanization and the acceptance of Keynesian economic ideas in the post-World War II period.

Canada grew in population and industrialized in the nineteenth century. The charitable practices adopted by the provinces, and later by the nation, were strongly influenced by British law and practice. Our colonial inheritance brought ideas associated with the English Poor Laws into Canadian society. Distinctions between the deserving and undeserving poor were reasserted in colonial practices. The notion of workhouses and indoor relief, which were first established in the English Poor Laws, also found their way into Canadian legislation and into the practices of most provinces. Quebec was the exception because of the singular role that the Catholic Church played in the history of charity in the province.

It is for these reasons that we have to look back into the history of British law and practice to understand the origins of modern Canadian social welfare. In fact, we have to look as far back as the fourteenth century to trace the rise of the system of social and economic organization called modern capitalism.

"People must know the past to understand the present, and to face the future."

— Nellie McClung (1873-1951), Canadian author, orator and political activist, was one of the "famous five" Alberta women who fought in the courts and in Parliament to have women declared "persons" so that they would be eligible for appointment to the Senate.

THE RISE OF CAPITALISM

The concept of social welfare developed in England and France when society shifted from feudal relations to capitalism. The shift began in the 1300s and culminated during the Industrial Revolution in the early 1800s. Prior to the fourteenth century, society was based largely on a system of obligations in a primarily agricultural society. This kind of social organization was known as feudalism. **Feudalism** was both an economic and a social system in which the owner of the property was responsible for the peasants working on the land. The lord was obligated

SOCIAL WELFARE HISTORY

The author's website provides an overview of the history of income security. The site is located at:
www.socialpolicy.cc/cash

to provide for the peasants' welfare, ensuring that everyone on their land had food and shelter. Under the feudal system, peasants were tied to the land on which they lived and worked. People lived on the land and were supported by the produce of the land, although land in the form of private property did not exist. Land was held as a trust from the monarch and ultimately as a divine entrustment. Feudalism in France was similar to the system in England.

With the shift from feudalism, lords were no longer obligated to ensure the economic security of peasants. As the shift advanced, many people increasingly found themselves poor and homeless. A long series of legislative acts, such as the Poor Laws, were enacted to address this new economic insecurity. A new economic system came into being known as **capitalism**, an economic and social system based on a monopoly of the ownership of capital rather than the ownership of land, as in the case of feudalism. Ownership of or access to capital (machinery and equipment, private property and money) provided the new industrialists with the basis for employing workers at a wage.

Several developments were key parts of what became known as the industrial capitalist system. First, the factory system began to develop in the late eighteenth century, bringing the production and assembly of products under one roof. The growth of the factory system led to other changes. As factories developed in the towns and cities, potential workers had to go to the cities to find work; it did not come to them. Factory work required the existence of what came to be called free workers – workers who were no longer obligated to a feudal lord, but were mobile and free to sell their labour.

The period that saw the rise of industrial capitalism was filled with new and rapidly changing ideas. New technology emerged in the form of complex and expensive mechanical means of production – machines that could do the work of several people. From steam power driven by coal, industry rapidly progressed to the use of other sources of fuel and machinery, such as natural gas, electricity and gasoline; and the electric and gasoline engines. Also, the ideas of individual ownership, portable money and storable wealth emerged in this period. The modern concept of the family also developed during this period. Women were seen as weak and subordinate and responsible for the home; men worked for wages at employment located outside of the home. Childhood began to be seen as a separate part of life requiring special care.

The nineteenth century was also a period of rapid European/American colonization of other peoples and societies. Much of Africa, Asia and the Americas were divided up between the European powers and the United States in their search to conquer and exploit the earth's natural resources and available labour. Colonization provided the resources on which European industrialization was built. Canada emerged in the last third of the nineteenth century – a country built on first the French and then the English desire for the wealth of the North American lands. This desire to conquer lands and extract wealth had a profound impact on the original inhabitants, or First Nations, of Canada, which we will discuss in subsequent sections.

It is in the era of industrial capitalism that the modern system of public and private social welfare was born. By the twentieth century, private markets and prices had become the key method of organizing economic and social life in Canada. Most individuals and households were dependent on the sale of their labour, and unemployment became the key insecurity. This new form of social organization created both wealth and financial uncertainty. A gradual transition took place for the unemployed as they moved from dependence on private charity to dependence on publicly organized and administered assistance.

EARLY ENGLISH SOCIAL WELFARE: THE STATUTE OF LABOURERS

The plague between 1347 and 1349 (known as the "Black Death") killed one-third of the British population and many people survived by living off the land as vagabonds or by begging for food. The deaths and the need to survive by begging resulted in a severe labour shortage – there were not enough workers for the emerging factories, such as those used by the weaving industry. It was the labour shortage that prompted the first piece of English social welfare legislation – the first example of social policy – known as the **Statute of Labourers**.

In attempting to address the problems of begging, vagrancy and the shortage of labour, the Statute of Labourers originated four ideas. It put forth the concepts that

1. as long as beggars can live from begging they will not work for wages but will remain idle,

2. those who are idle will also become involved in crime and vice,

3. beggars should not be supported so that they are compelled to work for their living and

4. people who give charity are contributing to the problem and should be prevented from doing so.

Income security today remains linked to the past by many of these same ideas. Many people believe that charity or social programs encourage idleness, and that workers will not work unless they are compelled to do so. At the root is the belief that humans are lazy by nature and will only work if they are forced to work due to lack of food and shelter. It is a belief still held by many Canadians, although the experience of mass unemployment in the 1930s convinced others that, more likely, it is the lack of employment, not the lack of initiative, that accounts for the inactivity of many of the able-bodied unemployed.

The Statute of Labourers originated the concepts of the **deserving poor** and the **undeserving poor**, a notion that persists to this day. Six hundred years ago, the goal was to ensure that those who were able to work did so and to allow relief for those unable to work. The ultimate goal was to ensure a supply of cheap labour. Those physically able to work were forced to work by law. Those not physically able to work were considered the deserving poor or paupers. As the notion

Homeless in Toronto, 1903 (William James/National Archives Canada/C4228).

developed, it became a problem to identify the deserving poor and control begging. Again, this is an issue that is still relevant.

From these early origins, the present welfare system developed, and several themes contained in the Statute of Labourers remain in our current social welfare legislation and practices. First, the notions of idleness and work as expressed in the Statute of Labourers are largely intact. Second, the contradiction between the impetus to help people and the impetus to punish them for not working when society views that they should is a view that remains with us. Third, just as the Statute took the point of view of the employer in search of cheap labour, and not necessarily the point of view of the welfare of the individual, today's legislation places priority on incentives to work.

The dislocation of the old feudal order provided a new freedom to the individual to sell his or her labour, but it also created instability. Many of these instabilities and insecurities have since shifted, but they still exist. The history of modern social welfare has been a history of dealing with such insecurities and instabilities.

THE COLONIAL INHERITANCE

Denis Guest, the first Canadian social work author to provide a comprehensive history of social security in Canada, traces the origins of modern social security legislation to the late sixteenth century in England and France (1999, 11). The famous **Elizabethan Poor Law of 1601** provided the bedrock of the modern welfare states in England, the United States and Canada. Until the sixteenth century, there were few resources for people without land or employment. People resorted to illegal begging, private charities and foundations, churches and craft organizations where employed workers helped those less fortunate. But in 1531, an important change took place in the legislation with respect to beggars and vagabonds, and that change has become a fundamental aspect of social welfare in Canada today.

Poor children were shipped to the colonies (National Archives Canada/C31018).

In sixteenth-century England, during the reign of Henry VIII, begging was legalized for all aged poor and "impotent persons." Herein lies the origin of the contemporary distinction between the able-bodied and the aged and disabled poor. The disabled poor were given permission to beg, and the citizenry were given sanction to provide charity. The able-bodied poor were still compelled to work. The same law required the lazy able-bodied to be tied to a cart and whipped until bloody, and then forced to work in the area from which they had most recently come.

The early Poor Laws were passed in 1597 and reiterated in 1601. They contained five basic principles:

1. The local government was responsible for the poor.

2. The local government was responsible for apprenticing children. Courts could place a child with a local family so he or she could learn a craft.

3. A distinction was made between the able-bodied unemployed and those deemed to be unemployable.

4. The construction of hospitals and almshouses for the poor was to be done locally using local or parish funds (there was no national government responsibility at the time).

5. Impoverished parents and children were responsible for each other.

Two key principles were established with the introduction of the Poor Law. First, the concept of less eligibility stipulated that the amount of assistance had to be less than the lowest paying job. This is described in more detail below. The less-eligibility principle continues today as a key idea in income security. The second principle dealt with the demarcation between outdoor and indoor relief. **Outdoor relief** was provided in place of residence to a select category of recipients: the sick, the aged, the disabled, the orphaned or the widowed – all groups that were seen as deserving of aid. The relief generally came in kind, meaning it was in the form of food, second-hand clothing or fuel. In contrast, **indoor relief** was provided to able-bodied men who were deemed employable. These recipients were obligated to live in a workhouse and undertake work duties in order to receive assistance. The objective was to limit relief and use work as a form of punishment.

In the seventeenth century, **workhouses** were erected as private enterprises, with the aim of making profit. Although the houses were officially called almshouses, the public referred to them as workhouses or poorhouses. In order to receive relief, the plan required the poor to undertake mandatory work in a centralized institution. Early in the nineteenth century, there were more than 4,000 workhouses populated by about 100,000 people, out of a population of 9 million (Webb and Webb 1927, 215). The work was supposed to make the ventures profitable, but little profit was being made, and the workhouses were an economic failure.

The Elizabethan Poor Laws drew a strict distinction between the unemployable and the employable poor. The employable poor were put to work so they could learn discipline. At the same time, the work they did was seen as a punishment for laziness. In addition, the work was meant to train beggars so they would have the skills to pull themselves out of their "disgraceful" state. Women's eligibility was largely dependent on their relationship to a man. Deserted and unmarried mothers were often denied support, while widows were deemed deserving of relief.

The three concepts of work in the Poor Laws were: discipline, punishment and training. When you listen to debates about workfare today, there are clear echoes of the Poor Laws. The key principle is that in a society where people are free to sell their labour, they are not to test this freedom by refusing to do so. This ensures that employers have a steady supply of labour, and reduces the benefits of being idle or not working.

In the seventeenth century, it was believed that the poor could be trained and employed and the surplus labour could be used for the prosperity of the nation. At the same time, there was a growing belief in the

PUNISHMENT FOR ILLEGAL BEGGING

King Henry VIII started licensed begging to ensure that the undeserving poor would not beg. He also instituted punishment for those illegally begging. A beggar was to be "tied to the end of a cart naked and beaten with whips ... till his body be bloody ... after which [he] shall oath to return to the place he was born ... and there put himself to labour."

In 1547, King Edward IV increased the punishment. He decreed that idlers and wanderers would have a "'V' marked with a hot iron in the breast" and be enslaved for two years. On their second offence, they would be marked with "S" on the forehead and enslaved forever.

Their third offence brought a sentence of death.

BUREAU DES PAUVRES

In New France (colonial North America), the parish priests became the welfare workers of the day. Those individuals who sought relief in New France went to their town's *Bureau des Pauvres*, or Office of the Poor, which was managed by the local priest.

responsibility of the individual for his or her own poverty. Poverty was understood as a defect in character. Because of this, charity to the poor was thought to increase idleness and dependency, and contribute to the growth of pauperization. In other words, the long-standing debate over individual versus social responsibility for poverty was resolved: it was the individual's fault. This is evident in the advent of the workhouse, a place where people were virtually incarcerated for their poverty as a form of punishment.

THE POOR LAW OF 1834

In 1834 a complete review of the Poor Law was undertaken in Britain. English poor taxes increased twofold between 1803 and 1818 and three-fold by 1832 (Webb and Webb 1927, 1037). Harsh criticism by the elite of the existing Poor Law and the rising poor rates led Parliament to appoint an investigative commission. The Commission began with a biased agenda, believing that the Poor Law was a path to indolence and vice, and that it needed a relief rates cut and drastic reforms. The Report presented an immense shift in thinking about the poor in English society. Rapid population growth, industrialization and the emergence of a new ethos of individualism culminated in recommendations for fundamental changes to the Poor Law. In 1834, several Poor Law reforms were introduced, which affected social thinking in England and continue to affect social thinking in present-day Canada.

The rather harsh new **Poor Law of 1834** had three main features. First, it forbade outdoor relief (relief outside the almshouse) for able-bodied persons and their families. The able-bodied (contemporary welfare institutions use the term "employable") were only to receive relief in a workhouse. Second, the new law aimed to dramatically cut relief rates. This proved difficult, as housing people in almshouses was expensive – costing almost twice as much as indoor relief. Finally, the new law aimed to tighten administrative rules and clean up what it saw as abuses of the system.

A slum in Montreal, c.1949 (National Archives Canada/ PA151688).

The dominant beliefs at the time were anchored in Reformation Protestant theology. Pauperism was thought to be a result of personal or family defects, and individuals were seen as responsible for their poverty. Idleness, worldly temptations and moral decline resulted in poverty. At the same time, the Protestant work ethic dictated that people could lift themselves out of poverty through discipline and hard work. John Graham, Karen Swift and Roger Delaney, three prominent Canadian social policy professors, outline how the ideas of several key theorists of the day reinforced Poor Law ideas: Thomas Malthus, Adam Smith and Jeremy Bentham (2003, 29). Malthus believed that if the poor were coddled they would multiply too quickly and threaten society's limited material wealth. Smith, known as the architect of capitalism, believed that the pursuit of individual well-being and wealth would benefit all people in society. Finally, Bentham's utilitarian beliefs proposed that society should promote the greatest possible good for the greatest number of people. These beliefs tended to leave the poor with minimal benefits.

KEY HISTORIC DEBATES

There have been continuing debates about the best way to accomplish social welfare goals. These historical debates – or juxtapositions (which refers to the contrast or dissimilarity between the opposing ideas) – continue to this day.

• Deserving versus Undeserving Poor

Anchored in the Statute of Labourers, reiterated in the Poor Laws and reasserted in colonial practices, the notion of deserving and undeserving poor is a fundamental premise of income security in Canada today. The idea is that those physically able to work should be forced to work by law. Those persons who are not physically able to work are considered deserving poor.

• Economic Security versus Disincentives to Work

The principle of **less eligibility** was debated with the rise of income security in Canada. The concept was based on the idea that the amount of assistance had to be less than that of the lowest-paying job. It stipulated that the "able-bodied pauper's" condition be less eligible (that is, less desirable or favourable) than the condition of the independent labourer. Less eligibility meant that the pauper received less by way of relief than the labourer did from his wages, and the pauper received it in such a way (in the workhouse, for example) as to make pauperism less respectable than work. The intention was to stigmatize relief.

• Bare Subsistence versus Adequate Standard of Living

To determine which applicants should receive bare subsistence levels of income, income security programs use either a means test or a needs test. A means test looks at the income and assets of an applicant – the applicant's means of supporting themselves. It is sometimes called an income test when only income (not assets) is considered. A needs test involves an assessment of the person's resources and budgetary needs. It generally includes a formula that calculates the gap between resources and budgetary needs. When this idea was implemented in the Unemployment Insurance program in 1956, it was thought that the new test would provide assistance that would allow for a social minimum or an adequate standard of living.

• Fact of Need versus Cause of Need

Early programs assumed that the unemployed were somehow personally defective. This came from the mind-set of the early settlers – a mind-set of rugged individualism and frontier mentality. Receiving relief had the stigma of failure attached to it, and involved humiliating inquiries into the personal affairs of the receiver. Although it was generally assumed that the person had a defect, the cause of need was important in determining eligibility. The fact of need approach establishes that the person is indeed experiencing risk, the person is assumed to be in need and benefits are paid without personal inquiry.

ADAM SMITH, 1723-1790

Adam Smith is one of the principal founders of the science of political economy. His 1776 book entitled *An Inquiry into the Nature and Causes of the Wealth of Nations* laid the theoretical basis of the modern capitalist economy.

Smith believed the most efficient market is composed of small, owner-managed enterprises located in the communities where the owners reside, and criticized large concentrations of economic power for distorting the market's natural ability to establish a price that provides a fair return on land, labour and capital.

Key Events and the Implications for Social Welfare

CANADA AND WORLD EVENTS	SOCIAL WELFARE
1940s • War-related state controls • Crown corporations • End of World War II • High labour unrest • International revolutions • Emergence of Keynesian economic ideas • Beginning of transition to public social welfare • Economic hardship of Great Depression remembered • Urbanization & rapid industrialization	• Universal social legislation • Unemployment Insurance Act (1940) • Marsh Report (1943) • Family Allowance (1944) • Veterans benefits (1944) • White paper on employment (1945) • Hospital construction • Organization of provincial departments of social services • End of federal grants for relief
1950s • Prosperity • High employment • Cold War purges of left • Low level of unrest • Liberal government • Acceptance of government intervention	• Expanded social programs • Old Age Pension for all at age 70 (1952) • Means-tested pension at age 65 (1952) • *Disabled Persons Act* (1955) • *Unemployment Assistance Act* (1956) • Allowances for blind disabled • Hospital care coverage (1957)
1960s • Grassroots unrest—growth of anti-poverty, Indian, labour, student, peace organizations • Founding of NDP • Quebec separatism • Economic growth & employment	• *General Welfare Assistance Act* (Ont) (1960) • *National Housing Act* (1964) • Canada/Quebec Pension Plan (1965) • Canada Assistance Plan (1966) • *Medicare Act* (1968)
1970s • Fiscal crisis of state • Conservative business ideas prominent • Shift to residual concept of social welfare • U.S. influence rises in Canada • Rise of women's movement • Rise in women's employment	• Cutbacks begin in health, education, welfare programs • More law and order • Rise of contracting out • NGOs funding of militant groups • *Unemployment Insurance Act* (1971) • Established Program Financing (EPF) legislation to finance education and health
1980s • Monetarist economics • Deepening poverty • Globalization on rise • Conservative policies • U.S. dominance in Canada • Cold War tensions • Third World unrest • Waves of refugees • Rise in militancy & popular coalitions	• Major contracting out, cutbacks, workfare • Period of cost control for social programs with significant spending cutbacks • Increases in punitive programs • Women's issues (day care, reproductive choice, pay equity, violence) discussed but little concrete progress • Rise of food banks, role of charities increases • Rise of free trade (NAFTA) • *Young Offenders Act* (1984)
1990s • Economic stabilization • Rising militancy of First Nations, women, visible minorities, disabled, etc. • Agenda: Jobs and Growth report (1994) • Environmental movement strong • Polarization of rich and poor • Popular demands for real social justice • Rising labour militancy at grassroots • Rise of information and communications technology (ICT) and knowledge-based economy • Labour market restructuring	• Attempts to dismantle welfare state, and transfer costs to provinces, cities • CHST and Social Union Framework Agreement (SUFA) • Canada Child Tax Benefit and National Child Benefit (1998) • Regressive taxes • The new *Employment Insurance Act* (1995) • Cuts in corporate taxes • Free trade • Privatization of universal programs • Cuts to women's, immigrant, Native rights and programs • Move to workfare and privatization (residual model)

THE RISE OF INCOME SECURITY IN CANADA

We can divide the rise of income security in Canada into four periods. These coincided with major political, social and economic changes. In each period, certain characteristics predominated and particular programs emerged:

1. the Colonial Period, 1840-1867
2. the Industrialization Period, 1868-1940
3. the Welfare State Period, 1941-1974
4. the Era of Erosion, 1975-Present

• Phase 1: The Colonial Period, 1840-67

This period spans from the arrival of settlers from France and England to confederation and the proclamation of the *British North America Act* of 1867. In this era, social welfare was local and private, and economic security was a matter for the family, not the government. Social welfare consisted of regulations about family, economy, charities and Aboriginal Peoples. Public income security provisions were extremely limited and consisted of poor relief, prisons and care for neglected children, the insane and the handicapped. The French settlers introduced quite different responsibilities, assigning the care of the elderly, sick and orphaned to the Catholic Church.

This period is characterized by

- local and limited relief for the poor,
- social welfare as a private service (little role for government),
- an aversion to taxes and
- a reserve system and *Indian Act* imposed on the Aboriginal Peoples.

As we have seen, the Poor Law approached poverty by regulating the poor rather than by addressing the causes of poverty. British Poor Law style relief was implemented in Nova Scotia (1758) and in New Brunswick (1786). Upper Canada (now Ontario) did not enact a Poor Law, but encouraged private charities to assist the poor and destitute. The First Statute of Upper Canada in 1792 stated that all British laws would apply, except the Poor Law. Lower Canada (now Quebec), with its French traditions, relied on charity through the church. Despite these varied laws, the underlying ideas of the Poor Law greatly influenced the basis for relief.

In colonies such as Canada, the pioneering character left the problem of poverty to a "help-thy-neighbour" principle. Vagabonds were often "warned-out" or ordered to leave a community, whipped and confined to jail or publicly auctioned to the lowest bidder. The townsperson that offered to take care of the person for the lowest amount – to cover food, clothing and shelter – would win the person's labour (Blyth 1972, 10).

Care of the poor was generally assigned to the smallest unit of government or the parish, and the principles of indoor and outdoor relief

ABORIGINAL PEOPLES

The term "Indian" is widely understood to have originated with explorers who thought they had reached India in their search for a passage to the East. Today the term is used to define a group of indigenous people registered as such according to the *Indian Act*.

Of course, the Aboriginal Peoples have their own names in their respective languages: Anishnaabe, Inuit, Innu, Nuu-chah-nulth and Métis. The Inuit are Aboriginal Peoples of Canada that have used and occupied the lands and waters ranging from the Yukon and Northwest Territories to northern Quebec and Labrador.

persisted in Canada. Indoor relief in Canada involved providing food and shelter in a poorhouse, where poor people would work for assistance. Examples of this include the Toronto-based House of Industry, formed in 1837, and the Halifax workhouse known as Bridewell. To make relief less appealing, applicants underwent a workhouse test; doing unpleasant work was a mandatory step in getting assistance, and was a way to judge whether or not need was genuine. Outdoor relief was provided in the residence of the person requesting aid by private charities or local governments. This type of assistance became more popular at the end of the 1800s, as it became difficult to find enough unpleasant jobs for people to do in poorhouses. There was also uneasiness about building too many large institutions filled with poor people. With this turn of events, the workhouse test became known as a work test. With the work test, a person would stay at home, but would be required to perform jobs such as cutting wood or breaking rock.

Although income security in Canada was supposedly available to every citizen who met the conditions of the particular program, there has been a double standard when it comes to Aboriginal Peoples. What we now know as Canada, of course, was not a vacant place during this period – the ancestors of First Nations, Inuit and Métis Peoples lived on the continent for thousands of years before the settlers came. Vibrant and diverse communities existed, with developed methods of social and communal caring.

During the sixteenth and seventeenth centuries, the relationship between Aboriginal Peoples and Europeans was harmonious and mutually advantageous. At first, Aboriginal Peoples served as partners in exploration and trading. As the English and the French became locked in an imperialistic struggle for control over the North American continent, the relationship with the Aboriginal Peoples evolved into a military alliance. Then, the presence of Aboriginal Peoples on lands needed for settlement became the "Indian problem," and an impediment to "civilization." Colonial representatives and, later, government officials, devised various schemes to address the "Indian problem," including land-cession treaties and assimilation policies.

Aboriginal child with an Indian Agent (J.F. Moran/National Archives/PA102608).

With the founding of Canada, the social relations between the Aboriginal Peoples and the colonizers were expressed in the *Indian Act* and the reserve system. These continue to shape contemporary relations between Aboriginal Peoples and Canadian governments. The introduction of the reserve system was similar in many ways to the poorhouse. The *Indian Act* was, and still is, a piece of social legislation of very broad scope, which regulates and controls virtually every aspect of native life. The so-called "Indian Agent" administered the Act directly in Aboriginal communities.

The *Indian Act* sought to strictly define who was considered to be an "Indian," so as to exert government authority over the Aboriginal Peoples. The Act fragmented the Aboriginal population into legally distinct groups with different rights, restrictions and obligations. Canada is one of the few countries to have legislated separate laws for a specific group based on race or ethnicity.

Early in the colonial period, officials issued rations to Aboriginal people. Eventually, a separate system of monetary assistance was established. This remained in place until the early 1900s. Any kind of monetary relief for "Status Indians" was taken from the trust accounts of Indian bands. Relief was granted at the discretion of the local Indian Agent, based on the practice of distinguishing between the "deserving" and the "undeserving" poor – and Indians were generally considered to be undeserving. Non-registered Indians, Métis and Inuit were on the margin of the Indian relief system, although their economic circumstances were similar to, or worse than, those of the "Indians." (Moscovitch and Webster 1995, 212).

• Phase 2: The Industrialization Period, 1868-1940

This phase covers the post-confederation period up until World War II. After 1867, Canada industrialized rapidly. This drew people from small, self-sufficient rural communities into towns and cities. Many people left the security of the family to look for greater economic opportunity, sometimes ending up with an insecure factory job. In terms of government aid for the poor, the pioneer values of independence and individualism still predominated. Poverty was still seen as an individual failure, and relief was minimal and carried a stigma.

This period is characterized by

- a transition from private to public social welfare,

- World War I,

- significant protest and social unrest,

- rapid industrialization and urbanization,

- the economic hardship of the Great Depression and

- the emergence of Keynesian economic ideas.

Until World War I, income security was minimal and slow to develop. As the country grew and the process of industrialization took hold, new ideas and initiatives were introduced. This did not occur without significant protest and social unrest. Rapid industrialization, the economic hardship of the Great Depression and the internal migration of Canadians from rural to urban centres not only increased the magnitude of social and economic needs, but transformed these problems from local issues into regional and national issues. At the same time, the cost of income security was becoming too burdensome for local governments and parishes. These factors instigated a shift in responsibility for income security provision and funding from local governments and parishes to provincial and federal governments. During this phase, the transition from private to public social welfare was important. Social welfare was no longer seen as the private domain of families. A new vision of public social welfare emerged. The perception was that the state had the potential to improve the economy and the lives of people. State policies and programs were used to promote economic stability and even family stability.

J.J. Kelso, founder of the Children's Aid Society, 1910 (National Archives/C-085882).

Unemployed workers demonstrate for more government action to create jobs, Ottawa, Ontario, 1950 (National Archives of Canada/PA93929).

The calamity of World War I produced intense changes in Canadian society. Relative to its population, Canada suffered huge losses, and as men returned from the war, they faced poverty and misery. It was also a time of spreading social unrest. People assumed that, if the government had the resources to finance the Great War, it also had the funds to alleviate suffering. The Russian Revolution occurred in 1917 and the European labour movement and their Social Democratic and Communist parties were growing rapidly. Fearing socialism, governments reacted to this unrest by enacting social security programs. The early programs were seen as security for the government against a revolution by men trained in the use of arms (Blyth 1972, 27).

The important provisions passed in this period were

- the *Government Annuities Act*: 1908,

- the *Workmen's Compensation Act*, Ontario: 1914,

- Mothers' Allowances, Manitoba: 1916; Ontario: 1920,

- *Old Age Pensions Act*: 1927 and

- the *Unemployment Insurance Act*: 1940.

The *Government Annuities Act* of 1908 made it possible for those who had the private funds to prepare for their old age; this was done by making periodical or occasional payments into a government-operated scheme. After retirement, the individual would receive regular payments representing the return of the original funds, plus accumulated interest. Government annuities were offered to the public in order to avoid the institution of a public pension, which was considered unnecessary in Canada by the politicians of the time. Between 1908 and the passage of the federal *Old Age Pensions Act* in 1927, about 7,713 annuities were issued (Guest 1999, 36).

A modern income security system in Canada began to emerge when the *Ontario Workmen's Compensation Act* was introduced in 1914. Around this time, the size and number of industrial accidents were beginning to increase, and so were the lawsuits against employers. Employers pressed the government for protection from such lawsuits. The government responded with a Royal Commission and federal legislation in 1914. The Act eliminated workers' rights to sue employers, and instead provided compensation according to a formula. This was the first state social insurance scheme in Canada. The *Workmen's Compensation Act* of Manitoba, enacted in 1916, quickly followed suit. The passage of British Columbia's *Workmen's Compensation Act* happened in 1902, but it did not come into force until 1917, when the Workmen's Compensation Board was created. Legislation followed in all other provinces and territories over the next 60 years. The Yukon did not pass legislation until the 1958 Workmen's Compensation Ordinance. Saskatchewan passed legislation in 1930, Prince Edward Island passed legislation in 1949 and Newfoundland passed legislation in 1950.

Programs of assistance for mothers appeared first in Manitoba in 1916, followed by Saskatchewan in 1917, Alberta in 1919 and British Columbia and Ontario in 1920. The Eastern provinces did not follow suit until later: Nova Scotia enacted its relevant legislation in 1930, followed by Quebec in 1937. In New Brunswick, legislation was enacted in 1930, but not implemented until 1944. These early Mothers' Allowance programs were developed in response to pressure from the emerging women's movement, led by the suffragette Nellie McClung. Canadian women obtained the right to vote in federal elections in 1918, and between 1916 (Alberta) and 1940 (Quebec), the provinces extended voting rights to women. It is not surprising, therefore, that similar benefit programs for women quickly followed. Protests by women's organizations against the poverty of families left fatherless after the war also led to the implementation of programs. The allowances were also a way of encouraging women to leave the workforce and return to the home after the war. The informal social security system of rural Canada was disrupted by industrialization, as was the family unit. This increased the need for assistance to one-parent families. During World War I, the federal government extended pensions to the widows and children of soldiers who gave their lives. There was an obvious difference in the treatment of war widows and single-parent women who were left alone for other reasons.

WOMEN'S RIGHT TO VOTE

1951	Northwest Territories
1940	Quebec
1925	Newfoundland and Labrador
1922	Prince Edward Island
1919	Yukon
1919	New Brunswick
1918	Canada
1918	Nova Scotia
1917	Ontario
1917	British Columbia
1916	Alberta
1916	Saskatchewan
1916	Manitoba

TRY A SHORT QUIZ!

In the 1930s, what social welfare programs existed?

• Workers' Compensation
• Old Age Pension
• Municipal Relief
• Mothers' Allowance
• Canada Pension Plan
• Family Allowance
• National Social Assistance
• Unemployment Insurance

For the answer, go to: http://www.socialpolicy.ca/cush /m2/m2-t15.stm

After the war, there was an increased concern for children. The large loss of life in the war, the loss of life during the post-war influenza epidemic and the extension of the vote to women increased support for Mothers' Allowance elsewhere in the country. By 1920, five provinces had instituted Mothers' Allowance.

The *Old Age Pensions Act* of 1927 was the first major intervention by the federal government in the area of income security. The Act permitted the federal government to assist the provinces that provided a pension to the elderly at the age of 70. By the 1930s, only a few provinces were using the new federal pension plan. In 1937, the Old Age Pensions were extended to blind persons aged 40 and over. Recommendations for Old Age Pensions were contained in several post-war reports on labour unrest in Canada. In the 1921 federal election, the first three labour Members of Parliament (MPs) were elected to the House of Commons. These MPs, who became known as the "Ginger Group," included J.S. Woodsworth, a former Methodist minister and social worker. Later, Woodsworth was one of the founders and the first leader of the Co-operative Commonwealth Federation (CCF), the forerunner of today's New Democratic Party. In a 1926 electoral deadlock, Woodsworth traded the support of the CCF to Mackenzie King and the Liberal Party in return for the passage of the Old Age Pensions legislation. The Liberal Party under King was elected to government and fulfilled its promise with the passage of the *Old Age Pensions Act*.

The *Old Age Pensions Act* of 1927 was the first foray by the federal government into the provision of a minimum income program, but it depended on the participation of the individual provinces. The Act provided federal funds to those provinces that were prepared to institute a public pension for Canadian citizens over the age of 70. The provinces were obligated to introduce means testing to limit the availability of the pension to the poorest of the elderly. The Act was explicit in stating that an Old Age Pension would not be available to Aboriginal Peoples (Guest 1999, 77). The Act remained in place until 1952.

Early in Canada's history, government officials issued rations to Aboriginal Peoples that were grossly inadequate and were used as a means to reward certain types of behaviour (Moscovitch and Webster 1995, 211). When "the first universal and statutory old age pension was enacted in 1927 it excluded Indians and Inuit, but was available to the Métis" (Scott 1994, 18). The first *Unemployment Insurance Act*, passed in 1940, also excluded most Aboriginal Peoples from eligibility from its benefits (Scott 1994, 20).

In 1932, the Conservative government of R.B. Bennett introduced a *Relief Act* to assist the provinces with relief funding. On the advice of the military, unemployment relief camps were introduced to provide work and shelter for single, unemployed and homeless men. The mandatory work of clearing bush, building roads, planting trees and building government buildings was done for 20 cents a day under the supervision of the Department of National Defence. The camps were formed in lieu of a job creation program. The Depression peaked and Bennett's government was seen as indecisive and ineffectual.

The government resisted doing anything else, and fully expected that natural forces would correct the market. Meanwhile, in the United States, Roosevelt's New Deal was putting people to work in public works projects. Taking a cue from this and the Canadian social unrest, Prime Minister Bennett went on the radio in January of 1935 and told Canadians he would bring in his own New Deal, which would include Unemployment Insurance.

Social unrest and political action precipitated the government's increased openness to social programs. Two events of social unrest, the "On to Ottawa Trek" and the "Regina Riot," motivated Bennett to act. Thousands of angry relief camp workers in Vancouver went on strike and moved by train to Ottawa to meet with the government. The trek was prompted by the poverty, dismal working conditions and poor benefits in the unemployment relief camps – and the federal government's inaction in getting people back to work. The trek was stopped in Regina and several people were arrested. This prompted the Regina Riot of July 1, 1935. One man was killed and hundreds were injured.

The culmination of all of these factors led Prime Minister Bennett to introduce the 1935 *Unemployment Insurance Act*. Canadian federalism and the division of powers specified in the *British North America Act* hampered its passing. The 1935 *Unemployment Insurance Act* was struck down by the courts, which argued that only the provinces could enact such legislation according to the rules of the *British North America Act*. Therefore, at the end of the 1930s, the new Liberal government formed the Royal Commission of Dominion/Provincial Relations to establish the roles of the federal and provincial governments. The Commission concluded that the provincial government should retain responsibility for unemployed people who were unemployable – or the "deserving poor" – such as seniors, single parents and the disabled. The Commission concluded that the federal government should take responsibility for the employable or "non-deserving poor." The Commission established the agenda for post-war discussions on social reform.

Under Mackenzie King, the Liberals reintroduced an amendment to the *British North America Act*. This allowed the passage of a new federal Unemployment Insurance bill with a national scope. By 1940, Unemployment Insurance was finally legislated. In 1945, the federal government made a series of proposals to the provinces for a more comprehensive approach to social welfare, based on federally funded social programs. However, one condition stipulated that the federal government would have exclusive use of the income tax and the corporate tax. The provinces refused and social welfare change came to a halt for a few years. Federal/provincial debates about jurisdiction continued to hamper social welfare progress, and these still persist today.

Reinforcing these changes was the emergence of Keynesian economic ideas. The British economist John Maynard Keynes provided an economic rationale to the government's intervention in the economy. As outlined in Chapter 3, Keynes's theory provided the foundation for demand-management through government spending and other fiscal policies. Fiscal policy continues to play a major role in the government's efforts to manage the ups and downs of the Canadian economy.

ON TO OTTAWA TREK

The On to Ottawa Trek began when men from the relief camps decided to ride freight trains from British Columbia to Ottawa to peacefully protest their treatment. Believing that the men should be grateful for any assistance at all, the government did not react to their demands.

R.B. Bennett, the Canadian prime minister at the time, ordered the RCMP to stop the trekkers in Regina, saying that they were a threat to the government. Bennett rejected their demands and riots broke out in Regina on July 1, 1935. Shots were fired and many trekkers and RCMP officers were injured. Police eventually halted the trek and the protest in Regina and the trekkers were provided with transportation back to the Western provinces. After the camps were turned over to the provinces, relief camp conditions improved significantly.

"On to Ottawa" Trek, June 1935 (National Archives of Canada/X29399).

R.B. Bennett, elected on his aggressive economic policies (Quaker Oats Co. Series).

The **Great Depression** was an important event in the rise of income security and social services in Canada. It was so financially devastating that people were shocked into changing long-held beliefs about why people are poor and what the state should do to help. People began to see that poverty and unemployment were not the result of individual inadequacy or laziness, but were common and insurable threats to everyone's livelihood. Public perception of the poor began to shift. Massive numbers of people were unemployed, and Canadians began to see that this could not possibly be due to individual fault, but had more to do with the operation of the economy. People started to recognize that social forces and government policy affected unemployment and impoverishment. The notion that help for the poor should be a local or family responsibility was replaced with the idea that the government should be responsible for providing relief to the unemployed.

• Phase 3: The Welfare State Period, 1941-74

This was a period of rapid development of social welfare in Canada. Dennis Guest, author of *The Emergence of Social Security in Canada* believes that World War II was the catalyst for social security advancement (1999, 103). The role of government in society had changed as a result of the Depression and the war, and Keynesian economic ideas had been firmly established. In terms of protecting the security of citizens, the government was seen as playing an important role in society and the economy. The urgencies of war had placed large responsibilities and fiscal powers with the federal government, and this was carried into the area of income security.

This period was characterized by

- a post-World War II desire for security,
- a rapid industrialization and urbanization,
- a remembrance of the lessons of the Depression,
- an acceptance of government intervention,
- an acceptance of Keynesian economics,
- a variety of landmark income security programs and legislation,
- the 1966 Canada Assistance Plan (CAP) and
- a growth of the socialist and reform movement (CCF).

Most importantly, World War II had a profound impact on the role of the federal government and the Canadian acceptance of deep government involvement in economic and social affairs. During the war, the government oversaw labour activities and gained far-reaching economic powers. It became the largest employer of labour and used significant taxation and spending powers to aid the war effort. Most Canadians viewed the government in a positive way – as an efficient and positive force in society. This perception, in association with the Keynesian theory of government intervention in regulating markets and social spending, provided the foundation for the welfare state. In fact, the term "welfare state" was coined to denote the shift from a "warfare state," concerned primarily with World War II, to a welfare state, concerned with advancing the welfare of its citizens. Canadians saw the government's deep involvement in economic and social affairs merely as a shift in government priorities.

By 1971, social programs had reached a point where they were touching the lives of most Canadians. Between 1930 and 1970, the change was nothing less than revolutionary. Unfortunately, by the mid-1970s many changes affected Canada – inflation and unemployment grew, oil prices went up and the global economy changed. This began a downward spiral in terms of government revenues and expenditures. As more people became unemployed, more people turned to Unemployment Insurance. This drove up the cost of insurance, yet fewer employed people were supporting the program. This was a very active period of social welfare legislation and reform. The following is a brief summary of some of the major events during the period, and the important social services and income security programs that were legislated.

The **Beverage Report** came out of Britain in 1943, the same year as the subsequent Canadian **Marsh Report.** These reports established the baseline for the rapid expansion of social welfare. Sir William Beverage wrote a comprehensive report on post-war social security for Britain. It included comprehensive health insurance and income security. This crucial report was followed by a Canadian equivalent written by Dr. Leonard Marsh. *The Report on Social Security for Canada* became commonly known as the Marsh Report and received extensive media attention. In it, he detailed the need for comprehensive and universal social welfare programs. His report sparked debate over universal income security benefits versus targeted income security benefits.

Many consider the Marsh Report to be the most important report in the history of the Canadian welfare state. Marsh suggested that the country should establish a "social minimum" – a standard aimed at protecting the disadvantaged through policies such as social insurance and children's allowances. At first, the study did not attract much attention from policymakers, but, by 1966, most of Marsh's recommendations had become law. His work served as the blueprint for the modern Canadian social security system. University of Toronto historian Michael Bliss described the Marsh Report as "the most important single document in the history of the Welfare State in Canada." Marsh himself viewed his report as the natural outgrowth of the decade of social studies he had directed at McGill University.

In the report, Marsh established the concept of a desirable living minimum income. He went on to outline proposals that meet the principle types of contingencies that characterize industrial society. He coined the three categories of contingencies, which are still used today to describe social welfare. He proposed a two-pronged system of social insurance to cover both employment risks and universal risks. The first covered wage-earners and the second covered all persons for old age, disability and death. He also proposed children's allowances and health insurance. Finally, he emphasized the importance of training and placement programs to help people, especially youth, prepare for employment.

IMPACT OF THE GREAT DEPRESSION

The Depression of the 1930s dramatically affected people's ideas of social welfare. For an audio description of the changes click the audio option at: http://www.socialpolicy.ca/cush/m3/m3-t15.stm

The report made headline news as the media spoke about the proposed social spending of billions of dollars. People sensed the beginning of a new era in which they would have medical insurance coverage and protection from unemployment. These were new ideas to most people, and these ideas sparked debate about what this would mean for Canadian society. While some stressed the positive impacts on citizenship and responsibility for one another, others spoke of the onset of communism. (Some social workers at the time, such as Charlotte Whitton, spoke negatively about the idea of social insurance. She advocated for Social Assistance in which trained social workers supervised and counselled people needing assistance.)

Between 1951 and 1966, the Indian relief system collapsed, and was replaced by access to the mainstream welfare state (Moscovitch and Webster 1995). This occurred after the development of several federal Acts related to income security, the amendments to the *Indian Act* in 1951 and the establishment of the Canada Assistance Plan. Having developed an administrative structure with huge discretionary powers that minimized community control, the government of Canada effectively came to control the day-to-day lives of Aboriginal Peoples. Despite their best efforts, however, the government of Canada still failed to assimilate or to eradicate the Métis, the Inuit or the First Nations.

This era marked the arrival and development of many of Canada's social welfare programs. These programs include

- the *Family Allowance Act*, 1944,
- the *Old Age Security Act*, 1951,
- the *Old Age Assistance Act*, 1951,
- the *Unemployment Assistance Act*, 1956,
- the Canada/Quebec Pension Plan, 1965,
- the Canada Assistance Plan, 1966 and
- the *Unemployment Insurance Act*, 1971.

We will discuss the form and content of these programs in later chapters. As you look at this list of social welfare programs, you can see how important this period was in establishing the essentials of the Canadian welfare state. Total expenditures on social welfare, health and education grew from 4 percent of Gross Domestic Product (GDP) in 1946 to 15 percent of GDP by 1976 (Moscovitch and Albert 1987, 31).

The first piece of government legislation for this period was the *Family Allowance Act* of 1944. It was the first universal income security program in Canada. When it was introduced, considerable debate took place over the feasibility of a universal program. The goals of this important piece of legislation were to protect the up-and-coming generation and to maintain purchasing power. By giving money to mothers of children, it was thought that the money would be spent, and this would subsequently stimulate the post-war economy.

The *Old Age Security Act* (OAS) of 1951 provided $40 per month to everyone, beginning at the age of 70. This was another universal program providing a minimal subsistence amount to elderly Canadians with little or no other income. At the same time, the *Old Age Assistance Act of 1951* provided a means-tested amount of $50 per month for those aged 65 to 69. The *Unemployment Assistance Act* of 1956 reformed the previous program and the federal government shared 50 percent of the cost. It was expanded to cover all persons not covered by existing categorical programs. It also replaced the means test with a needs test. Many believed that the new needs test would provide a social minimum as it filled the gap between resources and needs.

The Canada/Quebec Pension Plan of 1965 provided a wage-related supplement to OAS and was the first program to be indexed to inflation or the cost of living allowance (COLA). It provided wide coverage and advanced the concept of social minimum.

In 1966 the **Canada Assistance Plan (CAP)** was introduced (see Appendix A). CAP was instrumental in standardizing and funding Social Assistance nationwide, and was in effect between 1966 and 1996. This program was the consolidation of federal-provincial programs based on means tests or needs tests. Half the costs of all shareable items were assumed by the federal government, provided a needs test was given. Assistance was possible for the working poor, and the public was given the right to appeal decisions.

The historic debate concerning "fact of need" versus "cause of need" peaked when CAP was introduced. The Canada Assistance Plan was intended to meet needs regardless of the cause for need. This was a strong effort to reverse the long-held belief that those in need were somehow defective. Others debated this notion, stating that cause of need was necessary to prevent the undeserving from obtaining assistance. This fact-of-need concept combined with a needs-assessment procedure was first introduced with the *Unemployment Insurance Act* in 1956.

CAP was the basis for cost-sharing, not only for income security programs, but also for a range of social services and programs including health services, children's services, Social Assistance, disability allowances, old age assistance, services for the elderly and institutional care. This program was the cornerstone of Canada's social service funding until 1996 when it was replaced with the Canada Health and Social Transfer (CHST; see Appendix B). The CHST is discussed below.

The 1969 Senate Committee on Poverty discovered high poverty levels and recommended an income supplementation scheme for the working poor. The plan was rejected by the provinces as being too costly. In 1970 the federal government undertook a major review of income security programs, which resulted in two important reports: the White Paper entitled *Income Security for Canadians* and the White Paper on *Unemployment Insurance.* The former report called for greater emphasis on anti-poverty measures and stated that resources should be concentrated on those with the lowest incomes. In other words, it recommended that selective benefits replace universal programs. The debate between universal and targeted programs was re-ignited. The reports also advocated for benefits that provide an adequate standard of living, rather than poverty or subsistence level benefits. For the first time, significant government reports recommended benefit levels that

Unemployed men in Manitoba, 1933 (F. Man/National Archives of Canada/PA145949).

addressed poverty and provided adequate standards of living. This ignited heated debate about the role of income security programs in Canadian society.

These reports were followed by program expansions and increases in old age benefits and Unemployment Insurance. The *Unemployment Insurance Act* of 1971 extended Unemployment Insurance to cover more people and eased qualifying conditions. Benefits were raised to two-thirds of wages. These income security program changes created benefits that neared the level of an adequate standard of living.

• Phase 4: The Era of Erosion, 1975 - Present

The current period has seen a great decrease in the scope and influence of social welfare legislation. Many of the income security programs implemented in the previous phases have been eroded or terminated altogether. Expenditures on income security programs have been cut and greater restrictions have been placed on eligibility. Unemployment has been placed lower on the list of priorities, and old debates about issues such as fraud and workfare have been resurrected.

This period is characterized by

- a shift away from the institutional conception of social welfare,
- increases in economic integration or globalization,
- cuts to income security expenditures,
- greater restrictions built into the design of programs,
- an emphasis on work incentives,
- the Canada Health and Social Transfer (CHST),
- an expansion of corporate tax deductions,
- the growth of public debt and
- the implementation of monetarist policies.

Monetarist economics, representing a major move away from post-war Keynesian economic policies, took hold during this period. The 1980s began with double-digit inflation and the most severe economic recession (1981-83) since the Depression. Rising oil prices and growing unemployment created a situation where the economy experienced both high rates of unemployment and inflation. This led to a questioning of Keynesian economic principles and put substantial pressure on government expenditures. In order to return to economic prosperity, the preferred solutions included decreasing government expenditures and controlling inflation. The debate between universal and targeted benefits re-emerged and targeting benefits was seen as a way of cutting costs.

This period also began with rapid increases in international economic integration, also known as economic globalization. Large corporations expanded their access to global markets, and new international institutions and agreements were forged to facilitate the expansion, such as the World Trade Organization (WTO) and the North American Free Trade Agreement (NAFTA). Each new agreement limited the Canadian

A small group of anti-Olympic bid protesters set up tents at Victory Square in Vancouver's east side, vowing to stay until there are changes to welfare policy and more social housing, July 2003 (CP PHOTO/Chuck Stoody).

government's ability to address the income security needs of Canadians. Some have referred to this as an era of the post-sovereign state. The focus of the era was on free trade and expanding market forces, coupled with a retrenchment of public spending and programs. Debates about income security shifted from helping people face insecurities in a market economy, to debates about the effects on the economy and international competitiveness. This era saw the beginning of a harmonization of welfare states around the world, and the Canadian government quickly cut back on social programs in what its opponents referred to as a "race to the bottom."

After the election of Brain Mulroney's Progressive Conservative government in 1984, the way was paved for deep cuts to income security programs in Canada. This government was committed to reducing the

A BRIEF HISTORY OF THE CANADA HEALTH AND SOCIAL TRANSFER (CHST)

2000 September: First Ministers agreed on an action plan for renewing health care and investing in early childhood development. The federal government committed to invest $21.1 billion of additional CHST cash over five years, including $2.2 billion for early childhood development. Legislation of these investments became effective October 20, 2000. This brings total cash transfers to the provinces and territories through the CHST from $15.5 billion in 2000-01 to $18.3 billion in 2001-02, $19.1 billion in 2002-03, rising to $21.0 billion in 2005-06. In 2005-06, CHST cash will be 35% above 2000-01 levels. Combined with the growth in the value of the CHST tax points to $18.8 billion, the federal transfer to provinces and territories will grow to $39.8 billion by 2005-06. To ensure further predictability, by the end of 2003-04, the federal government will establish the CHST cash transfers for years 2006-07 and 2007-08.

February: Budget announced a $2.5 billion increase for the CHST to help provinces and territories fund post-secondary education and health care. This brings CHST cash to $15.5 billion for each year from 2000-01 to 2003-04.

1999 Budget announced increased CHST funding of $11.5 billion over five years, specifically for health care. Changes to the allocation formula to move to equal per capita CHST by 2001-02.

1998 CHST legislation put in place a $12.5 billion cash floor beginning in 1997-98 and extending to 2002-03.

1996 Budget announced a five-year CHST funding arrangement (1998-99 to 2002-03) and provided a cash floor of $11 billion per year. For 1996-97 and 1997-98, CHST entitlements were maintained at $26.9 and $25.1 billion respectively, thereafter to grow at GDP minus 2%; GDP minus 1.5% and GDP minus 1% for next three years. New allocation formula introduced to reflect changes in provincial population growth and to narrow existing funding disparities, moving halfway to equal per capita entitlements by 2002-03.

1995 Budget announced that, starting in 1996, EPF and CAP programs to be replaced by Canada Health and Social Transfer (CHST) block fund. For 1995-96, EPF growth set at GNP minus 3%, and CAP frozen at 1994-95 levels for all provinces. CHST entitlements set at $26.9 billion for 1996-97 and $25.1 billion for 1997-98. CHST entitlements for 1996-97 to be allocated among provinces in the same proportion as combined EPF and CAP entitlements for 1995-96.

1994 Budget announced that total CAP and EPF transfers in 1996-97 would be no higher than in 1993-94.

1991 Budget extended the EPF freeze and CAP growth limit, introduced in 1990-91, for three more years to 1994-95.

1990 Growth in CAP transfer for three non-equalization provinces (Ontario, Alberta and B.C.) limited to 5% annually for 1990-91 and 1991-92. EPF per capita transfer frozen for 1990-91 and 1991-92 for all provinces.

1989 Budget announced that EPF growth to be further reduced to GNP minus 3%.

1986 EPF growth reduced from GNP to GNP minus 2%.

1984 *Canada Health Act* (CHA) enacted. EPF funding conditional on respect for the CHA, and provisions for withholding introduced.

1983 Post-secondary education portion of EPF limited to 6% and 5% growth for 1983-84 and 1984-85 under the "6&5" anti-inflation program.

1977 Established Programs Financing (EPF) provided federal funding in equal parts through a tax transfer and a cash transfer. A federal tax transfer involves the federal government ceding some of its "tax room" to provincial governments. Specifically, a tax transfer occurs when the federal government reduces its tax rates to allow provinces to raise their tax rates by an equivalent amount. With a tax transfer, the changes in federal and provincial tax rates offset one another and there is no net financial impact on the taxpayer. Provinces received 13.5 percentage points of personal income tax (PIT) and 1 percentage point of corporate income tax (CIT). The value of the transferred tax points was equalized. The value of the tax points was to grow as economies expanded, and the cash transfer was escalated by the growth rate of per capita GNP. Entitlements were distributed equal per capita.

1966 Canada Assistance Plan (CAP) introduced — cost-sharing arrangement for Social Assistance programs. Conditions attached to federal funding.

Source: Department of Finance 2002. *Federal Transfers to Provinces and Territories*. Ottawa. Available on-line at: http://www.fin.gc.ca/fedprov/hise.html

deficit, shrinking the public sector and expanding the private sector. Several reports were commissioned, including the *Royal Commission on Economic Development*, the Forget Commission on *Unemployment Insurance* and the *Neilson Task Force Report on the Canada Assistance Plan*. The government identified four key problems with the income security system: (1) spending was too high, (2) programs were not targeted to those most in need, (3) public social benefits were becoming a disincentive to work and (4) public benefits were becoming a substitute for earned income.

The federal Liberals under Jean Chrétien were expected to expand the social agenda. They began by commissioning Lloyd Axworthy to examine social security. His 1994 Green Paper entitled *Improving Social Security in Canada* provided recommendations in a variety of areas, but resulted in the termination of the Canada Assistance Plan and an over $6 billion cut in annual transfers to the provinces for social programs.

A key piece of federal legislation introduced during this period was the **Canada Health and Social Transfer (CHST)**. The CHST, which is provided to provinces and territories through both cash and tax transfers, is a block fund providing support for health care, post-secondary education, Social Assistance and social services – including early childhood development. By the end of the 2002-03 fiscal year, the CHST will have provided $35.7 billion. The CHST was created by rolling together the former federal transfers under the Established Programs Financing (EPF) and the Canada Assistance Plan. The CHST had far-reaching effects on income security in Canada. It fundamentally changed the social safety net and the role of the federal government in the social policy field. Some believe that the CHST diminished the power of the federal government in order to ensure that social programs continued, while others believed it was necessary to put the financial house in order.

The most recent government legislation affecting income security is the **Social Union Framework Agreement (SUFA)** (see Appendix B) of 1999. The agreement was based upon mutual respect between different orders of government and their willingness to work more closely together. The agreement aimed to smooth out relations after the fallout from the unilateral discontinuation of CAP and the implementation of the CHST. The SUFA refers to a range of programs such as Medicare, social services and education. It also addresses how these programs are funded, administered and delivered. It remains to be seen how this new agreement will affect Social Assistance.

The particular shape and character of Canada's welfare state stems from an important shift in the concept of social welfare. The residual concept, which shaped policy until the 1940s, upheld the "Protestant work ethic" and relied on private relief agencies. The residual concept gave way to the institutional concept, which followed the Keynesian means of integrating income security into the fabric of the economy. The era of erosion began when social policy discussions became dominated by the notion that governments must cut back spending and rein in the debt. Income security programs were seen as being too generous and therefore affecting people's incentive to take employment, especially at the low end of the pay scale.

Food depot at the Salvation Army in Sydney, N.S., 2003 (CP PHOTO/Vaughan Merchant).

REFERENCES

* Blyth, Jack. 1972. *The Canadian Social Inheritance*. Toronto: The Copp Clark Publishing Company.

* de Schweinit, Karl. 1943 *England's Road to Social Security 1349-1947*. Philadelphia.

* Graham, John, Karen Swift, and Roger Delaney. 2003. *Canadian Social Policy: An Introduction*. 2nd ed. Toronto: Pearson Education Canada Inc.

* Guest, Denis. 1999. *The Emergence of Social Security in Canada*. 3rd ed. Vancouver: UBC Press.

* Manitoba. 1991. *Aboriginal Justice Inquiry of Manitoba*.

* Moscovitch, Allan, and Andrew Webster. 1995. Aboriginal Social Assistance expenditures. In Susan Philips, ed., *How Ottawa Spends: 1995-96: Mid-Life Crisis*. Ottawa: Carleton University Press.

* Moscovitch, Allan, and Jim Albert, eds. 1987. *The Benevolent State: The Growth of Welfare in Canada*. Toronto: Garamond Press.

* Polanyi, Karl. 1944. *The Great Transformation*. Boston: Beacon Press.

* Scott, Kimberly A. 1994. "Aboriginal Health and Social History: A Brief Canadian History." Unpublished.

* Webb, Sidney, and Beatrice Webb. 1927. *English Local Government: English Poor Law History*. New York: Longmans.

CONCLUSION

The ideas underlying Canada's income security programs have their roots in the Poor Laws and the Colonial period. The Elizabethan Poor Laws were enacted to address the large numbers of desperately poor, and to control workers entering the wage-based labour market. The laws also gave rise to the conceptions of the deserving and undeserving poor. Those considered deserving were people who were very old, sick or severely disabled. Able-bodied poor were thought to be capable of working and therefore undeserving of assistance. Canadian poor relief and subsequent income security programs were strongly influenced by the Poor Laws.

The emergence of our current system breaks down into four periods: the Colonial Period, 1840-67; the Industrialization Period, 1868-1940; the Welfare State Period, 1941-74 and the Era of Erosion, 1975-Present. The Colonial Period is characterized by limited and local charity, and the provision of outdoor and indoor relief to those seen as deserving. The Industrial Period saw a gradual shift from private to public social welfare, the emergence of Keynesian ideas and a shift from blame-oriented beliefs to socially-oriented beliefs (in order to explain post-Great Depression poverty). After World War II, Canada saw the development of the welfare state, as we have come to know it. In this period, the role of the government changed dramatically. There was general acceptance of government intervention in the economy and society following the war effort, and Keynesian economic ideas took hold. The era of erosion, from the mid-1970s to the present, brought this to an abrupt end. Monetarism and globalization fueled deep cuts to income security programs and caused changes that emphasized work incentives and restricted eligibility.

A new vision of social welfare now needs to assert itself – a vision that balances economic production and social equity. The creation of such a vision and social movement underlies the current debates over the future of the welfare system in this country, and is the subject of the next chapter.

CHAPTER 2: THE HISTORY OF SOCIAL WELFARE

Discussion Questions

1. What factors led to the emergence of income security in conjunction with the economic system of capitalism?
2. How do our current conceptions of social welfare remain linked to the ideas of early British society?
3. What are the five principles of the English Poor Laws, and how do they compare with the ideas underlying income security for the poor today?
4. What are the key historical debates in the rise of income security, and how do they continue today?
5. What are the four phases in the rise of income security in Canada, and what ideas and programs characterize each phase?
6. What factors have contributed to the decrease in scope and size of income security since 1975?
7. What are the three pieces of broad federal legislation that impacted all income security programs in Canada, and what were the specific impacts?

Websites

- **A State of the Art Review of Income Security Reform in Canada, 1998**
  http://idrc.ca/socdev/pub/social/contents.html

  By Jane Pulkingham and Gordon Ternowetsky of the International Development Research Centre. The entire report is on-line and presents an excellent overview of the major issues confronting our welfare state.

- **The Canada Assistance Plan: A Twenty Year Assessment, 1966-86**
  http://www.canadiansocialresearch.net/allanm.htm

  A 1998 publication by Allan Moscovitch that provides an excellent critical analysis of CAP's history.

- **Canada's Unique Social History**
  http://www.socialpolicy.ca/cush

  An overview of different aspects of the history of social welfare in Canada.

Key Concepts

- Feudalism
- Capitalism
- Statute of Labourers
- Deserving and undeserving poor
- Elizabethan Poor Law of 1601
- Outdoor relief
- Indoor relief
- Workhouses
- Poor Law of 1834
- Less eligibility
- Colonial period (1840-1867)
- Industrialization period (1868-1940)
- Great Depression
- Welfare State period (1941-1974)
- Beverage Report
- Marsh Report
- Canada Assistance Plan (CAP)
- Era of erosion (1975-present)
- Canada Health and Social Transfer (CHST)
- Social Union Framework Agreement of 1999 (SUFA)

A McDonald's sign in a poor neighborhood in Caracas, Venezuela. Most Venezuelans make the minimum salary per month. Even if two parents are working, it's still not enough to buy the basket of basic goods for the average family of five. Venezuela's economic crisis, the worst in decades, has spared no one (AP Photo/Natacha Pisarenko).

3

Social Welfare Theory

Why People Differ on What to Do

Canadians disagree about the nature and importance of social welfare programs. Some of this divergence of views is based on common myths about the programs and people these programs are designed to help. However, much of the disagreement rests in different political ideologies, basic values and theoretical understandings that people hold, either implicitly or explicitly. This chapter unravels some of these ideologies and theories.

Government officials, academics and social welfare activists differ widely on their views about social welfare and the role it should play in our society. Commonly, introductory textbooks examine such differences in terms of political ideologies (George and Wilding 1993; Djao 1983) or in terms of sets of ideals and beliefs (Mullaly 1993). Reducing differences in the overall approach to values and beliefs does not address the day-to-day complexities of implementing social welfare policy in a capitalist economy such as our own. Nevertheless it is important for students of social welfare to understand the ideas that lie behind the debates about how the social welfare system works. In this section, before getting into the more descriptive chapters, we will examine the differing ideologies and theories about social welfare.

In this chapter, we will examine four approaches to social welfare: (1) the political ideology approach, (2) the economic theory approach, (3) the welfare state models approach and (4) the gender-based approach. In most cases, there is considerable overlap between these orientations. All are discussed in detail later in the chapter.

"A free and open society is an ongoing conflict, interrupted periodically by compromises."

— Saul Alinsky (1909-72), U.S. community activist. Alinsky's 1971 book, *Rules For Radicals* was his impassioned advice to young people on how to bring about constructive social change, in which he stressed "the difference between being a realistic radical and being a rhetorical one."

1. The **political ideology approach** situates social welfare in the context of economic, social and political theory – in Canada, this is normally distinguished according to conservative, liberal, social democratic and socialist beliefs.

2. The **economic theory approach**, as its name implies, focuses on the influence of economic theories. Economists have differing theories about the root causes of unemployment and poverty that generally revolve around explanations derived from the three economic theories: Keynesian economics, monetarism and political economy. Each body of economic theory has a different view of the role of government and the impacts of social spending on the economy.

3. The **welfare state approach** classifies welfare states according to how social welfare is provided in a given society.

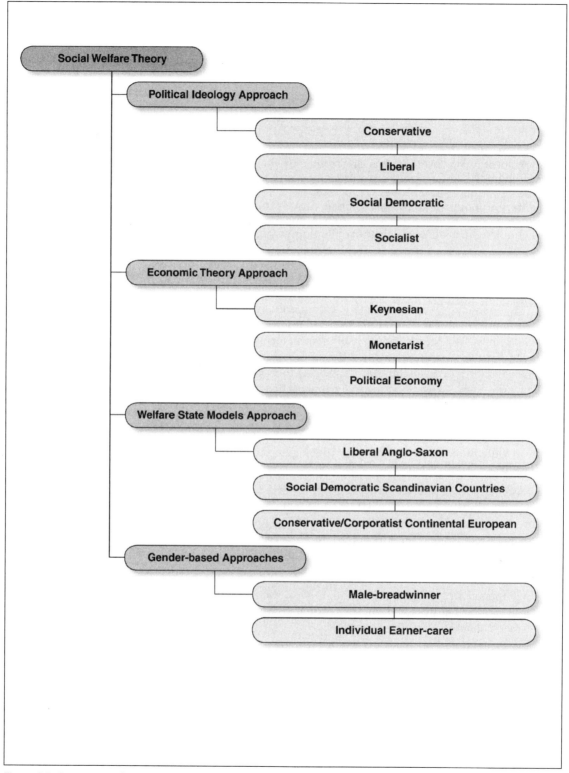

Figure 3.1: Four approaches to social welfare theory: (1) the political ideology approach, (2) the economic theory approach, (3) the welfare state models approach and (4) the gender-based approach. There is considerable overlap between these broad orientations.

4. The **gender-based approach** to social welfare takes the categorization a step further and identifies two additional regime types based on an analysis of the family and unpaid labour: the male-breadwinner regime and the individual earner-carer regime.

POLITICAL IDEOLOGIES APPROACH

One way to look at the different approaches to social welfare is to examine the political ideology underlying the approaches. These are normally divided according to conservative, liberal, social democratic and socialist belief systems. Most people present these ideologies in terms of "right wing" or "left wing," with the former referring to the conservative ideology and the latter referring to social democratic or socialist beliefs. Liberals are often referred to as "centrists," that is, somewhere between the right and left.

• Conservative Ideology (Anti-Collectivists)

Conservative ideology places emphasis squarely on individual freedom in the sense that it holds that each person knows best what he or she wants and therefore the individual should have the maximum opportunity to pursue his or her own interests. Adherents to this view accept that this may lead to inequality in terms of wealth and power, but see this as a necessary aspect of society.

The basic values of **conservative ideology** are

- freedom,
- individualism and
- social inequality.

According to this approach, the role of government (including interference in the free market economy) should be limited and the role of private property and private enterprise should be paramount. Conservatives believe that the best government is the one that governs the least. In other words, governments should establish the rules of the game (e.g., the pursuit of self-interest) but not be a primary actor – there should be a limited number of laws and regulations, and political institutions should not be involved in economic activity. Instead, conservatives say, the best system is a private system in which everything is bought and sold through the market. In short, free enterprise and all that follows, from this premise, is the most efficient way to organize society.

In accordance with this underlying philosophy, conservatives believe that social welfare interferes with the labour market and creates a dependency on government. They believe that much of social welfare is misguided and creates the opposite of freedom and individualism. They believe that many social programs hinder the operation of the market, and thereby limit efficiency and wealth creation. In their view, social welfare expenditures are often too generous, which results in inflated demands on the public purse. Insofar as welfare is necessary, they argue

THE CONSERVATIVE PARTY OF CANADA

The new Conservative Party of Canada began in 2003 with the merging of the Canadian Alliance and Progressive Conservative Parties. The merger was not easy as the two previous parties often disagreed on key policy issues, with the Alliance Party having a more right-wing conservative ideology. But in the end their common philosophies and the recognition that the right would never win an election if they continued to split the conservative vote in Canada resulted in a merger.

The beginning of the end? The 1976 PC leadership convention (National Archives/PA115204).

Photo by Duncan Cameron.

THE LIBERAL PARTY OF CANADA

The Liberal Party of Canada embraces the values of the liberal ideology. Their philosophy is committed to the view that the dignity of each individual man and woman is the cardinal principle of democratic society. The Party "is dedicated to the principles of individual freedom, responsibility and human dignity."

To learn more about the Liberal Party of Canada go to: http://www.liberal.ca

that private social welfare is better – it reduces social services and targets social program benefits to only the very needy.

George and Wilding refer to these people as "anti-collectivists" (1993, 19) due to their adherence to individualism and inequality. Individualism, as a belief system, is composed of two things. First is the belief that social phenomena can only be understood through an analysis of the actions of individuals. Secondly, individualism sees people as irrational, self-centred and fallible. According to this "anti-collectivist" ideology, competition is at the root of modifying the behaviour of irrational and imperfect citizens, and is the surer road to progress.

• Liberal Ideology (Reluctant Collectivists)

This group is more difficult to define. The liberals endorse the private (free) enterprise system, but at the same time they believe that the market needs a degree of government regulation.

The primary values of a **liberal ideology** are

- pragmatism,
- liberty,
- individualism,
- social inequality and
- humanism.

Pragmatism means that, as a government or an individual, you do what needs to be done. Liberals have often been described as less ideological, which means they are willing to do things that suit the circumstances, but may not exactly follow "liberal" principles. With liberalism, there is an acceptance of the basic tenets of conservatism – such as liberty, individualism and social inequality – but the inclusion of two other values, pragmatism and humanism, differentiate liberalism. Liberty, individualism and social inequality are tempered by a bottom line of social justice for the poor. So, competition and markets are tempered by a concern for people and the need for a certain basic level of social security.

The liberal view is that the government should regulate the free market to a degree and provide a minimum of income security benefits. George and Wilding refer to this group as the "reluctant collectivists" (1993, 44). The key idea here is that, despite the value of free enterprise and private markets, liberals believe that there is a tendency for economic power to concentrate in the hands of a few people and a tendency for markets to break down without government intervention. Liberals firmly believe that governments should intervene to ensure that the economy and the society remain stable and grow over time – private markets require regulation, and it is legitimate to restrict the freedom of the market in order to establish a social minimum and to preserve society by avoiding unrest.

Liberals are strong proponents of the insurance principle, particularly the idea of social insurance. They believe that the risk of unemployment

Trudeau at the 1968 Liberal convention (Duncan Cameron/ National Archives/PA41213).

and other interruptions in earnings – social contingencies – should be spread evenly across society. Everybody pays, and everyone benefits if and when they need to. This is not the same as a targeted program, insofar as it creates entitlements – in the sense that if you pay in, you have a right to take money out. In contrast, targeted programs are based on the principles of charity. At the same time, liberals advocate a social minimum program, such as basic welfare, to provide benefits for those who may not be covered by social insurance.

Liberals believe in a mix of targeted programs for those in need as well as universal programs, such as Medicare, that are available to all Canadians. They believe in "taking the middle ground" and "resisting extremes." In many ways, the famous inter-war economist John Maynard Keynes epitomized the liberal ideology. He believed in the free market economy, but also believed that there must be a way to organize it that would avoid unemployment and poverty. Writing in the depths of the 1930s recession, concern about unemployment was at the root of Keynes's work and it had a lasting effect on post-war economic and social policies in the West. (Keynes's ideas are described more fully later in this chapter.)

• Social Democratic (or New Democratic) Ideology

The ideology of the social democrat (or, in Canada, the New Democrat) is a middle ground between liberalism and fully-fledged socialism. It is characterized by beliefs in the democratic process and by adamant support for public social welfare programs.

The key values of **social democratic ideology** are

- social equality,
- social justice,
- economic freedom and
- fellowship and cooperation.

To the social democrat, social inequality wastes human ability and is inefficient in its distribution of resources. In an unequal society, issues of class, gender and race determine opportunities in the labour market. New Democrats argue for social justice on the basis that in "natural law" everybody has an equal claim to the wealth of society, and no one has a claim to immense wealth. Freedom for social democrats is not only political, it is economic – the kind of freedom that results from government intervention in maintaining a stable economy and stable employment.

Finally, New Democrats believe in cooperation and the common good. This is a very different understanding of what governments should be doing, particularly in the area of social welfare. Markets must be regulated and government enterprise has a substantial role. The economy itself, they believe, should be a mixture of public and private companies; hence, their notion of the "mixed economy."

The income security provisions of a social democratic government would highlight universal programs, full employment and citizenship. Full employment, the New Democrats believe, should be a matter of

THE NEW DEMOCRATIC PARTY

According to their official mission statement, the New Democratic Party seeks fundamental change. They state that they "will apply the resources of government and the strength of cooperation and community to advance our society toward the goals of equality, social justice and democracy."

The NDP believes that the Party is part of a greater national and international movement that seeks to challenge the dominant political agenda of market globalization and the resulting environmental, social and economic problems.

To learn more, explore the New Democratic Party website: http://www.ndp.ca

Founding convention of the NDP, 1961 (Federal Photos/ National Archives/PA149637).

KARL MARX (1818-1883)

Karl Marx is, without a doubt, the most influential socialist thinker to emerge in the nineteenth century. Marx held that the foundations of reality lay in the material base of economics rather than in the abstract thought of idealistic philosophy.

The core of Marx's economic analysis found early expression in the *Economic and Political Manuscripts* of 1844 and later in *Capital* (1867-95) and *Theory of Surplus Value* (1862). Marx argued that the conditions of modern industrial societies invariably result in the estrangement (or alienation) of workers from their own labour and conflict between the working class and the owners of capital.

"The worker becomes all the poorer the more wealth he produces, the more his production increases in power and range. The worker becomes an ever cheaper commodity the more commodities he creates. With the increasing value of the world of things proceeds in direct proportion to the devaluation of the world of men. Labour produces not only commodities; it produces itself and the worker as a commodity–and does so in the proportion in which it produces commodities generally."
– *Economic and Philosophic Manuscripts*, 1844

Marx: "Philosophers have only interpreted the world; the point is to change it" (TEP Archives).

government policy. New Democrats also support the use of national income for social programs. They feel that this kind of development represents a positive expansion of the idea of citizenship, encompassing not only voting, freedom of expression and access to the court system, but a range of universally provided social services. For this reason, they de-emphasize income testing and income targeting, and use these only when necessary. They believe that unemployment is a waste of the talents and capacities of citizens and a socially and economically destructive drain on our productive potential.

• Socialist Ideology

Socialists believe that the means of production and distribution in a society should be owned by that society. Modern socialist ideology has its roots in the influential writings of Karl Marx. Marx believed that socialism was a transitional state between capitalism and communism – a transition to a new society would come about by means of a social and political revolution.

Socialist ideology could be described as emphasizing

- freedom,
- collectivism and
- equality.

Socialists believe in equality and a society that operates to meet people's needs. Marx's saying, "From each according to their abilities, to each according to their needs," summarizes this view. In short, production should be organized according to social criteria and distributed according to need. Here, equality means the absence of special privilege.

Socialists believe that people cannot truly be free unless they are free from poverty and have the opportunity to develop as human beings – in other words, political and civil rights cannot be separate from economic and social rights. Socialists believe that individuals are social beings and have the potential to act cooperatively and harmoniously with each other – if society is organized in such a way that this is encouraged. Competition and consumerism in a capitalist economy, they argue, creates an unfavourable environment for collective action. Socialism has evolved and adapted to the changing times. Even countries such as Cuba and China that maintain a socialist approach are moving more towards a mixed economy with elements of state and private ownership of production.

Social democrats, or New Democrats, differ from the socialists in that they believe in the idea of a social welfare state. Socialists promote a view of society where the proletariat, or the workers, own the means of production (productive enterprises) through their own state. In other words, social democrats work within the bounds of capitalism in developing their social welfare programs, whereas socialists view state-instituted social welfare programs as mechanisms of social control – one that serves capitalism and fosters inequality by regulating and controlling the subordinate classes.

ECONOMIC THEORIES APPROACH

Another way to look at social welfare and social welfare systems is from the point of view of the economic theory that underlines them. As John Maynard Keynes wryly remarked: "Practical men, who believe themselves to be quite exempt from any intellectual influences, are usually the slaves of some defunct economist."

Certainly, economic theory has had a profound impact on the development of social welfare programs in all capitalist countries. In fact, social policy analysts would generally agree that without the theory of Keynes himself, we would not have developed a welfare state in the post-war period. Some even refer to this period as the "Keynesian Welfare State."

The Keynesians, the monetarists and the political economy theorists have fundamentally different views on the role of government in the social and economic sphere. They also have contrasting views on unemployment, the causes of poverty and the impact of social spending on society. The Keynesians believe that governments should use policies to combat unemployment and to maintain the income of consumers. The monetarists believe that governments should keep inflation in check and not discourage unemployment. Political economists believe that private ownership creates two classes that are structurally antagonistic and that unemployment results when unions are weakened and cannot protect the jobs of the working people. Let us look at each in more detail.

• The Keynesians

Keynesians is the name given to the followers of the economic theory of the British economist John Maynard Keynes (1883-1946). Much of Keynes's important work took place during the Great Depression in the 1930s, and his best-known work is the *General Theory of Employment, Interest and Money*, published in 1936. His theories, culminating in the publication of *The General Theory*, precipitated the "Keynesian Revolution," as it came to be known. His economic theories provided the intellectual rationale for the intervention of governments in economies and the transformation of social policy. Keynes's ideas were considered radical at the time, and some mistakenly called Keynes a socialist in disguise.

Aggregate demand is the total spending of consumers, business investors and public agencies. Keynes believed that any increase in aggregate demand in the economy would result in an even bigger increase in national income. Any increase in aggregate demand leads to more people being employed. If more people are employed, more people are spending their income. More spending leads to even more employment. With more income there is even more spending, and so forth. Keynes referred to this as the multiplier effect.

Keynes argued that markets would not automatically lead to full-employment equilibrium, but that the economy could settle into equilibrium at any level of unemployment. In other words, the economy could reach equilibrium even with high unemployment and impoverishment. Unemployment, according to Keynes, is a result of the

JOHN MAYNARD KEYNES (1883-1946)

Keynes revolutionized economics with his classic work, *The General Theory of Employment, Interest and Money* (1936), which is regarded as one of the most influential pieces of writing in the twentieth century. It quickly and permanently changed the way the world looked at the economy and the role of government in society. No other single book, before or since, has had such an impact.

A full electronic copy of *The General Theory of Employment, Interest and Money* is on-line at: http://cepa.newschool.edu/het/essays/keynes/gtcont.htm

overproduction of goods – that is, the previous output of products cannot be sold because those who would buy them are now unemployed and impoverished. This results in a general economic depression. According to Keynes, classical economic policies of government non-intervention in the economy would not work. Economies need prodding, and this means active intervention by the government to manage the level of aggregate demand.

Keynes's theory appealed to economists and governments of the day because it provided an alternative to the traditional view that unemployment can and should be eliminated by a drop in wage rates. Keynes's theory was much more politically palatable. According to Keynes, the solution to unemployment was a growth in government spending. Keynes advocated for the government to spend, purposely taking on budget deficits. Government spending to stimulate the economy was part of what Keynes called fiscal policy. Fiscal policy takes place when the government gets actively involved in the economy through spending in order to manage the level of demand – also known as demand management.

Demand management means adjusting the level of demand to ensure that the economy arrives at full-employment equilibrium. If there is a shortfall in demand, such as in a recession (a deflationary gap), then the government will need to reflate the economy. If there is an excess of demand, such as in a boom, then the government will need to deflate the economy.

Keynes also believed that unemployment decreases savings as the general population withdraws money from savings in the struggle to survive. Without saving, Keynes said, there is no investment; without investment, no employment; without employment, there is no spending; without spending, there is an overproduction of goods that cannot be sold. Reflationary policies to boost economic activity may include

- increasing the level of government expenditure,
- cutting taxation to encourage spending,
- cutting interest rates to discourage saving and encourage spending or
- allowing some money supply growth.

Deflationary policies to dampen the level of economic activity may include

- reducing the level of government expenditure,
- increasing taxation to discourage spending,
- increasing interest rates to encourage saving and discourage spending or
- reducing money supply growth.

Keynesian economics had a direct and major influence on the policies of most governments, including Canadian, in the period after World War II. Governments accepted the maintenance of a high and stable level of employment as one of their primary aims and responsibilities after the war to promote maximum production and purchasing power.

British economist John Maynard Keynes (Popperfoto/Metro Toronto Reference Library).

• The Monetarists

The **monetarists** are a group of economists known for their preoccupation with the role and effects of money in the economy. The most famous monetarist is Milton Friedman, who is responsible for elaborating most of the economic theory in this area. Simply put, the monetarist theory asserts that managing the money supply and interest rates (monetary policy) – rather than focusing on fiscal policy – is the key to managing the economy. According to the monetarists, the government should not stimulate the economy through government spending, but should maintain a steady money supply. Market forces would then adjust inflation, unemployment and production automatically and efficiently.

Monetarism is very closely allied with the "neoclassical school" of economic thought, the school of economics that dominated the field from the 1870s to the Keynesian revolution of the 1930s and 1940s. Monetarists share the same views as the neoclassical school insofar as they reject theories of demand management and emphasize the efficiency of free markets. The modern term "monetarist" was derived from the debate of the 1960s and 1970s about the role of the money supply in determining aggregate demand.

Modern monetarist theory was developed to try to explain a new economic phenomenon during this period – stagflation. Stagflation was an expression coined to try to explain two simultaneous economic problems: stagnation and inflation. Much of the monetarists' work revolved around the role of expectations in determining inflation, and a key part of their theory was the development of the expectations-augmented Phillips Curve. The Phillips Curve showed a trade-off between unemployment and inflation (more of one led to less of the other). Friedman argued that there were a series of different Phillips Curves for each level of expected inflation, hence the theory of the expectations-augmented Phillips Curve. The theory asserts that full employment is bad for the economy because it leads to inflation. If workers see other unemployed workers as ready and willing to take their jobs, then they are less likely to seek wage increases. Therefore, according to monetarist theory, some unemployment is good for the economy because it helps to control inflation caused by wage demands.

Monetarist economists formulated the idea of natural unemployment or NAIRU (non-accelerating inflation rate of unemployment). They believe that there is a natural, acceptable and beneficial level of unemployment. Attempts to lower unemployment below NAIRU will result in the risk of accelerating or increasing inflation. This is in sharp contrast to the Keynesian idea of full employment.

Two kinds of unemployment make up the idea of NAIRU: structural and frictional. With structural unemployment, the number of vacant jobs exceeds the number of persons unemployed, because the available jobs do not match the skills of the unemployed persons. Frictional unemployment is caused by workers moving between jobs to look for work that is more suitable.

The other aspect of the theory is control of the money supply. Money refers to anything that serves as a generally accepted medium of

MONETARY POLICY

Monetary policy significantly affects the social welfare of Canadians. It attempts to direct inflation by controlling the amount of money in circulation or the cost and availability of credit.

If money is readily available because, say, interest rates are low, people can afford to borrow and spend. But unless production keeps pace, there will not be enough goods and services to meet the demand created by this borrowing and spending. In the face of the excessive demand, producers and suppliers have incentives to raise their prices. As time goes by, prices spiral upward, leading to uncontrolled inflation, during which dollars lose their value.

The key to keeping inflation in check is to maintain stable interest rates and not to let the money supply grow too rapidly.

MONETARISM

The term "monetarism" was coined in 1968 by Karl Brunner. It refers to the macroeconomic theories and doctrines most closely associated with University of Chicago economist Milton Friedman.

Although "born" in 1956, monetarism only became a powerful intellectual force in the late 1960s and early 1970s, and had to wait until the late 1970s and early 1980s to be channelled into economic policy. By the mid-1980s, however, monetarism was largely a spent force and, today, one would have to search very far indeed to find an old-fashioned "monetarist."

exchange, a standard of value and a means of saving or storing purchasing power. The money supply is the total quantity of money in the economy. Governments can directly affect the money supply by printing or destroying currency, bills and coins, or indirectly by adjusting interest rates.

The key to monetarist policy is to control consumer and business spending by raising and lowering interest rates. The Bank of Canada (a government agency) controls prime interest rates. Lowering interest rates can stimulate the economy and slow money supply growth. Lower interest rates, for example, tend to increase spending (aggregate demand) and reduce savings. Conversely, higher interest rates tend to curb domestic spending. Strong demand for Canadian goods and services puts upward pressure on prices if the demand is larger than the economy's capacity.

Since the work of monetarists is mainly limited to their view of inflation, their policy recommendations emphasize fighting inflation. They believe that if inflation control is the main priority, then the economy will be more stable and be able to grow at its optimum rate. The key policy is controlling the money supply to control inflation. The government should not intervene to try to reduce unemployment because the economy will automatically tend to the natural rate of unemployment. The only way to change the natural rate is through supply-side economics.

Supply-side economics is the view that the best way to change the economy is to work on changing supply rather than demand. Rather than spending money to stimulate the economy, the government should not intervene – except to reduce taxes, to maintain a steady money supply and rate of inflation and to provide financial incentives to businesses. The end result, according to monetarism, is more business activity, and therefore more employment.

Supply-side economic policies may include

- reducing taxes (leads to more business profits, creates more businesses or creates more personal incentive to work);

- lowering interest rates (encourages more consumer spending and business expansion);

- privatizing government-owned companies (removes unfair competition in the marketplace);

- deregulating the economy (creates more cash flow in business and a more flexible business environment);

- providing financial incentives to businesses, such as direct grants of money, low interest loans or deferred taxes (encourages businesses to maintain or expand production and increase employment);

- improving education and training (makes the workforce more occupationally mobile);

- making people more geographically mobile by scrapping rent controls, simplifying house buying or

- reducing the power of trade unions.

For the past two decades, Canadian governments have largely adhered to monetarist economics. Monetary policy has been emphasized over fiscal policy, taxes have been cut and government social spending has decreased. Rather than viewing income security spending as part of demand management policy, Canadian governments have increasingly viewed it as a negative influence on work incentives. Governments at all levels have abandoned the notion of increasing spending during recessions in order to stimulate the economy.

• Political Economy Theorists

Among the economic theories, the third variant has wide-ranging economic, political and cultural components. **Political economy theorists** believe that the operation of economic markets is tied to private concentrations of ownership and is essentially exploitative.

Most adherents to the political economy perspective would argue that social spending serves to prop up and justify an unjust economic system. The welfare state, in their view, is seen as one of the contradictions of capitalism: it increases well-being, particularly for the rich countries of the world, but it also frustrates the pursuit of a truly just society. It reinforces the very institutions and values that the welfare state was established to do away with.

Many advocates of a political economy orientation go beyond a strictly Marxist analysis. They recognize that society is divided into social classes, the predominant one being workers and owners, but they also emphasize other sources of inequality and oppression, such as gender relations and ethnicity.

Political economy policies attempt to decrease the inequality in society by transferring the ownership of main sectors of production to ordinary workers and by expanding and developing high-quality and accessible health, education and social services. Such policies may include

- improving education and health services for all sectors of society,
- decreasing private ownership of productive resources,
- increasing the power of trade unions,
- encouraging community economic development initiatives to make capital available and
- increasing the provision of public goods.

The political economy perspective has never been a central tenet of government social policy in Western societies, but it has nevertheless shaped many of the critiques of the present-day welfare state. Political economy theorists would opt for nationalizing the major economic sectors and towards pursuing community economic development and worker-owned and state-owned enterprises. A well-developed social infrastructure – including free education, health care and other services – would also be central to this vision.

MILTON FRIEDMAN (1912-)

Milton Friedman, widely regarded as the leader of the "Chicago School" of monetary economics, which stresses the importance of the quantity of money as an instrument of government policy and as a determinant of business cycles and inflation.

Milton Friedman is the twentieth century's most prominent economist advocate of free markets. The following quotation succinctly captures his economic and political viewpoint:

"The basic long-run objectives, shared, I am sure by most economists, are political freedom, economic efficiency and substantial equality of economic power... I believe – and at this stage agreement will be far less widespread – that all three objectives can best be realized by relying, as far as possible, on a market mechanism within a 'competitive order' to organize the utilization of economic resources." ("A Monetary and Fiscal Framework for Economic Stability," 1948, AER).

Milton Friedman, one of the most influential monetarist economists (AP PHOTO/Eddie Adams).

WELFARE STATE REGIMES APPROACH

To this point, we have examined social welfare systems from the point of view of ideologies and economic theory. A third classification is based on how welfare is actually practiced in different countries. The "welfare state regimes" approach classifies nations or welfare state regimes according to established patterns of income security provision.

Building on the work of Richard Titmuss (1958), Gøsta Esping-Anderson identified three world regimes of social welfare state types: (1) liberal Anglo-Saxon welfare states, (2) social democratic Scandinavian countries and (3) conservative/corporatist continental European welfare states. It is important to point out that these were conceived as ideal types and that no welfare state exists in this pure sense. This categorization is meant to distinguish nations only according to their commonalities.

Welfare states are classified according to three criteria – public/private sector mix, extent of de-commodification of citizens and extent of inequality reduction or reinforcement. De-commodification occurs when a social program is delivered as a matter of right and when a person can maintain a livelihood without reliance on the market. People are "de-commodified," so to speak, when, due to the existence of income security programs, they do not need to rely on selling their labour as a commodity to survive.

Many social welfare theoreticians have added to or changed the Esping-Anderson dimensions. Others have rigorously critiqued the approach. In particular, many feminist scholars have focused on gender-relevant dimensions and others have examined racial dimensions. Fiona Williams, a British social welfare scholar, for example, has pointed out how the discipline of social welfare as a whole has marginalized gender and race. She developed a framework that accounts for patriarchy, imperialism and the international division of labour (Williams 1989).

The future of daycare due to inadequate funding (Shane/National Archives/C144992).

• Liberal Anglo-Saxon Welfare States

Esping-Anderson's **liberal welfare regimes** include countries such as Canada, the United States, Australia, the United Kingdom and Ireland. He used the term "liberal" to refer to the classical liberalism that is concerned with laissez-faire economics and minimal government interference (which is different from the use of the term "liberal" as a political ideology). Linked to many of the ideas of the early Poor Laws, welfare regimes of this type emphasize minimal benefits in order to discourage people from choosing public assistance instead of work. Overall, benefits would be residual, available only as a last resort and only to those in need. Income security programs have low benefit levels and are limited, needs-based and selective. As a percent of GDP, total expenditures would be low, and private sector delivery of programs is encouraged.

The overriding principles of the liberal model are privatization and targeting of benefits. In many of the countries within this model, the desire to reduce taxation and expenditures is paramount. Over the past decade, these aspects of this model have taken increased hold in many countries. Middle classes have opted for an increased level of private welfare and the government has sought to distribute benefits to the most needy. In addition, there has an been increased concern with ensuring that work incentives are strong.

• Social Democratic Scandinavian Countries

Esping-Anderson's **social democratic welfare regimes** include countries such as Sweden, Finland and Norway. This model emphasizes citizenship rights and the creation of a universal and comprehensive system of social benefits. The model is focused on optimum conditions for the citizen – as a right. This model would resemble an institutional approach to social welfare. Full employment, the elimination of poverty, access to high-quality and well-paying jobs, comprehensive health care, a safe working environment and a decent retirement are among the basic rights that would be guaranteed (Olsen 2002, 75).

The welfare states in Scandinavian countries emphasize universal income guarantees, maximum employment levels and highly developed programs for children, people with disabilities and the elderly. The principle underlying this model is that benefits should be provided to all citizens, regardless of their employment or family situation. Government authorities provide most of the income security benefits, and churches or charities fulfill a limited role. Intertwined with these comprehensive and universal income security benefits is a wide range of health and social services. These are either free or subsidized. Education services and health services are free in Scandinavian countries.

Such programs, however, are expensive and require a high level of personal and corporate taxation to function. This calls for broad support from the middle classes. The combination of high taxes and generous benefits results in the redistribution of income from high-income earners (who pay more taxes) to low-income earners (who receive more income security benefits). Because of these programs, citizens of these countries are more "de-commodified" than citizens in other advanced capitalist nations. In other words, they do not need to rely on income from the labour market to survive.

• Conservative/Corporatist Continental European Welfare States

Germany, Austria and France typify the **Conservative/corporatist continental welfare states** model. Esping-Anderson refered to these welfare states as "conservative" or "corporatist" at different times in his writing. Both terms refer to the basic principles of authority, tradition and resistance to change. Welfare states following this model provide income maintenance to uphold the status quo and maintain income difference between classes. They are not concerned with eradicating poverty or creating a more egalitarian society. Employment-linked social insurance programs financed through employee contribution are directed at income maintenance and do not seek to redistribute income between the classes.

SOCIAL DEMOCRACY IN SCANDINAVIAN COUNTRIES

During much of the twentieth century, many people associated social democracy with Scandinavia. The Swedish Social Democratic Party has been the most successful labour party in the world, and social democracy is the foundation of the development of the Scandinavian welfare state.

Despite some significant economic problems in the 1990s in Sweden and Finland, Scandinavian countries have fundamentally maintained, and even strengthened, their welfare states during the last decade. They largely escaped the shift to monetarism and were able to preserve social welfare protections.

Germany provided the ideas behind the first laws on social insurance. Underlying this approach, social benefits are given only to those who have been in the labour market. This evolved into the conservative or corporatist model, which emphasizes the protection of people with stable, lifelong employment. But people with a tenuous connection to the labour market, such as workers with irregular careers, face difficulties in being eligible for benefits. Continental welfare states have developed a variety of family support and ad hoc income security programs to build some kind of social minimum into the system. This provides little support for women. Northern European countries are inclined to address the concerns of poor families, but lack the necessary tax base for programs that redistribute wealth. These countries provide more generous benefits and a limited role for the private sector.

GENDER APPROACHES TO WELFARE STATE REGIMES

Patricia Evans and Gerda Wekerle, two Canadian social work scholars, view Esping-Anderson's "welfare state regimes" framework as flawed because it only considers the state-market dimension in meeting needs, and subsumes women within the family. According to Evans and Wekerle, this ignores the distribution of labour within the household and between the family and state (1997, 11). Many other feminist scholars have sought to address such weaknesses and have developed their own theories or models that take into account the very specific and unique contexts in which women, children and families find themselves in society.

Many aspects of social welfare policy and programming can and certainly should be examined in conjunction with gender concerns. In particular, there should be a recognition that the needs of the family and the unpaid work by women produces stratification along gender lines. The definition of de-commodification can be refashioned to include the capacity of women to maintain an autonomous household, free from the dictates of the market.

All social welfare theoreticians can also appreciate Sheila Neysmith's discussion of how the separation of family life, the labour market and state responsibilities in separate domains have hampered social welfare advancement. Her analysis demonstrates that public and private labour – or production and reproduction – need to be connected to achieve a complete theoretical understanding of the social welfare system (Neysmith 1991). In this view, it is crucial that our theoretical ideas do not separate the world into boxes that are different from the true experience of people.

Diane Sainsbury of the University of Stockholm, a prominent author in the field of gender and welfare studies, has outlined gender approaches to welfare state regimes. Her model is different from Esping-Anderson's in that it distinguishes regimes based on ideologies that describe actual or preferred relations between men and women, principles of entitlement and notions of caring. She distinguishes between the male-breadwinner regime and the individual earner-carer regime (her most recent work added the separate gender roles regime).

Sharing home duties contributes to gender equality (Health Canada/IMG0051-PCD2005).

• Male-Breadwinner Regimes

Male-breadwinner regimes are characterized by an ideology of male privilege based on a division of labour between the sexes that results in unequal benefit entitlements (Sainsbury 1999, 77). Men are seen as the family providers and thereby are entitled to benefits based on their labour force participation or their position as "head of the household." In such regimes, marriage is the preferred family form. Women are viewed primarily as wives and mothers and receive their entitlements as such – their primary role is to care for their husbands and children in the form of unpaid work. There is little state involvement in caregiving. Unmarried mothers and divorced women fall outside the confines of the "normal" policies of this type of regime.

• Individual Earner-Carer Regimes

In sharp contrast, **individual earner-carer regimes** are based on relations between men and women as shared roles leading to equal rights (Sainsbury 1999, 79). In this model, both sexes have equal rights to social entitlements as earners and caregivers. Paid work in the labour market and unpaid caregiving work have the same benefit entitlements, thereby neutralizing gender differentiation with respect to social rights. Both men and women are seen as equals. The state plays a central role in the provision of services and payments – whether it be caring for children, elderly relatives, the sick or people with disabilities.

The gender approaches to welfare state regimes provide a useful lens for analyzing social welfare. With this approach, we can see how entitlements are awarded and how this is often based on an ideology that supports a gendered division of labour, with men as breadwinners and women as caregivers. This approach goes beyond looking at relations in the market and takes into account relations within the family and relations between men and women.

SOCIAL INCLUSION

Before ending this chapter, it is necessary to touch on the idea of **social inclusion** as another way of looking at social welfare delivery. The concept of social inclusion emerged in Europe during the 1980s as a means of addressing growing social divides. It is now a central topic in Canadian social policy discussions. The concept challenges social welfare scholars to consider the non-economic aspects of society that lead to social disadvantages or social exclusion, such as education, community life, health care access and political participation. The concept is often referred to as being about "removing the bar" rather than "raising the bar." This idea refers to the need to remove barriers and sources of exclusion.

Mitchell and Shillington, two Canadian social policy researchers, define social inclusion as a process of investments and actions that will ensure that all children and families are able to participate as valued,

SOCIAL CITIZENSHIP: RIGHT OR INVESTMENT?

Underpinning social welfare is the idea of social citizenship, first espoused by T.H. Marshall. Marshall's social citizenship is based on a guarantee of rights partly realized through state intervention. It involves granting citizens civil, political and social rights. T.H. Marshall's lecture, "Citizenship and Social Class," has influenced social welfare thinking for decades. In it, he outlines the history of social rights, beginning first with the rights and obligations in feudal society. In feudal society, each person had a status (noble, commoner or serf) that meant certain rights and duties. With the transition to capitalism, these rights were dissolved and this started a series of conflicts. Struggles over rights resulted in the acquisition of civil rights in the eighteenth century, political rights in the nineteenth century and social rights in the twentieth century. This culminated in the notion of citizen rights and the post-war mind-set that underlies the welfare state.

According to Marshall, citizenship rights are best fulfilled through a welfare state and through that state's involvement in economic and social affairs. A key component of Marshall's citizenship rights are social rights. Social rights, according to Marshall, include the right to economic welfare and security, the right to share in social heritage and the right to live according to the standards prevailing in society. Social rights underpinned the development of post-World War II welfare states in Western industrialized countries, including Canada. The period was typified by a shift from a residual approach (seeing social welfare as a form of stigmatizing charity) to an institutional approach to social welfare (seeing social welfare as a right or entitlement). Social rights were placed on the agenda beside civil and political rights. But as time went on, some have argued that civil and political rights, including property rights, have tended to receive an enhanced importance while social and economic rights have declined.

In the past few years, social policy analysts have begun to outline social welfare within a "social investment" framework — the "third way." Some refer to it as "removing the bar" rather than "raising the bar." The goal of social investment is social inclusion. It therefore requires change at multiple levels — change that goes beyond meeting basic needs. One example of how a social investment approach would differ from a social rights approach is the provision of education for the homeless. Within a social rights model, the government might assign teachers for children located in a shelter for the homeless. The social investment approach would emphasize and respect the need for children to attend and participate in community school life. The new approach has merit because it uncovers the multiple aspects of social welfare. Others critique it for its "softness" on the need for structural change. They argue that the introduction of social investment and social inclusion may obscure the difficult issues of poverty, racism and other forms of inequality and powerlessness.

Table 3.1: Comparison of "Social Rights" and "Social Investment" Frameworks

	"Social Rights" Framework	"Social Investment" Framework
Vision	Social welfare is a right of citizenship	Social welfare is achieved by giving people equal opportunity
Time horizon	Meeting social welfare needs in the present	Improving the present to prepare for the future
Strategy	Provide income protection	Provide equal opportunity
Problem identification	Lack of income	Multi-dimensional nature of problems
Target	Raising the bar	Removing the bar

respected and contributing members of society by closing the physical, social and economic distances that separate people (2002, 6). Social welfare programs organized according to this perspective would go beyond providing material or income benefits. They would also include: (1) developing the capacities of people to earn their own income, (2) the direct participation of people in the decisions that affect them, (3) respecting and valuing of differences and (4) reducing the social and physical distance between people (i.e., mixed-income neighbourhoods and integrated classrooms).

In a market-based economy, income and other material resources are key to facilitating opportunities or capacities. The social inclusion perspective challenges us to move beyond income and material resources to consider other items that affect well-being and human development. For example, the well-known United Nations' Human Development Index (HDI), on which Canada has consistently scored high, measures more than income. The index also includes life expectancy, adult literacy and the gross enrollment ratio. It measures items that shape future opportunities, such as basic and advanced education and health, taking a social inclusion viewpoint on inequality. Amartya Sen, an influential scholar in this area, states that deprivation is determined by what people possess and by what it enables them to do. Therefore, when examining social welfare, it is important to consider access to housing, health, education, community life and political life.

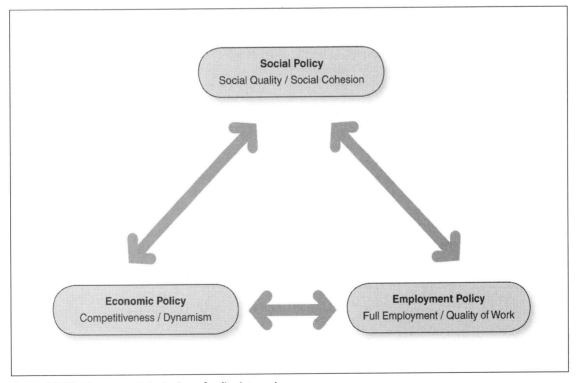

Figure 3.2: The European Union's view of policy interactions.
Source: Jane Jenson, *Redesigning the "Welfare Mix" for Families: Policy Challenges* (Ottawa: Canadian Policy Research Network, 2003).

REFERENCES

* Esping-Anderson, Gøsta. 1999. *The Three Worlds of Welfare Capitalism*. Princeton, NJ: Princeton University Press.

* Evans, Patricia, and Gerda Wekerle, eds. 1997. *Women and the Canadian Welfare State*. Toronto: University of Toronto Press.

* Djao, A.W. 1983. *Inequality and Social Policy*. Toronto: John Wiley & Sons.

* George, Vic, and Paul Wilding. 1993. *Ideology and Social Welfare*. London: Routledge.

* Mitchell, Andrew, and Richard Shillington. 2002. *Poverty, Inequality and Social Inclusion*. Perspectives on Social Inclusion Working Paper Series. Laidlaw Foundation.

* Mullaly, Robert. 1993. *Structural Social Work: Ideology, Theory, and Practice*. Toronto: McClelland & Stewart Ltd.

* Neysmith, Sheila. 1991. From community care to a social model of care. In *Women's Caring: Feminist Perspectives on Social Welfare*, Carol Baines, Patricia Evans, and Sheila Neysmith, eds. Toronto: McClelland & Stewart Ltd.

* Olsen, Gregg M. 2002. *The Politics of the Welfare State: Canada, Sweden, and the United States*. Don Mills, Ontario: Oxford University Press.

* Sainsbury, Diane, ed. 1999. *Gender and Welfare State Regimes*. Oxford: Oxford University Press.

* Titmuss, Richard M. 1958. *Essays on the Welfare State*. London: Allen and Unwin.

* Williams, Fiona. 1989. *Social Policy: A Critical Introduction*. Cambridge: Polity Press.

Overall, the concept of social inclusion as a solid framework for social welfare is a still a "work in progress." Some scholars and social welfare activists have cautioned that it is soft on the need for structural change, that it can be too general (thereby letting governments off the hook concerning issues such as poverty and racism), that it does not adequately confront historical exclusionary practices (such as the colonization of First Nations Peoples) and that the looseness of the concept allows governments to equate inclusion with employment (thereby ignoring the multiple dimensions of social exclusion). This book focuses on welfare programs that further income security, one of the pillars of social inclusion. But, this is not meant to minimize other aspects of social inclusion. These other aspects are the basic building blocks for survival, and they develop opportunities and the capacities of individual members of society. All of these work together to form social inclusion.

CONCLUSION

There are different ways to categorize the diverse ideas that underpin income security provision in Canada. This chapter provides a brief overview of some of the more prominent approaches. It is essential to understand that there is a range of theories and that no theory captures all the aspects of the welfare state – all have merit and together they help us understand how welfare provision works. While general theories and models can provide a context for understanding and critiquing social welfare policy, it is also important to keep sight of the useful contribution, at any given time, of particular policies targeted to individuals, within the welfare system through no fault of their own.

The next four chapters examine income security programs in Canada from differing perspectives: labour market, women and household, human rights and poverty. When reading these chapters, bear in mind that behind these programs may well be, to repeat Keynes's words, "some dead economist." Try wherever possible to identify the social welfare theory that stands in the background. Following these chapters, Chapters 8 to 11 describe specific income security programs. As you move through these chapters, you can draw upon some of the material presented in this chapter to see where the ideas and debates that guide these programs may have originated.

CHAPTER 3: SOCIAL WELFARE THEORY

Discussion Questions

1. What are the four approaches to social welfare, and how do they differ?
2. What is an ideology? What political ideologies exist in Canada, and how do they differ in their views of social welfare?
3. Keynesianism and monetarism are two different approaches to economic management. Define each approach and discuss two ways in which the two approaches differ.
4. Explain the political economy perspective, and discuss how its policies would differ from the other two economic approaches.
5. What are the welfare state regime types? Discuss two differences between them.
6. What dimensions are added by the gender-based approach to welfare state regimes? Based on this, what two types of welfare state regimes emerge?
7. Why do you think there are so many different ways to conceptualize social welfare?

Websites

- **Social Policy Research Centre**
  http://www.sprc.unsw.edu.au/dp/index.htm

  This is the discussion paper section of the SPRC. Look in particular at Paper #77 by Maureen Baker. The SPRC is an independent research centre of the University of New South Wales, with some Canadian content.

- **National Anti-Poverty Organization**
  http://www.napo-onap.ca/

  This website has updates on poverty issues of national interest.

- **National Council of Welfare**
  http://www.ncwcnbes.net/

  One of the most extensive collections of on-line reports on social welfare, poverty, welfare and other social issues. The National Council of Welfare is a citizens' advisory body to the Minister of Human Resources Development Canada on matters of concern to low-income Canadians.

Key Concepts

- Political ideologies approach
  - Conservative ideology (anti-collectivist)
  - Liberal ideology (reluctant collectivist)
  - Social democratic ideology
  - Socialist ideology
- Economic theories approach
  - Keynesians
  - Monetarists
  - Political economy theorists
- Welfare state regimes approach
  - Liberal welfare regimes
  - Social democratic welfare regimes
  - Conservative/corporatist continental welfare states
- Gender approaches to welfare state regimes
  - Male-breadwinner regimes
  - Individual earner-carer regimes
- Social inclusion

Striking CUPE workers demonstrate in a rally in downtown Prince Albert, Saskatchewan, in June 2001. A mediator was appointed to kick-start negotiations in the strike involving more than 12,000 Saskatchewan health-care workers (CP PHOTO/Prince Albert).

4

Labour Market and Employment

Economic and Social Perspectives

Social welfare and the labour market are inextricably linked. In our economy (a capitalist economy), one's social welfare is largely determined by attachment to the labour force. If all members of a society were able to consistently meet their needs through wages from employment, investment income or inheritance, the need for income security programs would be drastically reduced or eliminated.

Together, Employment Insurance (EI) and Social Assistance (SA) are the pillars of income support for those of working age in Canada. **Employment Insurance** provides a level of income replacement to those workers who are temporarily out of work and meet strict eligibility conditions. **Social Assistance** provides minimal income support to those who do not qualify for EI. A variety of factors can result in someone becoming unemployed. Demand for one's occupation may fall, one's training may become outdated, there might not be enough jobs to go around, the overall economy might dip or perhaps a life event results in a personal crisis. Regardless of the cause, an unemployed person in a market economy requires money to survive.

"Annual income twenty pounds, annual expenditure nineteen nineteen six, result happiness. Annual income twenty pounds, annual expenditure twenty pounds ought and six, result misery."

— Charles Dickens, *David Copperfield*, Chap. xii.

EI and SA help people who are unemployed, yet many Canadians living in poverty are underemployed and part-time employed. Income support is often not available in these cases unless earnings are extremely low, and even then it is a minimum amount. Underemployment occurs when the education and training required for the job obtained is less than the education and training of the worker that is doing the job. Part-time employment is also a growing sector of the labour market. Many people are working part-time involuntarily, and would prefer full-time work.

There is debate about the merit of income security programs such as EI and SA. Some people believe that these programs hurt the labour market and hinder economic growth, while others believe that the programs benefit both individual citizens and the economy. Still others, especially countries in the European Union, believe that social welfare programs are productive, rather than a drain on the economy. In this chapter, we will look at this debate by examining employment and unemployment and their relation to income security. Finally, we will look at the relationship between economic efficiency and social equity, and the role that income security can play in managing an efficient and fair economy.

EMPLOYMENT AND UNEMPLOYMENT

In the nineteenth century, the concept of unemployment did not exist. People who were physically able to work, but did not work, were assumed to be lazy. In modern times we define unemployment as the involuntary loss of wage income. In our economy, the possibility of losing wage income is a frightening prospect for individuals and their families.

Employment includes any activity carried out for pay or profit. It also includes unpaid family work, when it is a direct contribution to the operation of a farm, business or professional practice owned or operated by a related member of the household. Some employed people are self-employed. **Self-employment** is becoming prevalent as people provide services on contract, produce products or sell someone else's product. Self-employed people rely on their own initiative and skills to generate income, and undertake the risks and uncertainties of starting their own businesses. Official unemployment (as it is counted in the unemployment statistics) is made up of people in the labour force who do not have paid employment, are available to take work and are actively looking for a job. If an unemployed person has given up searching for a job, he or she is not considered to be part of the labour force and is not included in the unemployment statistics. As noted earlier, many Canadians also face **underemployment** – when the education and training required for the job is less than the education and training of the worker who is doing the job. Underemployment is generally not measured in Canada. Evidence indicates that underemployment increases as higher quality jobs become relatively fewer in number.

Anyone can lose his or her job, often when it is least expected. The notion of the unemployed being lazy has been replaced with a more realistic view as more people experience job loss or have a relative or friend experiencing it. Prior to the the economic downturn from 2000 to 2003, many high technology workers and managers thought that their jobs were secure and that they were in a booming sector of the economy. Many suddenly found themselves without a job, and did not find employment for a number of years. According to Statistics Canada data (Catalogue no. 89F0133XIE), 47.7 percent of those who became unemployed in 2002 were laid off. Twenty-three percent were unemployed in the previous year. Only 1.7 percent left their job for personal or family reasons (2.6 percent for women and 1 percent for men).

Some unemployment is unavoidable, due to people moving between jobs and mismatches between the skills of the unemployed and the skills for available jobs. Employees who move between jobs cause what is known as **frictional unemployment**. This includes new labour force entrants such as those returning to the labour force after completing school or raising children. **Cyclical unemployment** occurs due to a temporary downturn in the job market. The most common form of cyclical unemployment occurs when workers are temporarily laid off.

If, on the other hand, unemployed people do not have the skills for available jobs, do not live where jobs are available or are unwilling to

This experienced worker is unsure where workfare will lead (CP PHOTO/C. Schuler).

work at the wage rate offered in the market, this form of unemployment is known as **structural unemployment**. The extent of structural unemployment will depend on various things:

- **Mobility of labour.** If people quickly switch jobs from a declining industry to a rapidly growing one, there will be less structural unemployment.

- **The pace of change in the economy.** If demand, supply and people's tastes change at a fast rate, industry has to adapt quickly to change. This leads to more structural unemployment.

- **The regional structure of industry.** If declining industries are heavily concentrated in one area, this may make it much more difficult for people to find new jobs. For example, both the shipbuilding and mining industries were heavily concentrated. Some areas have taken many years to adapt to and reduce the level of structural unemployment.

A combination of frictional and structural unemployment results in what is referred to as **natural unemployment** or NAIRU (non-accelerating inflation rate of unemployment). According to monetarist economists, attempts to lower unemployment below NAIRU will risk the acceleration or increase of inflation. This is discussed in more detail in Chapter 3.

A recent study entitled *The Future of Work in Canada* explores the "pervasive public anxiety" that exists regarding jobs, the economy and our ability to cope with change (Betcherman and Lowe 1997). This anxiety is located in the individualization of the risk associated with trends of high unemployment, downsizing and restructuring. According to the study, individual Canadians are increasingly bearing the risks of unemployment at the same time that the social safety net – in the form of Employment Insurance and stable employment relations – disintegrates.

Some believe that we should completely reorganize our economic system so as to ensure that everyone who wants to work has a job. In 1945, the Canadian government issued a statement committing itself to full employment in the White Paper on *Employment and Income*, acknowledging that unemployment results from the unregulated operation of markets. The government committed to intervening in the economy to create jobs and control job losses. This was a recognition that the government could reduce unemployment by directly generating economic activity and assisting the private sector. At the time, this social policy commitment represented a strong break from the past, in which individuals were solely responsible for their own employment.

However, the notion of full employment as a government policy objective has slowly been abandoned. The *Unemployment Insurance Act* of 1971 addressed the concept of **full employment** and established that 4 percent unemployment was considered full employment. Subsequent to this, the idea of full employment has been rarely mentioned, and never directly applied in social policy.

THE GREAT DEPRESSION: 1929-39

The Roaring Twenties saw boom times in Canada. Unemployment was low; earnings for individuals and companies were high. But prosperity came to a halt with a decade-long depression. It was the beginning of the Dirty Thirties.

The Great Depression caused Canadians great hardship. There was massive unemployment – 27% at the height of the Depression in 1933. The Depression did not end until 1939, when the outbreak of World War II created demand for war materials.

The Great Depression was a turning point for Canada. Before 1930, the government intervened as little as possible, believing that the free market would take care of the economy, and that churches and charities would take care of society. But, in the 1930s, a growing demand arose for the government to step in and create a social safety net with a minimum hourly wage, a standard work week and programs such as Medicare and Unemployment Insurance.

**WHAT IS THE
UNEMPLOYMENT RATE IN
YOUR PROVINCE OR
TERRITORY?**

Use the Internet to find the
unemployment rate for your
province. Compare this to the
rate of unemployment for the
country as a whole.

UNDEREMPLOYMENT AND PART-TIME EMPLOYMENT

People that have paid jobs are considered employed. However, not all employed people are employed full-time. **Full-time employment** refers to people who usually work 30 or more hours per week or people who work less than 30 hours per week, but consider themselves to be employed full-time. **Part-time employment** refers to people who usually work less than 30 hours each week. The voluntary part-time worker chooses to work fewer than 30 hours a week, because he or she is a student, has personal or family responsibilities, wants to spend time in other pursuits or may not need the income of a full-time job. The involuntary part-time worker prefers full-time work but can only find part-time employment.

Dave Broad, director of the Social Policy Research Unit at the University of Regina, found that one of the most pronounced recent labour force trends has been the increase in the number of part-time workers. He found that part-time employment, as a percentage of total employment, has grown steadily from 3.8 percent in 1953, to 12 percent in 1973, to 16.9 percent in 1983, to 18.5 percent in 1999 (Broad 2000, 13). Part-time workers generally experience substandard living and working conditions, and a range of social problems resulting from holding several jobs while trying to balance paid work and family responsibilities. Many commentators believe that this shift to part-time work has resulted from the desire of employers to lower operating costs by substituting high-paying jobs with non-unionized, lower-cost, flexible labour.

Many people who take part-time work do so involuntarily – they would prefer a full-time job if one were available. Involuntary part-time work is defined as a job involving less than 30 hours a week that is held by a worker who has been unable to find full-time employment. These workers are dealing with an underemployment problem. According to Grant Schellenberg, author of *The Changing Nature of Part-time Work* (1997), half of all part-time workers would prefer to work more hours for more pay and about 35 percent want to work full-time. Between 1975 and 1994, the proportion of part-time workers who wanted a full-time job, but could not find one, rose from 11 percent to 35 percent. Sixty-eight percent of involuntary workers are women (Statistics Canada 2000, 11). This trend has increased significantly among mothers with children, indicating that part-time employment is more the result of a lack of employment options for this group, rather than a voluntary choice to balance paid and unpaid work.

The polarization of the workforce – with one group receiving good wages, benefits and job security, and another (including most part-time workers) receiving poor wages, no benefits and little security – is worsening. Since 68 percent of involuntary part-time workers are women, this labour market issue is a gender issue. Analyzing this data according to family characteristics produces disturbing results. The involuntary part-time rates of single mothers (18 percent) far exceeds those of the other groups (Statistics Canada 2000, 12). Comparing full-time full-year employment also finds women at a disadvantage, earning 71.7 percent of what a man earns, on average (see sidebar on page 114).

RATE OF UNEMPLOYMENT

The **unemployment rate** is the percentage of the labour force that is unemployed. The rate of unemployment can be determined by the following calculation:

$$Unemployment\ Rate = \frac{Number\ of\ Unemployed\ People}{Number\ of\ People\ in\ the\ Labour\ Force} \times 100$$

However, not all unemployed people are counted as unemployed. If you are unemployed, but have given up your search for a job, you are no longer counted as unemployed. In other words, many people including those who have given up the search for a job are not considered part of the labour force – they therefore are not included in the equation above.

The official definition of the **labour force** is the number of people in the country 15 years of age or over who either have a job or are actively looking for one. This excludes people living on reservations, full-time members of the armed forces and institutional residents (for example, prison inmates and patients in hospitals or in nursing homes who have resided there for more than six months). Retired people, students, people not actively seeking work and people not available for work for other reasons are also not considered part of the labour force, although they may be part of the working age population. **Discouraged workers** is the term used to refer to those individuals who are no longer looking for a job because they believe they will not find one. Discouraged workers are classified as not being in the labour force.

The rate of unemployment in Canada has varied over the years. During the Depression the rate was around 25 percent. In the 1960s, the rate was as low as 3.4 percent. Since the mid-1970s unemployment has risen to 10 percent and has stayed just above or below this level most of the time. Unemployment rates are higher for youth, women, persons with disabilities and Aboriginal persons. Unemployment rates also differ widely between provinces.

The unemployment rate in January 2004 was 7.4 percent (Statistics Canada, CANSIM, Matrices 282-0087). This means that, of those who were officially counted as being part of the labour force and actively looking for work, 7.4 percent could not find a job. The labour force consists of just over 16 million Canadians, or 65.6 percent of the adult population. Of this 16 million, 1.2 million could not find paid employment. The total number of employed Canadians was therefore 14.5 million. Of these, almost 3 million worked part-time (Statistics Canada, CANSIM, Matrix 3472).

Canada's unemployment rate is generally higher than that of the United States, Japan, Australia and New Zealand. It is also almost double for young people aged 15-24 (16.6 percent for men and 13.7 percent for women). As well, increasing numbers of Canadians are working part-time, many involuntarily. This is a form of partial unemployment that is not measured by unemployment statistics. For example, 38 percent of women and 12 percent of men work part-time (Statistics Canada, CANSIM, Matrix 3472).

INFLATION AND UNEMPLOYMENT

According to monetarist theory, inflation and unemployment have an inverse relationship under ordinary conditions. However, recent history has shown that the Canadian government has chosen to fight inflation, rather than unemployment. Canadians wonder why this is so.

People who have an abundance of money tend to store that money in the form of assets such as stocks and bonds, which pay a rate of return. They tend to benefit more when the rate of inflation is low because their return after inflation is higher. On the flip side, the average income earner does not own much in the way of assets, so they are less concerned with inflation. Keeping their job is crucial, therefore a low unemployment rate is desirable.

Some social policy analysts argue that the government's monetary policy is more concerned with protecting the interests of people with an abundance of money, rather than the average working person.

"Not everything that can be counted counts, and not everything that counts can be counted."
— Albert Einstein

Two alternative measures of labour force activity (in addition to the unemployment rate) are the labour force participation rate and the employment population ratio. The ratio of the labour force to the working age population (age 15+) is referred to as the **labour force participation rate**.

$$Labour\ Force\ Participation\ Rate = \frac{Labour\ Force}{Working\ Age\ Population} \times 100$$

In 1989, the labour force participation rate was 67 percent and in 2000 it was 65.9 percent (Statistics Canada, CANSIM Matrix 3472). This means that 66 out of every 100 persons aged 15 years and over were part of the labour force. The rate varies widely between provinces – with Newfoundland at 56.1 percent and Alberta at 72.6 percent. Even if both provinces had the same unemployment rate, Alberta would be considered to be better off because a greater part of its population was employed. A high participation rate means that a large proportion of the working age population is either employed or actively looking for work. A high participation rate can reflect optimism about the availability of jobs.

The **employment population ratio** is the ratio of employed to the working age population.

$$Employment\ Population\ Ratio = \frac{Employed}{Working\ Age\ Population} \times 100$$

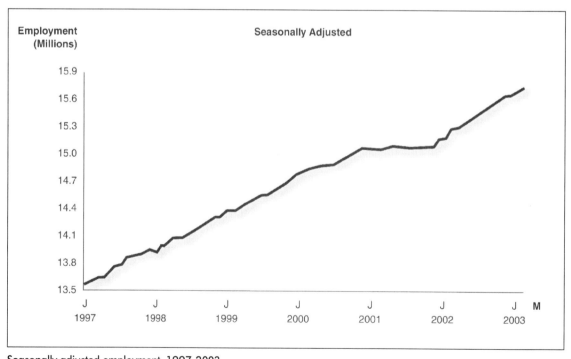

Seasonally adjusted employment, 1997-2003.
Source: Statistics Canada, *Labour Force Survey Release* (2004). Retrieved from: http://www.statcan.ca/english/Subjects/Labour/LFS/ifs-en.htm.

UNIONIZATION

The rise of industrialization in Canada spawned the development of the **trade union movement**. One in three employees in Canada belongs to a union. Trade unions are organizations that represent those individuals working in particular industries or industrial sectors, and they work to defend and advance the interests of these workers in terms of wages and working conditions as well as broader welfare concerns.

Workers first organized against the threat of mechanization, and later to improve working conditions. In 1886, the Trades and Labour Congress was formed. In 1902, this was changed to the Canadian Federation of Labour, as Canadian unionists sought to become more independent from the American union movement. These early union efforts appear to have had little impact on work conditions or wages. It was not until the 1920s that unions began to have an impact on the economy, but this was forestalled by the Great Depression of the 1930s. After the Depression, between 1940 and 1956, union membership quadrupled. After 1956, union membership grew more slowly due to the increase in white-collar workers, who were less inclined to organize. The period from 1967 to 1997 saw a renewed growth in union organization, as women increasingly entered the workforce. The percentage of women who are members of unions (29.2 percent) is now only slightly lower than that of men (30.6 percent). This high level is due, in large part, to the unionization of the teaching and health professions where women predominate.

Unionization has had an important impact on Canadian social welfare. Unionized jobs generally provide higher wages, greater non-wage benefits and better work arrangements. The role of unions also extends beyond the workplace setting. Unions often promote public income security provisions and other social and health services.

In more recent years, with globalization and greater economic instability, the organized labour movement has faced new challenges. Among these are the transfer of manufacturing jobs to Third World countries where labour is cheap and working conditions are unregulated, as well as a shift to low-paying, part-time and temporary jobs. All these have made union organizing more difficult and more urgent.

THE ECONOMIC AND SOCIAL COSTS OF UNEMPLOYMENT

There are social and economic costs associated with unemployment. Unemployment represents a loss of revenue for society and, more important, it has a negative impact on individual citizens.

First, let us examine the economic costs. Using human resources for work produces goods and services and allows the employed to earn a salary. Unemployment, on the other hand, leads to a reduction on the output of goods and services and a loss of income for employees. However, this is only a fraction of society's loss. For example, Human Resources Development Canada (HRDC) analysis points out that the 1994 total production loss associated with cyclical and structural unemployment was estimated by various studies to have ranged from

Protest for jobs, not soup kitchens, in Montreal (National Archives of Canada/PA93930).

GROSS NATIONAL/DOMESTIC PRODUCT

Growth in the economy is usually referred to as a growth in Gross National Product (GNP) or Gross Domestic Product (GDP). The GNP includes all economic activity or the monetary value of all goods and services produced in the world by Canadian-based firms. The GNP can be expressed including inflation (nominal GNP) and excluding inflation (real GNP). For example, if the GNP grew by 10 percent but the inflation rate was 8 percent, the real growth would be 2 percent. In this example, most of the growth is due to increases in prices and only 2 percent of growth is in real production. On the other hand, if the GNP grew by 5 percent and the inflation rate was still 8 percent, the economy contracted by 3 percent. Data on GNP is available in constant or current dollars. To compare GNP over a number of years, it is better to use constant dollars, because this accounts for inflation. The dollar value of the current year is known as the current dollar. Since the GNP includes products and services produced by Canadians outside Canada, it is not necessarily a good measure of the Canadian economy.

The GDP includes all economic activity (the monetary value of all goods and services produced) taking place within the geographical domain of any country or province. This indicator is available for both Canada and the provinces. The same rationale as for the GNP is used to compare the growth rates for GDP (in real terms and using constant dollars).

Many people throw around the terms GNP and GDP, but few of us know where this system of quantification originated. In her book *Counting for Nothing: What Men Value and What Women are Worth*, economist Marilyn Waring tells us that GDP and GNP come from a small calculation in the UN System of National Accounts (UNSNA). She believes that UNSNA has allowed women's work and much of the rest of life to be made invisible, and subsequently deemed unimportant in measures of economic progress. The UNSNA is described by its proponents as a coherent, consistent and integrated set of macroeconomic accounts, balance sheets and tables based on a set of internationally agreed concepts, definitions, classifications and accounting rules. The UNSNA presents economic data in a format that is designed for purposes of economic analysis, decision making and policy making. It is commonly used as a way of comparing the supposed economic well-being of countries. However, the UNSNA ensures that certain factors of

economic life appear far more important than others. Waring says that when economy includes only activities that involve monetary transactions, much of women's productive and reproductive work is excluded. Bearing children, mothering, tending a garden, feeding one's family, milking a family cow and raising sheep for wool you use yourself are all excluded as economic activities and do not find their way into any country's System of National Accounts. In other words, through a traditional understanding of the economy, much of the work of half of the population becomes invisible.

Here is how the UNSNA divides life, according to Waring:

Things with economic value:

- trees when they are cut down
- the tobacco industry
- arms and missile production
- the weight loss industry
- crime, the court system and imprisonment
- prostitution
- illness, clinics and hospitals
- death and the funeral business
- rebuilding countries after natural disasters or terrorist attacks
- war
- oil spills
- women's bodies used in media advertising

Things without economic value:

- rivers and forests (when they are not being harnessed for economic gain)
- health
- caring for your own children
- vegetables grown in your own garden and eaten by your family
- caring for the Earth
- a mother's contribution to the birthing process
- beauty (except if it is for sale in an art piece)
- doing your own dishes and laundry
- hunting, fishing, and trapping your own food.

3.8 ercent to 10.2 percent of the $748 billion GDP. That adds up to a loss of $29-$77 billion.

In addition to production losses, governments suffer revenue losses from personal and corporate taxes as well as increased expenditures on EI and SA. For all governments, the budget costs of Canada's unemployment rate of 10.4 percent in 1994, compared to an unemployment rate of 8.5 percent, might range from $8 to $12 billion (Human Resources Development Canada 1996, 1).

To summarize, the economic costs of unemployment include:

- **Loss of output to the economy.** The unemployed could be producing goods and services. If they are not, then GDP is lower than it could be.

- **Loss of tax revenue.** Unemployed people are not earning wages, and therefore they aren't paying tax. The government loses a potential source of tax.

- **Increase in government expenditure.** The government has to pay out benefits to support the unemployed.

- **Loss of profits.** With higher unemployment, firms are unlikely to perform better and make higher profits.

Perhaps the main costs of unemployment are those incurred by the unemployed themselves. Individuals lose their self-esteem and confidence. If they are unemployed for a long time, they may also lose their skills. In addition to these effects, unemployment often leads to poor health as well as a range of social and family problems not calculated in official statistics.

THREE ECONOMIC THEORIES ON UNEMPLOYMENT

Economists do not agree on the causes or solutions to unemployment. Debate generally revolves around explanations derived from the three economic theories: Keynesian economics, monetarist economics and political economy. Each has a completely different view of the role of government in the economy and the effects of social spending on the economy. We can summarize these approaches as follows (see Chapter 3 for a fuller discussion).

The Keynesian approach (based on the work of economist John Maynard Keynes) is based on the concepts of demand and labour. The premise is that unemployment results from a lack of demand for commodities, because people have less money to spend. This creates a vicious circle. Economists of this persuasion believe that the government should spend when unemployment is high to maintain consumer demand. The Keynesian approach was widely implemented after World War II, and provided the impetus and foundation for the development of modern social welfare programs.

In the last decade or so, the monetarist approach has dominated government policies in Canada and other industrialized countries. In this approach, inflation is considered to be the primary problem. Low

A demonstration for cash relief, in 1952 (National Archives/ PA93913).

WHO EARNS MINIMUM WAGE?

	1995 Male	1995 Female
Young (<24)	59.0%	46.3%
Old (>24)	41.0%	53.6%
Drop out	36.3%	36.7%
High school grad	24.3%	26.1%
College or trade	18.5%	19.0%
Univ. grad	6.7%	4.3%

Source: Nicole M. Fortin and Thomas Lemieux, "Income redistribution in Canada: minimum wages versus other policy instruments." Paper presented to the IRPP Conference on Adapting Public Policy to a Labour Market in Transition. Montreal, PQ, April 18-19, 1997.

inflation is seen as a condition that is necessary to attract investment, because people will not invest their money in countries that have high inflation. Monetarists tend to see unemployment as not necessarily a bad thing; they believe that the government can use unemployment as a tool to keep inflation in check – it cools inflation by keeping wage demands lower, and less income means that people are buying fewer commodities.

The political economy approach concentrates on the relationship between politics and economics and is generally critical of government employment policy. In this approach, the economic power belongs to the corporate elite, who influence the political powers to pursue the corporate elite's interests, rather than those of the unemployed. The political economy approach focuses on the large concentration of ownership of major corporations and the large spread and great inequality between employers at the top and the workers at the bottom.

MINIMUM WAGE AND SOCIAL WELFARE

Canada's provinces all set a standard **minimum wage**. This is the lowest wage rate, by law, that an employer can pay employees to perform their work. Wage laws were originally instituted to protect women and children from uncontrolled exploitation. Minimum wage laws were first instituted in Canada in 1918 in the provinces of British Columbia and Manitoba, but only women were covered. By 1920, four other provinces followed: Nova Scotia, Quebec, Ontario and Saskatchewan. British Columbia was the first province to include men, with the *Men's Minimum Wage Act* (1925). The Act set a higher minimum wage for men, reflecting the belief that the man should be the family's breadwinner and therefore should be paid more.

In 1993, about 6 percent of Canadians earned minimum wage (Foitin and Lemieux 1997). Many people believe that only struggling students or people without higher education make the minimum wage. This is not the case: 61 percent of minimum wage workers are adults, 64 percent are women and 48 percent have some post-secondary education (Goldberg and Green 1999, 4).

The minimum wage varies by province and territory. The general minimum wage in Ontario was $6.85 per hour in 2003. One of the actions by the newly elected Liberal government was to raise this by 30 cents to $7.15 and it will increase every year until it reaches $8.00 in 2007. The rates are set in the *Ontario Employment Standards Act*. In Alberta the minimum wage for most workers is $5.90 per hour. Nova Scotia has set the minimum wage for experienced employees at $6.00 per hour and for inexperienced employees at $5.55 per hour.

The rates are raised periodically to account for a portion of inflation, but the general purchasing power of the minimum wage has decreased over the past few decades. The real value of the minimum wage (after inflation) has fallen dramatically from its peak in the mid-1970s. Table 4.1 illustrates the decrease in purchasing power of the minimum wage between 1976 and 1995.

• Killer of Jobs?

The level of minimum wages has been the subject of considerable public debate. Some view it as a "killer of jobs" – hurting those it intends to help by pricing low-wage earners out of the job market. Others, specifically labour unions and anti-poverty groups, view it as a policy instrument for promoting greater wage equity and anti-poverty goals.

The impact of increasing the minimum wage on employment levels appears to be minimal. Analysis shows that large increases in the minimum wage have been followed by both increases and decreases in employment, demonstrating that other trends in the economy have greater influence on employment levels than do minimum wages. Thus, minimum wages are not a "killer of jobs," as some would have us believe (Goldberg and Green 1999, 17). Studies looking at the employment effects of minimum wage changes typically find that a 10 percent increase in the minimum wage produces declines in the range of 0 to 2 percent in the employment-to-population ratio. No negative effect on employment would be preferable, but the benefits, including the social benefits of increasing low-income wages by 10 percent, must be weighed against the costs of slightly higher unemployment.

Some social policy advocates state that minimum wages should be set at the poverty line. They believe that, in a just society, people working full-time should not find themselves living in poverty. Setting a higher minimum wage would raise the floor for low-income earners and reduce the costs for many of our income security programs. People would be getting their income from the labour market, rather than having to turn to government transfers, but governments must also consider possible negative impacts on the overall economy.

INFLATION: THE MONETARIST'S NEMESIS

Inflation is defined as the average rate of increase in prices by the federal Department of Finance. Inflation is usually measured as a percentage increase in the Consumer Price Index (CPI). Canada's inflation target, as set out by the federal government and the Bank of Canada, aims to keep inflation within a range of 1% to 3%. If the rate of inflation is 10% a year, $100 worth of purchases last year will, on average, cost $110 this year.

Table 4.1: Comparison Annual Minimum Wage Income (constant 1995$ based on 40-hour work week)

Province	1976	1995	% Change
Newfoundland	14,615	9,880	-32%
Prince Edward Island	14,031	9,880	-30%
Nova Scotia	14,615	10,712	-27%
New Brunswick	14,569	10,400	-29%
Quebec	16,573	12,480	-25%
Ontario	15,210	14,248	-6%
Manitoba	16,065	11,232	-30%
Saskatchewan	16,368	11,128	-32%
Alberta	15,851	10,400	-34%
British Columbia	17,537	14,560	-17%

Source: Christa Freiler and Judy Cerny, *Benefiting Canada's Children: Perspectives on Gender and Social Responsibility* (Ottawa: Child Poverty Action Group, 1998). Retrieved from: http://www.swc-cfc.gc.ca/publish/research/cbenef-e.html (September 23, 1999).

FACTORS INFLUENCING UNEMPLOYMENT

Unemployment occurs when the supply and demand for human resources or labour is out of synch. Supply and demand, in turn, are influenced by a range of forces created by the interaction of economic, structural and policy factors.

• Economic Factors

There is a range of more strictly economic factors that influence employment and unemployment levels. These affect the supply/demand equation for jobs. Consider the following:

- **Business cycles.** Agreement among economists is rare, but they do agree that market-driven economies move in cycles, and it is during the dips that unemployment may result. The cause of cycles is not as clear, but it is generally agreed that it is a function of supply and demand throughout the economy.

- **Industrial adjustment.** Production may move from high-wage countries to low-wage countries, from inefficient facilities to newer ones, and these moves can leave a trail of unemployed workers.

- **Cost of production and productivity.** Low productivity may result from obsolete plants and equipment, high cost of labour per unit, high transportation costs, bad management and high taxes. The value of the Canadian dollar relative to other currencies, particularly the U.S. dollar, also has a major impact on the business costs and competitiveness.

- **Technological changes.** Increased automation may result in a decreased demand for labour. It can also result in skills redundancies – situations in which the original workers do not have the technological skills necessary for the new types of occupations. (On the positive side, technological change can also result in new products, new markets or increased productivity.)

• Structural Factors

Unemployment levels are also affected by a number of quasi-economic factors, which we will refer to as "structural." These include the following:

- **Growing labour supply.** Since 1981, Canada's labour supply has grown more than at any time in its history. Women, persons with disabilities and Aboriginal Peoples have entered the labour force in growing numbers.

- **Imbalance between skills supply and demand.** People may not be able to take advantage of job opportunities because they lack the skills needed for the jobs available in their area. The mismatching of skills in demand with those available is a common and persistent cause of unemployment. As Canada shifts to a more knowledge-based economy, the availability of jobs for those without high levels of education will shrink.

Protesting for full employment and Unemployment Insurance (National Archives/PA125093).

Checking for jobs at a Human Resources Centre in Vancouver, 2002. Statistics Canada reported that same day that unemployment had jumped from 7.5 to 8 percent , the highest level in almost three years (CP PHOTO/Chuck Stoody).

- **Movement between jobs.** Called frictional unemployment, this phenomenon refers to people who switch jobs. While they are between jobs, they are considered unemployed.
- **Seasonal layoffs.** People get laid off in seasonal occupations such as the resource industries, construction and tourism. Canada is particularly affected by seasonal layoffs.
- **Internal migration.** Rural-to-urban migration can increase unemployment until the migrating people find jobs.

• Policy Factors

Government economic and social policies continue to be used as tools in effecting certain outcomes, such as the rate of inflation, deficit levels and international trade. The following affect employment:

- **Interest rates.** The use of high interest rates to combat inflation increases the cost of doing business and increases the cost of financing government deficits. This may lead to unemployment.
- **Exchange rate policies.** The exchange rate policy of keeping the dollar artificially high may make Canadian products less competitive.
- **Education and job training.** Government job training initiatives can influence employment levels. These include job-specific training and support to schools, colleges and universities, as well as apprenticeship programs.

WHAT IS THE "PERSONAL SECURITY INDEX"?

Developed by CCSD, the PSI is a five-year-old tool to measure annual changes in the security of Canadians according to three key elements:

• Economic security in the broad sense of job and financial security.

• Health security in the sense of protection against the threats of disease and injury.

• Physical safety in the sense of feeling safe from violent crime and theft.

The PSI measures changes in both empirical data and in people's perceptions of their personal security. The 2003 PSI results are available at: http://www.ccsd.ca/pubs/ 2003/psi/

THE EFFICIENCY/EQUITY DEBATE

Debates about economic efficiency and social equity are at the heart of much of mainstream social policy discussions. **Economic efficiency** generally refers to economic growth with a flexible and increasingly productive labour market. **Social equity**, on the other hand, refers to the existence of adequate levels of health and security for all people, and a reasonably equal distribution of income and wealth. For example, a society may consider the objective of redistribution to the poor a valued objective, but if such a redistribution comes at a substantial cost in terms of misallocated resources and income losses, it may not be politically or economically sustainable.

Statements such as "Canada cannot afford generous social programs" or "more taxes will just kill the economy" contain ideas about trade-offs between economic efficiency and social equity. On one side of the debate are organizations such as the Fraser Institute who believe that economic freedom is the key to prosperity. They quote monetarist theorist Milton Friedman to block their claims: "Freeing people economically unleashes individual drive and initiative and puts a nation on the road to economic growth," to back their claim (Gwartney and Lawson 2003). Key to economic freedom, according to the Institute, are low taxes and minimal social spending. At the other end of the debate are organizations such as the Canadian Council on Social Development (CCSD). They believe that Canada must "knock down the barriers to social exclusion by investing in well-designed social policies that can contribute to a healthy, productive and safe Canadian population – from cradle to grave" (CCSD 2003). The Fraser Institute has developed the "Economic Freedom Index" (see http://www.fraserinstitute.ca) to measure economic efficiency and the CCSD has developed the "Personal Security Index" (see http://www.ccsd.ca/pubs/2003/psi/) to measure social equity.

Social policy analysts are often confronted with the argument that social welfare programs cause inefficiencies in the economy, and that economic efficiency and social equity are incompatible goals. Some argue that social spending undermines the competitiveness of Canadian business by channelling valuable resources away from making business firms more competitive. Others counter that social spending helps improve employee skill levels, employee health and confidence, as well as family security, thereby making Canada more competitive. So what is the relationship between economic efficiency and social equity? Is there a direct trade-off, as many would have us believe?

Income security and social services increase the health and security of people. Whether or not this negatively or positively affects Canada's competitiveness is a scientific question. Many European countries have found that social spending has more beneficial impacts on economic growth than do tax cuts for upper-income earners.

In the end, the efficiency/equity trade-off debate is a question that can only be answered by examining the relevant empirical data. The largest collection of research on the issue is the Luxembourg Income Study (LIS) project, a database of household income surveys. These surveys provide demographic, income and expenditure information on three different levels (household, person and child), from 25 countries on four continents (Europe, America, Asia and Oceania). The LIS data generally shows that the "efficiency-equality trade-off associated with welfare state economies does not hold" (Bohácek 2002, 1). Many of the reports arising from LIS can be downloaded from: http://www.lisproject.org/publications/wpapers.htm. Perhaps there is no real inverse relationship (if one goes up, the other goes down) between economic growth and social equity. Well-designed social and economic policies should reinforce each other, building both a strong economy and a just society.

• From Welfare State to Social Investment State

New ideas have emerged about how to provide social welfare, and scholars worldwide are examining new approaches. For example, sociologist Anthony Giddens proposes a **social investment state** that focuses on social inclusion by strengthening civil society and providing equality of opportunity rather than equality of outcomes (*The Third Way*, 1998). Giddens believes that jobs that are not low paying and dead-end are essential to attacking involuntary social exclusion. Nevertheless, an inclusive society must also provide for the basic needs of those who cannot work, and must recognize the wider diversity of goals that life has to offer (Giddens 1998, 31).

Giddens rejects the ideologies of liberalism and socialism as workable options (see Chapter 3 for further explanation). The social investment state, according to Giddens, is a mixed economy with an interaction of state, family, work and community, with each area reinforcing one another. Giddens emphasizes investment in human capital to cultivate human potential wherever possible, rather than directly providing income support. He calls this a positive welfare society. In such a state the government would focus on providing employment-training opportunities for working-age adults and a positive educational and nurturing environment for children.

In the last decade governments worldwide have started to recognize that a new policy mix is required to respond to changing labour markets, an ageing population, worsening inequality, poverty and a knowledge-based economy. Governments in the European Union are now considering social policy, economic policy and employment policy in a new way – as being interrelated. Rather than seeing an inverse trade-off, they see each area reinforcing one another. With this in mind, they put forward a social welfare policy mix that addresses employment support, income support (especially for families with children) and service support (such as housing and child care). They call this an "activation for social inclusion strategy."

The social investment state and its variations focus on

- partnership investments in lifelong learning and training,

- encouragement for family-friendly workplaces and

- support for innovation, entrepreneurship and expansion of existing enterprises.

CASH VS. COERCION

In what may set an example for other provinces, on April 2, 2004, Quebec announced cash incentives to get welfare recipients into the workforce.

The Liberal government's new anti-poverty strategy ensures a minimum annual guaranteed income (as of April 1, 2005). The income will be fully indexed for those who are incapable of working and indexed at 50 percent for those who can work but refuse to do so.

The guaranteed income will also be fully indeed for those who show a desire to reintegrate into the job market. Coercive measures requiring welfare recipients to find work or be peanlized will be abolished.

"It is unique, unlike anything else in Canada," said Vivian Labrie, the head of the province's anti-poverty coalition. "But there are still no assurances that people will have enough money to pay for all the essential services under this plan … There is just no way that persons earning $503 a month can cover all their bills."

Poster created by "just1WORLD," which seeks to help those living in the world's poorest countries.

RACIALIZED GROUP

The term "racialized group" is preferred to the more commonly used "visible minority."

The term racialized group makes it clear that race is not determined by biology, but is socially constructed. It highlights the socially constructed differences, rather than the biological differences. To say that race-based work divisions are socially constructed means that reality is constructed in the activity of human beings.

Further, the term racialized groups more accurately reflects the process by which non-white groups are considered almost solely by race while white people are not.

Finally, the term "visible minority" is often used with the intention of negative connotation (Smith and Jackson, 2002)

LABOUR MARKET EXPERIENCES AND INCOMES OF RECENT IMMIGRANTS

Canada has always been a nation of immigrants (other than the original inhabitants of this land – the Aboriginal Peoples). Since 1967, there has been a major shift in the source countries from which immigrants have come to Canada. Fewer now come from Western Europe; most now come from the countries of Asia, Africa and Central and South America. In addition, today, three in four recent immigrants to Canada belong to visible minority groups, making them more vulnerable to racial discrimination and social exclusion. **Visible minorities** are defined as being neither Caucasian nor Aboriginal. Members of visible minority groups now make up about 11 percent of the total Canadian population, compared to just 6 percent as recently as 1986.

Chapter 7 details the broader aspects of poverty in Canada, but clearly employment and the labour market are crucial aspects of inclusion for recent immigrants. Poverty among recent immigrants stands at 27 percent, and their annual wages and salaries are one-third less than those of other Canadians. Many recent visible minority immigrants perceive themselves as having been discriminated against in the job market.

Ekuma Smith, senior research associate with the Canadian Council on Social Development (CCSD) and Andrew Jackson, CCSD research director, studied levels of employment, earnings, family incomes and poverty rates of recent immigrants, and compared them to the rest of the Canadian population over the economic recovery period from 1995 to 1998. Their key findings indicate that the "rising tide" of economic recovery in the mid- to late 1990s had a positive impact on the employment opportunities and incomes of recent immigrants. This indicates that a healthy labour market can provide a major impetus towards equality and the inclusion of recent immigrants into the economic and social mainstream. However, they also found that the gap between recent immigrants and the rest of Canadians remains large.

The non-recognition or the undervaluing of foreign education, skills and credentials are emerging as key factors that help explain why recent immigrants do not do as well in the job market. A variety of policies is required to assist the process of inclusion and confront discrimination. These policies include employment equity, credentials recognition, promotion of the "hidden skills" of new immigrants to prospective employers and provision of language and skills training to new immigrants.

A recent study by Statistics Canada (Frenette and Morissette 2003) discovered that recent immigrant men employed on a full-year, full-time basis saw their real earnings fall 7 percent on average from 1980 to 2000, even though they had a substantial increase in their educational attainment. During the same period, however, real earnings of Canadian-born men went up 7 percent. Earnings of recent immigrant women rose over the period, but not as quickly as among Canadian-born women.

The rapid integration of immigrants into the Canadian labour market is key to the country's future prosperity. To achieve successful integration, we must recognize that racism is a factor. Racism can be a subtle

NDP leader Alexa McDonough and candidate Olivia Chow cut into a Youth Unemployment "cake." (CP/1997, *Toronto Star*/Rick Eglinton).

REFERENCES

* Betcherman, G., and G. Lowe. 1997. *The Future of Work in Canada*. A Synthesis Report. Ottawa: CPRN.

* Boháček, Radim. 2002. *The Efficiency-Equality Tradeoff in Welfare State Economies*. Luxembourg Income Study (LIS) project. Available at: http://www.lisproject.org/publications/wpapers.htm

* Broad, D. 2000. Living a half life? Part-time work, labour standards and social welfare. *Canadian Social Work Review*, Vol. 17, No 1.

* Canadian Council on Social Development. 2003. Imagining a Future of Inclusion: CCSD's submission to the House Of Commons Standing Committee On Finance, Ottawa: CCSD.

* Fortin, Nicole M., and Thomas Lemieux. 1997. "Income redistribution in Canada: minimum wages versus other policy instruments." Paper presented to the IRPP Conference on Adapting Public Policy to a Labour Market in Transition. Montreal, PQ, April 18-19, 1997.

* Frenette, Marc, and Morissette, René. 2003. Will they ever converge? Earnings of immigrants and Canadian-born workers over the last two decades. Ottawa: Statistics Canada.

* Giddens, Anthony. 1998. Equality and the social investment state. In I. Hargreaves and I. Christie, eds., *Tomorrow's Politics: The Third Way and Beyond*. London, U.K.: Demos.

* Goldberg, Michael, and David Green. 1999. *Raising the Floor: The Social and Economic Benefits of Minimum Wages in Canada*. BC: Canadian Centre for Policy Alternatives. Retrieved from: http://www.policyalternatives.ca/bc/minwage.pdf on Dec. 23, 2002.

* Gwartney, James D. and Robert A. Lawson. 2003. Economic Freedom of the World: 2003 Annual Report. Vancouver: Fraser Institute.

* Human Resources Development Canada. 1996. Tallying the economic and social costs of unemployment. *Applied Research Bulletin*, Summer/Fall 2, No. 2.

* Schellenberg, Grant. 1997. The changing nature of part-time work. *Social Research Series Report No. 4*. Ottawa: Canadian Council on Social Development.

* Smith, E., and A. Jackson. 2002. *Does a Rising Tide Lift All Boats? Labour Market Experiences and*

phenomenon. It may be less about excluding candidates from consideration for a job because of their skin colour than about fearing that they will not "fit in." And it may be about seeing foreign credentials and experience as "obviously inferior," rather than assessing skills and abilities on an individual basis (Smith, presentation to SOWK 1000 class, 2003). Other crucial factors are language skills training opportunities, overall economic growth and well-designed and accessible settlement services.

YOUTH UNEMPLOYMENT

While they are working, young people gain valuable experience and life skills. In fact, young people who are employed part-time generally have better school performance and a lower dropout rate. By the same token, teens who lack skills and job experience are at a disadvantage when competing for jobs. Research confirms that teens that have dropped out of school are having much greater difficulty finding full-time jobs than even a decade ago, and many of those working earn minimum wage. **Youth unemployment**, the difficulty many young people have in finding meaningful work that will enable them to make a smooth transition to adulthood, is a major problem in Canada, and it is one that is unlikely to go away without conscious policy intervention.

Youth at Work, an extended study of the labour market experiences of teenagers (aged 15-19 years), found that the employment rate of teens fell sharply from 1989 to 1997. The lack of jobs during the recession and recovery sharply limited the opportunities for teenagers to find work. Overall, the teen employment rate in 1999 was 41.1 percent, up modestly from the low of 37.1 percent in 1997, but not near the rate of 51.6 percent in 1989. Employment rates were typically lower for teens from lower-income and immigrant families, and (not surprisingly) high-unemployment regions and communities.

*Incomes of Recent Immigrants.
Ottawa: Canadian Council on
Social Development. Retrieved
from: http://www.ccsd.ca/pubs/
2002/risingtide/index.htm on
October 4, 2002.*

* *Statistics Canada. 2002.
Longitudinal Aspects of Involuntary
Part-Time Employment. Ottawa.*

A key problem for teens (and young adults to a lesser degree) was that the recession and cuts to Employment Insurance forced many middle-aged and older workers with more skills and experience to accept low-income jobs. This effectively shut many employable teens and young adults out of the job market. Even after the recovery began, teens were still stuck behind 20- to 24-year-olds in the job queue. It is possible that welfare reforms in various provinces, such as making young adults ineligible for benefits, also heightened competition for relatively low-wage jobs.

A series of policy initiatives directed towards youth employment seems particularly urgent. The importance of young people having an opportunity to acquire work experience and skills, as well as to develop the personal confidence that accompanies employment, cannot be overemphasized if they and their families are subsequently to participate fully in the Canadian economy and society.

CONCLUSION

While Canada has sustained impressive economic growth over the past decade or so, it still does not generate or distribute enough employment to sustain all Canadians, and secure employment is key to reducing the incidence of poverty. Increasingly, those with jobs are in uncertain situations, working part-time or in temporary jobs. The "just-in-time" economy of the 1990s has resulted in less secure employment and fewer benefits.

There are social and economic costs to unemployment – costs often overlooked in the thrust to compete globally. Unfortunately, arguments for economic efficiency often preclude an intelligent debate about social equity and many assume that a direct trade-off between economic efficiency and social equity exists. However, unstable work, low wages and the decreasing purchasing power of the minimum wage have been obstacles to reducing and preventing poverty in Canada. Economic prosperity in Canada is increasingly polarized – corporate executive salaries and the use of food banks and shelters for the homeless are both hitting all-time highs.

Advanced capitalist economies such as Canada's are changing, and changes in social welfare policy need to keep pace. Rather than viewing social programs as a drain on the economy, there is a need to look more closely at the interactions between the economy, employment and social policy. There is a need for more government involvement in the economy to ensure that people actively participate in all aspects of community life.

Many social welfare analysts are now calling for a change in the direction of our economic and social policies, one that is premised on the idea of social inclusion. The belief underlying this premise is that social inclusion will lead to social cohesion, economic growth and, in the long run, a reduction in the number of individuals who require social welfare assistance.

CHAPTER 4: LABOUR MARKET AND EMPLOYMENT

Discussion Questions

1. What are some of the recent trends that are affecting the income and job security of Canadians?
2. Why are people who are discouraged or, in other words, have stopped looking for a job not counted in the official unemployment statistics?
3. What is the relevance of the social costs of unemployment to future government expenditures?
4. List and explain the three theories on unemployment. How would each theory differ in its approach to solving unemployment?
5. List the economic, structural and policy factors that influence unemployment.
6. Define what is meant by the concepts of "economic efficiency" and "social equity," and explain why some might regard the two as being in a trade-off relationship.
7. Describe the labour market experiences of recent immigrants and explain two possible reasons for these experiences.

Websites

- **The Centre for Social Justice**
  http://www.socialjustice.org

  The Centre is an advocacy organization that seeks to strengthen the struggle for social justice. Check out their free on-line books.

- **Just Labour: A Canadian Journal of Work & Society**
  http://www.justlabour.yorku.ca

  York University's Centre for Research on Work & Society is pleased to offer trade unionists, community activists, researchers, policymakers and students the first volume of *Just Labour: A Canadian Journal of Work & Society*.

- **Canadian Centre for Policy Alternatives**
  http://www.policyalternatives.ca

  The CCPA is a non-profit research organization, funded primarily through organizational and individual membership. It was founded in 1980 to promote research on economic and social policy issues from a progressive point of view. Check out the "Behind the Numbers" section.

- **Canadian Labour Congress**
  http://www.clc-ctc.ca

  The CLC conducts research and publishes employment- and labour-related reports, many of which are available on-line. A Work Rights website (http://www.workrights.ca) is also accessible from here.

- **Disability Research Information Page**
  http://www.ccsd.ca/drip/research

  The site contains a large collection of Information Sheets on disability issues, many specifically dealing with employment issues.

Key Concepts

- Employment
- Self-employment
- Underemployment
- Frictional unemployment
- Cyclical unemployment
- Structural unemployment
- Natural unemployment
- Full employment
- Full-time employment
- Part-time employment
- Unemployment rate
- Labour force
- Discouraged workers
- Labour force participation rate
- Employment population ratio
- Trade union movement
- Minimum wage
- Economic efficiency
- Social equity
- Social investment state
- Visible minorities
- Youth unemployment

Children sing during the welcoming ceremony at the "World Summit on Sustainable Development" in South Africa, August 25, 2002. The summit sought to develop a plan for lifting people out of poverty; providing health care, clean water and sustainable energy to those without them and protecting the environment (AP PHOTO/Dario Lopez-Mills).

5

Globalization and Human Rights

The Social Welfare Context

We have entered a period of tremendous economic transition. The world is being transformed into a vast global marketplace by complex financial systems and revolutionary information technologies. As global corporations gain more power and influence, they are preparing regulations to protect their interests, and they are relying on institutions such as the World Trade Organization to enforce them. In the face of this vast concentration of resources and power in fewer and fewer hands, human beings need new mechanisms to protect their rights and their welfare.

M ajor corporations that operate across the globe are growing larger and more powerful. This growth in power and influence is affecting social welfare in countries around the world, and Canada is no exception. Globalization is creating new patterns of interaction among people, states and private companies, but it is also threatening to compound many existing challenges and deepening the economic marginalization of those most vulnerable. As globalization progresses, social protections are being eroded. In this chapter we will see how the concept of human rights has become a key response – global-based standards of human rights can provide the structures for global social welfare, equality and justice.

Human rights became an international priority for the United Nations 50 years ago, and were addressed formally in the December 1948 Universal Declaration of Human Rights. In today's complex world, these rights have gained prominence as a universally recognized set of norms and standards that increasingly shape our relations as individuals and as collective members of groups, within communities and among nations. Human rights include

- the rights of political choice and association, of opinion and expression and of culture;
- the freedom from fear and from all forms of discrimination and prejudice and
- the freedom from want and the right to employment and well-being and, collectively, to development.

Today, there is near-universal recognition that respect for human rights is essential to achieving the three agreed-upon global priorities of peace, development and democracy. But achieving these priorities is

"Civil and political rights — the right to vote — is meaningless in the absence of having your basic needs met. An adequate standard of living is a right."

— Josephine Grey, formerly the Canadian observer for domestic issues to the World Summit on Social Development in Copenhagen, 1995. She is currently the Executive Director of LIFT (Low Income Families Together).

proving to be difficult. As nations compete to become more "investor friendly," social welfare is eroded in favour of tax cuts and government debt payment. Globalization has also provided capital with an exit option – if corporations do not like what they see in the policy of a particular country, they leave. This gives corporations more control over working conditions and civil society. In the global age, Keynesian policies of demand management, progressive social policy and full employment are no longer priorities.

The social welfare of people, whether it be in a country or worldwide, can be based on the idea of human rights or social standards. In this chapter, we will explore how a human rights-based approach to social welfare can act as a counterbalance to globalization. It provides a framework and mechanism to pursue global social welfare within increasingly limited confines. Corporations have globalized and protected their interests through free trade agreements and institutions. Social welfare must take a similar course, and at the same time it must hold corporations accountable to human rights standards.

As the international community becomes increasingly integrated, how can cultural diversity and integrity be respected? Is a global culture inevitable? If so, is the world ready for it? Can we respect cultural differences and have universal, worldwide human rights? These are some of the issues, concerns and questions underlying the debate over universal human rights.

CANADA IN THE WORLD

To this point, we have focused on economic disparity and social welfare in Canada, but it is also important to understand how Canada fits into the larger global picture. We have seen how in Canada a relatively small number of people own a large share of the resources and obtain a large share of total income. At the international level, the same phenomenon occurs.

Canada is a wealthy country, possessing more than its share of wealth per capita. Canada's rank in North America in 2002 is illustrated in the table below.

Table 5.1: Human Development Indicators, 2002

	CANADA	UNITED STATES	MEXICO
Life expectancy	78.8	77.0	72.6
GDP per capita	27,840	34,142	9,023
Population without improved water sources	0%	0%	14%
Proportion of population with less than $1 per day	0%	0%	10.1%
Proportion below 50% of median income	12.8%	16.9%	22.1%
Per capita health expenditures	1,939	4,721	236

Source: United Nation Development Programme, *Human Development Indicators* (UNDP, 2002). Retrieved from: http://www.undp.org.

These disparities of wealth among countries are not simply a matter of entitlement. It does not mean that as Canadians we work harder than our Mexican neighbours; in fact, the reverse may be true. Our consumer-driven lifestyle depends directly upon the production of cheap goods by our poorer neighbours. Bananas, coffee, clothing, electronics and sugar are among the many products that are produced outside of Canada, and Canadians routinely purchase them at a price that does not represent a fair trade.

Unless one is directly involved in international social work, it is a little difficult to grasp how what we do in Canada affects people in other countries. Knowledge about how the international economy operates – what is commonly referred to as economic globalization – is the first key to developing a deeper understanding.

CANADIAN POLICY RESEARCH NETWORK

This organization consists of a network of people conducting research on public policy. They have an extensive publications list available free on-line. It is located at:
http://www.cprn.org/

WHAT IS GLOBALIZATION?

Economic globalization is the growing integration of international markets for goods, services and finance. There are three main characteristics of economic globalization:

- **Free trade and investment expansion.** Globalization allows for expansion in the trade of goods and services between countries, and transnational corporations (TNCs) are expanding the geographical extent of their investments.

- **Concentrated TNC power.** Economic power is concentrated in the hands of large TNCs.

- **Enforcement and TNC rights protection.** International bodies, such as the World Trade Organization (WTO), are devising policies and enforcement practices to protect the rights of TNCs and their capital worldwide.

Globalization is essentially a new stage in the global expansion of the economic system of capitalism. Nowadays, the power of transnational corporations, combined with their concurrent control of the mass media, has led to a kind of "economic fundamentalism" – our lives are increasingly ordered to maximize corporate profits. Globalization means that products and services are increasingly flowing between countries. For example, a part for an automobile may be produced in five countries, assembled in another country, and sold around the world. Territorial units such as the nation state are decreasing in importance, and the idea of state and society is shifting.

• Free Trade and Corporate Power

Free trade refers to the lowering and dismantling of the barriers and regulations that might impede the international flow of capital and products, or restrict marketplace demand. Globalization opens domestic markets through the removal of international trade barriers. Free trade is embodied in the growing collection of free trade agreements and

WATCHING CORPORATE POWER

CorpWatch (www.corpwatch.org) has interesting studies and discussions about corporate power and globalization. They work to foster democratic control over corporations by building grassroots globalization – a diverse movement for human rights, labour rights and environmental justice. Here are a few interesting facts from a study by the Institute for Policy Studies regarding large global corporations:

The combined sales of the world's top 200 corporations are bigger than the combined economies of all countries minus the biggest 10.

The top 200 corporations' combined sales are 18 times the size of the combined annual income of the 1.2 billion people (24% of the total world population) living in "severe" poverty.

Corporations in the United States dominate the top 200, with 82 slots (41% of the total). Japanese firms are second, with only 41 slots.

international trade organizations, including the General Agreement on Tariffs and Trade (GATT), the Asia-Pacific Economic Cooperation (APEC) and the North American Free Trade Agreement (NAFTA). Powerful lobbying by big corporations are behind these developments. Globalization is also encouraging the trend towards the privatization and marketization of social services and health services.

As the economies of individual countries become increasingly interdependent, the political sovereignty of individual countries is slowly diminishing. New telecommunication technologies have enabled large corporations to move capital and productive capacity quickly to anywhere in the world. They have enabled TNCs to open new operations in various countries around the world, as opportunities present themselves, and to execute "lean production" to ensure maximum profitability.

Transnational corporations (TNCs) are organizations that possess and control the means of production or services outside of the country in which they were established. Two hundred corporations, most of them larger than many national economies, now control one-quarter of the world's economic activity, and have a combined revenue of $7.1 trillion (Rice and Prince 2000, 21). One-third of the world's trade is constituted by transactions among various units of the same corporation (Clarke 1996). The power of TNCs is increasing, as is the influence of the most powerful Western nations, and this power is increasingly being used to dictate how less powerful countries should be run.

Calculations by the Institute for Policy Studies (IPS) indicate that the top 200 global firms account for an alarming and growing share of the world's economic activity. Based on a comparison of corporate sales and country GDPs, of the 100 largest economies in the world, 51 are corporations; only 49 are countries (Anderson and Cavanagh 2000). The Philip Morris corporation is, economically speaking, larger than New Zealand, and it operates in 170 countries. Instead of creating an integrated global village, these firms are weaving webs of production, consumption and finance that bring economic benefits to, at the most, only a third of the world's people. Two-thirds of the world (the bottom 20 percent of the rich countries and the bottom 80 percent of the poor countries) is left out, marginalized or hurt by these webs of activity.

ENFORCEMENT AND RIGHTS PROTECTION FOR THE TRANSNATIONAL CORPORATIONS

In this new era of globalization, the rules for the global economy that were once made by national governments are increasingly being made by international organizations that are not accountable to anyone. International bodies such as the **World Trade Organization (WTO),** the **International Monetary Fund (IMF),** the **World Bank** and the **G8** are devising policies and enforcement practices to protect the rights of TNCs and capital. The traditional concerns of social welfare practitioners about addressing the basic needs of people are the last thing on the agenda.

These international institutions, along with the free trade agreements that they enforce, increasingly are shaping the policymaking and budgetary decisions of governments around the world. Social policy professors James Rice and Michael Prince (2000, 21) maintain that these institutions and agreements limit the ability of local and national governments to solve social problems. In effect, they shift economic thinking, placing free trade and narrow economic concerns ahead of social policy (moving from the Keynesian to the monetarist approach) and thereby provide direct limits on what local governments can do. Some have called this a "post-sovereign state," meaning that the state or government is no longer free to make its own decisions.

One of the primary vehicles for advancements in free trade is the World Trade Organization (WTO), created in 1995. As stated on their website at http://www.wto.org: "The World Trade Organization (WTO) is the only international organization dealing with the global rules of trade between nations. Its main function is to ensure that trade flows as smoothly, predictably and freely as possible." The WTO, for example, can rule that various environmental or social policies of countries are in violation of the WTO agreement, and can mandate elimination of what would then be deemed a trade barrier. According to critics, the WTO has ruled that every environmental policy it has reviewed is an illegal trade barrier that must be eliminated or changed. With one exception, the WTO has also ruled against every health or food safety law it has reviewed. An organization with this type of far-reaching power certainly affects Canadian social welfare.

With this much global power and influence, the regulation of TNCs is clearly necessary for the promotion of human rights. The UN bodies currently responsible for regulation of TNCs are the United Nations Conference on Trade and Development (UNCTAD) and the Division on Transnational Corporations and Investment (DTCI). Until 1993, the United Nations Centre on Transnational Corporations (UNCTC) held this responsibility. In 1988, after 20 years of discussion and redrafting, the UNCTC published the *Draft Code of Conduct on Transnational Corporations*. It was never adopted, due to extreme pressure from corporate lobby groups and Western governments. One of the last attempts to introduce international corporate regulation via the UN was at the 1992 UN Conference on Environment and Development (UNCED) – the "Earth Summit" – held in Rio de Janeiro. The UNCTC drafted recommendations to be included in Agenda 21 (UNCED's global plan of action) for the environmental regulation of TNCs. Again, pressure from a coalition of Western governments and corporate lobbies resulted in the removal of the recommendations.

At the present time, there is a TNC regulatory vacuum at the UN. The Bangkok Declaration and Plan of Action, adopted in 2000 at the 10th session of UNCTAD, provides the main thrust for the work of the current UNCTAD. The retooled UNCTAD has moved away from TNC regulation towards trade and investment policy. Its work now centres on analyses of economic trends and major policy issues of international concern, rather than dealing with the human rights violations of TNCs (as revealed on its new website at http://www.unctad.org).

G7/G8

Since 1975, the heads of state or government of the major industrial democracies have been meeting annually to deal with the major economic and political issues facing their domestic societies and the international community as a whole.

The six countries at the first summit, held at Rambouillet, France, in November 1975, were France, the United States, Britain, Germany, Japan and Italy. They were joined by Canada at the San Juan Summit of 1976 in Puerto Rico, and by the European Community at the London Summit of 1977.

From then on, membership in the G7 was fixed, although 15 developing countries' leaders met with the G7 leaders on the eve of the 1989 Paris Summit, and the USSR and then Russia participated in a post-summit dialogue with the G7 since 1991. Starting with the 1994 Naples Summit, the G7 met with Russia at each summit (referred to as the P8 or Political 8).

The Denver Summit of the Eight was a milestone, marking full Russian participation in all but financial and certain economic discussions; and the 1998 Birmingham Summit saw full Russian participation, giving birth to the G8 (although the G7 continued to function along side the formal summits).

At the Kananaskis Summit in Canada in 2002, it was announced that Russia would host the G8 Summit in 2006, thus completing its process of becoming a full member.

THE WTO CRITICS

Critics of the WTO outline a variety of problems:

- It operates in secret.
- It promotes free trade over social and human rights.
- It places priority on commercial interests.
- It makes poverty and inequality worse.
- It benefits large corporations and rich countries.
- It dictates the ideal path to development (in conjunction with the World Bank/ International Monetary Fund).
- It transforms citizens into consumers.

Given this new era of globalization, the traditional concerns of social welfare will need to be broadened to include a concern with the issue of global human rights. As noted earlier, **global social welfare** (a concern with justice, social regulation, social provision and redistribution between nations) is already a part of the activities of various supranational organizations or international governmental organizations of the United Nations.

Within this new world context, several new political strategies have emerged: regulating global competition. These involve making international institutions such as the World Trade Organization and G8 more accountable as well as empowering the United Nations and its international organizations to effect changes that enhance the welfare of individuals and communities around the world.

GLOBALIZATION IN OPERATION

Advocates of globalization would have us believe that freer trade will automatically benefit all countries of the world. The economic theory is that poorer countries would be able to specialize their production in areas where they have a competitive advantage, and they could export those products to richer countries. This theory may work in some cases, but in practice, it tends to enrich some countries and impoverish others.

• Structural Adjustment

Have you ever noticed that bananas are often cheaper than apples, even though apples could have been grown in your Canadian backyard? The process of **structural adjustment**, which is commonly forced upon countries that are seeking loans, helps to explain this phenomenon. The process operates as follows:

1. A country needs a loan due to a currency crisis, crumbling infrastructure or a variety of other reasons.

2. The country approaches monetary organizations such as the International Monetary Fund (IMF) and the World Bank (WB).

3. The IMF and WB agree to lend money if the borrowing country agrees to undertake what is called structural adjustment. The new economic policies focus on reducing social spending and other government expenditures, increasing GDP by decreasing labour and environmental regulations, lowering any trade barriers, specializing production, allowing currency to freely trade and encouraging foreign investment.

4. As part of the structural adjustment, the country may agree to change from subsistence agriculture to monocropping. Monocropping or monoculture occurs when agricultural land is used to grow a great deal of one product instead of a variety. So, the country converts a large percentage of their agricultural production from rice to bananas. The country becomes dependent on one or two crops.

5. Foreign corporations purchase large tracts of land and hire former farmers to work as agricultural workers. (The new mega-farms are known as agri-business.)

6. Labourers work long days, for very low wages, under poor conditions. The very best produce is shipped for sale to foreign markets, leaving the local market with bruised bananas or no local produce.

7. Environmental deregulation leads to increased use of pesticides and health risks for labourers. Soil is rapidly spent as a consequence of monocropping and overuse. As a result, the country turns to deforestation to expose rich, unused soil.

8. Western nations are able to import cheap bananas, and the profits benefit the shareholders of the foreign agri-business.

WHY INVEST IN A ZIMBABWEAN EPZ?

- Corporate tax holiday of five years.
- Free movement of investment capital.
- Duty free importation of capital equipment and machinery.
- Exemption from capital gains tax.
- Cost-competitive skilled and semi-skilled labour.

Source: From the Zimbabwean Export Processing Zone Authority: www.epz.co.zw

• Export Processing Zones

Globalization encourages people to do business wherever the conditions are most favourable. For large corporations, this means they can do business where their costs are minimized and profits are maximized. The deregulation of capital and freeing of trade barriers allow corporations to rapidly move their capital across international borders, making it easy for a company to set up a mobile factory in a place where labour regulations are relaxed, environmental legislation is weak and tax law is favourable. In fact, a country can set up in an export processing zone designed specifically for this purpose.

An **export processing zone** (EPZ) is a particular area in a country from which benefits come in the form of preferential financial regulations and special investment incentives. There are export processing zones all over the world. Have a look at the tags on the clothing you are wearing and imagine what the working conditions, environmental standards and wages were for the person who made your garment. Naomi Klein, activist and author of *No Logo: Taking Aim at the Brand Bullies*, examines how TNCs use migrant factories to move around to different EPZs in order to follow the tax breaks and incentives. She calls it "zero-risk globalization" (2000, 287).

According to Klein, corporations primarily produce brands, rather than products. Corporate brands are ideas, values, experiences and even cultures. Nike, Gap, Disney, Levi's and Starbucks are as much about branding as they are about products. Through the advertising and sponsorship of athletes and music stars, the TNCs create demand for their vision. In many cases, companies spend more on advertising and branding than on actually producing the product.

Most export processing zones employ a high proportion of women with minimal education. These women are subjected to pregnancy tests, locked out of washrooms, expected to work in conditions that strain their eyesight, forced to work overtime, paid low wages and are fired for pregnancy or joining a union (Ehrenriech and Fuentes 1992).

Protesting against superpower intervention in Philippines (photo courtesy of Steve Hick).

INTERNATIONAL DEVELOPMENT RESEARCH CENTRE (IDRC)

Created in 1970, IDRC is a Canadian organization that helps developing countries find long-term solutions for the social, economic and environmental problems they face. IDRC funds the work of researchers working in universities, private enterprise, government and non-profit organizations in developing countries. Their website contains volumes of research publications: http://www.idrc.ca

WHAT ARE HUMAN RIGHTS?

Before discussing how the human rights-based approach to social welfare can counterbalance and challenge the process of globalization, we need to understand what human rights are and how human rights protection operates in the world today.

Human rights are a common standard of achievement for human dignity, for all peoples and all nations. They are those inherent rights without which we cannot truly live as human beings. A right is a justified claim or entitlement by someone or some institution in society. A person or community claiming a right must offer the rest of society sufficient reason why the claim should be met. Rights are not a property of a person, but rather are a reason to treat a person in a certain respectful way. Many human rights advocates and writers would agree with Ronald Dworkin's famous declaration that "rights are trumps" – a rights claim "beats" all other competing social values.

Human rights are commonly considered as being universal, indivisible, inalienable and inabrogable (Ife 2001, 12). *Universality* means that human rights apply to all human beings. *Indivisibility* refers to the conception that all human rights must be pursued and realized – we cannot pick and choose which rights are enforced and which are abandoned. The *inalienability* of human rights means that human rights, as a general rule, cannot be taken away. Of course, there are emergencies that may necessitate the suspension of some human rights. For example, in a medical epidemic, a quarantined infected person may find that his or her rights to freedom of movement have been suspended. Finally, the *inabrogable* nature of human rights refers to the idea that one cannot voluntarily give up one's human rights or trade them for special privileges.

The belief that humanity has a duty to protect the universal and inalienable rights of all people is now a recognized part of the heritage of humankind. This recognition has led to international cognizance, declarations, legislative laws and regulations.

• International Human Rights Instruments

The **International Bill of Human Rights** is the primary basis of United Nations activities to promote, protect and monitor human rights and fundamental freedoms. The Bill comprises three texts: the *Universal Declaration of Human Rights* (1948); the *International Covenant on Economic, Social and Cultural Rights* (1966); and the *International Covenant on Civil and Political Rights* (1966) and its two optional protocols.

These instruments enshrine global human rights standards and have been the inspiration for more than 50 supplemental United Nations human rights conventions, declarations, bodies of international minimum rules and other universally recognized principles. These additional standards have further refined international legal norms relating to a very wide range of issues, including women's rights, protection against racial discrimination, protection of migrant workers and the rights of children.

The two covenants are international legal instruments. Thus, when member and non-member states of the United Nations ratify a covenant and become a "state party" to it, they are wilfully accepting a series of legal obligations to uphold the rights and provisions established under the text in question.

The 1948 **Universal Declaration of Human Rights (UDHR)** defined the fundamental expectations for freedom and dignity in a free and just society. It stated that "disregard and contempt for human rights have resulted in barbarous acts which have outraged the conscience of mankind, and the advent of a world in which beings shall enjoy freedom of speech and belief and freedom from fear and want has been proclaimed as the highest aspiration of the common people." Accepted human rights include freedom of expression, freedom of association, freedom from fear and persecution and freedom of religion, as well as the right to shelter, education, health and work, among others.

NEGATIVE, POSITIVE AND COLLECTIVE RIGHTS

Some distinguish between different human rights according to whether they are negative, positive or collective rights. Others refer to these dimensions as "generations" of human rights. The way human rights are viewed and analyzed is a topic of considerable debate, but let us consider the following three categories of human rights:

1. *Negative rights.* Civil and political rights (Articles 2-21 of the UDHR).

2. *Positive rights.* Economic, social and cultural rights (Articles 22-27 of the UDHR).

3. *Collective rights.* Social and international order rights (Article 28 of the UDHR).

• Negative Rights

The first category of human rights refers to civil and political rights. These are individually based and include the right to life, the right to liberty and security of person, the right to vote, the right to freedom of assembly, the right to equality before the law, the right to presumption of innocence until proven guilty, the right to freedom of movement and the right to own property, to name a few (Ife 2001, 25). These rights are detailed in Articles 2-21 of the *Universal Declaration of Human Rights.* They are further expounded in the *International Covenant of Civil and Political Rights,* the *Optional Protocol to the International Covenant on Civil and Political Rights* and a wide range of other covenants that add more detail to specific rights. (A list of the additional covenants is available on-line at: http://www1.umn.edu/humanrts/instree/ainstls1.htm.) They address protection from torture, ill-treatment and disappearance; the rights of women, indigenous peoples and visible minorities; the rights of prisoners and detainees; the rights of children and juvenile offenders; the rights of employment and forced labour and the rights of disabled persons, to name a few of the broad areas.

HUMAN RIGHTS AND WAR: WAR CHILD CANADA

Founded in 1999 by Dr. Samantha Nutt, Dr. Steven Hick and Frank O'Dea, War Child Canada is assisting thousands of children and youth in some of the most devastated areas on earth. They work with youth in North America to promote the awareness of human rights issues and the cause of war-affected children. War Child Canada also works closely with the music industry to help raise funds and build awareness for the cause of war-affected children and youth worldwide.

War Child Canada is helping children in war-ravished Bosnia (photo courtesy of Steve Hick).

INTERNATIONAL HUMAN
RIGHTS INSTRUMENTS

As part of an extensive website
at the University of Minnesota
Human Rights Center, a
complete list of the
International Human Rights
Instruments is available at:
http://www1.umn.edu/
humanrts/

These are referred to as **negative rights** because their emphasis is on protection. They are rights that need to be protected rather than realized through social security or provision. They are rights that call for inaction on the part of the person or institution fulfilling the rights. The right is met by merely refraining from acting in a way that would violate the right. When Canadians hear the phrase human rights, it is generally these rights that spring to mind. In fact, many people do not realize that the field of negative human rights also includes social, economic, cultural and collective rights.

This category of human rights has roots in the intellectual tradition of the eighteenth-century Enlightenment and the political philosophy of liberalism. Enlightenment thinkers such as Voltaire, John Locke and David Hume believed that human reason could be used to combat ignorance, superstition and tyranny, and to build a better world. Their principal target was the domination of society by a hereditary aristocracy. The liberal tradition has centred on religious toleration, government by consent, personal freedom and, especially, economic freedom. Based on these traditions, negative rights have emphasized individual liberties and freedom.

• Positive Rights

The second category of human rights concerns economic, social and cultural rights (ESCR). These rights are outlined in Articles 22-27 of the *Universal Declaration of Human Rights*. They are detailed further in the *International Covenant on Economic, Social and Cultural Rights*. These rights refer to the various forms of social provision, such as health, education, social services, food, housing, employment, adequate wages and the right to form trade unions. Article 25 directly addresses economic rights, stating that "everyone has the right to a standard of living adequate for the health and well-being of himself and of his family, including food, clothing, housing and medical care and necessary social services, and the right to security in the event of unemployment, sickness, disability, widowhood, old age or other lack of livelihood in circumstances beyond his control."

These rights are referred to as **positive rights** because they imply that the state plays a more positive and active role in ensuring that these rights are realized. A positive right requires action, rather than inaction, on the part of the duty-bearer or the person or institution fulfilling the right. For instance, for the right to an adequate income to be realized, the state must act to provide that income to those who do not have it. These rights are pursued by means of welfare state provision: universal health care, education, social housing and employment and labour legislation, among others. They require the state to play an active role in providing income security and services.

These rights generally have their roots in social democracy, socialism and social movements. There is less consensus in Western capitalist democracies about such rights. At times, the rights themselves seem to run contrary to models that emphasize the rule of market forces.

• Collective Rights

The third category of human rights are rights defined at a collective level and are referred to as **collective rights**. They are briefly mentioned in the *Universal Declaration of Human Rights*, Article 28: "Everyone is entitled to a social and international order in which the rights and freedoms set forth in this declaration can be fully realized." These types of rights generally have their roots in anti-colonial struggles, environmental activism and the efforts for self-determination of indigenous peoples.

There is a risk in equating human rights with only negative rights. Pervasive poverty and lack of access to basic survival necessities are ignored within such a framework. However, it is not always easy to get social, economic and cultural rights on the agenda of national governments and international organizations. Civil liberties, property rights and political rights are generally consistent with the demands of the marketplace, but often economic and social rights are at odds with these demands. Indeed, many governments are embracing "the market" as the solution to all of society's ills, and leaving economic and social rights to the private sector.

Canada's parliament passed the *Canadian Human Rights Act* in 1977. The purpose of the Act is to ensure equality of opportunity and freedom from discrimination in federal jurisdiction. In 1982 the *Canadian Charter of Rights and Freedoms* was enacted as part of the *Constitution Act*. It has sections pertaining to legal rights, democratic rights and equality rights, but it makes no mention of social and economic rights. Each province and territory also has a human rights act that applies to businesses and organizations within its jurisdiction. For example, discrimination in housing would be brought to the provincial/territorial human rights commission.

More recently, the *Modernization of Benefits and Obligations Act*, 2000, was brought about due to human rights challenges under the *Charter of Rights*. In its May 1999 ruling in *M. v. H.*, the Supreme Court of Canada made it clear that governments cannot limit benefits or obligations by discriminating against same-sex common-law relationships. Denying equal treatment before the law to same-sex common-law partners is contrary to the principles of equality enshrined in the *Canadian Charter of Rights and Freedoms*, as well as the *Canadian Human Rights Act*. Sixty-eight statutes involving some twenty departments are affected. Amendments will be made to statutes such as the *Income Tax Act*, the Canada Pension Plan, the *Criminal Code* and the *Old Age Security Act*. For example, under the Canada Pension Plan, the surviving spouse in a married relationship or the surviving partner in an opposite-sex common-law relationship may qualify for Survivor's Benefits.

However, the *Canadian Human Rights Act* does not protect the poor from discrimination. In 1998, the Senate Bill S-11 attempted to add the grounds of social condition to the *Canadian Human Rights Act*. The House of Commons defeated it. The 1998 UN Committee on Economic, Social and Cultural Rights stated in its concluding remarks that Canada should "expand protection in human rights legislation to protect poor people from discrimination because of social or economic condition."

SOCIAL CONDITION

One option being proposed for addressing inequality and poverty in Canada is to add "social condition" to human rights legislation. It would respond to the UN's criticism of Canada's lack of explicit recognition of social and economic rights in legislation. Adding social condition would mean that discrimination on the basis of social condition (level of income, occupation or education) would be prohibited.

Maher Arar, innocent victim of US's anti-terrorism campaign (CP PHOTO/Andre Pichette).

THE EUROPEAN SOCIAL CHARTER

The countries comprising the European Community (EC) have instituted the *European Social Charter*. It protects the social rights of people in the nations comprising the EC in seven areas, including housing, health, education, employment, social protection, movement and non-discrimination. A key element is the entrenchment of social protection and the elimination of poverty and exclusion.

SOCIAL WELFARE, GLOBALIZATION AND HUMAN RIGHTS

In this era of globalization, social welfare policies aimed at protecting the poor and disadvantaged members of society seem to be in retreat. Whereas capital is now freer to move across borders to seek higher and higher rates of return, local governments are no longer the main sites for social and economic activity. Athough the post-World War II consensus was to maintain high levels of employment and a welfare state based on a sense of social citizenship in a nation, the era of globalization has severely eroded this belief.

Overall, the future of the welfare state has become a central issue of contention between the forces of globalization and civil society in nations worldwide. In his 1999 book, *Globalization and the Welfare State*, Ramesh Mishra refers to this as "decentring the nation state." He sees the following globalization impacts on social welfare:

- Globalization undermines the ability of national governments to pursue (Keynesian) policies of full employment and demand management.

- Globalization is increasing inequality in wages and work conditions, and high-paying unionized jobs are shrinking as non-standard and part-time work grows.

- Globalization prioritizes deficit reduction and tax cuts over systems of social security.

- Globalization shifts power to capital or corporations and away from labour and civil society, thereby weakening the support for social welfare programs.

- Globalization constrains the social policy option of national governments, due to the threat of capital flight if one nation is not as "investor friendly" as another.

- The logic of globalization conflicts with the logic of community and democratic politics; it is eroding not only the welfare state, but also democratic politics.

The post-World War II welfare state was based on general consensus between labour, civil society and capital. It was believed that the welfare state was necessary to ensure steady economic growth and social stability. In this new era of globalization, governments and the owners of business have taken the position that labour should be subjected to market forces as much as possible, like any other commodity. TNCs generally resist policies that limit the reach of the market, such as minimum wages, employment insurance and health and safety legislation – policies that protect people from the negative impacts of the market.

To meet this challenge head-on, a new approach is called for, one that involves taking a **human rights approach to social welfare**. A human rights-based approach to social welfare would differ from traditional conceptualizations in several ways:

1. Programs and policies would be conceptualized as rights or entitlements rather than as needs or problems.

2. Collective rights to participation in community life would see social welfare as an investment in people.

3. The state-centric model of viewing the state or government as the exclusive provider of social welfare would have to be changed.

4. International bodies would be required to provide for global social welfare and ensure that TNCs uphold human rights.

The traditional needs-based model of welfare puts emphasis on the assessment of needs, and then on the process of addressing those needs. By framing the issue as a person's right to an "adequate standard of living for his or her health and well-being," it shifts income security away from a charity model, whereby only the deserving receive charity, for which they should be extremely grateful, towards the idea of social entitlements as a right of citizenship.

Some social welfare activists go farther, arguing that social inclusion must be addressed through a model of social investment (see Chapter 3 for more information on the social investment model). The social investment model emphasizes the need for change in a variety of institutions, policies and practices that deal directly with social inequality in the present and in the future. Many social welfare advocates see this as a means of going beyond the provision of income security to a more dynamic improvement and participation of traditionally marginalized individuals in community life.

With globalization working to limit the state's ability to meet basic needs, the transition from a needs orientation to a rights affirmation will be required. Whatever the language or relations involved, the notion of concern for members in one's community can be universalized across cultures and societies. In many non-Western countries, for example, the notion of individual rights is non-existent. In such countries, people are viewed in relation to one another, as a community, and social welfare entails interdependence and solidarity. In such countries, community standards, rather than individual rights, may be more relevant.

New trade discussions at the WTO are ringing alarm bells for many social policy analysts. Since February 2000, negotiations have been underway in the WTO to expand and "fine tune" the General Agreement on Trade in Services (GATS). GATS is an international trade agreement that came into effect in 1995. It aims to gradually remove all barriers to trade in services, such as banking, education, health care, rubbish collection, tourism and transport. These negotiations have aroused unease worldwide. Many believe that GATS will threaten the ability of governments to provide social security and protection to citizens. It may mean the privatization of education, health care and social insurance. It may also limit the capacity of governments to regulate health and environmental standards.

GLOBALIZATION FROM BELOW

The global discussion of human rights is dominated by the voices of the privileged – it is a discourse of the powerful about the powerless. This should not be surprising as the disadvantaged tend to be excluded from all discourses of power – human rights is no different from economics, politics and social work. But this denial of voice is, in fact, itself a denial of human rights. As in other fields of social change work, the human rights field requires more developed methods of participation. The voices of the disadvantaged must be included in the construction of human rights and what they mean. Some have called this a globalization from below.

An anti-globalization protest in the Philippines (photo courtesy of Steve Hick).

REFERENCES

* Anderson, Sarah, and John Cavanagh. 2000. *Top 200: The Rise of Corporate Global Power.* San Francisco: Institute for Policy Studies. Retrieved from: http://www.corpwatch.org/upload/document/top200.pdf

* Clarke, Tony. 1996. Mechanisms of corporate rule. In *The Case Against the Global Economy* by Jerry Mander and Edward Goldsmith (eds.), Sierra Club Books.

* Ehrenreich, Barbara, and Annette Fuentes. 1992. *Women in the Global Factory.* Boston: South End Press.

* Ife, Jim. 2001. *Human Rights and Social Work: Towards Rights-Based Practice.* Cambridge, UK: Cambridge University Press.

* Klein, Naomi. 2000. *No Logo: Taking Aim at the Brand Bullies.* Toronto: Vintage Canada.

* Mishra, Ramesh. 1999. *Globalization and the Welfare State.* UK: Edward Elgar Publishing Inc.

* Rice, James, and Michael Prince. 2000. *Changing Politics of Canadian Social Policy.* Toronto: University of Toronto Press.

CONCLUSION

In a recent speech, Professor John Polanyi stated that we shall never have peace as long as large segments of humankind are voiceless. Much of the world's population, being poor, is at the mercy of the rich. According to Polanyi, for the half of the world's population that lives on less than $2 per day, it would be better to be a European cow that receives $2.20 daily in subsidies from the European community taxpayer. He concludes that change will come from the clamour of the poor made effective through international agreements and law.

The trend towards economic globalization has crucial implications for social welfare activists throughout the world. Globalization means that national borders become less relevant to every aspect of our lives, including social welfare. Given this new era, the traditional concerns of social welfare practitioners in addressing the immediate needs of their clients will need to be broadened to include a concern with the issue of global human rights.

TNCs are increasing in size and power to the point that they threaten the sovereignty of nation-states. Freer trade adds to their power. Some question whether or not nation-states will be able to maintain the tax base necessary for adequate social welfare programs, especially in the face of pressures to lower taxes to appease transnational corporations.

There is an epic struggle between the forces of economic globalization and the forces of human rights and civil society. Its resolution may determine the fate of humanity for many generations to come. Human rights are inseparable from social welfare theory, values, ethics and practice. Rights corresponding to human needs have to be fostered and upheld, and advocacy for such rights should be an integral part of social welfare.

CHAPTER 5: GLOBALIZATION AND HUMAN RIGHTS

Discussion Questions

1. What are human rights? What are the three categories of human rights?
2. What is globalization, and how does it compare to economic globalization?
3. Why do some commentators see economic globalization as a problem for the social welfare of the citizens of the world?
4. How do developing nations become impoverished by structural adjustment programs?
5. How can a human rights-based approach to social welfare act as a counterbalance to economic globalization?
6. What three critical challenges result from a human rights-based approach?
7. What impacts of globalization on the welfare state have been observed? Are they negative or positive? Can you think of any positive impacts of economic globalization?

Websites

- **International Forum on Globalization (IFG)**
  http://www.ifg.org/
  The goal of the IFG is twofold: (1) expose the multiple effects of economic globalization in order to stimulate debate, and (2) seek to reverse the globalization process by encouraging ideas and activities that revitalize local economies and communities and ensure long-term ecological stability.

- **Council of Canadians**
  http://www.canadians.org
  Founded in 1985, the Council of Canadians conducts research and runs national campaigns aimed at putting some of the country's most important issues in the spotlight. Click on their trade campaign for information on globalization and its effects on Canada and the world.

- **Human Rights Internet**
  http://www.hri.ca
  This website lists human rights educational resources, subject-oriented rights talk forums, urgent human rights alerts and educational resource sites. It also includes publications and articles on children's rights. The World Calendar includes an international snapshot of human rights events each month.

- **Human Rights Research and Education Centre**
  http://www.cdp-hrc.uottawa.ca/index_e.html
  This website has an extensive collection of resources. Check out their virtual library, publications and links.

Key Concepts

- Economic globalization
- Free trade
- Transnational corporations (TNCs)
- World Trade Organization (WTO)
- International Monetary Fund (IMF)
- World Bank
- G8
- Global social welfare
- Structural adjustment
- Export processing zone
- Human rights
- International Bill of Human Rights
- Universal Declaration of Human Rights
- Negative rights
- Positive rights
- Collective rights
- Human rights approach to social welfare

Thousands participated in a march for equality and social justice in Montreal, October 14, 2000. The protest was organized by the Quebec Federation of Women. The white ribbons represent women killed by domestic abuse (CP PHOTO/Montreal La Presse/Bernard Brault).

6
Women and the Family

Changing Roles and Emerging Trends

Over the decades, social policy analysts have examined income security, paying special attention to women and families — and for good reason. A gendered division of labour exists in Canadian society that has resulted in women earning less than men, and in addition, many women bear the primary responsibility of caregiving for dependent family members. While there are income security programs in place to assist women and families, they are often based on outdated conceptions and can help perpetuate women's disadvantaged position.

ne of the defining social characteristics of the second half of the twentieth century has been the increasing labour force participation of women. Indeed, the participation rate for Canadian women more than doubled in a 30-year period, from 29 percent in 1961 to almost 60 percent in 1991. The social implications of this remarkable economic shift were phenomenal (Gunderson 1998). Among other things, it gave rise to the dominance of the two-earner family, increased the demand for child care, increased the need for part-time work and flexible work arrangements and heightened the pressure for legislation that would foster and ensure equality between men and women.

"There can be no significant or sustainable transformation in societies and no significant reduction in poverty until girls receive the quality basic education they need to take their rightful place as equal partners in development."

— Carol Bellamy, Executive Director, UNICEF

Nevertheless, by virtue of the primary role they are expected to play in caregiving and their disadvantaged position in the labour market, more women than men live in poverty. In the case of lone-parent families, the burden is even greater. Despite all the legislative changes in the area of pay equity and employment equity, there is a continuing need for social policymakers and social work practitioners to be aware of the economic problems women still face *as women*. This chapter examines the role that income security programs play in perpetuating or alleviating the challenging conditions that Canadian women and families face.

THE FEMINIZATION OF POVERTY

Even with advances in labour force participation, women dominate the ranks of those living in poverty. An examination of the situation reveals persistent problems for women in many areas of economic life.

- *Poverty.* Women constitute a substantial segment of the working poor. High poverty rates are concentrated in three family types: unattached women under 65 (40.3 percent, compared to 29.8 percent for men), unattached women 65 and older (45.6 percent, compared with 32.8 percent for men) and single mothers with

EMPLOYMENT EARNINGS FOR MEN AND WOMEN

Women still earn much less than men. The chart below compares the average annual earnings of men and women.

In 2001, the average wage earned by women was 64.2% of that of men. Even when we remove part-time employment (a higher percentage of women work part-time and this pulls down their average), women earn less.

Of the full-time and full-year employed, women earn 71.6% of the wage for men.

	All earners including full-time	Full-time full-year only
Women	$24,688	$35,258
Men	$38,431	$49,250
Earnings Ratio (%)	64.2%	71.6%

Source: Statistics Canada, Survey of Labour and Income Dynamics (SLID). Available at: http://www.statcan.ca/english/Pgdb/labor01a.htm

children under 18 (45.4 percent, compared to 10.8 percent for men) (Statistics Canada 2001).

- *Part-time work.* Women still constitute a large proportion of part-time workers in Canada and, as such, are usually underpaid and therefore particularly vulnerable to economic downturns. As we discussed in Chapter 4, part-time employment as a percentage of total employment has grown steadily from 3.8 percent in 1953, to 12 percent in 1973, to 16.9 percent in 1983, to 18.5 percent in 1999 (Broad 2000, 13). Seventy percent of these part-time workers are women.

- *Minimum wage legislation.* Because women hold 64 percent of minimum wage jobs, they are the group most in need of minimum wage legislation. Although Ontario's minimum wage was recently increased, it had been fixed since 1995. Providing a living wage for women can be a policy instrument for promoting greater wage equity and anti-poverty policy goals.

- *Maternity and parental leave.* Women still perform a double duty – even if they work outside the home, women are most often the primary caregivers for dependent relatives and therefore have to work another "full shift" with the family. Employment Insurance (EI) benefits can play a significant role in addressing this issue, if women are eligible for the benefits. As we discuss in Chapter 8, EI was expanded in 2000, allowing parents to receive benefits for up to one year while caring for a child, but many women find that they are not eligible.

- *Dependent care.* Because women are most often the primary caregivers of dependent relatives, Canada's lack of universal day care (child care) programs is a significant barrier to women's full participation in the labour force. Day care is a necessity for many employed mothers.

- *Free trade and globalization.* These global trends, involving competition from low-wage countries, particularly affect women who find themselves in low-wage jobs.

- *Pension programs.* These programs are of special significance to women, because women are often employed in jobs that do not give them access to private pension plans. (Chapter 11 highlights this.) Of the income of women aged 65+, 70 percent is from government transfers (compared to 52 percent for men). Of persons collecting C/QPP retirement benefits (September 1995), women averaged $274 per month while men averaged $477 per month.

- *Recessions.* Economic downturns affect women disproportionately – they are typically the last employees to be hired and the first employees to be fired.

- *Employment insurance programs.* Even those programs that are designed to assist workers can place women at a disadvantage. Increases in the required eligibility periods make it more difficult for women than men to collect Employment Insurance.

Almost 16 percent of adult women live below the Statistics Canada Low Income Cut-off, or LICO (Statistics Canada 2001). Women are falling further and further into poverty. In 1997, there was a total of 93,000 single-parent mothers with incomes at less than 50 percent of the poverty line. That was roughly double the number (47,000) in 1989, which was the year before the start of the 1990-91 recession (National Council of Welfare 1999, 54). In 1993, 81 percent of Canadian families living in poverty were headed by female single parents with children under the age of seven years (Hay 1997). The term now commonly used to capture this social phenomenon is the **feminization of poverty**.

Another way to look at the feminization of poverty is to calculate the severity of poverty, or the "poverty gap." This is done by examining how far below the "Low-Income Cut-off" (LICO) women fall. This type of analysis reveals that many women are not only poor, but they live far below the poverty line. Both unattached women and men who are below the poverty line have an income that is only 55 percent of the poverty-line income. Single-parent mothers earn 61 percent of the poverty line and unattached women over 65 earn 84 percent of the poverty line (National Council of Welfare 1999, 54).

WOMEN IN THE LABOUR FORCE

Women's poverty is caused by different factors than men's poverty. Many studies (Gunderson, Muszynski and Keck 1990; Townson 2000) found that men's poverty can be more directly related to low-wage employment, whereas women's poverty also arises from factors such as divorce and separation, and women's responsibilities as mothers, homemakers, caregivers and nurturers.

Since the 1970s, rapidly increasing numbers of women have entered the labour force. With this, there has been a shift in the policy representation of women from "stay-at-home mothers" to "worker-mothers." This shift has changed the idea of the economic dependency of women, but it has not significantly altered the disadvantages that women face. There are six main reasons for this:

- Women are overrepresented in part-time, temporary, low-paying jobs.

- Women still earn less than men for doing the same jobs. This is an inequality that "pay equity" legislation was supposed to address.

- Women still face discrimination in employment practices. This is an inequality that employment equity legislation was supposed to address.

- Women still tend to hold primary responsibility for care and household chores in the family.

- Child care provisions are deteriorating across Canada.

- Child support payments from absent fathers are often inadequate or are not paid at all.

CHILD POVERTY RATES

The United *Nation's Human Development Reports* consistently rank Canada in the top 10 countries in the world in the area of human development. When the number of children living in poverty is included, Canada's position drops significantly. Of the "Western" countries, Canada has one of the highest rates of child poverty.

Defence (munitions) workers during World War II (National Archives of Canada/C467).

FEMINIZATION OF HOMELESSNESS

Feminization of poverty means that more women than men are poor – so why are the majority of the homeless people we see on the streets men?

Only a minority of homeless people is seen on the streets during the day. Many of the homeless, in particular women, are not visible. Of the 26,000 people using emergency shelters in Toronto in 1996, half were in families and 5,000 were children (Faith Partners 1999). Young homeless women are particularly vulnerable to being recruited as prostitutes in order to make ends meet. You may not see them on the streets during the day, but you see some of them at night.

Most homeless people you never see at all.

Statistics reveal that an increasing number of women are active in the labour force, except for during short periods while they are on parental leave. The problem, then, is not that women are not working; the problem is in the pay that women receive. Christa Freiler and Judy Cerny (1998, 5) from the Child Poverty Action Group summarize the situation of women who work:

> Even when women do take responsibility for earning a living, they and their families remain economically vulnerable. *Women's Work, A Report* (Canadian Labour Congress, 1997) found that Canada has one of the highest incidences of low-paid employment for women and that 80 percent of women who are primary wage earners work in jobs in which they earn between $24,000 and $30,000 a year. Not surprisingly, lone-parent families headed by women run the greatest risk of poverty among all groups. The incidence of poverty has hovered around 56 percent to 57 percent since 1980, one of the highest rates in the industrialized world.

Of those who are employed full-time, women are more than twice as likely as men (34.3 percent as opposed to 16.1 percent) to be earning low pay (which is measured as less than two-thirds of the median wage). Over 70 percent of Canadian part-time workers are women earning much less than men.

• Women and Pay Equity

In the economic sphere, there were many legislative changes in the post-World War II period, and especially in the 1970s and beyond, aimed at fostering greater gender equality at work. In particular, important policy initiatives were taken that were intended to create a more equitable playing field for working women.

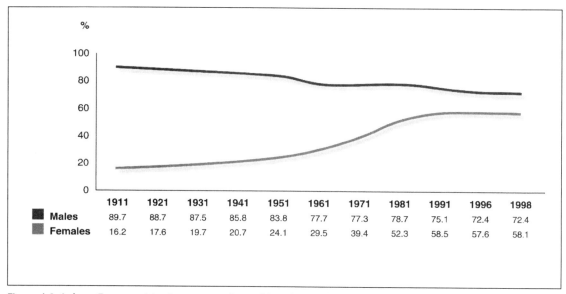

	1911	1921	1931	1941	1951	1961	1971	1981	1991	1996	1998
Males	89.7	88.7	87.5	85.8	83.8	77.7	77.3	78.7	75.1	72.4	72.4
Females	16.2	17.6	19.7	20.7	24.1	29.5	39.4	52.3	58.5	57.6	58.1

Figure 6.1: Labour Force participation rates, males and females aged 15 and over, 1911-1998.
Sources: For 1911-1971, Margrit Eichler, *Families in Canada Today,* 2nd ed. (Toronto: Gage, 1998). For 1981-1996, Statistics Canada, *Labour Force Historical Review* (1998), Catalogue No. 71F004XCB.

Among these policy initiatives were:

1. *equal pay policies* (including pay equity or equal pay for work of equal value) designed to improve women's pay;

2. *equal employment policies* (including employment equity) designed to help women's employment and promotion opportunities and

3. *other facilitating policies* (such as child care and parental leave) designed to put women on an equal footing with men in the labour market.

One of the fundamental issues facing women in the labour force is pay inequities – women being paid less than men for work of the same value. We have had **pay equity legislation** in Canada since the 1970s. An equal value provision was first legislated in 1976 in Quebec in its *Charter of Human Rights and Freedoms*. The federal government passed its equal value provision (section 11) under the *Canadian Human Rights Act* in 1978. Subsequently, all provinces, except Alberta, have enacted pay equity law or policy. Of these, six provinces have passed proactive legislation that mandates employers to comply with procedures to redress gender-based wage inequities. The policies of the other three provinces are complaint-driven – employees must file a complaint to address a pay inequity. These laws apply only to the public sector, and only Ontario, Quebec and the federal government extend pay equity into the private sector (Gunderson 1998).

Nevertheless, although more and more Canadian women entered the labour force in this period, they seldom did so on equal terms with men. The industries and occupations initially open to women were the less prestigious ones. Their incomes were far inferior to those of men in the same occupations, and all sorts of sexist justifications for this fundamental inequality were readily available. In addition to economic inequality, the patriarchal family model and social relations were still in full force, and in many households, women were expected to tend to children, husband and family affairs, as well as earn an income outside the home.

UNITED NATION'S REPORT ON CANADA

In considering Canada's adherence to Articles 16 and 17 of the *Covenant on Economic, Social and Cultural Rights* (see Appendix D), the United Nations concludes:

"The Committee notes with grave concern that with the repeal of CAP and cuts to Social Assistance rates, social services and programmes have had a particularly harsh impact on women, in particular single mothers."

Source: Report of the Committee on Economic, Social and Cultural Rights, United Nations, Concluding observations, Section 22 (1998).

DEFINING THE MODERN FAMILY

This text uses the term "family" with some caution. Many definitions of families exclude common-law couples, most exclude lone-parent families and pretty well all still exclude same-sex relationships. In Canada today, the term **family** is defined according to either structural criteria (what they look like) or functional criteria (what they do). Statistics Canada, for example, uses a structural definition of the family to count the number of families for census purposes. Statistics Canada defines a "census family" as

a now-married couple (with or without never-married sons and/or daughters of either or both spouses), a couple living common-law (again with or without never-married sons and/or daughters of either or both partners) or a lone parent of any marital status, with at least one never-married son or daughter living in the same dwelling.

FAMILIES ARE LESS TRADITIONAL

"Traditional" no longer describes the typical family in Canada. Traditional households consisting of four or more people – typically a mother, father and their children – accounted for only a quarter of all Canadian households in 2001. Two decades earlier, they accounted for a third.

The definition focuses on what can be objectively measured – who lives with whom and under what circumstances. Previous definitions of the family included specific reference to marriage and ignored common-law living.

The **Vanier Institute of the Family** (2000), a national, charitable organization dedicated to promoting the well-being of Canadian families, uses a functional definition of the family that emphasizes the activities of family members. It defines families as

> any combination of two or more persons who are bound together over time by ties of mutual consent, birth and/or adoption or placement and who, together, assume responsibilities for variant combinations of some of the following:
>
> • physical maintenance and care of group members,
> • addition of new members through procreation or adoption,
> • socialization of children,
> • social control of members,
> • production, consumption, distribution of goods and services and
> • affective nurturance – love.

This definition emphasizes the work and accomplishments of people who commit themselves to one another over time. It avoids many of the biases that have crept into definitions of the family. It acknowledges heterosexual and same-sex couples, lone-parent families, extended patterns of kinship, step-families and blended families, couples with children and those without, the commitments of siblings to one another and

A group of same-sex marriage supporters make their way to a rally organized by those opposed to changes in the definition of marriage in October 2003 in Fredericton, N.B. (CP PHOTO/*Fredricton Daily Gleaner*/David Smith).

the obligations and affection that unite the young and the old as their lives weave together. Included in the above definition are same-sex couples. Canadian federal law, however, defines same-sex couples as common-law relationships – different from marriage.

The Government of Canada defines marriage as the "union of one man and one woman to the exclusion of all others." **Same-sex couples** are currently fighting for the right to be legally married with all the benefits and responsibilities that opposite-sex couples have. In 1999, the Supreme Court of Canada ruled that same-sex couples should have the same benefits and obligations as opposite-sex, common-law couples and equal access to benefits from social programs to which they contribute. Although many laws were revised to comply with the Supreme Court's ruling, the federal legislature decided to retain the definition of marriage as the union of a man and a woman. To date, only the Netherlands and Belgium allow for same-sex marriage. The federal government in Canada is examining the issue.

• Seven Biases

Discussions about families are loaded with value judgements. These can be based on religious beliefs, moral beliefs, popular culture, advertising or media representations, as well as many other social and cultural forces. According to Margrit Eichler (1997, 7) there are seven types of biases that have crept into society's analysis of the family, and prevented social programs from keeping up with the changing nature of today's family.

1. *Monolithic bias.* The monolithic bias suggests that there is one basic, uniform type of household – the nuclear, breadwinner-dependent family with one or more children and a woman who maintains the home: the "Cleaver"-type family. As we will see later in this chapter, this is more of a myth than a reality.

2. *Conservative bias.* The conservative bias ignores changes taking place in family structures and relationships – for example, the blended family and the same-sex family.

3. *Sexist bias.* The sexist bias assumes a functional differentiation of work between men and women. Women taking care of children at home would be viewed as a natural role, rather than a role that is socially constructed.

4. *Micro-structural bias.* The micro-structural bias leads to a refusal to look outside the family in order to understand what is influencing them. Individual or family conduct is explained by looking only within the family unit, without considering extraneous factors. An example of this occurs when people express a concern for building "self-reliance" among welfare recipients without considering the availability of jobs, day care and other supports.

"A feminist perspective means inserting an additional level of understanding: that women stand at the crossroads between production and reproduction, between economic activity and the care of human beings."

— Isabella Bakker

5. *Ageist bias.* This bias shows up in discussions about families when only the perspective of middle-aged adults is considered. Here, the perspectives of children and the elderly are ignored.

6. *Racist bias.* The racist bias concerns a devaluing or discounting of culturally or ethnically different families. The treatment of First Nations families in Canada – where children were placed in residential schools – is a tragic example of this bias.

7. *Heterosexist bias.* The heterosexist bias treats the heterosexual family as "natural" and, therefore, the only legitimate form of family. Denying family status to lesbian and gay families typifies this bias.

Being aware of these societal biases helps policymakers design social welfare programs that reflect real, existing families, not just "ideal" families. Problems can occur when practitioners bring their biases into counselling or referral, because people must have access to services based on the family they live in, as opposed to the family the practitioner *thinks* they should live in. Families exist outside of these biases (whether we like it or not); acknowledging this enables practitioners to practice in a more reflective and appropriate manner.

In order to obtain an accurate and realistic definition of what a family is, these biases need to be challenged. The changing nature of families that define themselves as families, but are not recognized as such in social policy or government legislation, requires us to rethink our outdated and restricted notions of "family."

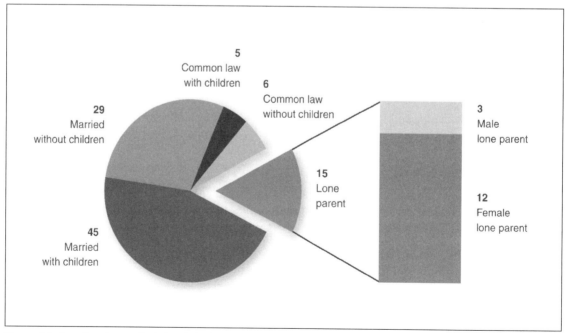

Figure 6.2: So, what does today's family look like? Out of 100 families, 1996.
Source: Vanier Institute of the Family, *Profiling Canada's Families II* (Ottawa: Vanier Institute of the Family, 2000).

CHANGING FAMILIES

In many ways, our income security programs are based on outdated, traditional notions of women and family. Although the vast majority of Canadians live in some kind of family setting, the contemporary Canadian family bears little or no resemblance to families of Canada's past. The "Cleaver" family ideal, based on the sitcom *Leave it to Beaver*, consists of two parents – a working father and a supportive non-working wife – and a couple of children. This ideal has remained dominant for many decades despite the fact that it has not really been reflective of reality.

Certainly, today's family is better protected than it was 30 years ago. For example, if a family member gets sick, our health care programs provide government-supported medical help. A myriad of government social programs are also available to provide external services to assist the family. Yet, family structures have changed dramatically.

Over the past 30 years, **male-breadwinner families** have decreased drastically, and are now well below 25 percent of the total of all Canadian families. Currently, it is **dual-earner families** that predominate. This change has led to a complete revision of family obligations in a very short time and, hence, a great deal of uncertainty. For example, there are no clear societal expectations with regards to an individual's responsibility to care for a step-uncle who gets sick. At the same time, fewer children are taking responsibility for the care of their ageing parents; this has made the question of government support to the elderly an issue where it once was not. Modern families take many different forms. The number of single-parent families is rising (up to 15 percent of the total), and many new entities are emerging, such as same-sex couples with children and blended families who bring with them other-family obligations.

According to Statistics Canada's Census (2001), there are 8.4 million "census families" in Canada, up from 7.8 million in 1996. Of these,

- 44 percent are married couples with children,
- 35 percent are married couples without children,
- 6 percent are common-law couples with children,
- 7.5 percent are common-law couples without children,
- 15 percent are lone-parent led (81 percent of lone parents are female),
- 44 percent are married or common-law couples,
- 41 percent are couples with no children at home and
- .5 percent are same-sex couples.

The 2001 Census showed that an increasing proportion of couples are living common law. Married couples accounted for 70 percent of all families in 2001, down from 83 percent in 1981. At the same time, the proportion of common-law couples rose from 6 percent to 14 percent.

The 2001 Census is the first to provide data on same-sex partnerships. A total of 34,200 couples identified themselves as same-sex common-law couples, accounting for .5 percent of all families with 55 percent of these being male couples.

BALANCING WORK AND FAMILY

At the beginning of this century, how people balance work and family is a central issue facing Canada. Often we address work, family and community issues as separate domains. But they are noticeably interrelated.

The model below demonstrates how we need to move beyond oversimplified models that make sweeping generalizations about the impact of work on family, or of family on work, and focus instead on the interconnections.

Source: Canadian Council on Social Development, "Work, Family and Community: Key Issues and Directions for Future Research." Prepared for the Labour Program Human Resources Development Canada (1999). Available at http://labour.hrdc-drhc.gc.ca/worklife/CCSD-CCDS/presentation-en.html

Conceptual Model:
Work, Family and Community

Figure 6.3: Conceptual model showing the interconnections of work, family and community.

• **Some Factors Changing the Modern Family**

The main factors that have led to changes in the family are: increased longevity, decreased fertility, industrialization of housework, labour force participation of women and increased rate of divorce. Let us look at each of these in turn.

• *Longevity.* Improved public health leads to increased longevity, and this has had implications for family structure. As well, women usually live longer than men, which has implications for pension and medical systems, as well as for relationships.

• *Fertility.* Decreased fertility in all age categories is a worldwide trend. In 1962, birth control pills were invented, but could only be prescribed for purposes other than contraception, until 1968 when the Criminal Code legalized access to birth control. This has meant that women are involved in childbearing for fewer years and therefore have time for other activities.

• *Household technology.* Especially since World War I, advances in technology have led to the automation of certain types of housework. This has drastically changed the family of the twentieth century. Electrification, hot water, central heating, air conditioning, refrigeration, vacuum cleaners, mass production of clothing and automobiles are all aspects of the industrialization of housework. These changes to domestic duties have contributed to the proportion of women working outside the home. Today, 73 percent of women who are married to men work and, of those, most contribute a significant share of total family income, as the chart below indicates.

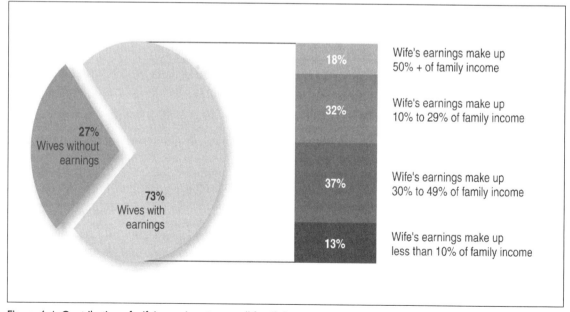

Figure 6.4: Contribution of wife's earnings to overall family income.
Source: Vanier Institute of the Family, *Profiling Canada's Families II* (Ottawa: Vanier Institute of the Family, 2000).

- *Divorce.* The increase in the proportion of women who are working outside the home has led to women, in general, becoming less economically dependent on their spouse or partner. In 1968, the grounds for divorce were expanded beyond adultery to include separation and incompatibility. Of those couples who married in 1996, 37 percent of marriages could be expected to end in divorce (Statistics Canada, 1996 Census). This increased divorce rate has, in turn, contributed to changes in family structures.

• The Women's Liberation Movement and Other Factors

There are additional factors that have caused changes in family composition. Consider the women's liberation movement.

The first wave of the women's movement occurred in the last 30 years of the nineteenth century and the first 20 years of the twentieth century. During this time, the movement was mainly political, and primarily concerned with the acquisition of women's right to vote. The second wave occurred in the 1960s, partly as a reaction to the rigidity of the male-dominated family structure with its fixed gender roles, and also as a result of the isolation of suburban life. The impact of this movement on improving women's lives has been phenomenal and far-reaching.

Consider also the decline of the extended family – the family "ideal" now consists of nuclear family units that by and large live in their own homes. Thus, housing has expanded rapidly, especially the suburban single-family home. There is also the decline of religious influence. This has meant that barriers to divorce have come down, and there has been a widespread acceptance of birth control (and a corresponding reduction in unwanted pregnancies, particularly among young women). Finally, increased cultural diversity in the Canadian population has caused us to become more familiar with different family types.

• Pressing Problems Today

All these changes to the Canadian family obviously have a direct bearing on how social programs operate and how income security programs are delivered. In devising programs that work for women and families, social analysts and policymakers now urgently need to take into account the following:

- Growth in the number of single-parent families, mostly led by women. (Single-parent families now account for approximately 15 percent of Canadian families.)
- Growth in the number of blended families.
- Growth in the number of same-sex families, some of which include children, now comprising 34,200 families.
- Growth in the number of mothers in the labour force, including women with children under the age of five.
- Decline in the number of extended family members who live in one family.
- Growth in the number of single-person households.

SAME-SEX MARRIAGE NOW LEGAL

Until now, only the Netherlands and Belgium had a law permitting legal marriages for gays and lesbians. Canada's 2003 *Act Respecting Certain Aspects of Legal Capacity for Marriage* states: "Marriage for civil purposes is the lawful union of two persons to the exclusion of all others." The Act does, however, permit religious groups to decide on their own if they will recognize same-sex marriages. (At time of press, this Act was still under consideration.)

THREE MODELS OF THE FAMILY

Women are now participating in the labour force in ever larger numbers, and many families could not survive if this were not the case. At the same time, however, government income security policy has continued to be based on the outdated assumption that women are available to care for family members and undertake domestic chores (as if they were at home all day).

Sociologist Margrit Eichler (1997) presents three conceptual models of the family upon which new policies directed at the work-family relationship can be based. In devising income security policy and programs, governments tend to use one of these three approaches or models. At present, the patriarchal family model perspective is losing popularity, and the individual responsibility model is gaining in influence. The following sections describe the characteristics of each model.

• Patriarchal Model of the Family

The **patriarchal model of the family** is based on perceptions that were dominant at the turn of the last century. Under this paradigm, the husband was considered the undisputed master of the family and the wife was economically and socially beneath her husband. Children were also treated as dependants of the husband/father. Within income security programs, this belief was reflected in the rule that a woman could not receive public assistance if her husband was alive. The wife/mother was seen as responsible for providing care and services to family members without pay. Finally, divorce did not exist (although there were separations not recognized by law), and because homosexuality was seen as an illness, same-sex couples were not recognized in any way.

• Individual Responsibility Model of the Family

Filipino mother and child struggle to survive (photo courtesy of Steve Hick).

The **individual responsibility model of the family** consists of three main elements: formal gender equality, gender-neutral policies and equalized caregiving. The *Canadian Charter of Rights and Freedoms* introduced gender equality and enshrined it in law, necessitating numerous changes in family policy. Some analysts point out that these legal gains constitute only "formal gender equality" – in other words, in the ideal world of policy, all people are treated "equally" despite continuing real-world inequalities. Within this model, the family unit is still treated as the normal unit of administration, but the husband and wife are seen as equally responsible for the economic well-being of themselves, each other and any children. Fathers and mothers are seen as equally responsible for caregiving. This model reflects the idea of gender neutrality or gender "blindness." In formulating social policy, gender neutrality ignores the differences in life experiences and caring responsibilities between men and women. The emergence of this model within provincial Social Assistance programs means that women can no longer make claims on the state as mothers. Either parent is assumed to be capable of fulfilling the care and provider functions in the family. The lack of recognition that one parent cannot care for dependent children and work full time has led to an erosion of entitlements for lone-parent families, which are predominantly led by women.

• Social Responsibility Model of the Family

As an alternative, the **social responsibility model of the family** directly addresses gender inequality, gender-sensitive policies and the social dimension of caregiving. According to Eichler (1997, 16), the model contains minimal gender inequality or stratification. It is important to note that this is different from the assumption of absolute gender equality. Eichler (p.124) believes that differentiation is a necessary aspect of our complex society, which in turn leads to stratification. The goal, therefore, should shift from moving towards a society based on equality to one where inequality is minimized.

This model sees the individual, rather than the family, as the societal unit of administration. Examples of this are our health care system, which treats every citizen as an individual, and our tax system, which is based on individual taxation. Within this model, familial caring and "housework" – which usually becomes the responsibility of women – is seen as a socially useful service (rather than a privately useful service). In this context, the public shares the responsibility with both parents for the care of dependent children. Similarly, the costs of care for dependent adults (such as elderly family members or individuals with disabilities) are a public responsibility, although family members may also provide the care.

A conference paper entitled *Family Making* begins the task of re-theorizing family (Baker 2002). The idea of "family making" was developed by Leslie Bella, a professor of social work at Memorial University of Newfoundland. According to Bella (2003), we can identify and value family, regardless of the living arrangements of family members. Family making is defined as the processes through which we develop relationships that are enduring, caring and intimate, that in turn nurture and support us. According to this definition, a family relationship exists to the extent that the relationship between two or more individuals is characterized by (1) endurance, (2) caring and (3) shared domestic space. Family making is the process through which individuals create, maintain and strengthen relationships that constitute "family" as thus defined (Bella 2003).

The idea of defining a family by identifying relationships and processes rather than family composition is useful for social welfare policymakers. Existing social policies have a tendency to disregard or invalidate non-traditional family forms and approaches to care. Conversely, policies based on family making include the wide range of family relationships. It enables social policymakers to address the concerns of those in diverse family forms and different cultural settings. It allows us to break away from policy based on limited or patriarchal definitions of the family. Such policies are more responsive to the diversity of family forms that actually exist in Canadian society.

WOMEN AND HUMAN RIGHTS

Canada has been a signatory to the United Nations *Convention on the Elimination of All Forms of Discrimination Against Women* (CEDAW) since 1981. In a single treaty, CEDAW brings together human rights standards for women and girls in public and in private life. The 2000 Optional Protocol to CEDAW (the "Optional Protocol") is a human rights instrument that creates new procedures to enhance oversight of compliance with CEDAW. It is hoped that the Optional Protocol will contribute to the recognition and protection of women's human rights and the promotion of gender equality in Canada and around the world.

Families are about caring above all else (Health Canada/IMG0073/PCD2005).

PAY THE RENT AND FEED THE KIDS

The 2003 Pay the Rent and Feed the Kids campaign was an effort to challenge the Ontario provincial government to raise Social Assistance rates to reflect the actual cost of living.

Many families often have to choose between paying the rent and eating, and for those with children, especially in families led by single mothers, the ultimate choice is often between paying the rent or feeding the kids. According to the campaign, inadequate shelter allowance rates are leading to increased hunger and homelessness.

For information on this campaign and many others, go to the Income Security Advocacy Centre at: http://www. incomesecurity.org

WOMEN AND CARING

Currently, the individual responsibility model underpins Canada's social welfare programs. However, to tackle women's poverty, governments need to develop strategies to deal with the unique problems faced by women – women's employment, child care, Social Assistance rates and general income security.

Patricia Evans, a professor of social work at Carleton University, has written extensively on this topic, and details several reasons why it is important to examine income security programs from the perspective and experience of women. First, she maintains that many programs are based on outdated assumptions about the roles and responsibilities of women and simply do not work. Second, it is women who dominate both sides of the social welfare encounter – as primary users of services and as service providers (Evans and Wekerle 1997, 4).

The exact relationship between social welfare and women's daily experiences is neither straightforward nor simple. Understanding women's responsibility for caring, and how income security programs play into it, is vital to the study of the Canadian "social safety net." It is important to note that women and men are benefiting differently from the income security system. Men tend to obtain their income security benefits from social insurance-type programs such as Employment Insurance or Workers' Compensation – programs that are less stigmatizing and more generous. Women, on the other hand, tend to draw benefits as citizens from minimum-income programs such as Social Assistance and Old Age Security. These programs provide bare minimums, are either needs tested or means tested and are more stigmatizing. If our society, and our income security programs, rewarded caring as highly as labour force participation, then a key aspect of women's inequality could be surmounted.

Not only are women the main recipients of minimum-income Social Assistance programs, but the programs themselves perpetuate certain biased models of the family. For example, what was once known as the "man-in-the-house" rule (now known as the "spouse-in-the-house" rule), stipulates that a woman who is living with a man is immediately not eligible for Social Assistance. The policy assumes that a man who lives with a woman should be financially responsible for her and her family, even when he is not the father of her children and has no other legal responsibility to support her or her children. Under the *Family Law Act*, people are not considered spouses until after three years of living together. The Ontario government deems that there is economic interdependence as soon as there is evidence of cohabitation – no matter the time period. This policy was widely criticized and changed for several years in some provinces (the rule was declared unconstitutional by the Ontario Supreme Court in 2002). The Ontario government is appealing the decision.

Other policies, many of which are presented as being gender-neutral, actually ignore the special circumstances of women. For example, workfare (viewing lone mothers as workers, rather than as mothers) ignores the circumstances that single mothers face. Lack of child support, lack of child care opportunities and a lack of jobs that will pay sufficiently to support a family on one income are ignored by this policy. When combined with the low levels of income support through Social Assistance, it is no wonder that the majority of single mothers and their children live below most definitions of poverty.

• Theorization of Women's Work and Caring

According to Statistics Canada, women comprise three-quarters of the adults who spend more than 30 hours per week caring for children in the home. Status of Women Canada, a federal government agency, has gone as far as to say that the unequal sharing of dependant care in the family may be the most persistent barrier to gender equality.

Beginning in the 1960s and throughout the following decades, a variety of theories were developed in an attempt to explain the nature and conditions of women's work and caring. Theorists disagreed about the extent to which gender-based work division was determined by ideas, biology, culture, material conditions or patriarchal family structures. Early debates were directed at rejecting the idea that women's work divisions, in both the workplace and the home, were determined by biological factors, such as physical size or shape, "natural" skills or aptitudes, maternal instincts or emotional make-up. Canadian feminist writers, such as Helen Levine, Pat Armstrong, Patricia Evans, Sheila Neysmith and Dorothy Smith, undertook extensive research to show that gender-based work and caring divisions were socially constructed or socially organized. In fact, today's feminist theorists use the term "gender" as opposed to "sex" to highlight the socially constructed differences, rather than the biological dichotomy.

To examine social welfare it is necessary to appreciate the dimension of gender. This text has drawn attention to the circumstances that contribute to the inequality of women, but more work remains to be done if we are to fully understand this relationship and be able to act on it. Sheila Neysmith, a leading social work scholar at the University of Toronto, shows how social welfare progress has been hampered by the separation of family life, the labour market and state responsibilities into separate domains. She believes that the public and private need to be connected in our theoretical understandings (Neysmith 1991).

Many feminist social policy experts and women in community-based organizations believe that caregiving by mothers should be recognized as work comparable in value to the work performed in the marketplace. In the same vein, Mothers are Women (MAW), an Ottawa-based grassroots group, advocates for a more equal sharing of the work between men and women, and responsibilities and rewards for paid and unpaid labour within families and within society. They believe that a fundamental recognition of the unpaid caregiving work of mothers is necessary to break the feminization of poverty.

Another unresolved issue is the dilemma of professional child care versus caregiving. Many believe that the current emphasis on supporting professional child care devalues caregiving and the women who do it, and prioritizes professionalization and the development specialist

REFERENCES

• Baker, Maureen. 2002. *Families, Labour and Love: Family Diversity in a Changing World*. Vancouver: UBC Press.

• Baker, Michael, and Nicole Fortin. 2000. *Does Comparable Worth Work in a Decentralized Labor Market?* Montreal: CIRANO.

• Bella, Leslie. 2003. "Family Making: A Framework for Anti-oppressive Practice." Conference paper presented at the University of Regina.

• Broad, D. 2000. Living a half life? Part-time work, labour standards and social welfare. *Canadian Social Work Review* 17, no 1.

• Canadian Human Rights Commission. 1997. *Annual Report of the Canadian Human Rights Commission*. Ottawa.

• Eichler, Margrit. 1997. *Family Shifts: Families, Policies and Gender Equality*. Toronto: Oxford University Press.

• Evans, Patricia. 2001. Women and social welfare: Exploring the connections. In Joanne Turner and Francis Turner, eds., *Canadian Social Welfare*. Toronto: Pearson Education.

• Evans, Patricia M., and Wekerle, G., eds. 1997. *Women and the Canadian Welfare State*, Toronto: University of Toronto Press.

• Faith Partners. 1999. *Poverty Hurts Series*. Ottawa: Faith Partners.

• Freiler, Christa, and Judy Cerny. 1998. *Benefiting Canada's Children Perspectives on Gender and Social Responsibility*. Ottawa: Status of Women Canada.

• Gunderson, Morley. 1998. *Women and the Canadian Labour Market: Transitions Towards the Future*. Ottawa/Toronto: Statistics Canada/ITP Nelson.

• Gunderson, Morley, Leon Muszynski, and Jennifer Keck. 1990. *Women and Labour Market Poverty*. Ottawa: Canadian Advisory Council on the Status of Women.

• Hay, David. 1997. Campaign 2000: Child and family poverty in Canada. In J. Pulkingham and G. Ternowetsky, eds., *Child and Family Policies: Struggles, Strategies and Options*. Halifax: Fernwood Publishing.

• Neysmith, Sheila. 1991. "From Community Care to a Social Model of Care," in *Women's Caring: Feminist Perspectives on Social Welfare*, Carol Baines, Patricia Evans, and Sheila Neysmith, eds. Toronto: McClelland & Stewart Ltd.

- Statistics Canada. 2001. *Income Distribution by Size in Canada.* Ottawa: Statistics Canada. CANSIM Table 202-0802.

- United Nations Fourth World Conference on Women (FWCW). 1995. *Platform for Action: Women and Poverty.* Beijing, China. Retrieved from: http://www.un.org/womenwatch/daw/beijing/platform/poverty.htm on November 2, 2001.

- Vanier Institute of the Family. 2000. *Profiling Canada's Families II.* Ottawa: Vanier Institute of the Family. Available at: http://www.vifamily.ca/profiling/contents.htm

over the caregiver. These and other issues are the subjects of ongoing debates and research. What remains undisputed is that the current welfare system is not adequately addressing the range of problems faced by women and that action is urgently required to establish basic equality between the sexes.

CONCLUSION

The term "feminization of poverty" depicts the phenomenon of women and families who are living in poverty in increasing numbers. Almost 19 percent of adult women, and around 50 to 60 percent of single mothers, live below Statistics Canada LICO measure. Income security programs have not adequately anticipated and adjusted to the changing nature of the family, and this has resulted in poverty issues for women.

Many social programs assume the existence of the traditional model of the family but, in reality, this model is not the norm. Currently, the individual responsibility model of the family governs social policy. For example, social welfare programs put in place in 1966, just two years before the *Divorce Act* of 1968, did not anticipate the rapid growth in the numbers of single-parent families resulting from the Act. Since then, the question has been asked: should single parents, who are mainly women, be considered employable and obligated to seek work, or should they be considered unemployable and, therefore, in effect be granted a pension during their child-bearing years?

Beyond the income security issues facing families, women are also disadvantaged in the labour market. Women generally receive lower pay than men, and other issues – such as divorce and separation, and women's responsibilities as mothers, homemakers, caregivers and nurturers – lower the earning potential of women. The shifting of women from "stay-at-home mothers" to "worker-mothers" has decreased the economic dependency of women, but it has not significantly altered the disadvantages they face. The problem is not that women are not working – the problem is the pay that women are receiving. In many respects, the legislative changes of the post-war period that were meant to foster greater equality at work have not improved the economic situation of women.

CHAPTER 6: WOMEN AND THE FAMILY

Discussion Questions

1. What factors contribute to the disadvantaged economic status of women in Canadian society? What are some of the solutions being proposed?
2. Define and describe the concept of "feminization of poverty."
3. List and describe the structural and functional definitions of the family.
4. Define the concept of "family," and describe how families have changed over the past decades. What factors have led to these changes?
5. What are the three models of the family, and how would adhering to a social responsibility model change the way we provide income security programs in Canada?
6. Why is it important to understand income security in relation to women?
7. The shift from "stay-at-home-mothers" to "worker-mothers" has not dramatically changed the disadvantaged status of women. Explain why this is so.

Key Concepts

- Feminization of poverty
- Pay equity legislation
- Family
- Vanier Institute of the Family
- Same-sex couples
- Male-breadwinner families
- Dual-earner families
- Patriarchal model of the family
- Individual responsibility model of the family
- Social responsibility model of the family

Websites

- **Status of Women Canada**
  http://www.swc-cfc.gc.ca/pube.html

  This federal government agency, which promotes gender equality and the full participation of women in economic, social, cultural and political life, has a publications section with a large selection of on-line documents.

- **Vanier Institute of the Family**
  http://www.vifamily.ca

  This website contains volumes of information about the family. Check out Profiling Canada's Families, located at: http://www.vifamily.ca/profiling/contents.htm.

- **WomenWatch (United Nations)**
  http://www.un.org/womenwatch

  WomenWatch is a gateway to information and resources on the promotion of gender equality throughout the United Nations system. If you want information about gender equality throughout the world, this is your stop.

- **DisAbled Women's Network Ontario**
  http://dawn.thot.net

  DAWN Ontario: DisAbled Women's Network Ontario is a progressive, feminist and cross-disability organization dedicated to social and economic justice. They are active in many areas of social welfare advocacy.

Widespread homelessness in Canada is considered a national disaster requiring immediate action on the part of all levels of government (photo courtesy of Dick Hemingway).

7

Poverty and Inequality

How Much Is Too Much?

One in six Canadians lives in "straitened circumstances," the Canadian government's euphemism for poverty. And statistics do not tell the whole story — most Canadians would be shocked if they knew how a large number of fellow Canadians survive. This chapter explores the extent of poverty and why poverty persists.

Canada is one of only a few countries without an official poverty line. However, Statistics Canada produces something called the Low Income Cut-off (LICO). These statistics on low income reveal that in 2001 around 4.4 million Canadians, or 14.4 percent, lived below the poverty level, including 1 million children (Statistics Canada 2002). Of course, certain populations, such as single mothers, unattached individuals, Aboriginal Peoples and recent immigrants, have a much greater risk of poverty. According to the 2001 Census, for example, the poverty rate of lone-parent families with children has dropped below the 50 percent mark for the first time in at least 20 years. For seniors, on the other hand, things have recently improved dramatically. The current poverty rate for seniors is 17 percent, which is nearly half that of the 1980s 30 percent rate.

"Today, 826 million people are chronically and seriously undernourished although the world can nourish 12 billion human beings — twice its present population — without any problem."

— Shukor Rahman, World Food Programme

The factors that result in poverty are varied and complex. Poverty is usually brought on by an unexpected turn of events, such as loss of employment, death or disability of a family breadwinner, family break-up or increased costs from a major illness or mishap. Changes in the economy and problems in the labour market can also result in limited employment opportunities, not enough hours of work, declining real value of minimum wages or wages so low that people cannot earn enough to live on. Furthermore, members of some groups in our society face a greater risk of poverty than others due to such things as discrimination, unequal opportunities, lack of recognition for their work (paid or unpaid) and inadequate income support for people who are unable to work or to find paid employment. In this chapter we examine ways of measuring poverty and inequality, which sectors of the Canadian population live in poverty and possible explanations for this. We will also look at global poverty, homelessness and hunger.

For the past century, governments and international bodies have attempted to reduce or eradicate poverty. Despite this, poverty at the national and international level has persisted, and indeed is rising overall. Increasingly, many are arguing that poverty is perhaps an impossible problem to solve, while others put forth the view that only a fundamental restructuring of the global economy will allow us to begin to address such deep-seated social problems.

INTERNATIONAL COUNCIL ON SOCIAL WELFARE (ICSW)

Founded in Paris in 1928, the ICSW is a non-governmental organization that represents organizations in more than 50 countries around the world. The ICSW undertakes research and organizes consultations to help analyze social problems and develop policies. Available on-line at: http://www.icsw.org

LET'S DISCUSS POVERTY, YET AGAIN!

It seems that poverty is continually discussed, defined and measured in an infinite number of ways. The United Nations Development Programme (UNDP) describes "human poverty" as "a denial of choices and opportunities for living a tolerable life," and the World Bank speaks of "income poverty" as living on less than $1 per day. There is also "absolute poverty," or those without the bare necessities, and "relative poverty," or those who are poor in relation to others. For governments, the latest term is "social exclusion," which is supposed to define what poor people experience. It seems that more time and money may be spent discussing poverty than actually trying to eradicate it. It is hoped that this chapter will not add to the malaise.

Certainly, one of the great failures of societies around the world, including that of Canada, is the perpetuation of poverty. Poor nutrition, poor health, a lack of shelter and in some cases death are directly related to poverty and contribute to the degradation of our social structures. The different approaches to addressing poverty have a long history in Canada and in the international community. Below, we will explore the different aspects of poverty, including how it is defined and the diverging explanations for its continued existence.

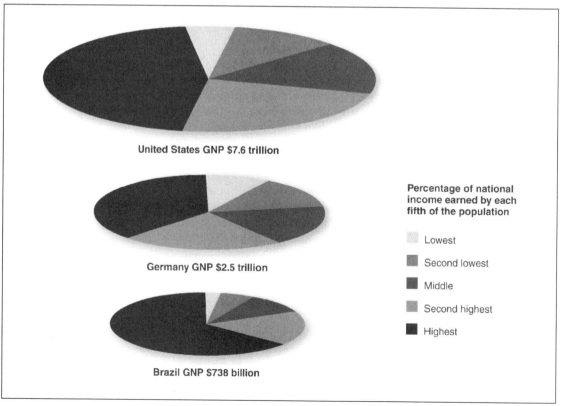

Figure 7.1: World Bank development indicators, showing the percentage of the national income of each country earned by each one-fifth of the population of that country.
Source: World Bank, *World Development Indicators 1999* (Washington D.C.: World Bank, 1999).

MEASURING POVERTY

Poverty traditionally has been defined using two different measurements: an absolute measure and a relative measure. The **absolute measure of poverty** is based on an essential basket of goods and services deemed necessary for survival or well-being. Using the term absolute is misleading, however, as there is not one "absolute" standard of needs. The bundle of goods and services considered essential to well-being is subject to numerous value judgements and is relative to local culture and context.

A measure of poverty based on the absolute approach generally leaves the door open as to what should be included in the essential basket for survival. Critics claim that the basket of goods and services should include items that bring a household beyond mere physical survival and up to a state that meets some kind of social or community norm. The essential basket may include adequate space, cooking facilities, storage for fresh food, furniture, transportation and even recreation and leisure. Other critics place strict boundaries on what should be included, based on the absolute approach. Christopher Sarlo, an analyst with the Fraser Institute, believes that poverty figures are exaggerated because of the level of poverty lines. He developed a new lower measure of absolute poverty by limiting the basket of goods and services to those deemed necessary. With this new lower poverty line, he found that only 4 percent of Canadians were actually living in poverty.

Growing income and wealth disparities in Canada and elsewhere will only serve to fuel social and political unrest. To prevent this happening, economic and social policies are needed that will foster greater levels of income equality and a greater sense of social inclusion (photo courtesy of Dick Hemingway).

On the other hand, the **relative measure of poverty** is based on how low one's income is relative to other people. It measures the number and proportion of persons and households whose incomes fall below some fixed percentage of average or median for the same household size and configuration. This measure reflects the differences in income between the poor and the majority of society, rather than being an abstract standard. Relative poverty is based on the income distribution within a particular society. It is established by setting a poverty line that is some fraction of either the mean or median income for a country or other reference group. When the mean income is used for the calculation, the poverty line changes when the incomes of the richest change. For this reason, many prefer to use the median income.

Some measures of poverty, such as Statistics Canada's **Low Income Cut-off (LICO)**, are based on both absolute and relative measures. This combined measure is often referred to as a "relative necessities" approach. It is based on the percentage of income that individuals and families spend on basic needs or necessities in comparison with the rest of Canadians. LICO is not explicitly put forth as a poverty line, but rather as a level of low income. Other jurisdictions use other measures. For example, the European Commission sets an explicit poverty measure at a poverty line of 60 percent of the national mean income. The United States, on the other hand, still uses an absolute measure of poverty, and the World Bank defines absolute poverty as living on less than $1 per day. In 2002, for example, the U.S. official poverty line for a family of four was US$18,100 (or CDN$28,000) (Federal Register 2002, 6931-6933). According to this measure, 10.4 percent of U.S. citizens live in poverty (see http://www.census.gov/hhes/www/poverty01.html).

Despite the continuous debate over poverty measures, it is safe to say that those scholars who research the causes of poverty are increasingly seeing a relative measure as appropriate for advanced capitalist countries. Although Canada does not have an official "poverty line," most consider the LICOs to be an adequate measure, including the United Nations.

POVERTY LINES: WHAT'S IN A DEFINITION?

For the past 30 years, Statistics Canada has produced LICOs for different household sizes in different regions. According to Statistics Canada, LICOs are used to distinguish "low income" families from "other" families. A family is considered to have a low income when it falls below the LICO for its family size and community population.

LICOs are set by taking what the average household spends on food, clothing and shelter and adding 20 percent. Today, the average Canadian household spends 35 percent of its income on food, clothing and shelter. Twenty percentage points are added to this to obtain a 55 percent threshold. This 55 percent threshold is then converted into a set of LICOs that vary with family and community size. The process is carried out for seven family sizes and five community sizes, providing a matrix of 35 cut-offs. In addition, Statistics Canada produces cut-offs for before-tax and after-tax incomes.

NAC's Sunera Thobani in Medicine Hat, AB (CP/1996/ *Medicine Hat News*/F. Webber).

For example, the 2003 LICO for a family of four in a medium-sized city of 100,000-500,000 is $31,952. A family of four living in a very large Canadian city with an before-tax income of less than $37,253 in 2003, would have been living below the poverty line.

Statistics Canada has another measure called the **Low Income Measure (LIM),** which is widely used for international comparisons of child poverty. It measures the relative low-income rates as one-half of the median income of the country. Because it is a straightforward calculation and can be collected in all nations, it allows for simple comparisons between countries.

Human Resources Development Canada (HRDC), in conjunction with a federal/provincial/territorial working group, has proposed yet another measure of poverty called the **Market Basket Measure (MBM).** This calculates the amount of income needed by a given household to meet its needs based on "credible" community norms. The calculation reflects changes in the cost of consumption rather than changes in income (HRDC March 1998). By defining income needs in this way rather than in bare subsistence terms, it goes beyond an absolute measure of poverty. The basic issue raised by the MBM is what to include and what not to include in the market basket. A limited market basket will result in a low poverty line, thus creating the assumption that fewer people are living in poverty.

MARKET BASKET MEASURE (MBM)

Statistics Canada's MBM calculates the cost of purchasing a basket of goods and services in 48 different geographical areas. It is an absolute measure of poverty.

Recent data on poverty levels are not yet available using the MBM; however, the overall incidence of low income in 2000 for the 10 provinces combined was 13.1% using this measure. This is slightly lower than it was for the pre-income tax version of the LICOs (14.7%).

Table 7.1: Pre-tax Low Income Cut-offs (LICOs), 2003

Family size	Population of Community of Residence				
	500,000 +	100,000- 499,999	30,000- 99,999	Less than 30,000*	Rural
1	$19,795	$16,979	$16,862	$15,690	$13,680
2	$24,745	$21,224	$21,077	$19,612	$17,100
3	$30,744	$26,396	$26,213	$24,390	$21,268
4	$37,253	$31,952	$31,731	$29,526	$25,744
5	$41,642	$35,718	$35,469	$33,004	$28,778
6	$46,031	$39,483	$39,208	$36,482	$31,813
7+	$50,421	$43,249	$42,947	$39,960	$34,847

Source: Prepared by the Canadian Council on Social Development using Statistics Canada's Low Income Cut-offs, from *Low income cut-offs from 1994-2003 and low income measures from 1992-2001*, Catalogue No. 75F0002MIE No. 002, March 2004. See: www.ccsd.ca/facts.html

SOCIAL EXCLUSION

Poverty is increasingly being understood as social exclusion — the result of many individual, family and social factors reinforcing each other in unhelpful ways. The new approach suggests the need for more coordinated, comprehensive solutions. Increasingly, the solutions are being viewed in the context of human rights.

In Canada, there is an ongoing debate about what the correct poverty line should be. Clearly, to some extent, what one person may consider to be adequate to survive will be different from what another person believes. In 1988, for example, Gallup conducted a survey asking what people thought was the minimum weekly amount of income required for a family of four. The amount was about $3,000 dollars less than LICO, but well above welfare rates. If one takes the approach that poverty is entirely based on the subjective belief of the citizens of a country, then LICO is fairly close to what Canadians believe is poverty.

In 1992, the Fraser Institute published *Poverty in Canada* by Chris Sarlo, a University of Nipissing professor. He proposed an alternative measure of poverty based on the costs of a list of necessities. The **Basic Needs Lines (BNL)** were widely criticized for being below most Canadian's idea of an adequate amount for survival. According to Richard Shillington, a social policy consultant, Sarlo's calculations of the costs of a body's minimum caloric requirements are chilling. In 1998, the amount for food for a single elderly women was $17.48 per week. This includes $2.11 for fruit and $1.33 for vegetables. For a single mother with two children, he allocates $50.47, including $7.82 for milk (including powdered milk) and $4.00 for vegetables (Sarlo 1992, 66). He provides no funds for school supplies, which are "assumed to be offset by part-time or summer earnings."

Sarlo recently updated the BNL. To address some of the critics, he scrutinized every item on the original list and reconfigured it from scratch. His new BNLs are higher and therefore find that income poverty in Canada is now in the range of 8 percent, compared to 4 percent with the old BNLs. He has set an annual food budget of $5,306 or $442 per month for a family of four (Sarlo 2001, 20). He does not provide a breakdown of the amount spent on each food item, as he did in the 1992 calculations. The BNLs are not generally taken seriously by the academic or international communities, and few Canadians would agree that people could actually survive on the amounts that are proposed for basic survival.

Precise poverty lines are by and large arbitrary. As we have seen, there is not even a basic conceptual agreement among the experts on what poverty means. Some, such as the Fraser Institute, argue for an absolute approach while others, such as the Canadian Council for Social Development, argue for a relative approach. The Organization for Economic Co-operation and Development (OECD) believes that absolute poverty measures have little meaning in advanced industrialized societies. They maintain that poverty should not be seen as a deprivation of very basic needs, but as an exclusion from the standards of living broadly available to others in the same society (OECD Employment Outlook, June 2001, 41).

Two things are clear, however. First, underlying these various academic debates about poverty and poverty lines are many unstated beliefs and assumptions about exactly how much inequality we should permit in our society. And, second, it is clear that there can be no debate that serious poverty exists in Canadian society today.

• More Than Income?

Many scholars, particularly in Europe, are increasingly conceptualizing poverty in terms of **social exclusion**. The concept refers to marginalization – having limited opportunities or abilities to participate in the social, economic and cultural activities of society. The use of social exclusion is an attempt to broaden the definition of poverty beyond simple income level calculations. It includes measuring the extent to which people have freedom of choice to achieve security. In short, social exclusion views poverty, not as matter of a low degree of well-being, but as the inability to pursue well-being because of the lack of opportunities.

How people themselves, particularly the poor, define poverty varies by gender, age, culture and other social aspects. For example, a young person may define poverty as a lack of job opportunities, while an elderly person may see it in terms of food security and health care. It becomes apparent, however, that poor people are acutely aware of their lack of power, voice and independence. Many poor people speak of poverty in terms of humiliation, isolation, safety and inhumane treatment – and, in some cases, poor people speak about these negative social aspects of poverty as being worse than the lack of income. Poor people also speak more about assets and less about income – having assets is perceived as providing opportunities to gain well-being. Clearly, poverty is more than a mere lack of income.

HOW MUCH POVERTY?

In discussing how much poverty exists, three dimensions need to be considered: *how many* people are poor (the headcount measure), by *how much* they fall below the poverty line (the poverty gap measure) and for *how long* they are poor (the poverty duration measure). Social workers and social policy analysts need to examine all three aspects of the problem to develop coherent and comprehensive income programs.

The **poverty headcount** measures the number and proportion of persons in poverty. Poverty is much more widespread than most people realize. Based on the 2001 LICO, there are 4.4 million people living in poverty or 14.4 percent of the total population. These numbers likely underestimate the number of poor Canadians, as they do not include Aboriginal Peoples on reserves, residents of the Yukon, Nunavut and Northwest Territories and people who live in homes for the aged or other institutions.

Provincial poverty rates also vary. Quebec has the highest rate (21.3%) and Prince Edward Island has the lowest (12.8%). Because so many Canadians reside in Ontario and Quebec, more than half of Canada's poor can be found in these two provinces. To determine if these rates are high or low, it is useful to compare them with those of different countries using a comparable measure. With poverty defined as 50 percent of the median income (adjusted), we find that Canada (11.9%) ranks 16th out of 22 countries (Jesuit and Smeeding 2002, 13). All European countries rank ahead of Canada, with the exception of Italy. Canada ranks ahead of the United States, Australia and the United Kingdom.

HUMAN DEVELOPMENT INDEX (HDI)

In 2003, Canada ranked eighth in the Human Development Index (HDI) annual survey by the United Nations Development Programme (UNDP). A component of the overall HDI is a poverty ranking. On this aspect Canada scored twelfth.

Canada's overall rankings can be found at http://www.undp.org/hdr2003/indicator/cty_f_CAN.html

HDI	Country	Poverty Rank
3	Sweden	1
1	Norway	2
14	Finland	3
5	Netherlands	4
11	Denmark	5
18	Germany	6
15	Luxembourg	7
17	France	8
19	Spain	9
9	Japan	10
21	Italy	11
8	Canada	12
6	Belgium	13
4	Australia	14
13	United Kingdom	15
12	Ireland	16
7	USA	17

Table 7.2: Persons in Low Income before Tax, Statistics Canada (prevalence* in %)

	1997	1998	1999	2000	2001
All persons	**18.0**	**16.5**	**15.8**	**14.7**	**14.4**
Under 18 years of age	20.0	18.7	18.0	16.5	15.6
18 to 64	16.9	15.3	15.0	13.7	13.6
65 and over	19.2	18.8	16.4	16.4	16.8
Males	**16.3**	**15.0**	**14.5**	**13.0**	**13.0**
Under 18 years of age	20.3	19.4	18.1	16.2	15.4
18 to 64	15.5	13.9	14.0	12.3	12.5
65 and over	11.9	11.9	9.6	9.8	11.1
Females	**19.6**	**17.9**	**17.2**	**16.3**	**15.8**
Under 18 years of age	19.8	18.0	17.8	16.8	15.7
18 to 64	18.4	16.6	16.0	15.1	14.7
65 and over	24.8	24.1	21.7	21.5	21.2
Persons in economic families	**14.3**	**13.0**	**12.2**	**11.2**	**11.0**
Males	13.2	12.2	11.4	10.2	10.3
Females	15.4	13.8	13.1	12.1	11.7
Persons 65 years of age and over	**8.3**	**7.8**	**5.2**	**5.0**	**6.1**
Males	7.7	6.9	4.9	4.6	6.3
Females	8.9	8.7	5.6	5.4	5.9
Persons under 18 years of age	**20.0**	**18.7**	**18.0**	**16.5**	**15.6**
In two-parent families	13.7	12.3	12.1	11.4	10.8
In female lone-parent families	58.7	55.1	52.2	47.6	45.4
In all other economic families	31.1	27.7	27.7	22.1	21.4
Persons 18 to 64 years of age	**12.7**	**11.3**	**10.9**	**9.9**	**9.9**
Males	10.9	9.7	9.5	8.5	8.8
Females	14.5	12.7	12.2	11.2	11.0
Unattached individuals	**42.1**	**39.7**	**39.3**	**37.3**	**36.3**
Males	36.7	33.9	34.6	30.8	30.2
Females	47.3	45.3	43.9	43.5	42.4
Persons 65 years of age and over	**44.4**	**44.1**	**42.4**	**43.0**	**42.2**
Males	31.1	34.2	31.6	33.3	32.8
Females	49.1	47.7	46.1	46.4	45.6
Persons under 65 years of age	**41.2**	**38.0**	**38.2**	**35.2**	**34.2**
Males	37.7	33.9	35.1	30.3	29.8
Females	46.2	43.7	42.5	41.7	40.3

* Prevalence of low income shows the proportion of people living below the Low Income Cut-offs within a given group. It is expressed as a percentage. *Source*: Statistics Canada, CANSIM Table 202-0802 and Catalogue No. 75-202-XIE. Available at: http://www.statcan.ca/english/Pgdb/famil41a.htm

Another dimension of poverty includes calculating the total shortfall from the poverty line – that is, the depth of poverty. Poverty rates do not show whether poor people are living in abject poverty or merely a few dollars below the poverty line. To determine this, we need to measure the **poverty gap**. The poverty gap is a measurement of how much additional income would be required to raise an individual or household above the LICO. Statistics Canada refers to this as the "average income deficiency." The number of people in Canada living at less than 50 percent of the LICO grew from 143,000 families and 287,000 individuals in 1989, to 277,000 families and 456,000 individuals in 1997 (National Council of Welfare 2002, 54). The average income for female-led lone-parent families was $9,051 below the poverty line. Of lone-parent families, 40 percent had incomes of $10,000 or more below the poverty line, and 33 percent of two-parent families in poverty had incomes of $10,000 or more below the poverty line.

Finally, it is important to consider **poverty duration**, or how long people experience low income. The Statistics Canada Survey of Labour and Income Dynamics (SLID) enables analysis of the duration of poverty. SLID follows the same set of people for six consecutive years and is designed to capture changes in the economic well-being of individuals and families over time. This data shows that, over the long term, poverty affects a greater number of Canadians than yearly poverty rates suggest. More than 7 million, or 29.5 percent, of all Canadians had experienced poverty in at least one of the six years between 1993 and 1998 (National Council of Welfare 2002). Lone parents, persons with disabilities, members of visible minority groups, recent immigrants, individuals with low levels of education and unattached individuals are more likely to experience lengthy spells of poverty.

Statistics Canada's survey of poverty duration, reported in *The Canadian Fact Book on Poverty 2000* (Ross, Scott and Smith 2002, Chapter 7), finds that, for roughly 60 percent of those in poverty in any given year, poverty proves to be a temporary situation, while it is a recurrent problem for the remaining 40 percent. On average, after counting both single and multiple spells, a poor individual will spend approximately five years in poverty, while 5 percent will stay in poverty for 10 or more years.

PERSISTENT POVERTY

Persistent poverty is highly concentrated in high at-risk groups, which include people with work-related disabilities, recent immigrants, single mothers, unattached older people (until they reach pension age), and Aboriginal Peoples.

THE WORKING POOR

There is a widespread assumption that people who are poor are unemployed, and that many of those who are unemployed are single parents staying at home with children. The reality is that many of the poor, including single mothers, are employed. The low-wage earners or **working poor** are people who are participating in the labour force through paid employment, but who do not earn enough income to lift them above the poverty line. (Some consider only those who are employed full-time to be the working poor, while others include those people with strong ties to the labour force, regardless of their hours of work.)

POVERTY MAKES ME SICK

The Children's Hospital of Eastern Ontario (CHEO), in partnership with 17 other hospitals, launched the video *Poverty Makes Me Sick*. This adds a hospital voice to the issue of child and youth poverty. They see firsthand the causes and effects of poverty on the health of children.

Last year, CHEO's Advocacy Committee of the Board of Trustees initiated an awareness campaign to draw attention to the link between child poverty and illness. The video includes statistics, lists of key resources and endorsements and ideas for action at local and national levels. You can obtain the *Poverty Makes Me Sick* package from CHEO at: http://www.cheo.on.ca

In 1998, there were 981,000 families living below the LICO with the head of the household being under the age of 65. Of this population, 26 percent worked full-time, 34 percent worked part-time, 31 percent did not work at all and 10 percent were unable to work. These statistics indicate that a large portion of those living with low incomes are employed, but working at jobs that provide such a low wage that they remain in poverty. As governments cut back on income security programs and tighten eligibility requirements, many find that the job opportunities do not provide an income sufficient for their family's well-being or even survival. The lack of good paying jobs has propelled increasing numbers of working Canadians into the category of the "working poor."

• Case in Point

The real issues facing people living in poverty frequently get lost in the barrage of statistics. The numbers are important, but people's accounts of their daily struggle do more to illustrate the situation. Mary-Anne's situation provides some insight into the problems faced by the working poor.

Mary-Anne became ill when she was pregnant with her daughter Clarisse. She lost her job, at which she was making $1,600 a month. She did not have enough hours to qualify for Employment Insurance, so she applied for Social Assistance. She received $1,200 per month. It was difficult having her income immediately decrease $400 per month, as well as having the expenses of a newborn child. After the Ontario Social Assistance cutbacks in 1995, her benefits were cut to $957 per month. She lost her apartment and moved in with her mother.

Living in poverty drove Mary-Anne and her mother apart. They found themselves accusing each other of spending too much on food. The thing Mary-Anne wanted most was to find a well-paying job to support herself and her daughter. She voluntarily entered the workfare program of Ontario Works, even though she was exempt because of Clarissa's age. Eventually, she located a job without the help of workfare, earning $1,235 per month. She receives $200 per month in child support and her Canada Child Tax Benefit amounts to $150 per month. Her total income is $20,120 per year, about 10 percent below LICO.

Mary-Anne's apartment ($700 per month) consumes almost half of her income, leaving little for other necessities. It is cramped, and she sleeps on a pull-out couch in the living room so that her six-year-old child can have her own room. After paying for the telephone, food, transportation, clothes and her student loan, nothing is left. She feels lucky to have a substantial child care subsidy, leaving her to pay only $30 per month. After paying $200 per month in payroll taxes, she cannot make ends meet.

She would like to save for Clarisse's education and open a Registered Education Savings Plan (RESP), but that is not possible with her income. She cannot even afford a drug prescription that her doctor recommended. She knows that, above all else, they have to pay the rent on time or risk losing their apartment. The only item that she can cut back on is food.

POVERTY AND CANADA'S CHILDREN

As mentioned elsewhere, in 1989 the Canadian federal government declared its commitment to "seek to achieve the goal of eliminating poverty among Canadian children by the year 2000." Campaign 2000, a national anti-poverty coalition, recently released *The Report Card on Child Poverty in Canada*, which indicates that one in five of Canada's children lives below the Statistics Canada LICO. The Campaign 2000 report summarizes the deteriorating economic situation of Canada's children since 1989. It further demonstrates a 43 percent increase in the population of poor children to 402,000, an increase of 27 percent in the number of families living with less than $20,000 per year and an increase of 49 percent of poor children in single-parent families.

According to Statistics Canada's 2001 Low-Income Cut-off, 10.8 percent of children in two-parent families and 45.4 percent of children in single-parent families were living in poverty. Infants were over 20 percent more likely than 11-year-old children to be living in poverty, primarily because statistics indicate that younger families have higher poverty rates. One in 10 Canadian children lives in a household that is supported primarily by Social Assistance. The odds of poverty are again increased by 56 percent if one family member is an immigrant, even when one equalizes other factors such as education, language skills and age (Kazemipur and Halli 2001, 231).

All of this indicates that different sectors in Canadian society are more likely to find themselves living in poverty. Simply put, the risk of being poor is higher when the head of the family is single or unattached, is a woman, lives with a disability, is a member of a visible minority, is an Aboriginal person or immigrated to Canada after 1979.

INCOME DISTRIBUTIONS

UNICEF produces an interesting annual report called *The State of the World's Children* that compares, among other items, poverty rates. See: http://www.unicef.org/sowc00

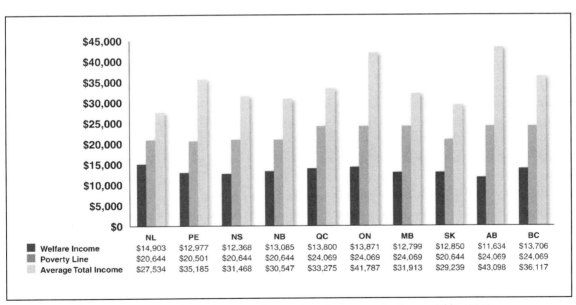

	NL	PE	NS	NB	QC	ON	MB	SK	AB	BC
■ Welfare Income	$14,903	$12,977	$12,368	$13,085	$13,800	$13,871	$12,799	$12,850	$11,634	$13,706
■ Poverty Line	$20,644	$20,501	$20,644	$20,644	$24,069	$24,069	$24,069	$20,644	$24,069	$24,069
Average Total Income	$27,534	$35,185	$31,468	$30,547	$33,275	$41,787	$31,913	$29,239	$43,098	$36,117

Figure 7.2: Welfare income, poverty line and average income for a single parent with one child in 2002. *Source*: National Council of Welfare, *Welfare Incomes 2002*, Volume 119 (Ottawa, 2003). Available at http://www.ncwcnbes.net/htmdocument/principales/onlinepub.htm

INEQUALITY AND INCOME DISTRIBUTION

Poverty and inequality are different concepts that should not be confused. As described above, poverty refers to some benchmark standard and how many people live below that standard. **Inequality** is concerned with the differences between income groups. The way in which total income in a country is divided between households is a measure of inequality (also known as income distribution).

Analysis of income distribution data illustrates that income is shared very unequally in Canada. First, we can examine the **quintile income distribution**. A quintile represents one-fifth (20 percent) of the total number of people being studied. If you took all Canadians and ranked them according to income, you could then divide them into five equal quintiles. The top quintile is the one-fifth (or 20 percent) of people with the highest incomes. The fourth quintile is the one-fifth with the second-highest incomes, and so on down to the bottom quintile, which is the one-fifth (20 percent) of Canadians with the lowest incomes. The quintile income distribution calculates the share of total income that goes to each quintile. If the Canadian population is divided into five sections (quintiles), the richest 20 percent or the richest fifth of Canadians receives around 40 percent of total income and the poorest fifth receives only 6 percent of the income.

Another measure of income inequality is the **Gini coefficient**, which measures the degree of inequality in income distribution. Values of the Gini coefficient can range from 0 to 1. A value of 0 indicates that income is equally divided among the population, with all units receiving exactly the same amount of income. At the opposite extreme, a Gini coefficient of 1 denotes a perfectly unequal distribution, where one unit possesses all of the income in the economy. A decrease in the value of the Gini coefficient can be interpreted as reflecting a decrease in inequality, and vice versa.

Table 7.3: Percentage Distribution of Total Income of Families by Quintiles, Canada, 1974, 1984, 1994 and 1996

Quintile	1974 (%)	1984 (%)	1994 (%)	1996 (%)
Bottom	6.3	6.1	6.4	6.1
Second	13.1	12.3	12.2	11.9
Middle	18.2	18.0	17.7	17.4
Fourth	23.6	24.1	24.1	24.0
Top	38.8	39.5	39.6	40.6

Source: Prepared by the Centre for International Statistics at the Canadian Council on Social Development, using Statistics Canada, *Income Distributions by Size*. Catalogue No. 13-207 (various years).

As shown in the following graph, each Canadian region falls within a similar range of income inequality. According to Gini coefficients, between 1980 and 1998 there was a significant increase in inequalities in each region except British Columbia and the Prairie provinces; however, they were already exhibiting high income inequalities.

Some analysts have attributed this increase in inequality to the effects of globalization (the increased integration of global markets and trade liberalization). In 2001, Bourguignon and Morrisson produced a benchmark study of world income inequality trends over the past two centuries. The study makes comparisons for 33 groups of countries between 1820 and 1992. They found that world inequality increased by 50 percent between 1820 and 1910, a period of rapid growth and globalization. Between 1919 and 1960, inequality remained stable, dipping in the 1950s, before resuming the rise after 1960. The period between 1960 and 1992 saw another era of rapid growth and globalization as well as substantial increases in inequality.

Others have criticized the premise of the study, maintaining that the growth in inequality during periods of economic growth and globalization may be merely a coincidence. But whatever the verdict, the promise of help for the poor trickling down from the rich when economic growth is strong seems unlikely.

WHO IS HUNGRY?

You might be surprised to know who uses your local food bank. The Daily Bread Food Bank in Toronto tracks food bank usage and found that, in 2002, 19% of those using food banks were working, 33% had at least some college or university education, 41% were headed by someone with a disability or long-term illness and 37% were children. But the food banks cannot possibly meet existing needs — 42% say they go hungry at least once a week.

Source: Daily Bread Food Bank, *Who Is Hungry Now?: The Demographics of Hunger in Greater Toronto* (2002).

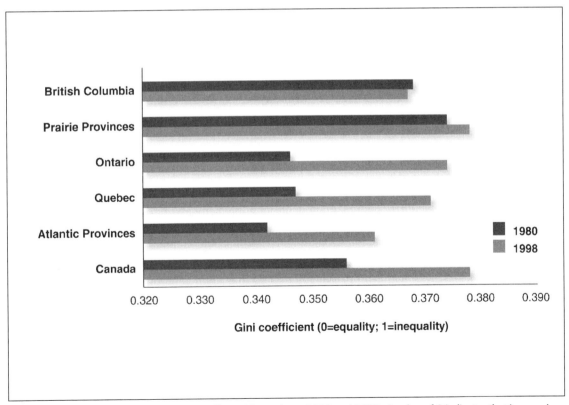

Figure 7.3: Disparities of revenues (Gini coefficient) by regions, 1980 and 1988. A value of 0 indicates that income is equally divided among the population, with all units receiving exactly the same amount of income.
Source: Calculated data from Statistics Canada, *Income trends in Canada 1980-1998,* Catalogue No. 13F0022XCB.

THREE EXPLANATIONS FOR POVERTY

Three explanations exist for the existence of poverty in Canada. Each takes a different viewpoint on how the economy and society interact, and therefore on how people end up in poverty. The first approach places more emphasis on the individual attributes of the person in poverty – what it calls human capital. The second explanation highlights the conditions of the labour market, such as the availability of jobs. The third, critical perspective takes aim at the unequal distribution of power and ownership within the economy and political institutions.

• Human Capital Perspective

The human capital perspective focuses on how the endowments of individuals determine their economic performance. Thus, low earnings that lead to poverty can result from factors such as less education, fewer job skills, old age, poor health and low geographic mobility. Beyond this, differences in earnings are ascribed to differences in individual preferences between income and leisure. This is known as the income-leisure choice theory: the view is that people will choose between paid employment and unpaid leisure. Those with lower incomes are said to have chosen the latter.

In this approach, it is thought that income distributions depend largely on the interaction of supply and demand in the market for labour. As such, workers receive what they contribute. The approach perceives income inequality as a result of the quality of labour supplied. Poverty largely results from a lack of skills or education; inability to plan for old age or unemployment; unwillingness to work, move or retrain or an unwillingness to compete. This approach places emphasis on education and job training in order to break the poverty cycle.

• Labour Market Perspective

In the labour market perspective, the emphasis is on the characteristics of society (demand-side) rather than the individual. Its historical basis is in Keynesian economics, as outlined in Chapter 3. It takes into consideration the barriers people face as a result of location, discrimination and lack of demand for their labour. This explanation emphasizes that the characteristics of the labour market determine income. Adherents to this perspective believe that both supply and demand in the market for labour are important. Markets are viewed as limited or constrained by institutional factors, social norms and other non-economic factors, such as:

- *Socialization.* People are conditioned to believe certain things about themselves and their position in society.

- *Discrimination.* Negative stereotypes and employment barriers may limit employment opportunities.

Within the labour market perspective, there is a variant referred to as *dual labour market theory.* This theory postulates that administrative rules and processes structure and shape labour markets into non-competing groups: the primary labour market and the secondary labour market. The primary labour market is composed of unionized or professional employment, with high wages, benefits, good working conditions and opportunities for advancement. It is generally closed to external competition or highly limited by qualifications. It is predominantly men who hold these jobs. The secondary labour market is composed of low-wage jobs with few benefits, and is open to external competition. Most often, women with part-time and unstable jobs occupy this market. According to this perspective, the large pool of unemployed workers keeps the wages down in the secondary labour market and poverty is generally associated with the secondary labour market. In today's society, there are fewer primary jobs and significantly more secondary jobs. The primary jobs are becoming increasingly knowledge-based; however, these jobs have become less stable and more people are working on contracts. One explanation for low incomes, therefore, is the growth of the secondary labour force. As well, many families living on one income are now considered low income. At the same time, the Canadian labour force is being pitted against the labour forces in other low wage countries, driving Canadian wages and benefits down.

• Political Economy Perspective

The political economy perspective presupposes a relationship between politics and economics (for more information on this perspective, see Chapter 3). The large concentration of ownership of major corporations affects the way in which governments operate in the regulation of industry and the labour market. Those who control the labour market control the wages of workers. Thus, there is a large spread and great inequality between owners at the top and workers at the bottom, leading to the poverty of some and the affluence of others.

Within this perspective, labour markets are segmented into competing camps. This enables employers to keep wages down. Stratification in the labour market is useful, it is argued, because employers pay some workers less than others pay, and create a group of flexible low-paid workers who can be moved in and out of employment as needed. Some feminist theories, for example, suggest that women are trapped in low-paying "women's work" in the labour market, which is viewed as an extension of their domestic work in the home.

Another factor that falls within the political economy explanation is discrimination. Discrimination based on race and ethnicity, both at interpersonal and at institutional levels, negatively affects the economic achievement of immigrants and people of colour. Some researchers have found that, even when immigrants are highly educated, their achievements are not recognized in the labour market.

Increasingly, social policy analysts are advocating an approach that considers all three explanations discussed above. This three-track method emphasizes accessible and quality education and training opportunities, job creation, employment equity and public participation in labour policy discussion and development.

WHAT ARE THE EFFECTS OF POOR BASHING?

• It hurts people in their daily lives.

• Adults and children are shunned, despised, pitied, patronized, humiliated and ignored.

• It blames individuals for being poor, and takes attention away from the overall state of the economy.

• It justifies policies such as workfare, which undermines wages and working conditions.

• It undermines support for social programs that benefit all Canadians and our communities.

• It encourages people to think in stereotypes and to discriminate against people who are poor.

• "Snitch" lines criminalize people on welfare and turn people against each other.

Source: Community Action on Poverty, Winnipeg, Manitoba.

THE COLOUR OF POVERTY

As noted earlier, aside from Canada's First Nations Peoples, we are a nation of immigrants. Moreover, "visible minority" groups now make up about 11 percent of the total Canadian population, compared to 6 percent in 1986. Poverty among racialized groups in Canada, particularly recent immigrants, is higher than for other Canadians. Census data from 1996 shows that the poverty rate for Canadians was 21 percent, whereas the rate for "visible minority persons" was 38 percent.

York University professor Michael Ornstein has researched poverty levels among racialized groups using the 1996 Census. The report, *Ethno-Racial Inequality in the City of Toronto: An Analysis of the 1996 Census*, found that, while 14 percent of European families live below the Low Income Cut-Off, the percentage is much higher for non-Europeans: 32.1 percent for Aboriginals; 35 percent for South Asians; 45 percent for Africans, Blacks and Caribbeans, and 45 percent for Arabs and West Asians. Similarly, a study by two university professors (Kazemipur and Halli 2001, 231) found that with everything else (such as education and language) being equal, the odds of poverty increase by 56 percent if one is an immigrant.

In *Does a Rising Tide Lift All Boats? Labour Market Experiences and Incomes of Recent Immigrants*, CCSD senior research associate Ekuwa Smith and former CCSD research director Andrew Jackson examined the issue in relation to recent immigrants. They found that the gap in employment and income between recent immigrants and other Canadians narrowed between 1995 and 1998, but the gap remains very large. In 1998, poverty among recent immigrants stood at 27 percent, double the 13 percent rate among the rest of the population; their annual wages and salaries were one-third less than those of other Canadians. They also found that three out of four recent immigrants to Canada now belong to visible minority groups, possibly making them more susceptible to racial discrimination.

Many studies have analyzed the possibility that the lower economic achievement of recent immigrants and racialized groups may be attributed, not to their lower level of education, language or skill (also known as human capital), but to diminishing returns for these factors. Immigrants have higher levels of education than Canadians overall, but do not earn income usually associated with their level of education. Some have attributed this to discrimination and of non-recognition or the undervaluing of foreign education, skills and credentials.

A major implication of this body of research is that labour market forces alone will not address such deep-seated problems, and a variety of initiatives are needed. Such policies include employment and pay equity, the recognition and promotion of the "hidden skills" of new immigrants to prospective employers, the provision of language and skills training to new immigrants and the expedited recognition of foreign credentials. These policies are especially needed to address the social exclusion of recent immigrants and racialized communities. Without such policies, the major social inequalities that currently exist will persist and even grow deeper as time goes on.

GLOBAL POVERTY

The circumstance of so many Canadians living in poverty is certainly appalling; however, the extent of **global poverty** and world inequality is infinitely worse. According to the World Bank, about one-quarter of the world's population lives on less than $1 per day and over half live on $2 per day. Such figures do not capture the suffering that can accompany poverty of this magnitude. While some people can adequately survive on such meagre incomes given the cost of living in their home countries, many suffer with health problems, low life expectancies, high infant mortality rates, low levels of education and malnutrition.

What is most startling about the situation of global inequality is that it is getting worse. Free trade and increased global investments have not decreased the gap between the rich countries and the poor countries. The *World Development Reports* of the World Bank state that the gap has widened considerably between 1960 and 1990. In 1960, the rich world average income was 20 times that of the poor world average income, whereas in 1990 the ratio had increased to 55 times.

The impacts of global poverty are enormous. According to the World Health Organization (WHO), more than 11 million children die each year before reaching the age of five; of them, 70 percent, or around 8 million children, die from one or more of five preventable causes of death that are all related to poverty: pneumonia, diarrhea, measles, malaria and malnutrition.

Beyond individual suffering, the existence of poverty affects world politics, warfare and terrorism. After the September 11 attacks on the World Trade Centre, Jean Chrétien, then prime minister at the time, told the UN that keeping people in poverty can lead to security risks for wealthy nations. In a CBC interview he said the attacks made him aware that the Western world faces a lot of resentment because of the growing divide between rich and poor nations. (See http://www.cbc.ca/stories/2002/09/16/chretien_UN020916 for text of the interview.)

Human development challenges remain large in the new millennium. Across the world we see unacceptable levels of deprivation in people's lives. Of the 4.6 billion people in developing countries, more than 850 million are illiterate, nearly a billion lack access to improved water sources, and 2.4 billion lack access to basic sanitation. Nearly 325 million boys and girls are out of school. And 11 million children under the age of five die each year from preventable causes — equivalent to more than 30, 000 a day. Around 1.2 billion people live on less than $1 a day, and 2.8 billion on less than $2 a day.

Such deprivations are not limited to developing countries. In OECD countries, more than 130 million people are income poor, 34 million are unemployed and adult functional illiteracy rates average 15 percent. Indeed, the late twentieth Century may go down in world history as a period of increasing global impoverishment. Some believe that the new economic order feeds on cheap labour and, with the freer movement of capital, corporations pick up and move when citizens begin to increase their earnings, leaving many people without a stable source of income.

GLOBAL POVERTY CHALLENGE

How much do you know about global poverty? Question: What percentage of the world's population do you think lives in absolute poverty? Answer: As unbelievable as it might seem, one in four people in the world lives in absolute poverty. Absolute poverty is defined as earning less than $1 per day. Go to this website and answer seven more questions: http://unpac.ca/globalization/1.html.

HOMELESSNESS AND FOOD INSECURITY

Symptomatic of the growing problem of poverty in Canada, homelessness is also on the rise. Simply defined, it is the absence of a place to live. A person who is considered to be homeless has no regular place to live and stays in an emergency shelter, in an abandoned building, in an all-night shopping area, in a laundromat, outdoors or any place where they can be protected from the elements.

Two types of homelessness can be distinguished: absolute homelessness and relative homelessness. **Absolute homelessness** is a situation in which an individual or family has no housing at all, or is staying in a temporary form of shelter. **Relative homelessness** is a situation in which people's homes do not meet the United Nation's basic housing standards, which are that a dwelling must

- have adequate protection from the elements,

- provide access to safe water and sanitation,

- provide secure tenure and personal safety,

- not cost more than 50 percent of total income and

- lie within easy reach of employment, education and health care.

The homeless you see on the streets are long-term or "chronically" homeless people who represent less than 20 percent of the homeless. The rest are families and individuals who find themselves without a place to live for a period of time.

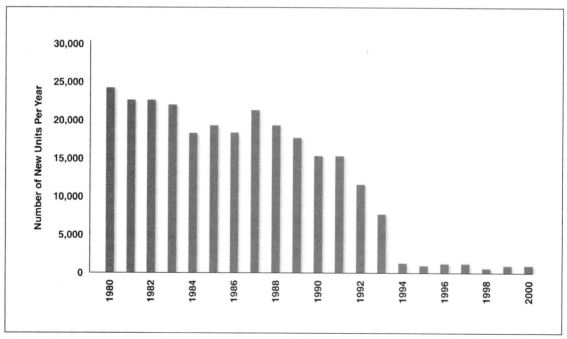

Figure 7.4: Affordable housing units created annually, 1980-2000.
Source: Canadian Housing and Renewal Association, presentation to the House of Commons Committee on Finance (2001).

People become homeless for a variety of reasons. The major reasons appear to be economic crises due to unemployment or low income, mental health problems, other severe health problems, violence or abuse in the home, eviction, a lack of support from family and friends and substance abuse problems. In some cases these factors can overlap and are precipitated by unemployment, health problems or a family crisis. Changes to government policy, such as the *Tenant Protection Act* in Ontario, have removed rent controls and made it easier to evict tenants. When combined with a decrease in affordable housing, homelessness becomes a growing problem.

According to Statistics Canada, about two-thirds of Canadians own their own homes – half without a mortgage. This is a testament to the wealth in Canada, for some. The problem, however, is for those with low incomes. Only 40 percent of households in the lowest quintile (the bottom 20 percent of income recipients) own their own homes. A report by the City of Toronto found that the number of families living in shelters is dramatically increasing. While the majority of people staying in Toronto's emergency shelters are still single men, the number of families is growing. The number of people using Toronto's shelters rose from 22,000 in 1988 to nearly 30,000 in 1999, an increase of 40 percent (City of Toronto 2001, 4).

However, such numbers do not capture the extent of the problem of homelessness. They do not include women staying in emergency battered women's shelters, people who are living in substandard situations (a relative's basement) or women who use sexual contracts to find shelter with a man (the latter is an increasingly common phenomenon, showing the extent to which women are desperate to avoid life in emergency shelters).

Homelessness has increased over the past decades as governments have cut back on social housing. In many cases people simply cannot afford the housing that is available in their community. What is called for is a program of investment in low-cost affordable housing.

• Food Security and Insecurity

With cutbacks in many income security programs, Canadians are having to rely on **food banks and feeding programs** in order to survive. In 2003, there were over 639 food banks in Canada, and 777,869 people received emergency food in one of these food banks (Canadian Association of Food Banks, 2003). This is a 1.2 percent drop from March 2000, when the number stood at 726,902 (Wilson and Steinman 2000, 1). The number of people who utilized food banks had doubled since March 1989. Over 40 percent of those being helped were under the age of 18, representing an estimated 294,516 children.

Of those Canadians using food banks, 81.2 percent relied on income security programs as their income source (65 percent Social Assistance, 12 percent Employment Insurance (EI) and 9 percent Disability Benefits). Only 12 percent were employed, and 4 percent reported no income (Wilson and Tsoa 2001, 3). As Social Assistance rates decrease and

REFERENCES

* Bourguignon, Francois, and Christian Morrisson. 2001. *Inequality among World Citizens: 1820-1992.* Working Paper 2001-25.

* Canadian Association of Food Banks. 2003. *Hunger Count 2003.* Toronto (retrieved from www.cafb.ca on December 15, 2003).

* City of Toronto. 2001. *The Toronto Report Card on Homelessness.*

* Department and Laboratory of Applied and Theoretical Economics, École Normale Superieure, Paris. *Child Poverty in Canada Report Card.* 2002. The UN Special Session on Children: Putting Promises into Action, A Report on a Decade of Child and Family Poverty in Canada.

* Federal Register, USA. 2002. Vol. 67, No. 31, February 14, 2002, pp. 6931-6933.

* Human Resources Development Canada. March 1998.

* Jesuit, David, and Timothy Smeeding. 2002. *Poverty Levels in the Developed World.* Luxembourg Income Study Work Paper No. 321.

* Kazemipur, A., and S. Halli. 2001. The changing colour of poverty in Canada. *Canadian Review of Sociology and Anthropology.* Vol. 38, No.2, pp. 217-38.

* National Council of Welfare. 2002. *Poverty Profile 1999.* Ottawa: National Council of Welfare. Available at: http://www.ncwcnbes.net.

* National Council of Welfare. 2002. Factsheet. Ottawa: National Council of Welfare. Available at http://www.ncwcnbes.net/ htmdocument/principales/ Factsheets.htm

* Ornstein, Michael. 2000. "Ethno-racial Inequality in the City of Toronto: An Analysis of the 1996 Census." Toronto: Chief Administrator's Office, City of Toronto.

* Ross, David P., Katherine Scott, and Peter Smith. 2002. *The Canadian Fact Book on Poverty 2000.* Ottawa: Canadian Council on Social Development.

* Sarlo, Christopher. 1992. *Poverty In Canada.* Vancouver: The Fraser Institute.

* Sarlo, Christopher. 2001. *Measuring Poverty In Canada.* Vancouver: The Fraser Institute.

* Smith, A., and A. Jackson. 2002. *Does a Rising Tide Lift All Boats? Labour Market Experiences and Incomes of Recent Immigrants.* Ottawa: Canadian Council on Social Development.

* Statistics Canada. 1998. *Income Trends In Canada 1980-1998.* Ottawa: Statistics Canada. Catalogue No. 13F0022XCB .

* Statistics Canada. 2001. *Income Distribution by Size in Canada.* Ottawa: Statistics Canada. CANSIM Table 202-0802.

* Statistics Canada. 2002. *Low Income Cut offs from 1992 to 2001 and Low Income Measures from 1991 to 2000.* Ottawa: Statistics Canada. Catalogue No. 75F0002MIE-2002005.

* Wilson, B., and C. Steinman. 2000. *Hunger Count 2000.* Toronto: Canadian Association of Food Banks.

* Wilson, B., and E. Tsoa. 2001. *Hunger Count 2001.* Toronto: Canadian Association of Food Banks.

eligibility requirements for EI tighten, it is estimated that food bank usage by Canadians will continue to increase.

Feeding programs provide cooked meals at specified times during the day. They often operate out of shelters or church basements and provide two meals per day. Such programs are operated by volunteers and by those who use the service. For example, The Well in Ottawa does not start providing meals until enough people volunteer to help. Many feeding programs are run in conjunction with emergency shelters. Feeding programs often also provide additional services, such as free laundry facilities, telephone access, newspapers and clothing. In certain instances, access to computers and the Internet is also available. At most times, social workers are available and may even work directly from within the feeding program.

There is difficulty in keeping pace with demand. Almost half, or 49 percent, of food banks report that they often run out of food and must turn people away. Many believe that the steady unravelling of the social safety net means that access to basic food is in jeopardy.

Food security is a basic right and all people in their community should have access to good, nutritious food at all times. Fundamental changes in benefit levels and eligibility requirements are still needed to address the hunger problem.

CONCLUSION

Regardless of how it is defined, serious poverty exists in Canada. People can find themselves in poverty due to the lack of employment, employment that pays inadequately or obligations to care for children or other family members. Economists and social scientists have put forth different explanations for the existence of poverty, so a variety of proposed solutions have emerged. Over the past few decades, Canadian policy has adhered to a human capital perspective.

While social scientists argue about the merits of their various measures of poverty, people must live in misery and with the problems created by poverty. Without a doubt, a market economy excels at maximizing the production of goods and services (as compared to other historical relations of production). However, the system, as it currently exists in Canada and most other industrialized countries, has not figured out how to address poverty. Some argue that with the new-found ability of corporations to move production from Canada to low-wage countries, the situation could get worse. What is alarming is that even with this shift in production, poorer countries on the whole are growing poorer, and the gap between rich and poor countries is widening.

CHAPTER 7: POVERTY AND INEQUALITY

Discussion Questions

1. How do the absolute and relative measures of poverty differ? Which one do you think produces a more accurate measure of poverty?

2. What is LICO, how is it calculated and what does it intend to measure? How is it different from the Low Income Measure and the Market Basket Measure? Which of these measures is an absolute measure?

3. Other than the rate of poverty, what other aspects of poverty are important to measure, and why?

4. What is inequality, and how is it measured? What share of total income goes to the top quintile of income earners in Canada? How does this compare to the bottom quintile?

5. What are the three explanations for poverty, and how would each differing explanation affect the method the government chooses to tackle poverty?

6. What are the two types of homelessness? What are the causes of homelessness? What do you think can be done to solve the homelessness situation?

Websites

- **Canadian Council on Social Development — Free Statistics**
  http://www.ccsd.ca/facts.html
  A large collection of statistics on poverty lines, poverty data and welfare incomes.

- **Policy.ca**
  http://www.policy.ca
  Check out the social policy issue area. Policy.ca is a non-partisan resource for the public analysis of Canadian policy issues. Go to the "Social Policy" area and scroll down to "Poverty" or "Social Assistance."

- **Centre for Equality Rights in Accommodation**
  http://www.equalityrights.org/cera/
  The Centre's website has reports on housing issues from a human rights perspective.

- **Toronto Disaster Relief Committee**
  http://www.tdrc.net/
  The TDRC has a good collection of resources on homelessness.

- **PovNet**
  http://www.povnet.org
  For people involved in anti-poverty work, this site has up-to-date information on a variety of pertinent issues related to the persistence of poverty in Canada.

Key Concepts

- Absolute measure of poverty
- Relative measure of poverty
- Low Income Cut-off (LICO)
- Low Income Measure (LIM)
- Market Basket Measure (MBM)
- Basic Needs Lines (BNL)
- Social exclusion
- Poverty headcount
- Poverty gap
- Poverty duration
- Working poor
- Inequality
- Quintile income distribution
- Gini coefficient
- Global poverty
- Absolute homelessness
- Relative homelessness
- Food banks and feeding programs

Over 4,000 people participated in this trade union demonstration in Shawinigan, Quebec, in March 1996. The Quebec workers were calling for provincial authority over Unemployment Insurance programs (CP PHOTO/ *Trois-Rivieres Le Nouvelliste*/Sylvain Mayer).

8

People in the Labour Force

Understanding Income Security

Two pillars of our income security system, Employment Insurance and Workers' Compensation, provide income loss protection for those in the labour force. Without these benefits, both employees and employers would face uncertainties and the operation of our economy would be hindered. They not only insure workers, but protect employers from lawsuits and enhance their competitiveness through labour market flexibility.

Since the post-war years, the recommendations of the 1943 Report on Social Security for Canada (known as the Marsh Report) and the rise of Keynesian economic ideas, there has been considerable debate about how the government should address the problem of unemployment. Debates centre on how much the government should interfere with a "free market" economy and whether emphasis should be on job creation, employment training or income support. In a market economy such as ours, unemployment is one of the most important risks faced by Canadians. Without a job, a person confronts poverty: loss of social status, less access to health, possible loss of housing and a multitude of other problems. In fact, many difficult social problems in our society can be attributed, to a large extent, to the repercussions of unemployment (or low wages).

Two income security programs provide social insurance against interruption in earnings: Employment Insurance (EI), delivered by the federal government, and Workers' Compensation (WC), offered by the provinces. Employment Insurance insures against a short-term loss of employment income – Canadians unemployed for longer periods will exhaust their EI benefits and will turn to Social Assistance (SA), which is discussed in detail in Chapter 9.) Workers' Compensation, on the other hand, protects the employed from work injuries and health-related risks. It was the first social insurance program in Canada – and in many other industrialized countries.

The fundamental element of a modern welfare state is its **social insurance schemes**. You pay your premiums and you have a right to benefits. This chapter outlines the historical and current EI programs and provides an overview of Workers' Compensation.

"The average number of fathers receiving parental benefits each month reached 7,900 in 2002, five times more than the average of 1,600 two years earlier."

— Statistics Canada, *The Daily* (March 21, 2003).

EMPLOYMENT INSURANCE AND WORKERS' COMPENSATION: AN OVERVIEW

In Canada over the past 50 years, overall unemployment has risen fairly steadily. The unemployment rate has increased from under

HOW MUCH WOULD I GET ON EMPLOYMENT INSURANCE?

Average Weekly Benefits, 2002

All benefits	$288.71
Regular	$287.91
Sickness	$257.52
Maternity	$296.99
Fishing	$398.84
Work sharing	$86.47
Adoption	$353.71

Source: Statistics Canada, CANSIM II, Table 276-0016. Available at: http://www.statcan.ca/english/Pgdb/labor17.htm.

2 percent in 1942 to over 9 percent through the 1980s, and over 7 percent through the 1990s and into the 2000s. **Employment Insurance (EI)** is a social program that contributes to the security of all Canadians by providing assistance to workers who lose their jobs and by helping unemployed people get back to work. However, Employment Insurance is much more than protection from unemployment. It provides temporary financial help to eligible unemployed Canadians while they look for work or upgrade their skills, while they are pregnant or caring for a newborn or adopted child, while they are sick or while they care for a gravely ill family member. It also provides employment assistance to help people return to the workforce. Individuals who have paid into the EI account can qualify for regular benefits of 55 percent of their average weekly insured earnings, to a maximum of $413 per week – provided they have worked the minimum required number of insurable hours within the last 52 weeks or since the start of their last claim, whichever is shorter.

But EI does not cover all unemployed Canadians. In fact, fewer and fewer people are finding that they can draw benefits when they need them. This can be a shock for someone who has paid into the insurance fund for years. Changes to EI eligibility requirements during the 1990s has severely limited the number of people who are eligible for benefits. From 1989 to 1997, the percentage of unemployed people that actually received benefits dropped from 83 to 42 percent (Human Resources Development Canada 1998). This increasingly affects women who, due in part to additional family responsibilities, work less than the required 35 hours per week. In 1999, 68 percent of employed women were ineligible for EI benefits (Canadian Labour Congress 2000, 3). Details on the program and how it has changed are discussed later in the chapter.

Workers' Compensation (WC) is an insurance system for employers and workers, established to replace the tort system (the courts) in determining compensation for workplace injuries and health-related risks. It provides no-fault compensation. This means that benefits are paid to injured workers whether or not negligence on the part of the worker or employer is considered to have contributed to the accident. With this coverage, workers give up their right of legal action in return for certainty of compensation. A worker injured in the course of employment cannot sue his or her employer for damages. Early programs were instituted due to employers' concerns about lawsuits resulting from injuries in the workplace where the employers were negligent. Factories in the late 1800s and early 1900s were dangerous places, and injuries and work-related illness were commonplace. Earlier programs were called "Workmen's Compensation," but have since been replaced with gender-neutral terms.

Roughly 85 percent of the Canadian labour force is covered by provincial workers' compensation programs (Human Resources Development Canada 1999b, 5). First, WC covers the risk of incurring costs for the rehabilitation from an injury or illness contracted at or caused by their workplace or because of working. Secondly, WC provides insurance against the interruption of income or the impairment of earnings capacity, whether temporary or permanent, that arises from an illness or accident at work. This includes support for dependants in the case of the death of a worker at the workplace or arising out of work.

On average, one Canadian worker out of 16 was injured at work in 1997 and one worker out of 31 was injured severely enough to miss at least one day of work. In 1997, Workers' Compensation Boards (WCB) paid over $4.5 billion in benefits (Human Resources Development Canada 1999b, 7). If the indirect costs (the time lost by uninjured workers trying to help an injured worker, lowered staff morale and damage to materials and equipment) are included, the total cost of occupational injuries to the Canadian economy could be estimated at over $9.1 billion (ibid.). These rates do not include those not covered by Workers' Compensation and may be underestimating injuries and costs by 15 to 20 percent.

Every province has its own Workers' Compensation program. Eligibility criteria, benefit levels and coverage all vary considerably between provinces. Coverage, for example, varies from 60 to 90 percent of the workforce between provinces. Quebec and Manitoba have even used WC to indemnify victims of criminal acts. This covers the costs of injury of victims of criminal acts or innocent bystanders. Programs are generally financed by employer contributions. The Workplace Safety and Insurance Board (WSIB) in Ontario is entirely financed by employer premiums. They receive no money from the Ontario provincial government. In 2000 employers paid $2.29 per $100 of payroll.

Through the changes introduced by the *Workplace Safety and Insurance Act* (1998), the WSIB in Ontario oversees workplace safety education and training. Some provinces and territories, such as the Yukon, the Northwest Territories, Nunavut and Newfoundland have added both workplace health and safety to their titles and to their missions. Other provinces, such as Manitoba, Alberta, Nova Scotia and British Columbia work exclusively in injury compensation, and they have retained the traditional organization title of Workers' Compensation Board.

Workers' Compensation programs nationwide are facing new challenges. Knowledge of work-related injury and disease causation has changed the nature of claims. When Workers' Compensation systems first began, far less was known about the intricate relationship between work and health. In the early days, work injuries were usually readily identifiable by specific traumatic incidents. Today, many claims relate to occupational diseases. Claims for items such as occupational cancer due to prolonged exposure to tobacco smoke at the workplace are more common than they used to be.

This new knowledge has implications for prevention. We are discovering the relevance of work factors that have not been adequately addressed by our prevention and compensation systems. There is a widening gap between our knowledge of how work causes disease and our strategies in preventing and compensating for it. Ontario is one of the few provinces that has begun to address prevention issues as part of its WSIB program, but so far, programs have related more to educating workers on how to avoid workplace disease rather than directly addressing its occurrence.

Protesting against EI cutbacks in Nfld. (CP PHOTO/*St. John's Evening Telegram*/J. Gibbons).

FEDERAL LEGISLATION
ON-LINE

The federal Department of
Justice keeps up-to-date and
historical copies of all of
Canada's laws and legislation.
The *Employment Insurance Act*
and the old *Unemployment
Insurance Act* can be obtained
at this site:
http://laws.justice.gc.ca/

THE HISTORY OF UNEMPLOYMENT INSURANCE

Unemployment Insurance (UI) – now called Employment Insurance (EI) – came into being during the high-employment era of World War II. It began with a narrow focus on the income support needs of regular, full-time, year-round workers who might find themselves temporarily without work. Over the next 30 years, it expanded to cover almost all employed workers and became the federal government's primary vehicle to address a wide range of income support and social policy issues.

The history of Employment Insurance begins in 1940 with the *Unemployment Insurance Act*. The federal government obtained the unanimous consent of the provinces to amend the *British North America Act*, making a national UI program possible. Before this amendment, such an insurance system was the exclusive domain of the provinces. On August 7, 1940, the *Unemployment Insurance Act* was given Royal Assent and, with it, Canada became the last Western industrialized nation to have Unemployment Insurance. As mentioned, the 1940 program was narrow in scale, and eligibility requirements were limiting. For example, weekly benefit rates for a single person were between $4.08 and $12.24. Throughout the period between 1940 and 1960, numerous amendments to the UI legislation expanded eligibility and increased benefits and coverage. In general, the 1950s and particularly the 1960s saw greater involvement of government in most areas of Canadian life. Growth in government revenues and increased expectations from Canadians led to an expansion of the social safety net, and this included UI.

The 1970 White Paper on *Unemployment Insurance* recommended an extended and enhanced UI program, including universal coverage for all workers who could be considered employees, increased benefits that should be related to income and lower contribution rates. Sickness and pregnancy benefits were also recommended. Bill C-229, introduced early in 1971, legislated a revamped UI that followed many of the White Paper recommendations. This was part of Prime Minister Pierre Elliott Trudeau's "Just Society" initiative. Due to these changes, 80 percent of unemployed workers were covered by UI.

New maternity and sickness programs were also introduced, providing financial support to new mothers who worked before they had their children and to workers with short-term illnesses. The government assumed full responsibility for the cost of extended UI benefits due to high unemployment (above 4 percent). In 1977, the government introduced a number of training measures for unemployed workers drawing benefits, such as work sharing and job creation programs.

The introduction of Bill C-21 in 1990 reversed several of these enhancements. The Bill increased the number of weeks of work required to receive benefits, reduced the maximum duration of benefits for most regions and reduced the replacement rate from 60 to 50 percent of insurable earnings for those who declined "suitable employment," quit "without just cause" or were fired. In 1993, benefits were tightened further. Bill C-113 cut the regular benefit rate from 60 percent of insurable earnings to 57 percent, and benefits for workers who quit or were fired from their jobs were eliminated.

A much-touted 1994 review of social security in Canada resulted in numerous changes to UI. The review resulted in the Green Paper called *Agenda: Jobs and Growth – Improving Social Security in Canada*. The Green Paper recommended the name change from Unemployment Insurance to Employment Insurance to represent the goal of encouraging employment (Human Resources Development Canada 1994, 42). The paper recommended a smaller, better-targeted program with tighter rules and lower premiums. With this in hand, the Liberal government announced a round of cuts to UI to save a projected $5.5 billion over three years. The changes included a reduction in benefits for most claimants from 57 to 55 percent of insured earnings, a further increase in the number of weeks needed to qualify and a decrease in the benefit period – in sum, extensive alterations to the benefit structure. Perhaps most controversial was the two-tier system of benefits that had lower benefits for frequent claimants – known as the *intensity rule*. (This was discontinued in 2001 due to findings that it was ineffective in discouraging repeat use, and was also seen as being punitive.)

On January 5, 1995, changes to the Employment Insurance system took effect with Bill C-12, *The New Employment Insurance Act*. The new system replaced the previous Unemployment Insurance system on July 1, 1996. Beyond the name change, there were five key differences:

1. **Hours**. Income benefits based on hours worked rather than weeks worked.

2. **Earnings**. Benefits more closely tied to earnings.

3. **Intensity Rule**. The basic benefit rate of 55 percent declines according to the number of weeks of benefits drawn in a five-year period (lowering benefits for frequent recipients).

4. **Employment Benefits**. Increased concentration on benefits intended to equip an unemployed person to return to work.

5. **Family Income Supplement**. Enhanced protection for low-income families.

The new Bill also reduced the dollar benefits payable, reduced the premiums to be paid into the EI fund by employees and employers, increased the length of work time required to be eligible and shortened the maximum periods for which benefits can be paid. These changes have been criticized by the labour community and by social welfare advocates for hurting those who need the program most – single-parent families (mostly led by women) and children.

In their report entitled *Analysis of UI Coverage for Women*, the Canadian Labour Congress found that the gap in UI coverage between men and women has widened due to the 1997 changes. They claim that the portion of women now getting UI is 10 percent lower than for men, and that women under the age of 45 have lost most heavily, since only 28 percent of them are covered (March 2000 http://www.clc-ctc.ca/policy/ui/wom-ui-00e.html).

COMPASSIONATE CARE BENEFITS (2004)

Bill C-28 amends the EI Act to provide up to six weeks of compassionate care benefits for workers with 600 hours of insurable earnings.

Workers can leave work to care for:

- spouse or common-law partner,

- child or the child of their spouse/partner,

- parent or the spouse/partner of their parent, or

- any other person who may be defined as a "family member" in subsequent regulations.

The person requiring care must have a serious medical condition with significant risk of death within 26 weeks and must require care.

SOCIAL INSURANCE NUMBER: YOURS TO PROTECT!

The Social Insurance Number (SIN) was introduced in 1964 as an identifier for Unemployment Insurance and the Canada Pension Plan. Over the years, a number of other federal departments have also begun to use the SIN. Every person who works in Canada is required to have a SIN. Keep your SIN private and do not show it to just anyone. While there is no law that prevents businesses from asking you for your SIN (for example, for a credit rating), you should not reveal it to them. The SIN can be used to gain access to your personal information.

THE HISTORY OF WORKERS' COMPENSATION

The concept of Workers' Compensation originated in England and the United Sates in the late 1800s and early 1900s. Early laws in England made it extremely difficult for workers to successfully sue an employer for negligence. The employers' defenses, which developed earlier in the nineteenth century, were based on the assumptions that contracts between workers and their employers were the same as commercial contracts between people of equal bargaining power. If workers did not like the employers' terms and conditions, they could simply find work elsewhere. The defenses later became known as the "unholy trinity:"

- **Voluntary assumption of risk.** The worker assumed the usual risks of the job. The rate of pay for each job was assumed to reflect its level of risk.

- **Fellow servant rule**. A worker's injury was related to a co-worker's negligence, and the employer was not responsible. The second defense was a variation on voluntary assumption of risk — one of the risks a worker assumed was the possible negligence of a co-worker. The injured worker could sue the co-worker, but considering the income levels of workers at the time, that was an ineffective option. It also pitted worker against worker.

- **Contributory negligence.** If the injured worker's own conduct contributed to the injury in even the slightest way, the employer completely escaped legal responsibility.

By the end of the nineteenth century, the situation began to change. Unions were becoming more powerful and political parties of the day competed for the labour vote. The government passed legislation that slightly loosened the hold of employers' defenses and it became somewhat easier for workers to succeed in the courts. A spate of successful lawsuits concerning the dangerous factories of the era put many employers in a panic. Employers began to push for legislation that protected them from these lawsuits.

To some extent, this was a worldwide problem, and it resulted in England's 1897 *Workmen's Compensation Act* and numerous state acts in the United States between 1908 and 1915. Germany enacted the first Workers' Compensation law in 1884, followed by Poland in 1884 and England, Czechoslovakia and Austria in 1887. The new laws were the first instance in history of a compulsory social insurance program. The German program was based on a non-profit system that required employers, through trade associations, to operate a collective liability system of insurance guaranteed by the government.

In Ontario, increasing accident rates and pressure from labour unions led the government to appoint a Royal Commission to study the matter, headed by Mr. William Meredith. The Royal Commission report was submitted in 1913. Meredith rejected the assumptions underlying employers' legal defenses. He maintained that workers had few choices concerning their place of work. He condemned the fellow servant rule as a "relic of barbarism." Meredith recommended abolishing what he called "this nuisance of litigation" and proposed the "historic compromise" that became known as the **Meredith principle**. The Meredith principle is a compromise in which workers give up the right to sue for work-related injuries, irrespective of fault, in return for guaranteed compensation for accepted claims. He concluded the Meredith Report as follows:

> In these days of social and industrial unrest it is, in my judgement, of the gravest importance to the community that every proved injustice to any section or class resulting from bad or unfair laws should be promptly removed by the enactment of remedial legislation and I do not doubt that the country whose Legislature is quick to discern and prompt to remove injustice will enjoy, and that deservedly, the blessing of industrial peace and freedom from social unrest (Meredith 1913).

As a result of Meredith's report, Ontario's *Workmen's Compensation Act* received Royal Assent in 1914 and was implemented in 1915. The *Workers' Compensation Act* of Manitoba quickly followed suit and was enacted in 1916. British Columbia's *Workmen's Compensation Act* was passed in 1902 but it did not come into force until 1917, when the Workmen's Compensation Board was created. Legislation followed in all other provinces and territories over the next 60 years. The Yukon did not institute legislation until the 1958 *Workmen's Compensation Ordinance*; Saskatchewan's legislation came in 1930, Prince Edward Island's in 1949 and Newfoundland's in 1950.

The passage of these early Acts in Ontario, British Columbia and Manitoba was revolutionary. At the time, no social welfare programs existed – nor did the income taxes to fund them. The social welfare programs were also revolutionary in that they broke away from the English common principle of individual fault and prescribed a collective responsibility.

The Meredith principle still forms the basis of Workers' Compensation systems across Canada. It was the first legislative challenge to the idea that free enterprise without government interference would be just and fair. Until the 1960s, changes to programs consisted mostly of revising benefit levels and clinical rating schedules to enable the Boards to more easily determine benefit rates and prevent litigation. The use of schedules provided a kind of rough-average justice, but also provided benefits based on a presumed wage loss related to the nature and extent of the injury – rather than the impact of the injury on one's earnings.

In the 1960s, compensation was expanded to include injuries that developed over time, as long as they were work related. This means that conditions such as occupational cancer and chronic stress could now be claimed. Conditions such as these are currently giving the Boards difficulty, because it is hard to be sure whether or not such conditions are work related. Some governments are removing such items from their lists and refusing to accept related claims. The problem with this approach is that it merely places the problem back into the courts and employers find themselves in litigation – situations Workers' Compensation Boards were created to avoid.

THE HISTORY OF UNEMPLOYMENT INSURANCE

For a complete review of the history of Unemployment Insurance check out: http://www.hrdc-drhc.gc.ca/insur/histui/hrdc.html

**CANADIAN LABOUR
STANDARDS**

The *Canada Labour Code*
applies only to employment
under federal jurisdiction – just
10% of the Canadian
workforce. Provincial laws
apply to the other 90% of
workers. The Canada Labour
Code differs in many areas
from the provincial legislation.
The codes deal with issues such
as hours of work; minimum
wage; general holidays;
termination or severance pay;
unjust dismissal and various
types of leave such as vacation,
maternity, bereavement or
illness.

EMPLOYMENT INSURANCE: THE DETAILS

There are different **types of Employment Insurance benefits**:

- **Regular benefits.** These are paid to people who have lost their job and want to return to work. To receive them, one must be actively looking for another job and be willing and able to work at all times. In October 2003, 579,900 Canadians were receiving benefits.

- **Maternity/parental and sickness benefits.** In addition to regular benefits, Employment Insurance provides maternity/parental and sickness benefits to individuals who are pregnant, have recently given birth, are adopting a child, are caring for a newborn baby or are sick. Maternity benefits are payable to the birth mother (or surrogate mother) for a maximum of 15 weeks. To receive maternity benefits, you are required to have worked for 600 hours in the last 52 weeks or since your last claim. You need to prove your pregnancy by signing a statement declaring the expected due date or actual date of birth. Sickness benefits may be paid for up to 15 weeks to a person who is unable to work because of sickness, injury or quarantine. To receive these benefits, you are required to have worked for 600 hours in the last 52 weeks or since your last claim.

- **Compassionate care benefits.** In 2004, a new type of EI benefit was introduced, called the compassionate care benefits. These benefits are paid for a maximum of 6 weeks to workers who have to be away from work temporarily to provide care or support to a member of their family who is gravely ill with a significant risk of death within 6 months. To qualify, you must have 600 hours of insurable employment during your qualifying period.

- **Family Supplement.** The Family Supplement (FS) provides additional benefits to EI to low-income families with children. Families with children with a net income up to a maximum of $25,921 per year have the FS benefit automatically added to their Employment Insurance payment. As income increases, the FS gradually decreases.

- **Fishing benefits.** These are paid to self-employed persons engaged in fishing, and who earn insufficient earnings from that activity.

The Employment Insurance program has a few other special features such as skills development assistance, self-employment assistance and EI for Canadian workers or residents outside Canada. The skills development assistance aims to help individuals obtain skills for employment, ranging from basic to advanced, by providing them with financial assistance to select, arrange and pay for their own training. Self-employment assistance helps provide unemployed individuals who are eligible for EI with financial support, planning assistance and mentoring to help them start a business. Finally, Employment Insurance for workers and residents outside Canada provides EI benefits to people working outside Canada for a Canadian company or with the Canadian government.

Table 8.1: Average Weekly Employment Insurance Benefits ($)

	1997	1998	1999	2000	2001
All benefits	259.59	257.27	259.52	268.72	279.89
Regular	249.72	255.30	261.08	265.15	279.36
Sickness	232.73	236.40	241.65	247.53	253.49
Maternity	272.42	274.35	279.79	285.3	290.05
Fishing	365.63	363.01	362.79	366.79	399.65
Work sharing	86.25	94.18	94.79	89.15	91.76
Adoption	335.75	343.23	351.33	351.96	351.43

Source: Statistics Canada, CANSIM II, Table 276-0016.

• Benefit Levels

The amount of EI benefits paid has dropped dramatically since the 1996 changes to the Act, with a 50 percent drop between 1993 and 1999. During the height of recession in 1993, EI (then UI) provided $19.6 billion in benefits. In 2003, total benefits amounted to $19.6 billion. (Human Resources Development Canada 2003).

This breaks down as follows:

• Regular benefits: $8.9 billion.

• Employment benefits: $211 million.

• Work-sharing benefits: $25 million.

• Fishing benefits: $348 million.

• Special benefits: $3.5 billion (includes sickness, maternity and parental)

Regular benefits can be paid if you lose your job through no fault of your own (for example, due to shortage of work or seasonal or mass lay-offs), and you are available for work and able to work but cannot find a job.

• Insurable Hours

If you have paid into the Employment Insurance account and you have worked a minimum number of hours of work (420-700 hours) you are eligible for EI. The number of insurable hours needed to qualify for EI depends on the rate of unemployment in your region. A 2001 change to the EI legislation allows EI claimants to exclude low-earning weeks (less than $150) for benefit calculation purposes, which encourages people to accept all available work.

Regular benefits are 55 percent of average weekly insured earnings to a maximum of $413 per week. Average is $265.13 (in the year 2000). The allowed amount of time you can be on EI, known as the **claim period**,

In 1996, significant changes
were made to EI. Qualifying
requirements were increased
from a minimum of 12 weeks
of work at 15 hours per week
(180 hours), to 420 hours or
700 hours, depending on the
local unemployment rate.

If you are in the workforce for
the first time, or are
re-entering the workforce after
an absence of two years, you
now need 910 insurable hours
to qualify – compared to 15
hours a week for 20 weeks
(300 hours) under the old
system.

varies depending on the number of weeks you have worked and the local unemployment rate. The maximum claim period is 45 weeks.

The basic benefit rate is 55 percent of your average insured earnings, up to a maximum of $413 per week. You may receive a higher or a lower benefit rate depending on your personal circumstances. If you are in a low-income family (an income of less than $25,921) with children and you receive the Child Tax Benefit (CTB), you could receive a higher benefit rate.

• Clawback Rule

The new Employment Insurance system has a **clawback rule**, which specifies that benefits must be repaid if net income is over $48,750. The maximum repayment is limited to 30 percent for a person with a net income in excess of $48,750. Claimants are exempt from benefit repayment (clawback) if they have received maternity/parental and sickness benefits. This is meant to ensure that parents who stay home with their newborn/newly adopted children or workers who are too sick to work are not penalized. The intent of the clawback is to discourage individuals with higher annual incomes from repeatedly collecting benefits.

Before the elimination of the intensity rule in 2001, if you had previously received EI benefits, it could have affected your benefit rate. Basic benefits are calculated at the rate of 55 percent of a claimant's weekly insurable earnings. When a claimant had drawn regular benefits in the past, the benefit rate was reduced by 1 percent for every 20 weeks of regular benefits collected in the previous five years. The maximum reduction was 5 percent for a claimant who had collected more than 100 weeks of benefits in the previous five years. Numerous studies of the intensity rule found it ineffective. In 2001, it was eliminated, helping many workers, especially those relying on seasonal employment with limited opportunities for additional work.

Table 8.2: Insurable Hours Required

Regional rate of unemployment	Required number of hours of insurable employment in the last 52 weeks
0-6%	700 hours
6.1-7%	665 hours
7.1-8%	630 hours
8.1-9%	595 hours
9.1-10%	560 hours
10.1-11%	525 hours
11.1-12%	490 hours
12.1-13%	455 hours
13.1% and over	420 hours

Source: Employment Insurance website at: http://www.hrdc-drhc.gc.ca/ei.
Retrieved on November 15, 2003.

CANADA'S FIRST NATIONS

Aboriginal people are more reliant on various forms of Social Assistance as a major source of income than the rest of the Canadian population (Royal Commission on Aboriginal Peoples 1996, 168). A primary reason for the high rates of poverty among Aboriginal people is unemployment. In 1995, only 25.3 percent of Aboriginal people had full-time, year-round employment, and 38.4 percent of working-age Aboriginal people were unemployed (Lee 1999, 11). The average annual income of Aboriginal women is about $11,900, compared to $17,400 for Aboriginal men, and $17,600 for all Canadian women.

A lack of economic development, unemployment and reliance upon Social Assistance, as well as a host of other social problems, relate to a long history of colonialist government policies. Aboriginal people are incarcerated in correctional centres and penitentiaries more than other groups. Aboriginal people are twice as likely to be imprisoned and are more likely to receive a full prison sentence than non-Aboriginal people. The rate of suicide and suicide attempts is at least three to four times higher among Aboriginal Peoples, especially among those 15-20 years old, than the rest of Canadians (Royal Commission on Aboriginal Peoples 1995).

These poor social conditions have caused many Aboriginal people to leave their own communities for urban centres, particularly within the last 30 years.

However, poverty does not disappear in cities. In 1996, 44.5 percent of Aboriginal people lived in metropolitan areas of Canada. Half of these lived in the Prairie provinces. Winnipeg has by far the largest Aboriginal population at 43,200 or almost 20 percent of the total urban Aboriginal population (Lee 1999, 9). Of the total Aboriginal urban population, 50.4 percent live below Statistics Canada's Low Income Cut-off (LICO), sometimes referred to as the poverty line, as compared to 21.2 percent of the non-Aboriginal population. Perhaps the most shocking statistic is that 77 percent of Aboriginal single-parent families live below this line. The poorest urban Aboriginal people live in Saskatoon (63.7 percent), Regina (62.2 percent) and Winnipeg (60.5 percent) (p.10).

The Final Report of the **Royal Commission on Aboriginal Peoples** in 1996 brings together six years of research and public consultation on First Nations issues. Among the many issues discussed, the Report examines the need for Aboriginal people to heal from the consequences of domination, displacement and assimilation. The foundation for a renewed relationship, according to the Report, involves recognition of Aboriginal nations as political entities.

For many First Nations communities, the actions of Canadian governments and the churches, particularly in the establishment of the infamous residential schools in the nineteenth and early twentieth, were an important part of the erosion of traditional cultures (National Archives of Canada/C24289).

THE FREE MARKET AND THE RISKS OF UNEMPLOYMENT

The economic system of capitalism has been a system of relative abundance, but it also carries the risk of unemployment.

The Canadian government's commitment to a policy of full employment following World War II represented a strong break from the past. Full employment, as a policy, was recognition that unemployment results from the unregulated operation of markets. It was also recognition that unemployment was not a natural phenomenon, but a human and social phenomenon that could be dealt with by social institutions.

In Canada, the commitment to full employment lasted between 1945 and 1984, at which point the new Conservative government issued a "Strategy for Economic Renewal." This ended the commitment to full employment and brought inflation and the deficit forward as key issues. Full employment was no longer supported as public policy.

Premiums collected from employees and employers fund the EI account. In 2001, employees contributed $2.25 per $100 earned, up to a maximum of $39,000 insurable earnings. Employers contribute 1.4 times the employee contribution as stipulated in federal government legislation. For employers, this amounts to $3.15 per $100. In total, both parties contribute $5.30 per $100 of wage.

Premiums paid are reported as being part of a special EI account, but in reality they are lumped in with all other government revenues. The Auditor General of Canada reports that EI premium revenue has exceeded program costs since 1994, resulting in a surplus of $43 billion (2002). This surplus will increase, probably reaching over $50 billion in 2003. According to the Auditor General, these funds have contributed to a large part of other government expenditures, including tax cuts and paying down government debt. Some question the practice of collecting premiums for designated insurance benefits, but actually using the monies for other purposes. Others believe that collecting premiums from working people and then using the funds for tax cuts that predominately benefit wealthier Canadians is a form of income redistribution from the poor to the rich.

Workers and employers both criticize the use of the EI surplus for other purposes. Employers complain that artificially high EI rates place a burden on labour-intensive industries and penalize employers for creating jobs. They want the premium rates lowered. Workers and their unions, on the other hand, criticize what they call the theft of EI premiums, and they want decreased eligibility requirement and higher benefits.

MATERNITY AND PARENTAL BENEFITS

In 1984, the Unemployment Insurance legislation began to provide for the payment of benefits to a claimant, man or woman, who remained at home to care for a child who was being adopted. Three years later, paternity benefits were introduced so as to provide support (under very specific conditions) for the father of a newborn who stayed at home to care for his child. In 1990, adoption and paternity benefits were replaced by parental benefits, which allowed payment of benefits for 10 weeks, with the possibility of extension to 15 weeks.

Important changes to the Employment Insurance Act were introduced in 2000 that increased **parental leave benefits** from 10 weeks to 35 weeks, increasing the total maternity and parental paid leave time from six months to one year. In addition, the threshold for eligibility was lowered from 700 to 600 hours of insurable employment. The 35 weeks of benefits can be taken by one qualifying parent, or split between both qualifying parents, with only one waiting period required between them. The benefit entitlement remains at 55 percent of average insured earnings, up to a maximum of $413 per week. In 2003, maternity benefits paid amounted to $873 million, with parental benefits totalling $1.9 billion. Only women can claim maternity leave benefits, administered in the same way as parental leave, for 15 weeks and up to eight weeks before the birth. The combination of maternity and parental benefits now enables parents to receive up to one year of paid leave to care for their infants. A mother can start collecting benefits either up to eight weeks before she is expected to give birth or at the week she gives birth. Maternity benefits can be collected within 17 weeks of the actual or expected week of birth, whichever is later. Parental benefits are payable either to the biological or adoptive parents while they are caring for a newborn or an adopted child. To receive either benefit, one is required to have worked 600 hours in the last 52 weeks or since the last claim.

Social policy author Richard Shillington, in his survey of maternity and parental benefits, found that recent significant increases in duration of benefits (now up to 50 weeks) has benefited families with newborn children. In researching maternity benefits, he found that only 58 percent of new mothers reported receiving EI benefits in 2001 (2000, 6). Of those that did not receive maternity benefits, about half reported that they did not work in the year before, and half did not have enough hours or had jobs that were not insured (p.12).

Some have said that recent enhancement to parental benefits has brought Canada close to the Swedish model of family policy. In Sweden the benefits are universal and administered through health insurance, unlike Canada, where only about 58 percent of parents are eligible. Other differences include coverage for 450 days for 80 percent of previous salary up to a maximum ceiling. Parents who continue to stay off work after the 450 days can receive a so-called guarantee amount of $60 per day. Parents with no previous income receive the guaranteed amount for all the 450 days (Swedish Institute 2001). Clearly, Canada's parental leave EI policy has a long way to go before it mirrors the Swedish model.

MATERNITY LEAVE FOR CANADIAN WOMEN

Since the extension of parental benefits in 2001, qualifying mothers are staying home longer with their newborn infants, and more fathers are claiming benefits. Canada is tied with Denmark as the fifth-best country for parents wanting time off, following Sweden, Norway, New Zealand and Australia. Canada offers one year maternity leave for mothers to raise their newborns, but Canada ranks fifteenth when it comes to the amount of benefits offered. During the year allowed for maternity leave, the government pays Employment Insurance to a maximum of $413 per week.

EI BENEFIT COVERAGE

One way to measure the extent to which people who become unemployed in Canada are covered by Employment Insurance is to calculate the proportion of unemployed who actually receive EI benefits. This is known as the **B/U ratio** – the ratio of unemployed EI beneficiaries to the unemployed without benefits.

In 1998, a study released by Human Resources Development Canada found that the B/U ratio declined by almost 50 percent in the 1990s, falling from a level of 83 percent in 1989 to 42 percent in 1997. This means that only 42 percent of the unemployed in 1997 actually received regular benefits. Many social policy analysts see this as a major cutting of costs. The HRDC study goes on to say that the B/U ratio is a poor indicator of how effective the EI program is in serving its clientele, because it is not an objective of the EI program to cover the unemployed who have little or no previous attachment to the labour market or who quit their job without cause.

Moreover, it is largely the growing number of Canadians who are unemployed but do not have recent work experience (and are therefore not eligible for EI) that is lowering the B/U ratio so dramatically. The category of unemployed without recent work, which includes young

THE KELLY LESIUK CASE: ARE EI ELIGIBILITY RULES A VIOLATION OF HUMAN RIGHTS?

Part-time and low-income workers have been particularly hard hit by the change from using insurable weeks to insurable hours as the basis for meeting minimum eligibility requirements. Since women comprise over 70 percent of the part-time labourers, only 32 percent of unemployed women in 1999 qualified for benefits — 10 percent lower than the comparable figure for men.

Many social policy advocates see this as a violation of human rights. Ms. Lesiuk has launched a *Charter* challenge to the EI eligibility requirements, arguing that they discriminate against women and mothers. Kelly Lesiuk was denied Employment Insurance benefits because, as a mother working part-time, she was unable to accumulate the number of work hours necessary to qualify. In 1998, Kelly Lesiuk moved from Brandon to Winnipeg, Manitoba — where her husband had recently found employment. For almost five years prior to the move, Ms. Lesiuk had been a part-time registered nurse at the Brandon General Hospital. She was also the primary caregiver for the couple's daughter. When Ms. Lesiuk applied for EI benefits shortly after arriving in Winnipeg, the Employment Insurance Commission determined that she had worked fewer than 700 insurable hours in the previous 52 weeks, and therefore could not qualify for regular, pregnancy or sickness benefits. Under the new EI rules, she was 33 hours short. Significantly, under the old *Unemployment Insurance Act* she would have had enough insurable weeks to qualify.

Assisted by the Community Unemployed Help Centre in Winnipeg and the Public Interest Law Centre, Ms. Lesiuk appealed the Commission's decision to the Employment Insurance "Umpire," arguing that the new EI eligibility rules discriminated against women and parents. In March 2001, she won a dramatic victory when the rules were found to violate the equality guarantee in section 15 of the *Charter of Rights and Freedoms*.

Kelly Lesiuk's case represents an important achievement for the equality rights of unemployed women in Canada. Finally, the federal government is being taken to task for its punitive, regressive and discriminatory Employment Insurance legislation — legislation that denies hundreds of thousands of unemployed women adequate income security.

Disappointingly, the federal government continues to defend its discriminatory rules. It appealed the Umpire's decision to the Federal Court and the case

was heard on November 19 and 20, 2002. ISAC appeared as an intervener to support Ms. Lesiuk's efforts at the hearing. On January 8, 2003, the Court released its decision, overturning the Umpire's verdict that EI rules violate the *Charter* (a copy of the decision can be found in the "resources" section). Ms. Lesiuk appealed this decision to the Supreme Court of Canada.

On July 17, 2003, the Supreme Court of Canada decided not to hear the case, thereby closing off the legal system as an avenue to address the issue. The Supreme Court also ordered Ms. Lesiuk to pay the costs associated with her appeal application. This will certainly provide a disincentive to any low-income person hoping to use the Supreme Court to enforce their rights. Here is an excerpt from the Federal Court Ruling:

> Ms. Lesiuk's case is an example of the complexity of the employment insurance program. Hers, and many other cases regularly heard by umpires, are sympathetic and I understand the frustration that Ms. Lesiuk must have felt, having met the minimum number of qualifying hours in Brandon but not in Winnipeg. Perhaps this argues for an adjustment to the Regulations applying the minimum number of qualifying hours where the hours were earned rather than in the location to which an individual moves. Undoubtedly, there are counter-arguments also.
>
> What this points out is that in a complex program such as employment insurance, the Court, with no expertise in the area, is not well equipped to propose changes to such programs. In my respectful opinion, this is not a case in which the Court should superimpose upon an already complex program additional required adjustments. I do not say that a differential between minimum threshold requirements as between the respondent's group and men may not be desirable. However, such a change will obviously give rise to other considerations. Should the threshold for the respondent's group be lowered or should the threshold for men be increased? If a differential is material, should there be other minimum requirements for the respondent's group and what should they be? Are there other groups who can justify lower requirements? What groups should they be compared to and what additional requirements should be imposed upon those groups, if any? How is this Court to assess and minimize the amount of disruption to the economies in different regions?

Available under the heading "Legal Challenges" at: http://www.incomesecurity.org

Source: Taken with permission from the Income Security Advocacy Centre legal challenges dossier.

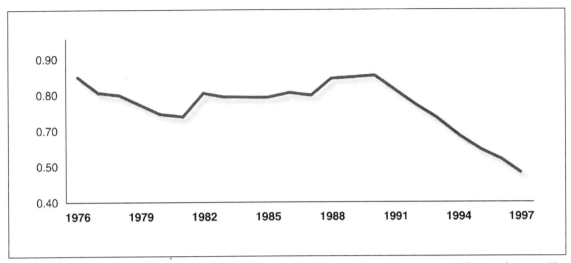

Figure 8.1: The B/U ratio, showing the ratio of regular Employment Insurance beneficiaries to total unemployment. The B/U ration has declined by almost 50 percent over the 1990s, hitting low-paid workers the hardest.
Source: Human Resources Development Canada, *Analysis of Employment Insurance Benefit Coverage* (Ottawa, HRDC, 1998) 13.

people looking for their first job and those looking for a job after an extended period of absence from the labour market, is the largest category of unemployed workers ineligible for Employment Insurance; it is also the group that grew the fastest during the 1990s. Their percentage doubled between 1989 and 1997 from 19 percent to 38 percent, before dropping to 34 percent in 1999 (Bédard, Bertrand and Grignon 2000).

According to the Canadian Labour Congress (CLC), the drop in EI protection has the most impact on the lowest-paid workers and women. Their data indicates that 41 percent of the $7.4 billion in reduced benefits (from 1993 to 1999) came from workers earning less than $15,000 per year, and two-thirds came from workers earning less than $20,000 (Canadian Labour Congress 2002, 2).

THE CURRENT STATE OF THE LABOUR MARKET

Jobs can be defined as standard and non-standard. Standard jobs are those that are full-time, full-year with a single employer. They usually offer benefits and career opportunities. Under one-half of Canadian workers hold standard jobs. The rest are part-time, self-employed contract workers and temporary help. The just-in-time workforce is a new reality. Employers are hesitant to commit to full-time, full-year "permanent" jobs and increasingly prefer to hire on a project-by-project basis.

In his book *Job Shift*, William Bridges (1994) coined the phrase "dejobbing" to describe this trend to non-standard employment. He says that workers are going to become more like independent business people (or one-person businesses) than conventional employees. Not only are there fewer standard jobs, but those that remain are changing. No longer do people have stable 9-5 jobs with good pay. People are left with what are called "McJobs," a term meant to reflect the sub-standard nature of jobs at McDonalds.

REFERENCES

* Bédard, Marcel, Jean-François Bertrand, and Louis Grignon. 2000. *The Unemployed Without Recent Employment*. Ottawa: HRDC.

* Canadian Labour Congress. 2000. *Left Out in the Cold: The End of UI for Canadian Workers*. Ottawa: Canadian Labour Congress (CLC). Available at: http://www.clc-ctc.ca/publications/mag_archive/ei-ac2002winter.pdf

* Canadian Labour Congress. 2000. *Analysis of UI Coverage for Women*. Ottawa: CLC. Available at: http://www.clc-ctc.ca/policy/ui/wom-ui-00e.html

* Canadian Labour Congress. 2002. *Unemployment Insurance Bulletin*. Ottawa: Canadian Labour Congress (CLC).

* Human Resources Development Canada. 1994. *Agenda: Jobs and Growth — Improving Social Security in Canada*. Ottawa: HRDC.

* Human Resources Development Canada. 1998. *An Analysis of Employment Insurance Benefit Coverage*. Ottawa: HRDC.

* Human Resources Development Canada. 1999. *Occupational Injuries and Their Cost in Canada, 1993-1999*. Ottawa: HRDC.

* Human Resources Development Canada. 2003. *Employment Insurance Monitoring and Assessment Report*. Ottawa: HRDC.

* Lee, K. 1999. Measuring Poverty among Canada's Aboriginal People. *Insight*, Vol. 23, No.2. Ottawa: CCSD.

* Meredith, W.R. 1913. *Meredith Report*. Toronto: Legislative Assembly of Ontario.

* Royal Commission on Aboriginal Peoples. 1995. *Aboriginal Self-Government: Legal and Constitutional Issues*. Ottawa: Canada Communications Group Publishing.

* Royal Commission on Aboriginal Peoples. 1996. *Perspectives and Realities*. Volume 4. Ottawa: Canada Communications Group Publishing.

* Shillington, R. 2001. *Access to Maternity Benefits*. Ottawa: Trisat Resources.

* Swedish Institute. 2001. *Facts Sheets on Sweden*. The Swedish Institute. Available at: http://www.si.se/E_infoSweden/1008.cs?dirid=1265

• EI: The Economy Stabilizer

A major portion of contemporary social welfare has to do with people who are out of work or are not making a wage that permits them, or those who depend on them, to live at the standards established in our society. People may be unable to work for a wide range of reasons. It may not have anything to do with their individual capacity to be employed, and instead may be based on the labour market's capacity to employ them. The Canadian UI/EI system has generally played a positive role as an automatic stabilizer for the economy. In employment terms, this translates into 11-14 percent of job losses being averted because of UI/EI.

There is indeed a strong correlation between the net UI/EI spending and the performance of the economy. This is especially true with respect to UI/EI benefit payments but much less so with respect to UI/EI premiums. The analysis suggests that the UI/EI premium rate (which is, arguably, not automatic but changed by policy choice) appears to have moved pro-cyclically – that is, its rate has been raised in downturns and reduced in upturns. The stabilizing impact of the UI/EI system has varied over the last 15 years, reflecting the changes in the size of the program relative to that of the economy. An average estimate of the stabilizing effect of the program is about 10-12 percent. This means that the program has prevented about 10-12 percent of the total output gap at the point of the maximum output loss.

CONCLUSION

Social insurance programs for those in the labour force are meant to protect workers from the consequences of particular risks, such as injury on the job or unemployment. Workers' Compensation programs represent the first legislated recognition of collective responsibility for social welfare in the world. A healthy, well-trained and secure labour force is essential for our economy to grow. Cuts to Canada's EI program threaten to weaken these positive aspects of our labour force. As the Canadian government strives to cut back expenditures, it has tightened and targeted the EI program. It is clear, however, that Canada requires a strong EI program in order to maintain a vibrant workforce.

In the past two decades, Canada has faced new challenges as the world economy shifted to an information- and knowledge-based economy with rapid globalization. Throughout the 1980s and 1990s governments cut social spending, pushed people off income security programs into paid employment and moved towards free trade in the hope that this would solve the problem. It is clear as we enter the 2000s that this is not sufficient.

New ideas are emerging that respond to these changing circumstances. Labour market participation does not guarantee an exit out of poverty. Governments are recognizing that families have particular needs, and there is new activity in the area of income supplements for low wages. There is a clear need to have better integration of EI, Social Assistance and child benefits.

CHAPTER 8: PEOPLE IN THE LABOUR FORCE

Discussion Questions

1. Who in Canadian society benefits from EI and WC, and in what ways do they benefit?
2. What was the primary impetus for the introduction of Workers' Compensation in the rising industrialized countries of the world, including Canada? Explain.
3. What are the "unholy trinity" defenses that made it extremely difficult for employees to successfully sue an employer? Define and explain each defense.
4. What is the Meredith principle and what is its significance?
5. In what ways did Bill C-12, *The New Employment Insurance Act*, change Unemployment Insurance in Canada in 1995? What have been two significant negative impacts on employees?
6. What maternity and parental benefits are available to Canadians?
7. What is the B/U ratio and how has it changed over the past decade?

Key Concepts

- Social insurance schemes
- Employment Insurance (EI)
- Workers' Compensation (WC)
- Voluntary assumption of risk
- Fellow servant rule
- Contributory negligence
- Meredith principle
- Types of Employment Insurance benefits
- Claim period
- Clawback rule
- Parental leave benefits
- B/U ratio

Websites

- **Social Policy in Ontario**
  http://spo.laurentian.ca/

  The On-line Guide to Social Policy in Ontario has information with five points of entry: service sectors, policy issue roundtables, the history of program development, Ontario's social context and community planning.

- **The History of Unemployment Insurance:**
  http://www.hrdc-drhc.gc.ca/insur/histui/hrdc.html or
  http://www.clc-ctc.ca/policy/ui/factbookreform.html

  A complete history of EI on-line.

- **Human Resources Development Canada**
  http://www.hrdc-drhc.gc.ca/ae-ei/employment_insurance.shtml

  Government website on EI.

- **Canadian Policy Research Networks (CPRN)**
  http://www.cprn.org/

  Founded in 1994, the CPRN's mission is to create knowledge and lead public debate on social and economic issues important to the well-being of Canadians. They currently have four themes or networks in the areas of Family, Health, Public Involvement and Work.

Part of a worldwide women's protest against poverty and violence that took place in Jonquiere, Quebec, in October 2000. The protesters presented twenty demands to the Quebec premier at the time (Lucien Bouchard), including an increase minimum wage and pay equity (CP PHOTO/Le Quotidien de Chicoutimi/Michel Tremblay).

9

People Living in Poverty

The Policy Context

Why do some people in Canada continue to live in poverty when public income security programs exist? Many believe that a new approach to poverty is needed. Building the labour market is obviously important, but financial support for families that are undergoing difficult transitions in their lives is also vital. This is largely the role of minimum income programs such as Social Assistance. But are they doing what is needed?

Many families and individuals experience difficult life events, challenges or changes that may affect their capacity to function effectively in their private and public lives. Incidental and unexpected events in any aspect of an individual's life can lead to stress, coping difficulties and loss of employment. The reaction of individuals and families to stress will vary. People may lack coping mechanisms, they may come up against a particular type of challenge that is too serious or difficult to deal with, or they may lack internal and external support systems. In some cases, these difficulties result in job loss, alienation and isolation.

When a person has no source of income, he or she is entitled to what is commonly known as **Social Assistance (SA)** (otherwise known as welfare). SA is a province-based minimum income program for people defined as "in need." Strict eligibility criteria, known as a needs test, are applied to determine if people are in need. If the person has a disability, he or she is entitled to disability support, normally with higher benefits. In Ontario this is called the Ontario Disability Support Program (ODSP). Social Assistance is a program of last resort with roots in early charity relief and the English Poor Laws.

Generally, Canadians access Social Assistance only when all other public and private means of support are exhausted. In 2000, 2 million Canadians, or 6.6 percent of the Canadian population, received Social Assistance. This compares to 2.7 million in 1996, or almost 10 percent of the Canadian population (Human Resources Development Canada 2000a). The cost of these benefits was $10.5 billion in 2000, compared with $14 billion in 1996 (Human Resources Development Canada 2000b).

Each of Canada's 10 provinces and three territories designs, administers and delivers its own Social Assistance program. Entitlement is based on a test, which takes into account the assets and income of the applicant's household and its basic needs (food, clothing, shelter and utilities, household necessities and personal needs) as defined in provincial legislation. Each province also establishes its own administrative and categorical eligibility requirements for those applying for benefits.

"No one would seriously contemplate allowing a free-for-all unregulated elementary school system or health care system, and neither should we continue to allow such a thing with child care ... Let us learn from successes — especially those in Québec — and develop a reliable system of regulated child care, one that respects specific provincial and territorial needs and responsibilities, and assures that a real pan-Canadian program exists.

— Social Council on Welfare, Presentation to the Standing Committee on Finance for the 2003 Pre-Budget Consultations

The federal Department of Indian and Northern Affairs is responsible for the Social Assistance for registered Indians living on reserves. Programs are delivered either by the provincial government or by an Aboriginal agency (depending on the province) in accordance with the prevailing Social Assistance rules and regulations of that province. The Department of Indian and Northern Affairs covers the entire cost of such assistance.

THE RISE OF POOR RELIEF AND SOCIAL ASSISTANCE

Before the twentieth century, the dominant explanation for poverty was that people who were poor had a defect in their character. The general public consensus was that persons living in poverty were unwilling to seek employment and had to be forced to work.

As we saw in Chapter 2, after the Elizabethan Poor Law legislation of 1601, unemployed people were harshly punished to discourage vagrancy and begging. If people could not be coerced to work through punitive efforts, they were forced into corrective and common jails (Guest 1999). Another widespread belief was that offering relief to the poor encouraged them not to work and, as a result, it was illegal to assist the able-bodied poor. In the nineteenth century, after the reform of the Poor Laws, relief was available only through the almshouse (commonly referred to as the poorhouse) or the workhouse, which offered work at miserable wages in order to discourage people from being lazy.

In the 1800s and earlier, caring for the poor in Canada was the responsibility of the family, churches or the local community. In Quebec, the Catholic Church was responsible for income security for the poor, whereas in the Maritimes, the application of Elizabethan Poor Laws gave the responsibility to the local authorities. Collective self-help was essential to survival in sparsely settled pioneer communities in the West. The western provinces relied on public programs run by municipalities for health care and aid to the poor. Towards the end of World War I, Manitoba and British Columbia offered Mothers' Allowance programs. These programs were the first provincial measures to aid the poor in the West.

Canada's first public income security provisions for the poor were based on the Elizabethan Poor Laws. This style of relief was implemented in Nova Scotia in 1758, in New Brunswick in 1783 and in Ontario in 1791. There were two styles of relief offered by private charities and municipalities – indoor and outdoor relief. Outdoor relief was available to the recipient in his or her own home, and indoor relief was given in an institution, such as a House of Industry. Rather than cash, most relief during the 1700s was in the form of food or food vouchers, clothes and fuel.

The concept of less eligibility was established in the English system of poor relief. According to the concept of "less eligibility," relief benefits had to be lower than what could be earned by the lowest paid labourer. Relief administrators were concerned that higher levels of relief would encourage workers to become dependent on the benefits. During this

Finding such simple comforts as warmth is a constant struggle for the homeless (photo courtesy of Dick Hemingway).

era, the concept of less eligibility was a significant factor in the high rates of unemployment and residual concept of social welfare. Not only did less eligibility ensure that no one would receive in relief more than what might be available from the poorest paying job, but it also kept people poor and provided few employment options other than low-paying and often dangerous jobs. Workers during the time of less eligibility described their workplaces in terms of detention rather than employment. Records from the labour commission reveal a pattern of exploitation, unhealthy workplaces and immutable laws of supply and demand (Guest 1999).

Welfare systems were dominated by political practices in which social policies were used as instruments to regulate the poor (Rice and Prince 2000). The earliest studies of poverty were not concerned with how the poor lived in relation to those better off; they were concerned with establishing the minimum income necessary for survival. The early laws of poor relief were not intended to raise the standard of the poor; they were intended to keep that standard low to ensure a plentiful supply of cheap labour. This attitude is evident throughout history. It is especially evident during periods of economic growth and increased immigration of foreign workers who were expected to roam the country, take work wherever it was available and be thankful for the wages offered. A typical example of this occurred during the advancement of the railway system. The Canadian Pacific Railway felt that immigrants could serve as a cheap and plentiful source of labour in the expansions of new branch lines.

THE NATIONAL COUNCIL OF WELFARE (NCW)

NCW is a citizens' advisory body to the Minister of Human Resources Development Canada on matters of concern to low-income Canadians. Their annual Welfare Incomes report details welfare rates by province and compares this to LICOs.

All of their publications are available at: http://www.ncwcnbes.net.

In Canada during the nineteenth century, this view was accompanied by the idea that there were unlimited work opportunities, and therefore there was no need for poor relief. The first constitution of Ontario, for example, did not carry any provision for poor relief. But conditions of misery became increasingly obvious in cities and towns during the Industrial Revolution of the late-nineteenth and early-twentieth century. Canadian people reacted accordingly. Social unrest led to the Canadian trade union movement and the widespread appeal of radical political ideas and parties. Poverty and inequality became an important issue in churches in Canada, and this spawned the Social Gospel movement. As a result, committees were formed, conferences were held and coalitions such as the Moral and Social Reform Council of Canada were organized to denounce capitalism and its effects on wages, sweatshops and child labour (Guest 1999).

To an extent, the wealthy began to fear the consequences of poverty, which led to efforts to deal with the problem in Canada. One of the first efforts to look at the conditions of the poor was initiated by the Royal Commission on the Relations of Labour and Capital in 1889. This report contained numerous pages of testimonies about the deplorable living and working conditions prevalent at the time. These testimonies and other observations led reformers to demand the involvement of the state and the public in a wide range of activities to curtail poverty.

Industrial development and the growth of poverty eventually led to demands for the development of public social welfare. In the early part of the century, a transition took place from private to public social welfare. Social welfare was no longer seen as the private domain of families. Before the Great Depression of the 1930s, the country had very limited public Social Assistance measures. The government avoided intervening in the economy – it believed that the free market would look after everyone. Lessons learned from the Depression changed this outlook. During the Depression, people began to see that poverty was due less to individual inadequacy or laziness, and was more the result of common and insurable threats to the livelihood of all people. Following the two world wars, there was a desire for economic security and more of an acceptance of government intervention in society. After World War II, Keynesian economic ideas (discussed in detail in Chapter 3) provided an economic rationale for substantial government intervention in the economy. At this time, there was a communal desire by citizens and governments to devise government-funded income security assistance for the poor. Eventually, welfare or Social Assistance was instituted in all provinces as a program of last resort.

By the 1960s, a wide range of programs had been instituted to assist the poor. Each province had a different program and there was little coordination and consistency between provinces. In an effort to consolidate Social Assistance and other income security and social service programs, the federal government introduced a new cost-sharing arrangement with the provinces in 1966 – the Canada Assistance Plan (CAP) – named by Judy LaMarsh. CAP brought together a range of cost-shared income security and social services into one system. It also included several national standards. In April 1996, the Canada Health and Social Transfer (CHST) replaced CAP as a vehicle for federal funding. It is a block grant and includes health and post-secondary education.

Current welfare programs, now called Social Assistance, income support or employment and financial assistance, provide additional support in the form of cash to help recipients meet expenses over and above basic needs, depending on the province.

MYTHS ABOUT THE POOR

Programs of income security for the poor often have been based on myths about the poor. The 1988 study by the Social Assistance Review Committee in Ontario, entitled *Transitions,* discovered a series of common misperceptions about people who use Social Assistance. As well, the National Anti-Poverty Organization (NAPO) and the Canadian Council on Social Development (CCSD) have documented a variety of myths. The following myths are prevalent today:

- *Poverty is the failure of the individual.* This is a stereotype or blame-oriented belief that has a long history. It began with early religious attitudes of the sixteenth century, and was reinforced by Calvinist ideas. The reasoning was that paupers were being punished for hidden sins. This perception gradually shifted to beliefs underpinned by the Social Darwinism of the nineteenth century, which applied Darwin's biological theories to social life. This blame-oriented idea proposed that people of any energy and ability could make their way in life, and that incompetence and poverty were clear signs of biological and social inferiority. Although it is clear that increases in unemployment in Canada during the Depression and over the last few decades did not result from personal inadequacy, but rather from economic factors, there is still a sense that poverty results from personal failure. Many workers have lost their jobs for reasons beyond their control and cannot find work because it is not available. Many people are on welfare because they are temporarily unable to provide for themselves, often due to some personal or economic crisis beyond their control.

- *People on welfare do not have basic education.* In 1997, almost 60 percent of heads of households on Social Assistance attended secondary school and 11 percent had post-secondary education (National Council of Welfare 1998, 41). The evidence also shows that heads of households on Social Assistance with a high-school education or better tend to have job-related reasons for being on welfare. People with less than a high-school education are more likely to be on welfare because of a disability.

- *The majority of welfare recipients are able-bodied men who are simply lazy.* There is a straightforward rebuttal to this myth. One needs only to examine the demographic characteristics of individuals on Social Assistance. Studies have found that only 14 percent of Social Assistance recipients are "employable" men. According to the National Council of Welfare, as of March 31, 1997, children were the largest single group of Social Assistance or welfare recipients, making up

By any measure, the persistence of poverty is disturbing (*Toronto Star/* National Archives/ C145008).

1,163,000 or 38 percent of the total estimated 3.1 million individuals on welfare. Of the heads of households on Social Assistance, 27 percent reported a disability as their reason for being on welfare in 1997 (National Council of Welfare 1998, 3).

- *The poor do not want to work.* Most poor people do work full- or part-time, including over 60 percent of heads of poor households, and over 70 percent of poor unattached individuals. Of this population, 26 percent worked full-time, 34 percent worked part-time, 31 percent did not work at all and 10 percent were unable to work. If we look at the people who are dependent on welfare, we see that about 38 percent are children. Another 16 percent are single mothers, many still caring for young children. If we look at the number of welfare cases, we find that about 27 percent are disabled people (National Council of Welfare 2002).

- *Most people who have incomes below the poverty level get most of their income from Social Assistance.* In fact, a full 60 percent of the families living below the poverty line are dependent on work for their income. The number of people known as the "working poor" is growing in Canadian society.

- *Long-term dependence on welfare is rare in Canada.* In March 1997, 54 percent of the people on welfare had been on welfare continuously for 25 months or more (National Council of Welfare 1998, 24). According to the National Council of Welfare, there had been a rise in long-term cases in the years after 1990. The shorter-term cases tend to rise in bad economic times and fall in good times. A study by the HRDC called *Low Income Dynamics in Canada* (Finnie 2000) found that half of those earning low incomes from 1992 to 1996 were doing so temporarily. By contrast, 40 percent were in poverty throughout the entire period.

- *Most female-led, single-parent families depend on Social Assistance.* In 1997, about one-third of single-parent families led by women relied on Social Assistance (National Council of Welfare 1998, 24). The other two-thirds were in the labour force. In 1996, 61.6 percent were living below the Low Income Cut-off (LICO). The rate in 2000 was 47.6 percent (Statistics Canada 2003). As these numbers indicate, many female-led, single-parent families are poor, but they are working (known as the working poor). The labour force participation rate of lone parents has increased from 56 percent in 1973 to 66 percent in 1997 (Phipps and Lethbridge 2002, 6).

- *Unmarried teenagers make up most of the single-parent mothers on welfare.* In March 1997, only 3 percent of the single parents on welfare were under the age of 20 (National Council of Welfare 1998, 34).

- *People on Social Assistance do not pay very much rent because they all live in subsidized housing.* There is not nearly enough public or assisted housing; only 7 percent of the welfare cases in March 1997 were in subsidized housing (National Council of Welfare 1998, 3).

- *Poor people do not pay taxes.* In Ontario, poor people pay about $160 million in income taxes. The requirement of having to pay income tax starts far below the poverty line. In 1991, a single mother with two children started paying federal tax when her income reached $11,601; a single person without dependants was taxed at an income level of $6,532. Although people on welfare do not pay income tax on their Social Assistance, they still pay sales tax, GST and property taxes. Refundable credits reduce the cost of tax, but do not cover the total tax paid.

- *Welfare rates are too generous.* All welfare rates are well below LICO. Welfare benefits for single employable people are the least adequate, with 1999 rates ranging from 9 percent of LICO in Newfoundland to 41 percent of LICO in Ontario. Welfare benefits for single-parent families ranged from 42 percent of LICO in Alberta to 70 percent of LICO in Ontario (National Council of Welfare 2000, 24). Even using the Basic Needs Lines (BNL), developed by Chris Sarlo at the Fraser Institute, welfare income is either below the BNL for single employable people or just above it. The BNLs are the lowest poverty lines ever calculated in Canada and are not taken seriously by Canadian policy experts or the international community.

- *Poor people need to be taught basic life skills, such as budgeting.* Many who live far below the poverty line must spend all or most of their income on basic needs. Anyone who manages to feed and clothe a family on a very limited income already has budgeting skills.

- *The welfare system is rife with cheating and fraud.* A study conducted by a national auditing firm estimated fraud to be within the range of 3 percent of the welfare budget (on the other hand, there are estimates that income tax fraud is in the order of 20 percent). The Ontario government reports that $46 million was saved due to catching people committing welfare fraud. Analysis of the government's claim (see discussion later in this chapter) reveals that, of the 15,680 reductions or terminations due to "fraud," very few were actually convicted of fraud. Most of what the government reports as fraud is actually administrative error.

- *Poor families are poor because they have too many children.* Most poor families do not have any children or they have one or two children. Only 15 percent have three or more children under 18. Nearly half of all single-parent families on welfare in 1997 had only one child and another 31 percent had only two children (National Council of Welfare 1998, 39).

- *We cannot afford the social programs needed to eliminate poverty.* This statement stems from the efficiency/equity trade-off concept discussed in Chapter 4. Canada is a very prosperous country with high rates of economic growth and GDP per capita. But, Canada spends less on social security and other income support measures (including EI and welfare) as a share of the GDP than most European countries. In Canada, all "social protection" government transfers add up to only 18 percent of the GDP (Bohácek 2002, 26), whereas France transfers 29 percent, Germany transfers 27 percent, the

Residents on James Bay reserve say workfare violates their rights (CP/1999/Kevin Frayer).

A "soup kitchen" for the poor in Montreal, 1931 (National Archives of Canada/PA168131).

Netherlands transfers 33 percent, Finland transfers 36 percent and Sweden transfers 40 percent. Countries with economies similar to ours have refused to tolerate high levels of family poverty. These countries provide more income and employment support to help families with children, and their economies still grow and thrive.

• *All children in Canada are assured a decent start in life.* Recent studies show strong links between poverty and poor health and poor achievement at school. While infant mortality rates for all income groups are about half of what they were 20 years ago, according to the 1986 Census, the rate for the lowest income group was still about double that of the highest. Children in poor families are more likely to suffer chronic health problems than other children. They are almost twice as likely to drop out of school. According to the Canadian Council on Social Development, there is finally hard statistical data showing that family income has a major effect on a child's well-being (see http://www.ccsd.ca/pubs/recastin.htm for more information). To date, they have examined 31 outcomes and living conditions, and in each case they found a statistical association with family income levels.

The list is long, but these are not the only myths about individuals and families that receive Social Assistance or live in poverty. It is important to be aware of such stereotypes and blame-oriented beliefs and to explore the possible reasons for their existence. The short paragraphs above, and other information and data throughout the text, should provide facts that help to refute myths about the poor.

SOCIAL ASSISTANCE: A MINIMUM INCOME PROGRAM

As noted in Chapter 1, there are four broad categories of public income security programs: social insurance, minimum income, demogrants and income supplementation. Social Assistance belongs in the minimum income category. It transfers income to people who have no employment or other income and it supplies a bare minimum of funds for survival. The transfer is conditional, based on a needs test. A needs test looks at what the person needs in terms of both expenditure and income – or the difference between what they have and what they are required to spend to survive. It also considers the assets that could be sold to provide an income.

Constitutionally, Social Assistance is the jurisdiction and responsibility of the provinces. Although people talk about welfare as a single entity, there are really 13 welfare systems in Canada: one in each province and territory, including the new territory of Nunavut. Despite the fact that each of the 13 systems is different, they have many common features. They all have complex regulations, including regulations about the eligibility for assistance, the rates of assistance, the amounts of other income recipients are allowed to keep and the appeals process for applicants and recipients to question decisions regarding their cases. In Ontario, Social Assistance is currently legislated through the *Ontario Works Act*, 1997. Ontario is the only province where municipalities are responsible for delivering the program.

Welfare is a provincial responsibility, but all three levels of government fund it: the city or municipality, the province and the federal government. For example, in Ontario, a typical city paid approximately 15 percent of the costs, the province paid approximately 57 percent and the federal government paid approximately 28 percent.

Some provinces also have special provisions for people with disabilities. The Ontario Disability Support Program (ODSP) is available to Ontario residents who can prove they have a disability that meets the legislated definition: "A substantial physical or mental impairment that is continuous or recurrent, is expected to last one year or more and results in a substantial restriction in his/her ability to: attend to personal care; function in the community or function in the workplace." Applicants must prove they qualify by obtaining a health status report from a registered health professional. To qualify for disability benefits, people must undergo a needs test. This means that an applicant's income and assets must be below a certain amount to qualify. The amount varies by family size, and in some provinces, housing costs. In Ontario, individual applicants must have less than $5,000 in cash, RRSPs or in insurance policies. Benefit amounts are higher for people on ODSP and provincial disability benefits than they are for other Ontario Works (OW) recipients. Some believe that this has origins in the Elizabethan Poor Law concepts of the deserving and undeserving poor (outlined in Chapter 2).

Eligibility for Social Assistance is based on general administrative rules that vary widely throughout the country. For example, applicants must be of a certain age (usually between 18 and 65). Full-time students of post-secondary educational institutions may qualify for assistance in

ONTARIO WORKS

In Ontario, we have the 1997 *Ontario Works Act* available on-line at: http://192.75.156.68/DBLaws/ Regs/English/980134_e.htm some provinces and territories, if they meet stringent conditions. In other provinces and territories, students cannot apply for assistance without leaving their studies. Parents must try to secure any court-ordered maintenance support to which they are entitled. People who are disabled require medical certification of their conditions. Strikers are not eligible in most jurisdictions. Immigrants must try to obtain financial assistance from their sponsors.

• The Poverty Gap

One way the adequacy of Social Assistance benefits can be calculated is to compare the welfare rates to LICO. The difference between the two is the poverty gap (see Chapter 6). The table below shows the total Social Assistance income per type of household, as compared to LICO, and the large gap between the two.

Researchers calculating the adequacy of Social Assistance compare benefits with the costs of basic necessities such as food and shelter. According to professors at the Department of Nutritional Sciences at the University of Toronto, a nutritional diet — as defined by the Ontario Ministry of Health standards — is out of reach for Toronto's Social Assistance recipients (Vozoris, Davis and Tarasuk 2002, 38). The three professors calculated the affordability of a nutritious diet by comparing the monthly costs considered essential for a basic standard of living with the average monthly income of three household types: one-person, single-parent and two-parent households. They found that if households live in market rental accommodations, income was insufficient to enable the purchase of a nutritious diet along with all the other essential items. (p.36). "This speaks to the need for a review of welfare benefit levels and housing policies to ensure that people on these programs are not put at risk," says Tarasuk (e-mail correspondence, October 2003).

The large discrepancies between welfare incomes and the cost of basic needs puts the health and well-being of Canadian children at risk. This not only affects their daily lives, but also their ability to keep pace with classmates in school and their future opportunities.

Table 9.1: Difference between Social Assistance and LICO (Ontario, 2002)

Type of Household	Total Income	LICO	Gap
Single Employable	$6,833	$19,256	($12,422)
Single Disabled	$11,763	$19,256	($7,492)
Single Parent One Child	$13,871	$24,069	($10,198)
Two Parent Two Child	$18,400	$36,235	($17,835)

Source: National Council of Welfare, *Welfare Incomes 2002.* (Ottawa: National Council of Welfare, 2003), 28. Available at: http://www.ncwcnbes.net

A CASE STUDY

To provide an example, let us examine the benefit amounts in Ottawa, Ontario. In Ottawa, the Ontario Works calculations for establishing financial eligibility is based on basic needs, the presence of a spouse or same-sex partner, the number of members in the benefit unit and the age of any dependent children. Shelter allowance is then added to this amount. It includes actual costs for rent, mortgage, taxes, board and lodging, utility and fuel costs, up to the maximum levels. Emergency assistance is also considered. The following chart is used by welfare workers (who are generally called case workers or case coordinators) in Ontario to calculate the amount that an individual or family would receive for basic needs. By adding this basic need amount with the basic shelter allowance amount in the second chart, the total monthly benefit is determined.

Shelter is calculated based on the maximum amount payable in accordance with the benefit unit size as indicated below. This is a maximum amount. One would get a lower amount if their actual shelter costs were lower. Using the two charts you can calculate the maximum total Social Assistance benefits as follows: single person at $520 per month ($195 basic allowance plus $325 maximum shelter allowance); family of four with two children under 12 at $1178 ($576 basic allowance plus $602 maximum shelter allowance).

Table 9.2: Ontario Works Basic Need Allowances

No. of dependants other than a spouse	No. of dependants 13 years and over	No. of dependants 0-12 years	Recipient	Recipient and spouse or same-sex partner
0	0	0	$195	$390
1	0	1	$446	$446
	1	0	$486	$512
2	0	2	$532	$576
	1	1	$572	$612
	2	0	$608	$648

For each additional dependant, add $136 if the dependant is 13 years of age or over, or $100 if the dependant is less than 13 years of age. *Source: Ontario Works Policy Directives 2001*. Ministry of Community and Social Services. Available at: http://www.cfcs.gov.on.ca/CFCS/en/programs/IES/OntarioWorks/Publications/ow-policydirectives.htm

Table 9.3: Basic Shelter Allowance

Benefit unit size	Maximum monthly shelter allowance
1	$325
2	$511
3	$554
4	$602
5	$649
6 or more	$673

Source: Ontario Works Policy Directives 2001. Ministry of Community and Social Services. Available at: http://www.cfcs.gov.on.ca/CFCS/en/programs/IES/OntarioWorks/Publications/ow-policydirectives.htm

CHILD TAX BENEFIT

In addition to Social Assistance or welfare, families with children living on low income are eligible for the Canada Child Tax Benefit (CCTB) basic benefit, but not the National Child Benefit Supplement (NCBS). As detailed in Chapter 10, the federal government began paying child-related benefits to low-income families in 1998. The maximum Canada Child Tax Benefit (CCTB) or basic benefit is available to families whose net income is below $32,000, including those on welfare. Until June 2004, the maximum basic benefit was $1,169 per year ($97.42 per month) for first and second children and $1251 for the third and each additional child. In addition, low-income families *not* on welfare received the National Child Benefit Supplement (NCBS) or supplemental benefit of $1,463 per year for the first child, $1,254 per year for the second child and $1,176 per year for each additional child.

A controversial aspect of these benefits is the "clawback" of the NCBS portion for Social Assistance recipients. The CCTB portion is received by all families with children whose net income is below a certain level, including families on Social Assistance, but the NCBS is taken away from families on Social Assistance (in most provinces). The term "clawback" refers to this taking back of the monies.

Only those families on welfare who live in Newfoundland and New Brunswick see an increase in their incomes because of the National Child Benefit Supplement (NCBS). The other provinces and territories claw back the money in different ways. In Prince Edward Island, Nova Scotia, Ontario, Manitoba, British Columbia, the Yukon and the Northwest Territories, the welfare departments consider the supplement to be non-exempt income that triggers a cut in the family welfare cheque. In Quebec, Saskatchewan and Alberta, the provincial governments have actually cut welfare benefits by the amount of the supplement (see Chapter 10 for more information).

Table 9.4: Annual Social Assistance Amounts by Type of Household (Ontario, 2002)

Type of Household	Social Assistance	Other Benefits*	Total
Single Employable	$6,240	$593	$6,833
Single Disabled	$11,160	$603	$11,763
Single Parent One Child	$10,210	$3,662	$13,871
Two Parent Two Child	$12,223	$6,177	$18,400

Source: National Council of Welfare, *Welfare Incomes 2002* (Ottawa: National Council of Welfare, 2003), 16. Available at: http://www.ncwcnbes.net

* Other benefits include additional Social Assistance benefits, the Federal Child Tax Benefit, the Provincial/Territorial Child Benefits, the Federal GST Credit and Provincial tax credits.

LIVING ON WELFARE: CASES

Bare numbers do little to illuminate the challenges facing people on Social Assistance. The following scenarios may reveal what life on welfare or disability benefits is actually like.

• Dorothy: Working on Welfare

Dorothy and her husband Harry managed to survive on their combined earned income along with some Social Assistance. Dorothy wanted to leave her husband because of his alcoholism and his "temper fits." She could not afford to rent her own apartment, so she applied for subsidized housing and was placed on the waiting list. Five years later her name came up on the list and she separated from her husband.

Dorothy and her four children now live on $950 per month from Social Assistance and $550 per month from the Canada Child Tax Benefit – $1,500 in total. Recently, Dorothy obtained part-time employment at a hamburger chain and makes about $350 per month. Welfare recipients are allowed a certain earnings exemption, so she is allowed to keep her entire earnings. In her case, with the four children, she is allowed to keep up to $423 per month. If she were single, her flat-rate exemption would only be $143. If Dorothy earns more than her exemption, she will lose some of her income. For the first 12 months that she has earnings, a full 25 percent variable exemption applies. This means that she retains 25 percent of her earnings above $423. Between the 13th and the 24th month, the variable exemption falls to 15 percent, and for the months over 24 it falls to zero.

The extra earnings allow Dorothy to survive, especially given the health problems of her youngest child. He has asthma and the extra medical supplies and transportation cause her expenses to exceed her income. Dorothy's ex-husband is supposed to pay $900 per month in child support, but Dorothy has yet to see a cheque. He says that he does not have any income, but Dorothy suspects that he is working in construction and is being paid in cash. Even if she did get support from her husband, her welfare benefits would be reduced dollar-for-dollar. Dorothy wants to find a job that pays more or offers more hours. She has been on Social Assistance for over two years now, so she knows that even if she finds a job that pays well, she will only be able to keep $423. She feels trapped and wonders if her situation will ever change.

• Carlos: Educated Poor

Carlos is 26 and came to Canada as a refugee five years ago, settling in Toronto. His homeland had been completely destroyed and he fled for his life. His younger sister is developmentally challenged and she lives with him. Any job that he gets just barely covers the cost of paying for someone to take care of his sister. She needs special care and does not speak English, so it is very difficult to find care.

WORKFARE WATCH

The Workfare Watch website monitors the implementation of workfare. Check out their latest bulletins: http://www.welfarewatch.toronto.on.ca

CANADIAN SOCIAL
RESEARCH LINKS

This website always has an
up-to-date and comprehensive
collection of web links on
welfare:
http://www.canadiansocial
research.net/onwelf.htm

He is a well-educated man and worked as a physician in his home country. When he arrived in Canada he found that the Canadian Medical Association did not recognize his medical degree, and he was forbidden to work in his profession. He was immediately placed on Social Assistance, and encouraged to "upgrade his skills." He was unable to find a way to gain Canadian medical credentials so he enrolled in a college nursing program.

He was enrolled as a full-time student, but found it impossible to dedicate himself to full-time work and full-time study. He did get a $2,500 Special Bursary, but that made him ineligible for the Ontario Student Assistance Program (OSAP) loans. Eventually, Carlos changed to part-time studies. His job pays $7.50 per hour – that is only $14,625 per year without holidays. He found that it was impossible to live in Toronto on that money, and pay tuition on top of it. He was left with no choice but to postpone his studies.

• Mary, Amira and Marie: Different Women Surviving

Mary, a single woman, spends $350 per month on rent for her bachelor apartment. She spends a further $30 per month on utilities. Since Mary lives in Ontario, she will receive a maximum of $195 per month for basic living expenses and a maximum of $325 per month for rent, even though her rent exceeds this. She will receive a total of $520 per month – this is the provincial maximum (or the maximum barring exceptions – more money could be possible if a physician recommended a special diet, or if Mary lived in the far north of Ontario, for example). After rent and utilities, this leaves Mary with $140 each month with which to pay for food, clothing, transportation and other expenses.

Amira, a single mother, has one five-year-old daughter. Their one-bedroom apartment costs $450 per month, and their utilities cost a further $50 per month. Amira receives $446 per month as a basic needs allowance and another $500 to pay for shelter. The maximum she can receive is $957 per month. Amira also receives a back-to-school allowance for her daughter each July. She receives $69 for this allowance since her daughter is under age 13 – when she is over age 13, Amira will receive $128 to pay for her school-related costs. Each November, Amira receives $105 as a winter clothing allowance for her child. For all other expenses, including child care, Amira must rely on the $446 dollars per month she has left after paying her rent.

Marie is homeless. Although she is eligible for the $196 per month in basic needs allowance, in order to receive her $325 per month shelter allowance, Marie must provide receipts to prove she is using the money to pay for shelter. If Marie does find housing, she will become eligible for the Community Start-Up Fund, which will help her with paying the last month's rent and other start-up costs, such as new dishes and furniture. She will only be eligible for this fund once within a 12-month period and is allowed to draw a maximum of $799 from the fund within that year. A family moving into new housing would be able to request up to $1500 within a 12-month period.

DETERMINING ELIGIBILITY

In order to qualify for Social Assistance, Canadians must meet the criteria for three eligibility tests: financial eligibility, administrative eligibility and categorical eligibility.

- To meet the **financial eligibility** requirement, an applicant must show the need for Social Assistance. A needs test compares the household's assets with its needs. Initially, the household's non-exempted assets are examined to confirm that they do not exceed the maximum level set by each provincial regulation. These levels vary both among provinces and across application categories. For example, a single person must have fewer assets than a single parent in order to qualify for Social Assistance. Once it has been established that an applicant's assets do not exceed the maximum, the household's income is compared with its needs. When the cost of a household's needs is greater than its available income, Social Assistance may be granted. In some provinces, Social Assistance may be granted even if the household has surplus income. An applicant must prove that the surplus is necessary in order to pay for recurring special needs.

- **Administrative eligibility** calls for Social Assistance applicants to fulfill certain administrative requirements. In most provinces, this entails the completion of an application (although, in Ontario, the process is now undertaken through an automated phone system). In addition, applicants are required to provide evidence that they meet other eligibility criteria. Evidence may be in the form of bank books, pay stubs or doctors' notes to support claims of disability. An applicant must meet with a worker in order to discuss his or her situation and must sign a waiver giving permission for the worker and the Social Assistance authority to contact other agencies to verify information. Finally, an applicant must agree to contact the office immediately should any change in circumstances result in an increase of household income.

- **Categorical eligibility** refers to the different types of reasons why applicants might request assistance. While all applicants are presumed to be in need, different criteria for needs are considered. Criteria can depend on whether the applicant is elderly, disabled, a single parent or otherwise employable. There are consistent policies across all provinces with regard to individuals in certain categories. For example, in the case of a single parent who is in need due to lack of child support payments, the parent must take on the responsibility of pursuing the absent parent. "Employable" applicants must agree to undergo training (or community work projects in Ontario) in order to receive assistance. Some categories of people are ineligible for Social Assistance. For example, sponsored immigrants and nominated relatives are considered the responsibility of the sponsor and would only be granted Social Assistance under very special circumstances.

B.C. Supreme Court strikes down residency requirement, 1996 (CP PHOTO/D. Nethercott).

WELFARE IN B.C.

The B.C. government introduced two Bills in 2002 that dramatically changed welfare legislation in British Columbia: Bills 26 and 27. British Columbia is the latest province to restrict and cut welfare.

Bill 26, the *Employment and Assistance Act*, includes the following changes:

- Eligible employable singles and couples will receive assistance for a maximum of two years out of every five years.
- People convicted of welfare fraud will be ineligible for income assistance for the rest of their lives.
- The independent Income Assistance Appeal Board will be eliminated and replaced with a tribunal directly appointed by the Minister of Human Resources.

These legislative changes are being made in the context of other dramatic cuts to welfare:

- The requirement to undertake a three-week work search before being eligible to apply for welfare.
- University and college students will no longer be eligible for income assistance.
- Seniors aged 55-59 will have their rates reduced by $50 a month, while seniors aged 60-64 will have their rates reduced by nearly $100 a month.
- Single parents will now be expected to seek work when their children are three, not seven.
- Homemaker services have been entirely eliminated.

Bill 27, the *Employment and Assistance for Persons with Disabilities Act*, includes the following changes:

- There will be a reassessment of all people on disability benefits.
- There are new, stricter definitions of "disability."
- The disability designation will no longer be permanent.

Welfare rates in B.C. were reduced with the new legislation. Single parents have seen their benefits reduced by $43 per month, while payments to employable individuals aged 55-59 have fallen $47 per month. Employable individuals aged 60-64 have had their benefits reduced by $98 per month, and those of employable couples age 55-59 have fallen $94 per month. The benefits of employable couples aged 60-64 have dropped by $145 per month.

Shelter allowances were also reduced by between $55 and $75 per month.

One of the most punitive changes to the B.C. legislation is the assistance limit of two years out of every five years. Once the two-year time limit has been exhausted, income assistance will be discontinued for employable singles and couples without children, and reduced by $100 per month for single parents and $200 for two-parent families. This two-year maximum rule is unprecedented in Canada. It denies welfare when in need as a basic human right. The rule will force people with nowhere else to go for income assistance into emergency shelters and food banks. The only possible benefit from such a policy is a decrease in welfare caseloads and government expenditures. Many analysts question whether this is the correct way to cut government spending.

Another rule states that applicants aged 19 and over must demonstrate that they have been financially independent for two consecutive years (including any time spent receiving Unemployment Insurance benefits) before they are eligible to apply for welfare. There is no defensible rationale for this rule, except perhaps to send a message to youth that they should either be in school or working at any available job. Some believe that it is causing an increase in the numbers of youth living on the streets. David Carrigg reported in the January 22, 2003, edition of *The Vancouver Courier* that, in the winter of 2003, the Dusk to Dawn youth drop-in centre in downtown Vancouver stated that the number of youths using its facilities had reached 75 per night, up from an average of from 40 to 50 per night six months earlier (itself an increase over the previous year). Deena Franks of Family Services of Greater Vancouver attributes this jump in part to B.C.'s new welfare rules.

THE LEGISLATIVE AND POLICY CONTEXT

The nature of Canadian federalism and disputes over funding and delivery of income security programs has led to legislation that attempts to define federal-provincial responsibilities.

The **Canada Assistance Plan** (**CAP**), mentioned earlier, was instrumental in standardizing and funding Social Assistance nationwide. The CAP was in effect between 1966 and 1996. From the Plan's inception until 1991, the federal government paid 50 percent of the cost of welfare in all the provinces and territories. Further details on the history and development of CAP can be found in Chapter 2.

Under CAP, provincial Social Assistance legislation contained conditions that clients had to respect to stay eligible for welfare. With regard to Social Assistance, the federal government established certain rules or standards that the provinces had to adhere to in order to receive CAP funding:

1. Welfare must be given on a test of need (not means).

2. No work for welfare. When somebody applies for welfare they cannot be told that they must take a specific job offered by the welfare agency in order to get a cheque. This does not mean that there is no obligation on the part of the recipient to work. If an "appropriate" job comes along, the recipient must take it. In addition, work activity or training is permitted.

3. No residence requirement. This means that a person needing welfare can claim it in any city or province.

4. There must be an appeals system, formalized in provincial law.

Beginning in 1991, the Canada Assistance Plan began to change. The first change was the so-called "cap on CAP" under which the three wealthiest provinces received a limited amount of federal support rather than the full 50 percent initially guaranteed by CAP. The amount contributed by the federal government was clawed back until 1996, at which point the Canada Assistance Plan was replaced with the **Canada Health and Social Transfer** (**CHST**).

The replacement of one federal subsidy program with another may not seem like a dramatic change, but the major drop in federal monies to the provinces resulted in the federal government's inability to maintain the national standards. A key change is the shift from cost-sharing with CAP, where the federal government paid a 50 percent share of the province's social spending, to a per-person transfer that is fixed regardless of actual costs. In addition, Social Assistance funds were now being drawn from the same pool as money for education and health. As a result, four of five standards previously outlined under the Canada Assistance Plan were dropped under the CHST.

The most notable and immediate change was the introduction of "workfare" in Ontario. Work for welfare was not allowed under CAP, but this standard was dropped under the CHST funding plan. Ontario immediately adopted a workfare scheme in the wake of this standard

This House "seek(s) to achieve the goal of eliminating poverty among Canadian children by the year 2000."

— House of Commons, unanimous all-party resolution, November 24, 1989

Table 9.5: Estimated Annual Basic Social Assistance Income by Type of Household and Province/Territory, 2002

Newfoundland and Labrador		Saskatchewan	
Single Employable	$3,048	Single Employable	$5,808
Person with a Disability	$7,140	Person with a Disability	$7,416
Single Parent, One Child	$11,436	Single Parent, One Child	$9,036
Couple, Two Children	$11,916	Couple, Two Children	$12,192
Prince Edward Island		**Alberta**	
Single Employable	$5,757	Single Employable	$4,764
Person with a Disability	$7,602	Person with a Disability	$6,384
Single Parent, One Child	$9,814	Single Parent, One Child	$8,505
Couple, Two Children	$14,473	Couple, Two Children	$12,678
Nova Scotia		**British Columbia**	
Single Employable	$4,980	Single Employable	$6,166
Person with a Disability	$8,580	Person with a Disability	$9,437
Single Parent, One Child	$8,760	Single Parent, One Child	$10,300
Couple, Two Children	$11,520	Couple, Two Children	$12,253
New Brunswick		**Yukon**	
Single Employable	$3,168	Single Employable	$11,990
Person with a Disability	$6,696	Person with a Disability	$11,990
Single Parent, One Child	$8,772	Single Parent, One Child	$15,816
Couple, Two Children	$9,828	Couple, Two Children	$12,253
Quebec		**Northwest Territories**	
Single Employable	$6,444	Single Employable	$11,490
Person with a Disability	$9,312	Person with a Disability	$14,830
Single Parent, One Child	$8,712	Single Parent, One Child	$18,050
Couple, Two Children	$10,939	Couple, Two Children	$23,036
Ontario		**Nunavut**	
Single Employable	$6,240	Single Employable	$10,148
Person with a Disability	$11,160	Person with a Disability	$12,288
Single Parent, One Child	$10,210	Single Parent, One Child	$24,802
Couple, Two Children	$12,223	Couple, Two Children	$28,431
Manitoba			
Single Employable	$5,352		
Person with a Disability	$7,157		
Single Parent, One Child	$9,636		
Couple, Two Children	$12,849		

Source: National Council of Welfare, *Welfare Incomes 2002* (Ottawa: National Council of Welfare, 2003), 25-28.

change. The federal government no longer requires the provinces to provide financial assistance to everyone in need, or to consider the question of need.

The CHST had profound impacts on welfare. There is a fundamental difference between the reciprocity condition that was inherent in programs under CAP, and the workfare that emerged after the CHST was implemented. The difference is the "extent of compulsion." CAP supported provincial rules that required employable people on welfare to do *something* to help themselves. This could involve participating in an activity to improve their employability, such as going back to school, participating in a training program or even working in a job placement or apprenticeship. It might also involve actively looking for a job. In the latter case, CAP even tolerated provincial rules requiring proof of job search efforts by clients. What CAP did not support was workfare in its formal sense – the requirement to work for a specific number of hours in a designated job for basic welfare benefits. The CHST allows provinces to implement formal workfare (to be discussed shortly).

The latest government act that affects Social Assistance is the 1999 **Social Union Agreement (SU).** This is an agreement based upon mutual respect between the federal and provincial orders of government and a willingness to work more closely together. After the unilateral discontinuation of CAP by the federal government, it aimed at reducing the fallout and smoothing out relations. The SU agreement covers a range of programs such as Medicare, social services, education and the manner in which these programs are funded, administered and delivered (policy). How this new agreement will affect Social Assistance remains to be seen. Further information is available at http://www.socialunion.ca.

ABORIGINAL PEOPLES AND SOCIAL ASSISTANCE

Social Assistance for Canada's First Nations is rife with struggle between federal and provincial governments over who should pay. Although welfare in Canada is supposedly available to any citizen who meets the conditions of a particular program, a double standard has existed for Aboriginal Peoples. The *Indian Act* gave the federal government total control over Indian monies and the government exercised this power.

The first system of income security for Canada's First Nations was a ration system based on confiscated Indian monies that were placed in a band trust account. Until the early 1900s, monetary relief was taken from the trust accounts, and was granted at the discretion of the local Indian Agent. These monies were grossly inadequate and were used as much as a means to sanction behaviour as for relief (Moscovitch and Webster 1995, 211). The decision to grant relief was based on the old practice of distinguishing between the "deserving" and the "undeserving" poor – and Indians were generally considered undeserving. This system applied British Poor Law principles until the mid-1960s. "Non-registered Indians, Métis and Inuit were on the periphery of the Indian relief system although their economic circumstances were similar to, or worse than, those of the Indians" (p.212).

Inuit mother and child signing up for family allowance, NWT, 1949 (National Archives/PA12879).

FIRST NATIONS STATISTICS

Total population of Canada:
31,414,000

Total people of Aboriginal
origin: 1,319,890

Origin

- North American Indian:
  957,650
- Métis: 266,020
- Inuit: 51,390
- More than one Aboriginal
  origin: 44,835

Reserves

- People of Aboriginal origin
  living on reserve: 285,625
- People of Aboriginal origin
  living off reserve: 1,034,260
- People of non-Aboriginal
  origin living on reserve:
  36,230

Source: Statistics Canada, *2001
Census.* Available at:
http://www.cbc.ca/news/
indepth/firstnations/

The first Old Age Pension of 1927 excluded Indians and Inuit, but was available to the Métis. The first *Unemployment Insurance Act,* passed in 1940, also excluded most Aboriginal people from eligibility. *The Family Allowance Act* of 1944 did apply to Aboriginal Peoples, but only provided "in kind" rations. The first income security program to apply to Indians was the 1951 Old Age Security. The *Unemployment Assistance Act* of 1956 was supposed to be a cost-shared program available to Aboriginal people, but the provinces refused to pay any part of what they saw as federal government responsibility. With the *Unemployment Assistance Act* of 1956, the federal government attempted to mirror the standards and procedures of the provincial systems. In most cases, however, they had lower benefit rates. This was the beginning of a process of parallel income security systems: one for mainstream society and one for Aboriginal people. The provinces remain unwilling to fund on-reserve Social Assistance.

Between 1951 and 1966, the Indian relief system collapsed and was replaced with access to the mainstream welfare state (Moscovitch and Webster 1995). This occurred after the development of several federal Acts related to income security, amendments to the *Indian Act* in 1951 and the establishment of the Canada Assistance Plan (1966). Through the development of an administrative structure with huge discretionary powers that minimized community control, the Canadian government effectively came to control the day-to-day lives of Aboriginal Peoples. The Department of Indian Affairs and Northern Development (DIAND) began administering Social Assistance on reserves in July 1964. This was passed under the authority of Treasury Board Minute Number 627879 and since carried out following provincial regulations and standards for Social Assistance. The Indian Agents were replaced by DIAND, now called Indian and Northern Affairs Canada (INAC).

The majority of First Nations now administer Social Assistance under the provincial guidelines, but under the direct supervision of INAC. The federal government continues to fund on-reserve Social Assistance, but the benefits are tied to provincial rates. Some off-reserve Aboriginal communities also deliver their own programs according to provincial standards. Urban Aboriginal people receive Social Assistance through the mainstream system. First Nations' Social Assistance usage rates vary widely across the country, from 20 to 30 percent in Quebec, Ontario and the Yukon, to 48 to 58 percent in the four Western provinces, to a high of almost 75 percent in the Atlantic provinces. These rates, on a national basis, have been increasing each year, from an average of 35 percent in 1982 to 45 percent in 1994.

INAC itself has acknowledged that the current welfare system for First Nations people living on a reserve must be replaced by a more dynamic and progressive system. The Royal Comission on Aboriginal Peoples (RCAP) proposed several recommendations to that effect. Canada's response to the recommendations made in RCAP, *Gathering Strength*, outlined a commitment by the government to take a "bottom-up" approach with First Nations to reform on-reserve Social Assistance programs. Past programs have failed and many attribute this to the "made-in-Ottawa" style of devising solutions.

WELFARE REFORM DEBATES

Several reforms of Social Assistance have been tried or considered over the past few decades. In some cases these reforms have sparked controversy. Three of these reforms will be discussed: workfare, the "spouse-in-the-house" rule and the zero tolerance of welfare fraud rule. Many of the recent reforms have been directed at increasing work incentives or decreasing eligibility.

• Workfare

Some provincial welfare programs require applicants to work as a term of eligibility. This is commonly known as **workfare**, and it has drawn criticism. Refusal to participate in the program results in some sort of penalty. For example, workfare could require people to work at specific jobs in order to get a government cheque, or it could mean that people receive a smaller cheque if they refuse to accept work through a government program. It might also require applicants to select retraining or pursue self-employment programs. Workfare placements could involve working in a community or social service agency. Applicants may also choose community work placements as a workfare option for the purposes of increasing skills, knowledge and networks in the labour market.

Critics equate workfare as a return to the "work test" of the Elizabethan Poor Laws. Others cite research to show its failure in other countries – particularly the United States. It has also been criticized for being expensive to administer, and for taking away jobs from the paid labour force. Others see workfare as a blame-oriented approach that ignores job creation, arguing that people want to work, but that there are not enough good jobs.

It is difficult to discuss the issue of welfare without confronting the concept of workfare. Most of what is discussed under the rubric of workfare is actually a combination of tighter eligibility criteria, benefit cuts, a broadening of the definition of "employable" and more stringent enforcement of job search rules. These requirements are generally not new. Before we can debate whether workfare helps or hinders the poor, we need to delineate what workfare really is.

It is important to distinguish between two types of workfare: formal workfare and de facto workfare. *Formal workfare* is officially prescribed in policy and procedures. It states that employable benefit recipients must work for a specific minimum number of work units (usually measured in hours per week) in a job that is approved by the welfare authority.

As of 2003, the province of Ontario is the closest to requiring formal workfare. All employable people in the Ontario Works program (single people, couples with and without children, single parents and people aged 60-64 years) must agree to participate in one of the program's three active parts: employment supports (job-search services, referral to basic education and job-specific skills training), employment placement (referral to a job placement or self-employment development agencies) or community participation (unpaid community service activity).

NATIONAL WORKFARE SURVEY

The National Welfare to Work Study produced a comprehensive inventory of the different types of welfare to work programs across Canada. For the details of all provincial programs, go to:
http://publish.uwo.ca/~pomfret/wtw

Table 9.1 – Welfare-to-Work Programs across Canada

Province/Territory	Title of Program	Program Description
Newfoundland	• Supports to Employment Program, 1996	• Continuum of services • Incentives, rather than requirement
Prince Edward Island	• Employment Enhancement Program and Job Creation Program, 1995	• Participation expected of employable people • Sanctions for non-compliance
Nova Scotia	• Employment Support Services, 1997	• Array of services, including work placements • Participation mandatory or benefits discontinued
New Brunswick	• New Brunswick Works, 1992-1998 • New strategy being developed, 1999	• Extensive voluntary training and education • New strategy unknown
Quebec	• APIE (Positive Action for Work and Employment) since 1989 • Dept. of Employment and Solidarity, 1997	• Provision of higher benefits to participants
Ontario	• Ontario Works, 1997	• Employment supports • Employment placement • Community placement (workfare) • Mandatory participation or sanctions imposed
Manitoba	• Employment First, 1996	• Variety of training and employment programs • Mandatory participation by employable people
Saskatchewan	• Saskatchewan Assistance Plan, 1997	• Plan for independence by employable people • Benefits withheld for non-compliance
Alberta	• Supports for Independence, 1990 • Welfare Reform, 1993	• Employable people must seek or prepare for work • Refusal may result in loss or reduction of benefits • Initial applications "diverted"
British Columbia	• Welfare-to-Work, 1996	• Job search assistance — mandatory participation • Employment preparation — voluntary • Employment-based activities — voluntary
Yukon	• Employment Training Services Head Start, 1993	• Program participation — voluntary • Self-sufficiency plan — mandatory
Northwest Territories	• Productive Choices, 1997	• Participation required • Self-employment and volunteerism accepted

Sources: C. Gorlick and G. Brethour, *Welfare-to-Work Programs: A National Inventory* (Ottawa: Canadian Council on Social Development, 1998); C. Gorlick and G. Brethour, *Welfare-to-Work — Program Summaries* (Ottawa: Canadian Council on Social Development, 1998). Reproduced by permission.

Community participation is the stream most readily identified with the concept of workfare. In this stream, welfare recipients can be required to work from 17 to 70 hours per month in a not-for-profit or public sector workplace approved under the program, in order to receive their basic welfare benefit.

Examples of community placement can include working with non-profit organizations: this may require helping with administration, fundraising, marketing and promotional strategies or working as support staff in child care. Other duties may include assisting the program staff with the delivery of specific programs, such as supervision of youth or providing transportation to seniors.

Workfare is hotly debated and a variety of new terms are used to describe it, such as formal or *de facto* workfare, welfare-to-work and even trainfare. All provinces except Ontario like to call their programs welfare-to-work programs. *De facto workfare* is more common and occurs when provinces stringently enforce job-search and training requirements for employable people. The government pays monthly supplements to people who actively train for and find employment. Some provinces pay extra benefits to recipients who are participating in an approved training program or job-search activity. Other provinces deduct benefits from those who do not participate in mandated employment-related programs.

Terminology aside, it is clear that across the country, a significantly more coercive and disciplinary approach is being used in employment and training programs for welfare recipients. The programs are defining increasing numbers of people as employable. For example, in most provinces, single parents with children are now considered employable depending on the ages of their children. In addition, the programs have mandatory participation requirements and sanctions for non-compliance and generally operate with the mind-set of "any job is a good job."

The welfare system in Quebec (as of 2003) provides a good example of provisions that deduct benefits for non-participants. For those who do not participate in an employability measure (such as schooling, training or job integration), the Quebec government deducts $120 per month for a single employable person and $200 for a two-adult household. This "non-participating" category includes those who refuse to participate and those who live in an area where no appropriate measures are available.

Sadly, most workfare schemes, whether de facto or formalized, rely on the same myths that have always plagued Social Assistance policymaking: that the average user is lazy and unmotivated, and will stay on Social Assistance indefinitely if not forced to do useful work. On the contrary, Christopher Clark (a policy analyst for the Canadian Council on Social Development) points out that most households are simply finding it impossible to support basic needs while working in low-income jobs. As Clark writes, "if the alternative for most people on Social Assistance is a minimum-wage job, the labour market offers little hope for avoiding the poverty trap" (Clark 1995).

WELFARE-TO-WORK PROVINCIAL AND TERRITORIAL SUMMARIES

A National Welfare-to-Work Study being completed by Carolyne Gorlick at the University of Western Ontario has produced an inventory of the different types of welfare-to-work programs emerging across the country. Go to the Phase 2 section and you can obtain a detailed description of the welfare-to-work programs that exist in your province. Available at: http://publish.uwo.ca/~pomfret/wtw/index.html

WORKFARE IN THE COURTS: THE GOSSELIN CASE

Between 1985 and 1989, the Quebec government slashed welfare benefits to all those under 30 deemed able to work and who were not in workfare or job retraining. The reduced rate, however, actually preceded any workfare and training programs.

Louise Gosselin, a Montreal woman on Social Assistance, had her welfare benefits reduced due to the introduction of the reduced assistance. Gosselin saw her benefits plunge from $434 to $170 per month. This drop, she says, forced her into soup kitchens and into prostitution. She took the Quebec and Canadian governments to the Supreme Court. Her lawyer asked the court to grant compensation, arguing that Quebec violated Gosselin's fundamental right to a decent standard of living. The plaintiff argues that under section 7 of the *Canadian Charter of Rights and Freedoms*, everyone has the right to "security of the person and the right not to be deprived thereof."

This was the first claim under the *Canadian Charter of Rights and Freedoms* and the first claim under human rights legislation — a right to an adequate level of Social Assistance for those in need.

The Gosselin case provided the first opportunity for the Supreme Court to consider whether denying members of a disadvantaged group adequate financial assistance, which results in homelessness and deprivation of other basic necessities, is a violation of the *Canadian Charter of Rights and Freedoms*. The case raised the critical issue of whether the right to "security of the person" in section 7 of the *Charter* and the right to equality under section 15 oblige positive legal responsibilities upon governments to ensure an adequate level of income for Canadians when they are unable to provide for themselves.

In 2002 the Supreme Court ruled against Louise Gosselin, but many social rights advocates saw positive elements in the ruling. For example, the decision overruled the lower courts, which were reluctant to review compliance of government policies with economic and social obligations under the *Quebec Charter of Rights*.

In future cases, economic and social rights will be interpreted to include positive obligations on the part of the government.

Members of Poverty Action Network (PAN) demonstrate in April 1999. The group was demanding more welfare money for longer months (CP PHOTO/Nick Procaylo-str).

Consider the scenario of a single mother with an eight-month-old child who is offered a minimum paying job. In order to take the job she must find child care and pay for her own transportation. The parent must deal with the increased stress of not being with the child, the increased expenses related to child care and employment needs and the discouragement of making equivalent or less income than she was receiving from assistance. The parent then begins to question the sense of working and succumbs to feelings of being trapped.

• The "Spouse-in-the-House" Rule

Social workers and welfare advocacy groups have long been critical of the so-called **spouse-in-the-house rule**. In some cities welfare workers were trained to determine if a person of the opposite sex had stayed overnight at a welfare recipient's home (they looked for things such as an extra toothbrush or shoes). If it was determined that there was someone staying in the home, that person could have been deemed financially responsible for the person receiving welfare. Until 1986, the definition of "spouse," under Social Assistance legislation, required a determination of whether opposite-sex co-residents were living together as "husband and wife." A Canadian *Charter of Rights and Freedoms* challenge to this definition prompted the Ontario government to bring in a new definition in 1987. The 1987 definition allowed welfare recipients to have up to three years of cohabitation before an economic interdependence was deemed to exist. This three-year rule matches the rule in the *Family Law Act*, which views unmarried couples as spouses if they have cohabited for at least three years.

Thus, under the 1987 definition, an individual welfare recipient cohabitating with a person of the opposite sex had a grace period of up to three years before being considered a spouse. After three years, to maintain an individual entitlement to Social Assistance, the recipient had to produce evidence to show that the social, familial and economic aspects of the relationship did not amount to cohabitation. No legal challenge was made to the 1987 definition.

In 1995, the Ontario government replaced the 1987 definition of spouse with a new definition. A person could be a spouse in one of four ways. Three of those ways were similar to the previous definition: a person could be a spouse by self-declaration, by being required to pay support under a court order or domestic contract and by having a support obligation under the *Family Law Act*. The Ontario government defined the fourth way to be a spouse more expansively than it had in the past. Under this provision, economic interdependence is deemed to exist as soon as there is evidence of cohabitation. This is the provision that is at issue.

This policy was deemed unconstitutional in 2000 by the Divisional Court and in 2002 by the Ontario Supreme Court. The definition of "spouse" is overly broad, and captures relationships that are not spousal or marriage-like. The 2002 court decision has ruled that citizens on welfare cannot be discriminated against just because they collect Social Assistance. The Ontario government is appealing the case to the

KIMBERLY ROGERS

Sudbury resident Kimberly Rogers died on August 11, 2001. She was convicted of welfare fraud for not declaring student loans she received while collecting Social Assistance. The penalty she received was

- six months under house arrest;
- only three hours per week to be spent outside of her hot apartment;
- repayment to welfare of $13,648.31;
- 18 months' probation;
- loss of the right to have part of her student loan forgiven and
- no income at all for three months.

At the time of her conviction, she was five months pregnant. A coroner's inquest into her death concluded that the zero tolerance lifetime ineligibility for Social Assistance, as a result of the commission of welfare fraud, pursuant to Ontario Works Act, 1997, O. Reg. 134/98 Section 36, should be eliminated. Further information is available at: http://dawn.thot.net/Kimberly_Rogers

A rally in front of the provincial building in Sudbury, Ontario, in August 2001 to remember Kimberly Rogers and to protest government welfare policies. Kimberly Rogers, who was confined to her apartment for welfare fraud, was found dead during a recent heat wave (CP PHOTO/*Sudbury Star*/Gino Donato).

Supreme Court. Updates can be found on the web at the following address: http://www.canadiansocialresearch.net/spouse.htm.

The Government of Ontario and the Fraser Institute (a public policy organization) seem to agree on the implication of the court decisions. According to Ontario's Attorney General David Young, the finding that Social Assistance recipients are among the protected groups covered under the equality provisions of the *Charter of Rights and Freedoms* is without precedent in Ontario. The Fraser Institute published a similar conclusion in its *Fraser Forum*. The Canadian Civil Liberties Association argued that the regulation violated the privacy and dignity of people who collect Social Assistance and unfairly discouraged them from taking roommates or from forming intimate relationships with members of the opposite sex.

The Women's Legal Education and Action Fund (LEAF), a national, non-profit organization working to promote equality for women and girls in Canada, agrees and further maintains that it directly affects single mothers who may want to form relationships. They believe that the law forces women and their children to be economically tied to a man, or that women must give up having live-in relationships or even sharing accommodation with men. The Charter Committee on Poverty Issues, an anti-poverty organization, says that Canada falls short in a number of areas stipulated in international human rights law, and this regulation is just one example.

This is an issue that has been debated by social policy analysts for decades, and it seems that whenever governments aim to cut spending on Social Assistance, they turn to this rule.

• Welfare Fraud

The Ontario *Welfare Fraud Control Report 1999-2000* shows that a total of 55,041 frauds were reported. Of these, 43,900 were followed up. This resulted in 15,680 reductions or terminations of assistance and 557 criminal convictions. The government report says that $46 million was saved as a result of reducing or terminating assistance. They do not state the cost of tracing these funds. The most prevalent reason for the reduction or termination of assistance is listed as "incarceration" (45.5 percent of cases in 1999-2001 and 43.6 percent in 2001-02). This means that most of the savings comes from terminating people who were receiving assistance while in prison. Other reasons include "spouse not declared" (10.9 percent), "undeclared income" (14.8 percent), "undeclared earnings" (9 percent) and "not at a stated address" (8.5 percent).

Several problems become evident when one analyzes the Ontario **welfare fraud** statistics. First, almost half of the fraud cases were instances of people collecting welfare while in prison. Many of the other reported frauds were overpayments and administrative errors, or cases where documents were missing.

The Ontario government introduced a zero-tolerance policy for welfare fraud. Anyone convicted of Social Assistance fraud (as of 2000) is permanently ineligible for welfare. Between April 1, 2000, and March 31, 2001, there were 17 convictions for welfare fraud, resulting in permanent ineligibility. The government of British Columbia introduced similar anti-fraud legislation in 2002 with Bill 26, the *Employment and Assistance Act*. The Act stipulates that eligible employable singles and couples will receive assistance for a maximum of two years out of every five years, and that people convicted of welfare fraud will be ineligible for income assistance for the rest of their lives.

It is safe to say that no one knows all the rules surrounding welfare. The rules are so complex, unrealistic and impossible to follow that recipients are in a situation where they are always breaking some rule at some time. And it is not only recipients breaking the rules – welfare workers cannot possibly know, and therefore follow, all of the rules and are left breaching key ones daily. In the eyes of some provincial governments, this amounts to fraud.

REFERENCES

* Bohácek, Radim. 2002. *The Efficiency-Equality Tradeoff in Welfare State Economies.* Luxembourg Income Study (LIS) project. Available on-line at: http://www.lisproject.org/publications/wpapers.htm

* Centre for International Statistics. 2002. *Incidence of Child Poverty Among Children in Female Lone-parent Families, by Province, Canada, 1990-1996.* Ottawa: Canadian Council on Social Development (using data from Statistics Canada, Cat. 13-569-XPB). Retrieved from: http://www.ccsd.ca/factsheets/fscp90s.htm on December 23, 2002.

* Clark, Christopher. 1995. Work and welfare: Looking at both sides of the equation. *Canadian Council on Social Development, Perception.* Vol. 19, No. 1. Available at: http://www.ccsd.ca/perchris.html #table1

* Guest, Denis. 1999. *The Emergence of Social Security in Canada.* 3rd ed. Vancouver: University of British Columbia (UBC) Press.

* Human Resources Development Canada. 2000a. *Provincial Social Assistance and Child Welfare Programs Table 435: Number of Beneficiaries (including Dependants) of Provincial and Municipal Social Assistance, as of March 31, 1997 to 2000.* Strategic Policy Branch. Ottawa: HRDC. Retrieved from http://www.hrdc-drhc.gc.ca/stratpol/socpol/ on November 21 2002.

* Human Resources Development Canada. 2000b. *Provincial and Municipal Social Assistance Program Expenditures, 1980-81 to 1999-2000, Table 438.* Strategic Policy Branch. Ottawa: HRDC. Retrieved from http://www.hrdc-drhc.gc.ca/stratpol/socpol/ on November 21, 2002.

* Moscovitch, Allan, and Andrew Webster. 1995. Aboriginal Social Assistance Expenditures. In Susan Philips, ed., *How Ottawa Spends 1995-96: Mid-Life Crisis.* Ottawa: Carleton University Press.

* National Council of Welfare. 1998. *Profiles of Welfare: Myths and Realities.* Ottawa. Available at: http://www.ncwcnbes.net

* National Council of Welfare. 2000. *Welfare Income 1999.* Ottawa: National Council of Welfare. Available at: http://www.ncwcnbes.net

* National Council of Welfare. 2001. *The Cost of Poverty.* Ottawa: National Council of Welfare. Available at: http://www.ncwcnbes.net

* National Council of Welfare. 2002. *Welfare Income 2000 and 2001.* Ottawa: National Council of Welfare. Available at: http://www.ncwcnbes.net

* Phipps, Shelly, and Lynn Lethbridge. 2002. *Fitting Kids in: Children and Inequality in Canada.* Luxembourg Income Study Working Paper No. 322.

* Statistics Canada. 2003. *Persons in Low Income before Tax: CANSIM II, Table 202-0802 and Catalogue No. 75-202-XIE.* Ottawa: Statistics Canada. Retrieved from: http://www.statcan.ca/english/ Pgdb/famil41a.htm on March 31, 2003.

* Vozoris, N., Davis, B., and Tarasuk, V. 2002. The affordability of a nutritious diet for households on welfare in Toronto. *Canadian Journal of Public Health,* Vol. 93, No. 1: 36-40.

CONCLUSION

Provincially delivered Social Assistance programs intend to provide a minimum income, as a last resort measure. The costs of these programs are the responsibility of all levels of government. With the 1996 discontinuation of CAP and its replacement with the CHST, the federal government ceased to play a role in setting national standards for Social Assistance, and cut transfers to the provinces that would cover Social Assistance. This opened the door to the workfare that several provinces have instituted.

Social Assistance rates in all provinces are below LICO. Rates in some of the provinces and territories, especially rates for single "employables," reach only one-fifth or one-third of LICO. The situation of single-parent families on Social Assistance is particularly dismal. Incomes for 2001 were at least $10,000 below the estimated average total income for all single-parent families.

The cost of poverty to all Canadians is high. There is evidence that poverty causes individual problems, lost opportunities and harms a nation's economic performance. In *The Cost of Poverty* (National Council of Welfare 2001), a number of studies in the areas of health, justice, human rights and human development, work and productive capacity and child development are reviewed. The report found that reducing inequality between rich and poor, and especially helping the extremely poor, has positive individual and societal effects. According to the National Council of Welfare, this would help Canada better manage the cost of health care, reduce crime, develop a productive labour force, advance human well-being and foster social cohesion and public confidence in governments and in the economy.

CHAPTER 9: PEOPLE LIVING IN POVERTY

Discussion Questions

1. What factors or events in Canadian society led to the implementation of public social welfare for the poor?
2. List and explain five myths or blame-oriented beliefs about the poor. Why do you think that these myths persist?
3. Describe the three types of eligibility tests that a Canadian must meet in order to qualify for Social Assistance.
4. List the three federal pieces of legislation that have affected Social Assistance in Canada. What was the impact of the move from CAP to the CHST on Social Assistance?
5. Outline the history of Social Assistance for Aboriginal Peoples in Canada.
6. List and describe the three key debates in discussions about Social Assistance.
7. Define workfare, and discuss criticisms put forward by social policy advocates.

Key Concepts

- Social Assistance (SA)
- Financial eligibility
- Administrative eligibility
- Categorical eligibility
- Canada Assistance Plan (CAP)
- Canada Health and Social Transfer (CHST)
- Social Union Agreement (SU)
- Workfare
- Spouse-in-the-house rule
- Welfare fraud

Websites

- **National Council of Welfare**
  http://www.ncwcnbes.net

  A one-stop location for information on welfare and poverty.

- **Statistics Canada**
  http://www.statcan.ca/english/Pgdb/

  This page contains links to free statistics. Click on "families, households and housing" for statistics on low income by family type.

- **End Legislated Poverty**
  http://www.endlegislatedpoverty.ca/

  ELP is a coalition of 36 organizations in B.C. working together to ensure that governments reduce and end poverty. ELP believes that unemployment and poverty are not the fault of individual people living in poverty. They believe poverty is created by laws that are passed by government legislatures.

- **Campaign 2000**
  http://www.campaign2000.ca/

  This is an extensive site that contains report cards on child poverty, resources and suggestions for taking action. Campaign 2000 was an across-Canada public education movement that aimed at building Canadian awareness and support for the 1989 all-party House of Commons resolution to end child poverty in Canada by the year 2000.

The unjust enrichment of the government and corresponding deprivation of vulnerable others is immoral & illegal

A 1996 rally on Parliament Hill designed to bring the government's attention to the millions of Canadians living in poverty. The anti-poverty rally in Ottawa was organized by the National Action Committee on the Status of Women and drew a crowd of about 5,000 (CP PHOTO/*Ottawa Sun*/Jim Young).

10

Children and Families in Poverty

A Call to Action

The persistence of child poverty in Canada is a threat to our future. Financial and social supports for families and children have recently changed with decreasing welfare rates in many provinces and the addition of the National Child Benefit. But what is lacking is a comprehensive and integrated approach to family income policy. Without it, children and working families in Canada will remain in a precarious position.

For most Canadians, child poverty is considered something that happens in another country. However, as of 2002, one in six Canadian children, or 16.5 percent, lives in poverty. This translates into 1,100,000 Canadian children. Canadian governments have recognized that Canada's children need help – not only is it the ethical thing to do, but our economic and social well-being depends on it. But not all attempts to effect change have been successful, as we will see in this review of Canada's income security for families with children.

One cannot examine the welfare of Canada's children without addressing the situation of families since, up to a certain age, children are dependent on the households in which they live. Not surprisingly, social researchers are finding that the income security of children's families in the early years of life is especially important for the children's health, education and personal well-being.

"I do not want to be the angel of any home; I want for myself what I want for other women, absolute equality. After that is secured, then men and women can take turns at being angels."

— Agnes Macphail, Canada's first female Member of Parliament.

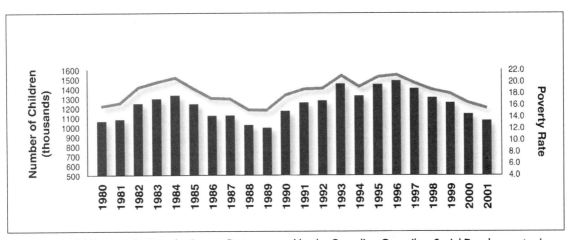

Figure 10.1: Child poverty in Canada. *Source*: Data prepared by the Canadian Council on Social Development using Statistics Canada's *Survey of Consumer Finances*, microdata files (1996-1999), and *Survey of Labour and Income Dynamics* (1999).

A WORLD FIT FOR CHILDREN

In 2002, the Special Session of the UN General Assembly on Children culminated in the official adoption, by some 180 nations, of the document *A World Fit for Children*. It emphasizes

- putting children's needs first,
- eradicating poverty and investing in children,
- committing to leaving no child behind,
- caring for every child and
- listening to children and ensuring their participation.

For more information see: http://www.unicef.org/specialsession

Some of the income security benefits to families with children have been, and continue to be, delivered through the tax system in the form of tax credits and exemptions. Others have been distributed through direct cash transfers. In 1944, a universal benefit called the Family Allowance was instituted, and this benefit went to all families with children regardless of income. Over time, this benefit became targeted toward middle- and low-income families. In 1993, it was eliminated entirely. The Canada Child Tax Benefit and the National Child Benefit are now used as the major child-related benefits for families with children. It is applied through the tax system, with eligibility determined by family income.

While Canada does not have an official family policy, it does have a collection of income security measures directed solely at families with children. In this chapter, we will examine these programs and explore their impact on Canada's children.

CANADA'S CHILDREN

Child poverty diminishes life chances for children. The National Council of Welfare and the Canadian Council on Social Development have reported extensively on the negative effect of poverty on children and their families. Good health and development during childhood are among the most important factors in making sure that individuals grow up healthy enough to learn, find work, raise families and participate fully in society throughout their lives. Children in low-income families have higher risks of poor health and poor developmental outcomes than do children in middle-income and high-income families.

The less income a family has, the less they can afford health care costs not covered by public health insurance. Less educational opportunities exist for these children and their parents, which makes it difficult to secure employment or upgrade to better employment. Financial strain can also lead to family breakdown, and contribute to social problems such as crime. As Children's Aid and group homes become involved, this can translate into higher social services costs. In short, there is a clear need for strong measures to eliminate child poverty in Canada.

In 1989, the House of Commons declared its commitment to eliminate poverty among Canadian children by the year 2000. At the time, the child poverty rate was estimated to be 14.5 percent. It now stands at just under 17 percent and has reached as high as 21 percent. **Campaign 2000**, an across-Canada public education movement to build Canadian awareness and support for the 1989 all-party House of Commons resolution, reports yearly on the progress towards the goal of eliminating child poverty. In their report on the situation of children in the year 2000, they found that about 1.1 million Canadian children live on incomes below Statistics Canada's Low Income Cut-off, and found that many families live far below these lines (see http://www.campaign 2000.ca/rc). The report notes that it is a positive sign that the rate of child poverty dropped for the fourth consecutive year, but goes on to point out that child poverty has actually increased since the resolution in 1989, when Canada's child poverty rate was 14.4 percent.

Anti-poverty protestors in downtown St. John's, Nfld., November 1999 (CP PHOTO/*The St. John's Telegram/* Gary Hebbard).

This dire situation exists despite the federal government's tax and income security policies. Many of these children live in modest-income households whose earnings have declined over the last decade. At the same time, the cost of raising children has risen, and the supply of secure, full-time employment has dropped.

Child poverty rates tend to rise in economic downturns and fall during economic growth. This trend is illustrated in Figure 10.1. In the 1980s, the child poverty rate rose with the 1981-82 recession, peaking in 1984 at 21 percent and then declining for the rest of the 1980s. By the recession of 1990-91, child poverty was again on the rise. The percentage of children in poverty peaked in 1993 and 1996 at over 21 percent. Then, a modest decline began in 1997 and continued in 1998 as the child poverty rate fell to 19 percent. As the poverty rate declined, so did the number of poor children. In 2002, there were 1,100,000 Canadian children living in poverty (16.5 percent).

It is instructive to examine the extent to which poor families live below LICO (what is known as the **poverty gap**). The poverty gap for two-parent families with children increased in the years from 1999 to 2000. As mentioned, 16.5 percent of children lived below the 2000 LICO. Within this number is a large discrepancy between children in two-parent families and children in single-parent families. The poverty rates for families headed by single-parent mothers have consistently been five to six times higher than the poverty rates for two-parent families. According to Statistics Canada, about 11.4 percent of children in two-parent families and about 47.6 percent of children in female single-parent families lived below LICO in 2000 (see Table 10.2).

CHILD POVERTY: A NATIONAL DISGRACE

Photosensitive is a collective of photographers who are exploring the use of photography in contributing to social justice.

For an on-line photography exhibit portraying child poverty in Canada, go to: http://www.photosensitive.com Click on "Child Poverty."

Table10.1: Child Poverty in Canadian Provinces, 2001

	RATE	NUMBER
CANADA	15.6%	1,071,000
NF	21.6%	24,000
PE	12.5%	4,000
NS	19.2%	38,000
NB	14.5%	23,000
PQ	17.8%	276,000
ON	13.0%	355,000
MB	22.5%	58,000
SK	17.6%	42,000
AB	14.1%	104,000
BC	17.0%	146,000

Source: Statistics Canada, *Income Trends in Canada*, Catalogue No. 13F0022XCB (2001).

UNICEF'S MEASURE OF POVERTY

The measure of poverty used by UNICEF is different from the Statistics Canada LICO measure, and therefore provides different rates.

The UNICEF measure calculates poverty as living below one-half of the median income in a country. The measure allows for international comparisons.

Nowadays it is necessary for families to have an actual or potential second wage earner and two adults to support each other with family responsibilities. For example, a single mother in Ottawa that works full-time as a cashier at minimum wage ($7.45 per hour in 2004) does not make enough to be above the poverty line established by LICO. Based on a 40-hour work week, she earns just over $15,000 in one year. Even with only one child, she would need to make over $24,077 in gross income to be above LICO. This rate is based on the 2002 LICO for a family living in a city with 500,000 people or more. Even if she lived in a much smaller city with a population of less than 30,000 people where living costs are lower, she is still below the poverty line. To be above LICO she would need to live in a rural area and work more than 40 hours per week at minimum wage.

For single mothers with more than one child, it is even more difficult to get out of poverty. For example, a single mother of two children (a three-person family), living in a city with over 500,000 people, needs to earn over $29,944 to be above LICO. If she lives in a rural area (where the LICO level is the lowest), she would need to earn over $20,694. For a four-person family (a single mother with three children, or two adults and two children) living in a medium-sized city of 100,000-499,999, the LICO is $31,090. Clearly, work does not guarantee that families will not be living in poverty.

One might think that, in a country with enormous wealth and resources, child poverty would not be an issue. Yet, Canada's child poverty rates are higher than most other countries. Using a conservative

Table 10.2: Persons in Low Income Before Tax, 1996-2000

Prevalence (%) of low income in:	1996	1997	1998	1999	2000
Persons under 18 years of age	21.1	20.0	18.7	18.0	16.5
Two-parent families	14.7	13.7	12.3	12.1	11.4
Female single-parent families	61.6	58.7	55.1	52.2	47.6
All other economic families	29.0	31.1	27.7	27.7	22.1

Note: Prevalence of low income shows the proportion of people living below the Low Income Cut-off within a given group. It is expressed as a percentage. The measures above are "before tax" and, therefore, do NOT include tax-based income security transfers such as the CCTB.

Source: Statistics Canada, CANSIM II Table 202-0802 and Catalogue No. 75-202-XIE. Retrieved from: http://www.statcan.ca/english/Pgdb/famil41a.htm on December 23, 2002.

measure of poverty to compare child poverty rates, the UNICEF study *Child Poverty across Industrialized Nations* (Bradbury and Jantti 1999) found that Canada's rate (11.2 percent) for children is the fourth worst, falling behind Russia, the United States and Italy. Using the United Nations measure of less than half of medium national income, Canada has the second highest rate of single-mother poverty in the world at 45.4 percent. Canada falls behind all countries except the United States, including Russia, Slovakia and Taiwan.

The face of child poverty is changing from the lone mother on welfare to that of the working-poor mother who is holding down at least one job. While just 6.8 percent of poor children lived with mothers who worked full-time in 1996, 11.5 percent of all poor children did so in 1998. Unfortunately, single mothers who are taking up the challenge of welfare departments across the country in trading a welfare cheque for a pay stub are not finding that the transition raises them out of poverty.

The downward trend in child poverty since 1997 is encouraging, but many analysts are concerned that child poverty may increase again the next time there is an economic crisis. To achieve a sustained reduction in child poverty, governments need a multi-pronged strategy. Delineating such a strategy is complex, but experts in the field (panel discussion in SOWK 1000 class at Carleton University) believe that such as strategy should include: consistent and adequate income security for families with children, improvements in the availability of living-wage jobs, early childhood education and care, and affordable housing programs that provide housing for the most vulnerable families.

POVERTY QUIZ

Test your knowledge of child poverty and family poverty in Canada. Go to:
http://www.campaign2000/quiz2

"We know quality of life when we see people working, with dignity, with good pay, with the opportunity to move ahead."

— Prime Minister Paul Martin, 2003 (victory speech at the Liberal leadership convention).

MARKET POVERTY: CHILDREN IN WORKING POOR FAMILIES

Not all children who live in families with a low income are on Social Assistance. Many families struggling to survive on low income are employed. Increasingly, the marketplace is not providing adequate income for Canadian families.

Market poverty refers to a situation in which a household remains below some measure of poverty, even though one or more members of the household earn a market income or are employed. These are referred to as the "working poor" on p. 139. There are two basic causes of market poverty: (1) low wages and (2) lack of access to the labour market. Low wages contribute to market poverty when wages do not provide an adequate income to support families. Market poverty continues to exist, despite people's commitment to seek paid employment.

Increasingly, the expectation is that families should become more self-reliant through labour market participation, whether it is a lone-parent or two-parent family. There is little consideration as to how realistic this is in terms of the level of minimum wages and the high costs of day care for these families. For example, a single mother with a very young child that is not in school needs full-time day care if she has a full-time job. At the Ontario minimum wage of $7.45 per hour (2004), the cost of day care takes up a large percentage of her earnings, particularly since full-time day care can cost from several hundred to several thousand dollars per month, depending on the day care provider. Even when her child is in school and she works full-time during the school hours, her income is so low that the family still falls below the LICO. Two-parent families are not much better off, especially if both parents earn wages at a low hourly rate and have to pay for day care. Even if their combined income places the family above the LICO, the cost of day care can be high enough to plunge them into poverty.

Table 10.3: Patterns of Poverty for Lone-Parent Families, Selected Countries

	Share of All Children in Lone-Parent Families (%)	Poverty Rate Income below 50 percent of national median	
		Lone-Parent Families (%)	Other Families (%)
France	7.7	26.1	6.4
Germany	9.8	51.2	10.4
Netherlands	7.4	23.5	5.5
Sweden	21.3	6.7	1.5
United Kingdom	20.0	45.6	12.3
United States	16.6	55.4	15.8
Canada	12.2	51.6	10.5

Source: UNICEF, *A League Table of Child Poverty in Rich Nations, Innocenti Report Card #1* (Florence, Italy: Innocenti Research Centre, 2000). Available at: http://www.unicef-icdc.org

Provincial and regional figures for families experiencing market poverty can vary significantly. For example, in 1994 Ontario faced a 20.3 percent market poverty rate in comparison to Newfoundland's rate of 34.5 percent. The average "market-poor" family in Ontario lived $14,749 below the poverty line, and the earnings of the average "market-poor" family in P.E.I. were $10,362 below the poverty line (Schellenberg and Ross 1996).

The current poverty statistics raise many questions. Why are so many working families still left with inadequate incomes? Does Canada have an official government policy that is addressing the problem?

APPROACHES TO CHILDREN'S SOCIAL WELFARE

It is helpful to examine where Canada's policy fits within the two main approaches to children's social welfare. These two approaches are: (1) the family responsibility approach and (2) the investing in children approach.

According to the **family responsibility approach**, parents are solely responsible for making decisions and providing for their children's well-being. The role of income security and social services is to facilitate decision making and provide support when the family's ability to provide fails. Within this approach there is little recognition of the contribution of parents to the future of society. This approach therefore sees labour force attachment for family members as the primary focus of concern. Programs are designed to intervene only when the family resources and abilities fail. Programs using this approach provide tax deductions for families with children, employment leaves and targeted minimum-income programs.

The **investing in children approach**, on the other hand, believes in building supports for families and households that enable them to attain positive outcomes for children. This approach holds that social spending on income supports and child education and care is an investment that benefits all of society in the long run. There is a recognition that the decisions open to families are increasingly limited and that the options for parents have narrowed insofar as most families need two incomes to adequately provide for themselves and their children. The market is also increasingly unable to provide sufficient incomes for families; hence, the increase in children living in low-income situations. This approach parallels aspects of the social responsibility model discussed in Chapter 6.

The Canadian government's focus on child poverty is generally consistent with an individual responsibility approach to social welfare. Many social workers and policy analysts have been at the forefront in advocating a policy shift in the direction of the social responsibility model. The approach recognizes that parents cannot always stay at home full-time, so there is a need for day care and early childhood development programs. There is also recognition that not all parents are employable and that they may require income assistance or child care assistance in order to access education and attend programs (to develop their skills so that they can become employable).

GETTING PEOPLE OFF WELFARE

"The Council [National Council of Welfare] believes that a far more constructive approach to getting people off welfare would be to provide real incentives to work. The most obvious incentive for parents on welfare is the provision of high-quality affordable child care. It is overwhelmingly clear to the Council that the provision of child care is the very first step in making it possible for a parent on welfare to complete an education or training program, and then find and keep a job."

Source: National Council of Welfare, *Welfare Incomes 2002 Report* (Ottawa: National Council of Welfare, 2003). Available online at: http://www.ncwcnbes.net/htmdocument/reportwelfinc02/Welfare2002.htm

FOUR PURPOSES OF CHILD-RELATED INCOME SECURITY

Amazingly, in a society in which we repeatedly hear about the importance of the family, there is no direct national family-related social policy, only indirect programs. At times, Canada's collection of programs has had aspects of both of the above approaches. The 1944 Family Allowance, for example, tended towards an investing in children approach. Recently we have moved further towards a family responsibility approach, whereby policies such as the National Family Benefit emphasize incentives to get parents working. Today, Canada can be squarely placed within the individual responsibility model.

Child-related income security benefits have four main purposes:

- *To deal with child poverty by providing a minimum income.* The labour market does not differentiate wages according to family size so this has always disadvantaged households with children. The first purpose is to supplement the income of lower-income families with children and help to fill the gap between wages and the poverty line.

- *To generate horizontal equity for households with children to have income equal to those without children.* **Horizontal equity** is based on the recognition that parents have heavier financial demands than childless households and single persons with the same income.

- *To act as an economic stimulus by putting money in the hands of those most likely to spend it.* The idea behind economic stimulus is that putting more money in the hands of parents who will spend it helps to stimulate consumer demand. This was one of the main purposes of the 1944 Family Allowance program. The idea was to give every mother a monthly cheque, which she would spend on necessities for her child or children, thereby stimulating the post-war economy.

- *To recognize parents as contributing to the future of society.* The children of today are the future leaders and workers of tomorrow, and families with children contribute something to society that people without children do not. Parental recognition is an acknowledgment by society of the contribution parents make to society in terms of raising future citizens, workers and taxpayers. It is a way of assisting all parents.

At various times, Canadian governments have implemented programs that attempt to address one or more of the above purposes. An approach that emphasizes investing in Canada's children would involve a set of programs that address all of the above purposes simultaneously. In this regard, Canadian policies have been lacking. In the beginning, programs were intended to create economic stimulus, such as with the 1944 Family Allowance. Now, child poverty is increasingly being addressed with employment incentives and income security policies targeted at poor families.

HISTORY OF BENEFITS FOR FAMILIES WITH CHILDREN

The current system of income security benefits directed specifically at children has had a long history in Canada. Indeed, the Family Allowance in 1944 was the first universal income security program, prior to being changed to an income-based program in 1978. The overall history can be divided into four phases.

• Phase 1: Recognition of Family Needs, 1918-40

In the 1700s and early 1800s, children were treated harshly under the Common Law of England. Early legislation, such as the *Orphans Act* in 1799 and the *Apprentices and Minors Act* of 1874 gave town wardens the power to bind a child under the age of 14 as an apprentice or labourer. The *Indian Act* of 1876 demonstrated the colonizer's view of First Nations children and many were placed in residential schools administered by Christian churches with the overriding aim of assimilation.

Income support to families with children began in 1918 with the introduction of the **Child Tax Exemption** in personal income tax. The exemption provided income tax savings that increased with taxable income. The after-tax benefit was of greatest absolute benefit to those in the highest tax brackets. The exemption provided no benefits to families that did not owe income tax. Dual-earner couples with the same family income as single-earner couples generally pay less tax. This is due to the progressive nature of our income tax system and the fact that taxes are levied on individuals and not families. (This is a problem that has never been adequately addressed and remains with us to this day.)

Concern about widowed mothers with small children after World War I led to Mothers' Allowance, first in Manitoba in 1916, in Saskatchewan in 1917, and in Ontario and B.C. in 1920. This provided a needs-tested monthly income support. All provinces followed suit within the next decade. Eligibility requirements varied between provinces, but one element remained steadfast – any mother deemed to be of bad character was not eligible, which was a throwback to the Poor Law concerns of distinguishing between the deserving and undeserving poor. The term "pension" was demanded from women's groups that wanted to avoid the stigmatizing effects of "assistance." They also demanded, but did not obtain, a non-discretionary pension.

• Phase 2: Universal Benefits, 1941-74

The *Family Allowance Act* of 1944 introduced the universal **Family Allowance (FA),** providing benefits to all Canadian families with dependent children. The FA was also popularly known as the "baby bonus." As noted above, it was the first universal income security scheme. The FA provided a monthly payment of $5.94 to the mother of every child under the age of 16 (changed to the age of 18 in 1973). If of school age, the child had to be attending school. The stated purpose of the plan was to assure children of their basic needs and to maintain purchasing power in the post-war era.

CONVENTION ON THE RIGHTS OF THE CHILD

Since its adoption in 1989, the Convention on the Rights of the Child has been ratified more quickly and by more governments (all except Somalia and the U.S.) than any other human rights instrument. Its basic premise is that children (below the age of 18) are born with fundamental freedoms and the inherent rights of all human beings.

Family allowance office in PEI, where FA was first introduced (National Archives/CA5315).

CONSUMER PRICE INDEX (CPI)

The Consumer Price Index (CPI) is an indicator of the consumer prices in Canada. It is calculated, on a monthly basis, using the cost of a fixed "basket" of commodities purchased by a typical Canadian consumer during a given month. The CPI is a widely used indicator of inflation (or deflation) and indicates the changing purchasing power of money in Canada.

The Family Allowance provision was introduced one year after the Marsh Report, which indicated that an allowance for the parents of children was central to a social security system. The majority of social workers and the Canadian Association of Social Workers strongly supported the plan. Interestingly, Charlotte Whitton, a leading social worker and director of the Canadian Welfare Council at the time, deemed the plan wasteful as both poor and wealthy families benefitted. She believed that any such program should target the most needy with social utilities, such as health and housing, rather than cash. Perhaps surprisingly, many trade unions also tended to oppose the benefit, seeing it as a substitute for adequate wages.

Historians continue to debate why the Mackenzie King Liberal government at the time introduced a universal children's benefit. Several factors have been suggested: (1) a desire to maintain purchasing power in the economy as a whole, (2) as an alternative to the wage freeze that was in place at the time, (3) to stave off the threat from the leftist Co-operative Commonwealth Federation (CCF) Party that was endorsing such a program and (4) to win Liberal support in Quebec where the conscription issue was problematic.

The Family Allowance remained completely universal until 1973 when various reforms made it taxable income in the hands of the recipients. In the 1973 Act, the benefit was made taxable and was indexed to the **Consumer Price Index (CPI)**. Why make the benefit taxable? The argument was that people with more income pay higher marginal tax rates and keep less of the benefit, which is the underlying idea behind a progressive income tax system. Reforms in 1989 increased the tax rate with a clawback, and the Family Allowance met its ultimate demise in 1993.

• Phase 3: Erosion and Growing Poverty, 1975-90

Beginning in 1978, Finance Minister Jean Chrétien announced a merging of social security programs and income tax provisions. The Liberal government introduced the **Refundable Child Tax Credit** as a way to target families in need of government assistance. Upon the creation of the Child Tax Credit, FA benefits were reduced from an average of $25.68 per month (which would have increased to $28 with indexing) to an average of $20 per month. The stated goal of the benefit was to help families meet the costs of raising children. It was income tested and varied according to the number of children in a family.

Unlike universal benefits, the use of the tax system to target low-income families was a fundamental shift in thinking from an institutional view of social welfare to a residual view. It was also the first time that the tax system was used to redistribute income.

The tax credit provided the maximum benefit to low-income families, a declining amount to middle-income families and no benefit to wealthy families. It provided a credit in the income tax account with the federal government. The whole credit was payable to families with a net income below a certain threshold. The credit was gradually reduced until the family's income reached the national average, at which point it was reduced to zero. If the family's tax credit was more than the amount they owed in taxes, the difference was paid in the form of a monthly cheque. This is what is meant by the term "refundable" – the tax credit is paid out if the taxpayer does not owe income tax. Benefits paid in this way are called "tax expenditures." They are made up of foregone taxes or taxes that go uncollected. In the case of a tax credit, it can become a reverse tax. This was the first major program of its type in the field of income security. Previously, it was used in the investment arena, in which governments would use it to induce certain types of investment behaviour and support for various industries.

The **Child Care Expense Deduction** was first introduced in 1971 and was originally intended for one-parent families. It was designed to offset the incremental costs of child rearing for parents in the labour force. When first introduced, this deduction was limited to $2,000 per child under the age of 14, subject to a maximum of $8,000 per family. Statistics from Revenue Canada for the 1996 tax year indicate that this deduction was being used by about 760,000 claimants, with about $2 billion in total deductions in 1996.

In 1986, the FA benefit, which still existed in its reduced form, was "partially de-indexed," meaning that there were no increases in benefit levels until inflation reached 3 percent. This meant the value of the FA would lessen over time. In 1989, benefit clawbacks were introduced. The clawback came in the form of a higher tax rate for FA benefits. This meant that higher income earners would pay back their FA. This marked the end of FA as a universal program in all but name and eventually led to the elimination of the Family Allowance in 1993 – and, many argued, to the end of universality as a principle of Canadian social security.

• Phase 4: Targeting Poverty and Work Incentives, 1991-Present

The idea of the welfare wall entered the government lexicon during this period. The term **welfare wall** refers to the disincentives that hinder the move from welfare to work because of financial and other supports that are lost when families accept employment.

In 1993, the Government of Canada consolidated its child tax credits and the Family Allowance into a single **Child Tax Benefit (CTB)** that provided a monthly payment based on the number of children and the level of family income. In addition to a basic benefit, the Child Tax Benefit included a **Working Income Supplement (WIS)** to supplement the earnings of working poor families.

The CTB included a supplement of $213 per year for each child in a family who was under the age of seven. The maximum basic benefit was $1,020 per child per year, plus an additional $75 for the third child and each subsequent child in a family. The maximum basic benefit was payable to all families with annual incomes of less than $25,921. The benefit was reduced at a rate of 5 percent of family net income in excess of $25,921 for families with two or more children, and at a rate of 2.5 for families with one child. Families with one or two children no longer received basic benefits once the net family income exceeded $67,000.

TAX BENEFIT CASUALTIES

Check out an interesting article by well-known social policy analyst Richard Shillington entitled "Two Casualties of The Child Tax Benefit: Truth and The Poor" published by *Policy Options* (November 2000).

It is available online in the Back Issues section at:
http://www.irpp.org/po

.

The maximum Child Tax Benefit per child per year in 1994 was broken down as follows:

- Basic benefit: $1,020

- Supplement for third and each additional child: $75

- Supplement for children under age seven: $213

- Working Income Supplement: $500

The WIS gave an additional benefit to those working at low-income levels. This benefit was not available to unemployed parents. The benefits were paid out at the rate of 8 percent of all earnings. Families began to receive benefits from the WIS once their earnings exceeded $3,750. A maximum annual benefit of $500 was provided for families with annual incomes between $10,000 and $20,921, regardless of the number of children in the family. The WIS was reduced at a rate of 10 percent of family net income in excess of $20,921, with a cease in benefits when income reached $25,921.

In 1998 a new initiative called the **Canada Child Tax Benefit (CCTB)** was introduced. The CCTB has two main elements: a Canada Child Tax Benefit (CCTB) basic benefit and the **National Child Benefit Supplement (NCBS)**. The NCBS is an additional tax credit that adds to the CCTB. The NCBS is the federal contribution to the CCTB. It provides low-income families with additional child benefits on top of the basic benefit. The terminology is confusing as the federal government, at times, refers to the overall program (CCTB and NCBS) as the National Child Benefit, instead of the Canada Child Tax Benefit (see http://www.nationalchildbenefit.ca). Finance Canada refers to the overall program as the CCTB.

Since 1998, the federal investment in the CCTB has risen dramatically. It is the first joint federal/provincial/territorial initiative under the Social Union Agreement, and the first national social welfare program since Medicare and the Canada Pension Plan in the 1960s. The 2000 federal budget announced that CCTB funding would automatically rise with inflation.

The critics contend that the reform discriminates against welfare families in particular because they will see no net increase in their child benefits, and only the working poor and other low-income families (such as families not on welfare or those collecting Employment Insurance) will enjoy an improvement in benefits.

THE CURRENT SYSTEM: NATIONAL CHILD BENEFIT

By the end of 1997, there was a growing concern that many Canadian children did not have the opportunity for a healthy start to life and the support to maintain a healthy, happy and educated future. This growing consensus recognized that the previous child benefit system was lacking. As a result, Canada's First Ministers and their governments examined various ways to improve assistance to children of low-income families.

• Canada Child Tax Benefit (CCTB) Configuration

The program is currently the primary mechanism for addressing child and family low income and poverty in Canada. It attempts to reduce overlap between provinces and promote labour market attachment by ensuring that families will always be better off as a result of working.

The CCTB has three stated objectives. The objectives are to

1. prevent and reduce the depth of child poverty,

2. promote attachment to the labour market by ensuring that families will always be better off as a result of working and

3. reduce overlap and duplication by harmonizing program objectives and benefits and simplifying administration.

With these objectives, the CCTB aims to help low-income families by increasing federal benefits for families with children. The program provides a **tax credit** to those who qualify based on an income test. A tax credit is an amount deducted directly from income tax otherwise payable. Examples of tax credits include the disability tax credit and the married credit for individuals, and the scientific research and experimental development investment tax credit for corporations. This is different from a **tax deduction**, which is an amount deducted from total income to arrive at taxable income. Child care expenses and capital cost allowances are tax deductions. Tax deductions are worth more to people with higher incomes as they are in a higher marginal tax bracket.

The CCTB basic benefit provides a platform of child benefits to all low- and middle-income families with children. More than 80 percent of Canadian families with children receive this basic benefit. In 2002, families with a net income under the threshold of $32,960 received a tax credit base benefit of $1,151 per child, with additional amounts for children under age seven and for families with more than two children.

Some families are eligible for an additional benefit. The NCBS provides low-income families with additional child benefits on top of the basic benefit. The supplement is targeted at low-income families, and provided over $1,000 per child for families with a net income under the $22,397 threshold in 2002. It is reduced with income above the threshold, and is fully phased out when family net income exceeds $32,000. Some of the above amounts incorporate changes that took effect in 2001. At that time, the supplement was increased from the previous year by a substantial 28.4 percent. The basic benefit was increased by a mere 1.2 percent, not even meeting the cost of living. As a result, for the first time since the inception of the NCBS, the amount of the supplement exceeded the amount of the base benefit.

At the time, the federal government stated that the NCBS was designed to address the welfare wall phenomenon. As mentioned, for families receiving Social Assistance, it is difficult to make the transition from welfare to work without losing financial and other supports. For example, many low-income working families may not be eligible for benefits and services, such as the prescription drug coverage that is provided through Social Assistance for families on welfare. As such, these

Anti-poverty rally in Halifax in 2002 (CP PHOTO/*Halifax Daily News*/Scott Dunlop).

A SUMMARY OF THE FEDERAL HISTORY OF CHILD BENEFITS IN CANADA

1918. Child Tax Exemption: This exemption provided income tax savings that increased as taxable income increased. It provided no benefits to families that did not owe income tax.

1944. Family Allowance (FA): This benefit was provided to all Canadian families with dependent children.

1973. The benefit levels of the Family Allowance were tripled, indexed to the cost of living and made taxable.

1978. Refundable Child Tax Credit: This more targeted and income-tested approach to child benefits provided the maximum benefit to low-income families, a declining amount to middle-income families and no benefit to upper-income families.

1993. Child Tax Benefit (CTB): This benefit consolidated child tax credits and the Family Allowance into a monthly payment based on the number of children and level of family income.

1993. Working Income Supplement (WIS): This additional benefit was provided to supplement the earnings of low-income working families with children. Federal child benefits in 1993 totalled $5.1 billion.

1998. National Child Benefit Supplement (NCBS): The NCB Supplement replaced the Working Income Supplement and was provided to all low-income families as part of the re-named Canada Child Tax Benefit (CCTB). As its initial contribution to the National Child Benefit initiative, the Government of Canada committed to an additional $850 million per year for the NCB Supplement. This was on top of the $5.1 billion per year that was already provided through the CCTB.

The 1998, 1999 and 2000 federal budgets and the October 2000 Economic Statement and Budget Update provided additional investments in the NCB Supplement and the CCTB basic benefit. As a result, the Government of Canada's investment in the CCTB was $7.7 billion in 2001-02, including an investment of $2.5 billion in the NCB Supplement.

The 2000 federal budget committed to continue investing in the CCTB by restoring full indexation of benefit levels and eligibility thresholds to protect their value against inflation.

Source: Federal, Provincial and Territorial Ministers Responsible for Social Services, *National Child Benefit Progress Report* (Ottawa, 2002), p.11. Available at http://www.nationalchildbenefit.ca/ncb/NCB-2003/ncb-report2002_e.pdf

barriers create the welfare wall, preventing some families from leaving Social Assistance and making it difficult for low-income working families to obtain necessary support for their children.

The NCBS attempts to address the problem of the welfare wall by augmenting family income only for low-income families not on welfare (such as the working poor and low-income families drawing from Employment Insurance). It provides no increases for families on welfare. The NCBS is designed to promote labour force participation by funding significant income supplements for low-income working families, and supports and services, such as child care and extended health benefits. In essence, it encourages and supports parents who enter and stay in the workforce.

Though the NCBS is administered through the tax system (individuals must file a tax return to apply), according to the federal governments it is fundamentally an anti-poverty program rather than a tax provision. While it is a federal tax provision, as noted above, it was designed as a joint initiative with provincial and territorial governments. The federal and provincial governments, with the exception of Quebec, support the NCBS.

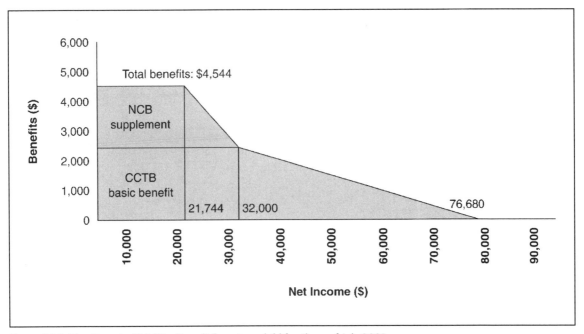

Figure 10.2: The Canada Child Tax Benefit for a two-child family as of July 2001.
Source: Federal, Provincial and Territorial Ministers Responsible for Social Services, *National Child Benefit Progress Report* (Ottawa, 2002).

Until 2002, the CCTB was not indexed. **Indexation** is an arrangement in which periodic adjustments are made to benefits based on changes in an index of some kind, most often the Consumer Price Index (CPI). The lack of indexation of CCTB and NCBS benefits enabled the government to ignore increases in the cost of living and thereby reduce the benefit surreptitiously. Non-indexation of benefits has the effect of reducing the benefit each year by the amount of any increases in the Consumer Price Index (CPI). The benefit is now indexed to the CPI.

• Clawbacks and Drawbacks

In comparison to the basic benefit, the distinctive feature of the supplement is that, by agreement with the provinces and territories, there is an **NCBS clawback** for Social Assistance recipients. The money taken back by the provinces is then supposed to be used for other programs that benefit low-income persons. Only Newfoundland and New Brunswick have increased Social Assistance benefits using NCBS funds. In all other provinces and territories, the supplement is clawed back from Social Assistance recipients in different ways.

Ontario and Prince Edward Island treat the NCBS as non-exempt income and reduce Social Assistance by the full amount. Other provinces, such as Nova Scotia and Manitoba, initially treated the NCBS as non-exempt income, but have since allowed families to keep the benefit while cutting back in other areas. In the case of Nova Scotia, families are worse off, as they have lost other, more generous, provincial allowances. More than anything, this treatment has allowed provinces to publicly

Table 10.4: Federal Child Benefit Parameters, 2002

	1996	1999	2002	2004
Base Benefit	**CTB**		**CCTB**	
Benefit per child	$1,020	$1,020	$1,151	$1,195
Supplement for third and each additional child	$75	$75	$80	$83
Supplement for children under age seven	$213	$213	$228	$237
Threshold	$25,921	$25,921	$32,960	$35,000
Benefit reduction rate				
One child	2.50%	2.50%	2.50%	2.00%
Two or more children	5.00%	5.00%	5.00%	4.00%

Supplement	**WIS**	**NCB Supplement**		
First child	8% of employment income above $3,750, up to a maximum of $500	$785	$1,293	$1,342
Second child		$585	$1,087	$1,128
Each additional child		$510	$1,009	$1,048
Threshold	$20,921	$20,921	$22,397	$23,256
Supplement reduction rate				
One child	10.00%	11.50%	12.20%	11.40%
Two children	10.00%	20.00%	22.50%	21.00%
Three or more children	10.00%	27.50%	32.10%	30.00%

Source: Finance Canada, *Tax Expenditures and Evaluations* (2002). Retrieved from: http://www.fin.gc.ca/taxexp/2002/taxexp02_4e.htm on October 26, 2002.

state that they are now allowing welfare families to keep the NCBS, but, in fact, no extra benefits are being paid. A few other provinces have since allowed some families on welfare to keep a fraction of the supplement. For example, Quebec no longer deducts annual increases to the supplement from the Family Allowance. According to a reinvestment agreement, the provinces that claw back the NCBS must use the money for provincially designed and delivered programs and services for families with children, particularly low-income families.

While the clawback is the issue that receives the most attention, there are other critical issues to consider when examining the effects of the CCTB, and the NCBS in particular. Two critical issues negatively influence the effectiveness of the CCTB: the way it defines a family and the use of net income as opposed to gross income in calculating benefits.

First, the CCTB calculation of benefit is based on net family income as reported on the income tax form. This is a compelling incentive not to report oneself as part of a couple on the tax form. In the case of a single mother, the tax rule stipulates that if she shares a dwelling with a person of the opposite sex for more than 12 months, then her CCTB could be substantially reduced.

Second, basing the benefit calculation on net income, and not gross income, has negative consequences for low-incomes families. Many tax deductions exist that can lower the net income or taxable income of middle- and high-income earners. These include Registered Retirement Savings Plans (RRSPs), child care expenses, professional dues, employment expenses, interest expenses, investment losses and even various tax shelters and investment funds. Low-income families are less likely to make these deductions. Basing the CCTB benefit calculation on net income, or income after these deductions, enables upper-income families to obtain the benefit, and may even mean that borderline eligible families do not receive benefits.

POLICY IMPACTS ON POVERTY

Many critics believe the NCBS will not eliminate poverty because it is clawed back from recipients of Social Assistance (the CCTB is not clawed back). The result, argue the critics, is that the majority of single mothers, who are most in need of the benefit, are denied the supplement. As well, there is no evidence that programs are improved by the reinvestment of funds in the provinces that take back benefits from Social Assistance. Indeed, many view the clawback of the NCBS as more of a discriminatory denial of necessary benefits than a mechanism to address the difficulties of the transition to work.

Supporters of the program point out that the benefit simply levels the playing field by providing benefits to those who are working. Prior to the NCBS, parents on welfare were reluctant to take a job because it would lead to the loss of prescription drug and other benefits for their children. Supporters of the program argue that the process of determining eligibility is superior with the CCTB and the NCBS. Eligibility is determined through an income test as reported on the income tax return rather than through an intrusive needs test as used by welfare. The supporters believe that the chance of improving benefits under an income-tested program with wide public appeal is far superior to obtaining increases in welfare benefits.

The **National Council of Welfare**, a citizens' advisory body on matters of concern to low-income Canadians, is on the other side of the debate. A 1998 report entitled *Child Benefits: Kids Are Still Hungry* estimated that, of the more than a million single-parent families in Canada, only 17 percent would receive the NCB Supplement, as compared to 59 percent of two-parent families. The remainder of the single-parent families – 83 percent – would not benefit from the supplement at all. In 1997, families headed by single mothers comprised 67 percent of families in receipt of Social Assistance (388,426 families), whereas families headed by single fathers comprised only 6.4 percent (37,374 families) and couples with children comprised 26.6 percent (157,675 families). The report concluded that the clawback was largely applied to single mothers. The Council argues that, despite the fact that women on Social Assistance may be most in need and most unable to pay for housing and related expenses, they were excluded from the federal government's only initiative to address child/family poverty.

CHILD BENEFITS: THE KIDS ARE STILL HUNGRY

The National Council of Welfare applauds the federal government for providing additional financial support to families with children but at the same time they believe that the government should not deny the additional income to roughly half a million poor families with children who are on welfare. This, the Council states, denies families headed by single-parent mothers who face the highest risk of poverty of any family type year after year. Most of these families are effectively cut off from the extra money provided by the federal government.

Available on-line at: http://www.ncwcnbes.net/htmdocument/reportchild/repchild.htm)

REFERENCES

* Battle, K., and Michael Mendelson. 1997. *Child Benefit Reform in Canada: An Evaluative Framework and Future Directions.* Ottawa: Caledon Institute. Retrieved from: http://www.caledoninst.org/cbr-toc.htm on November 11, 2002.

* Bradbury, B., and M. Jantti (UNICEF). 1999. *Child Poverty across Industrialized Nations.* Italy: UNICEF.

* Kazemipur, A., and S. Halli. 2001. The changing colour of poverty in Canada. *Canadian Review of Sociology and Anthropology,* Vol. 38, No. 2, pp. 217-238.

* National Council of Welfare. 1998. *Child Benefits: Kids Are Still Hungry.* Ottawa: National Council of Welfare.

* Ross, David, Katherine Scott, and Mark Kelly. 1996. *Child Poverty: What are the Consequences?* Ottawa: Canadian Council on Social Development.

* Schellenberg, Grant, and David P. Ross. 1996. *Left Poor by the Market: A Look at Family Poverty and Earnings.* Ottawa: Canadian Council on Social Development. Available at: http://www.ccsd.ca/es_left.htm

* Statistics Canada. CANSIM II, Table 202-0802 and Catalogue No. 75-202-XIE. Retrieved from: http://www.statcan.ca/english/Pgdb/famil41a.htm on Dec. 23, 2002.

* Unicef. 2000. *A League Table of Child Poverty in Rich Nations,* Innocenti Report Card #1. Florence, Italy: Innocenti Research Centre. http://www.unicef-icdc.org.

* United Nations. 2002. *The UN Special Session on Children: Putting Promises into Action.* Available at: http://www.campaign2000.ca/rc/unsscMAY02statusreport.pdf

The Caledon Institute (http://www.caledoninst.org) and its president, Ken Battle, believe that the NCBS should not be passed through to families on Social Assistance. They believe that any successful anti-poverty strategy must be based on a diverse range of social programs that have broad appeal and acceptance. They see the lack of public response to the severe cuts to welfare as an indication that welfare programs do not have public support. Therefore, the Caledon Institute argues that replacing child benefits in the welfare system with a broad, income tax-based, non-stigmatizing system of benefits is the first step in building an acceptable anti-poverty program.

In their report, *Child Benefit Reform in Canada: An Evaluative Framework and Future Directions* (1997), Ken Battle and Michael Mendelson even say that the argument against the clawback is naive. They argue that the provinces know the other income of welfare recipients, and generally, with the current climate of cutbacks, it is unlikely that many provinces would have actually passed the extra child benefits through (see http://www.caledoninst.org/cbr-toc.htm, Chapter 7).

CONCLUSION

In 1992, Canada ranked first among all countries in the world on a composite **Human Development Index** (created by the United Nations Development Programme) that combined life expectancy, educational attainment and standard of living. Canada has recently dropped on this list primarily due to child poverty and single-mother poverty levels. In 2002, Canada ranked third behind Norway and Sweden. Recent statistics show that Canada is one of five industrialized nations with child poverty rates of more than 10 percent (Ross, Scott and Kelly 1996). That translates into one in six, or 1,100,000 Canadian children who live in families that are below the LICO. The government in Canada has not overlooked this.

The CCTB and NCBS were expressly directed at addressing the low-income situations of families. The poverty levels of children is inextricably linked with the incomes of their parents or guardians. Several factors appear to be keeping the child poverty rate high. First, the number of single mothers is increasing, and this family type is the most likely to live in poverty. It is clear that in today's economy most families require the income of two people. Second, increasing numbers of working poor translate into more children living in poverty. Finally, decreased levels of income security benefits, such as Social Assistance in Ontario, Alberta and B.C, and difficult eligibility criteria for Employment Insurance, have lowered the incomes of the poor in Canada.

Without a comprehensive and integrated approach to family income policy, it is unlikely that this situation will change. Canada must see that helping children is an investment in the future. Social workers frequently see the effects of poverty on children and families, and clearly the long-term costs far outweigh the investment that can be made today.

CHAPTER 10: CHILDREN AND FAMILIES IN POVERTY

Discussion Questions

1. What is the current poverty situation of Canada's families and children?
2. What is market poverty and what are its basic causes?
3. What are the two general approaches to children's social welfare? What approach most closely resembles the approach followed by the Canadian government?
4. There has been a new reframing of the issue of poverty. What is this new reframing and how has it impacted the government's response to poverty and the explanations of poverty?
5. Explain the four purposes of child-related income security.
6. List and describe four key changes that took place over the history of income security for children in Canada.
7. What federal programs currently provide income security for Canadian families with children? What are two of the criticisms of the programs as they pertain to families on Social Assistance?
8. What is the welfare wall?

Websites

- **National Child Benefit website**
  http://www.nationalchildbenefit.ca/
  A federal government website providing the government's perspective on the success of the NCBS.

- **The Canada Customs and Revenue Agency (CCRA)**
  http://www.ccra-adrc.gc.ca/benefits/menu-e.html
  This site has information about the Canada Child Tax Benefit (CCTB). The GST/HST (goods and services tax/harmonized sales tax) credit is a tax-free payment to help individuals and families offset the cost of the GST/HST and Children's Special Allowances.

- **The Progress of Canada's Children**
  http://www.ccsd.ca/pubs/2002/pcc02/index.htm
  Every year the Canadian Council on Social Development produces the Progress of Canada's Children report, presenting a portrait of family life and the social, educational, physical and economic security of children.

- **Child Poverty Overview**
  http://www.policy.ca/archive/20001127.php3
  An overview of child poverty presented by author Steven Hick.

- **Child Rights Information Network**
  http://www.crin.org
  The Child Rights Information Network (CRIN) is a global network that disseminates information about the Convention on the Rights of the Child and child rights among non-governmental organizations (NGOs), United Nations agencies, inter-governmental organizations (IGOs), educational institutions and other child rights experts.

Key Concepts

- Campaign 2000
- Poverty gap
- Market poverty
- Family responsibility approach
- Investing in children approach
- Horizontal equity
- Child Tax Exemption
- Family Allowance (FA)
- Refundable Child Tax Credit
- Child Care Expense Deduction
- Welfare wall
- Child Tax Benefit (CTB)
- Working Income Supplement (WIS)
- Canada Child Tax Benefit (CCTB)
- National Child Benefit Supplement (NCBS)
- Tax credit
- Tax deduction
- Indexation
- NCBS clawback
- National Council of Welfare
- Human Development Index

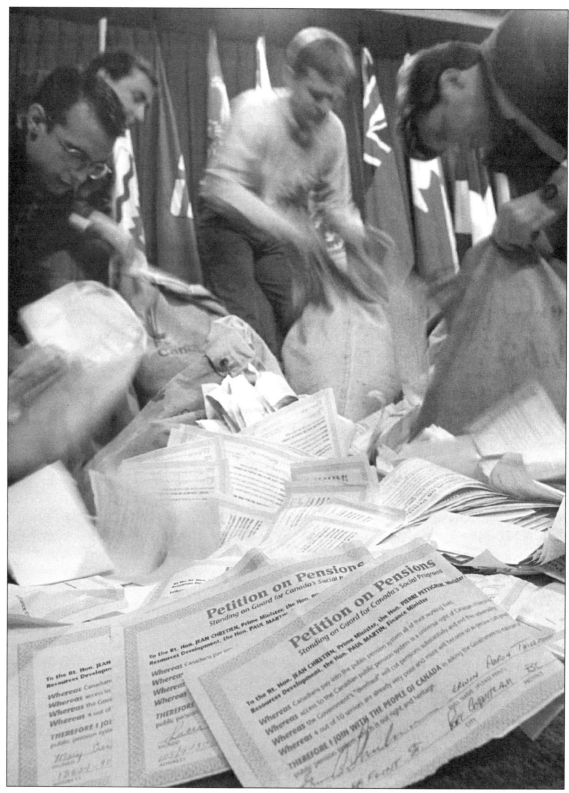

Members of the Council of Canadians gather up petitions opposing cuts to the Canada Pension Plan. They delivered the more than half a million petitions to the office of the then Finance Minister (now Prime Minister) Paul Martin (CP PHOTO/1997/Tom Hanson).

11

The Elderly and Retired

Pensions, Health Care and an Ageing Population

Although income security for the retired and elderly in Canada expanded rapidly in the 1950s and 1960s, leading to a large reduction in old age poverty, the current system may be strained over the next 35 years by the doubling of the percentage of persons over age 65. In particular, the challenge of combating old age poverty for elderly unattached women, people with disabilities and Aboriginal Peoples still remains. Continuing vigilance will be needed if we are to maintain recent gains and resolve these outstanding concerns.

A Canadian born in 1960 can expect to live 20 years longer than a Canadian who was born in 1900. Birth rates have been declining, and a growing proportion of the population is over 65. By the year 2031, approximately 20 percent of Canada's population – one in five – will be seniors. These facts have important consequences for Canadian society and income security programs. What are the needs of these older Canadians? How will they be taken care of? What are their income security needs?

Good health and financial security help to ease the changes that ageing and retirement require. Factors such as forced retirement, ill health and lack of money all contribute to lessened satisfaction with this period of life. Canada's income security system for the elderly and retired consists of three main "pillars" or components: basic minimum income allowances such as Old Age Security, Guaranteed Income Supplements and Spouse's Allowance; social insurance benefits such as the Canada/Quebec Pension Plan; and private pensions and publicly supported and regulated private savings plans such as Registered Retirement Savings Plans (RRSPs).

Canada's income security programs have had significant impacts on low income rates for the elderly and retired. The percent of elderly living below the Statistics Canada Low Income Cut-off (LICO) before tax fell from 29.3 percent in 1982, to 21.1 percent in 1990, to 16.8 percent in 2001. For men, the rate between 1992 and 2001 fell from 12.8 to 11.1 percent (Statistics Canada, *The Daily*, Tuesday, June 25, 2003).

Nevertheless, Canadians still have much to learn about the special issues of ageing. This chapter looks at the various income security programs that are currently in place for old age and retirement with a view to maintaining and improving the system for the challenging years that lie ahead.

"Old age pensions have been a recurring issue in Canadian politics since the beginning of the twentieth century and now have more government resources devoted to them than to any other single public program."

— Kenneth Bryden, 1974, author of *Old Age Pensions and Policy-Making in Canada*

THE AGEING POPULATION

The percentage of persons over age 65 will almost double over the next 35 years – from 12 percent today to 23 percent by the year 2030. As the "baby boomers" (born between 1946 and 1965) age, the senior population is expected to reach 6.7 million in 2021 and 9.2 million in 2041 (nearly one in four Canadians). The fastest growth is occurring among those 85 years of age or older. In 2001, over 430,000 Canadians were 85 years of age or older – more than twice as many as in 1981. The proportion of Canadians aged 85 or older is expected to grow to 1.6 million in 2041 (Health Canada 2002, 3).

A number of social changes have affected the needs and composition of the retired population in Canada. These include

- improvement in health care and extension of life expectancy,
- long-term decline in the birth rate,
- establishment of retirement age and
- establishment of the value that the elderly deserve a rest.

The first change has been the improvement in health care, which has resulted in a large extension of life expectancy. In 1997, life expectancy for Canadians was 75.8 years for men and 81.4 years for women. Life expectancy is expected to continue to grow, although more slowly, reaching 81 years for men and 86 years for women in 2041. This will continue to contribute to an increase in the number of elderly people in Canada (Health Canada 2002, 5).

The second change is the long-term decline in the birth rate. In 1997, Canada's fertility rate reached a record low at 1,552 births per 1,000 women aged 15-49. It now stands at less than half of the peak reached in 1959, when there were 3,935 births per 1,000 women. The current fertility rate of 1.5 children per woman is expected to remain relatively

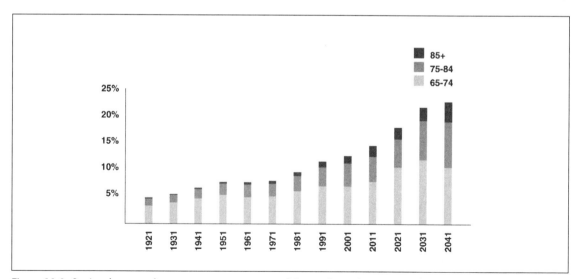

Figure 11.1: Seniors by age sub-groups, as a percentage of the total population, Canada, 1921-2041.
Source: Statistics Canada, *Population projections for 2001, 2006, 2011, 2016, 2021 and 2026* (Ottawa: Statistics Canada, July 1, 2002).

constant in the near future (Health Canada 2002, 4). Combined with the extension of life expectancy, this has resulted in an increase in the proportion, or the relative size, of the older population. These trends are expected to increase for several decades. Furthermore, female life expectancy is higher than that of males – women are living longer, and this too has implications for the income security system.

Third, a retirement age to leave the labour force was established in the age of industrialization. Initially, it was set at 70 years of age, and now it is set at 65. The concept of retiring from paid employment at an elderly age came about because people eventually reach an age when their level of productivity does not sufficiently maintain the demand for their labour. Whereas previously, with extended families, the elderly relied on their family for support, industrialization also changed the traditional nature of the family.

Finally, Canadian society realized that, when a person's productivity becomes insufficient, they should be given a phase in their lives in which they can rest. This notion is also tied to the concern that older workers should make way for the next generation of young and more productive workers.

All of these social changes have significant implications within Canada's income security system. By 2030, for each person receiving income security benefits, there will only be three working Canadians to support these benefits, compared to the five of today. As the proportion of retired Canadians receiving benefits keeps increasing, economic expenditures will continue to rise steadily.

WOMEN AND OLD AGE

Due to their longer life expectancy, women form the majority of the Canadian elderly population. In 2001, women comprised 56 percent of the elderly, and their proportion increases with age. In 2001, women made up 60 percent of seniors aged 75-84, and 70 percent of seniors aged 85 or older (Health Canada 2002, 6).

The effects of a variety of factors inhibit women from amassing adequate resources to support their later life and retirement. The present economic trends of downsizing, enforcing involuntary retirement and the growth in the service sector (where many women work) mean fewer benefits and pension coverage for many workers, particularly women. Due to factors listed below, many elderly and retired women find themselves living with low income and insufficient income security.

- The labour force itself is ageing, and a large proportion of women workers are aged 45-64; thus there are sizeable numbers of women "pre-retirees." There has been a longstanding trend for men to take early retirement, and many Canadian women retire at ages 60-62. Women work in lower paying occupations and sectors, such as community, business and personal services and trade. Women earn approximately 65 percent of male earnings (full-time workers). Contrasted with 10 percent of men, 28 percent of women work part-time.

THE CHALLENGE OF AGEING POPULATIONS

Around the world, headlines are warning that when the "baby boom" generation starts retiring in earnest, the labour force will shrink and economic growth and material well-being will be threatened.

To limit the impact, some policy analysts believe that innovative policies are needed to allow people to spread work across the full span of their lives — people can increase their leisure time in their early years and spend more time working and learning in their later years.

- Many women are unattached or single in old age – the risk of widowhood increases with age; 30 percent of Canadian women are widowed at age 65 and 50 percent by age 75. Older men are nine times more likely to remarry than older women. Thus, more women grow older alone, and many find themselves living below the Low Income Cut-off (LICO). The rate for unattached women aged 65 or over living below LICO in 2001 was 45.6 percent (Statistics Canada 2002).

- Fewer women are covered by their employer's pension plans than men, and many such plans have no survivor's benefits. Compared with 52 percent for men, 70 percent of the income of women aged 65 and over is from government transfers. Of persons collecting C/QPP retirement benefits (in September of 1995), women averaged $274 per month while men averaged $477 per month.

ELDERLY POVERTY RATES

The rate of low income among the elderly in Canada has declined noticeably since 1980. In 1982, 17.5 percent of seniors had after-tax incomes below Statistics Canada's Low Income Cut-off line (LICO). The rate had fallen to 7.3 percent by 2001 (Statistics Canada 2002). Low-income rates for Canadian seniors are among the lowest in all countries studied by the Organization for Economic Co-operation and Development (OECD) (OECD 2001).

The incidence of low income has fallen sharply among both senior women and senior men in the past decade and a half. This is due primarily to the effect of income security transfers. In 2001, the after-tax below LICO rate was 7.3 percent, compared to a before-tax rate of 16.8 percent. When measuring low income rates for the elderly population in

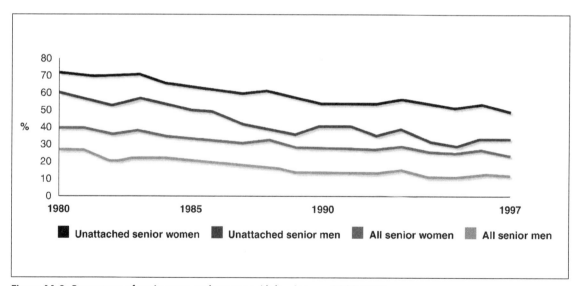

Figure 11.2: Percentage of senior men and women with low income 1980-1997.
Source: Compiled from Statistics Canada data.

Canada it is important to consider after-tax income. In 2001, elderly households received on average an estimated $19,900 in government transfers, accounting for 43 percent of their total income before taxes. According to Statistics Canada, the after-tax income of elderly households remained stable for the last decade, in part because of the high proportion of government transfers in their income. Nevertheless, there is a particularly wide gap in the likelihood of unattached senior women and unattached senior men having low incomes. In 2001, about half of these women (45.6 percent) lived in a low-income situation, compared with 33 percent of unattached senior men. The incidence of low income among both unattached senior women and men, however, has dropped sharply since the early 1980s. Among women, the figure fell from 70 to 45.6 percent between 1980 and 1997, while among men it dropped from 52 to 33 percent (Statistics Canada 2002).

Elderly poverty rates have decreased over the past few decades, largely due to the development of comprehensive income security programs for seniors. To a large extent, this has resulted from political pressure brought to bear by this powerful and growing lobby group.

HISTORY OF INCOME SECURITY FOR THE ELDERLY AND RETIRED

As the caring capacities of families shifted, pensions became a major issue in many industrializing countries. The elderly could no longer rely on an extended family support structure, as they once had within an agrarian society. Denmark led the way in 1891 with its means-tested plan and New Zealand followed in 1901. Social advocates and reform-minded politicians in Canada argued that the federal government should use its new power and financial capacities to extend the pension provisions that were currently offered only to war veterans.

In 1921, a minority government was elected federally for the first time in Canadian history, making it impossible to pass any pension legislation. The 1925 election saw similar results, and Prime Minister William Lyon Mackenzie King needed the support of the Progressive Party and the only two elected Labour members of Parliament – members James S. Woodsworth and Abraham A. Heaps. Woodsworth and Heaps, in cooperation with Progressive leader Robert Forke, presented Mackenzie King with a number of policy initiatives, including an Old Age Pension program. The prime minister agreed to pursue the reforms in return for the support of the two parties, thus ensuring his government would not fall. In 1926, Mackenzie King won a majority Liberal government and was able to undertake reforms. This led to the first major piece of income security legislation for the elderly – the *Old Age Pensions Act* of 1927.

The 1927 plan authorized the federal government to form agreements with the provinces to pay half of the costs of pensions paid under provincial legislation that met the requirements of the federal Act. Administration was to be entirely a provincial responsibility. The pension was not to be available to Aboriginal people, as defined by the *Indian Act*. The amount of the pension was set at $240 a year, subject to a means test. The pensioner was allowed to have a total income of $365 per year,

William Lyon Mackenzie King, 1935 (National Archives of Canada/C24309).

CHILD REARING DROP-OUT PROVISION (CRDO)

The amount of your CPP benefit is based on how long and how much you have contributed. Historically, this has negatively affected women who opt to stay at home and care for newborn children. Periods when they had no earnings or their earnings were low resulted in a lower benefit. The CPP now has a special provision to prevent this. Months of low or zero earnings spent caring for children under the age of seven are excluded from the calculation of a pension.

meeting what the government of the day determined to be an adequate income of $1 per day.

Kenneth Bryden, a CCF politician and professor of economics, wrote the definitive history of old age pensions (Bryden 1974). He attributes the emergence of public pension policy in Canada to two opposing forces: the social and economic needs of an emerging urban-industrial society and the influence of a deep-rooted set of cultural values, referred to as the market ethos. He argues that the struggle between these two forces – one demanding pensions and the other resisting – led to means-tested pensions in 1927, universal pensions in 1951 and contributory pensions in 1965.

The *Old Age Security* (OAS) and *Old Age Assistance Acts* of 1951 moved the government into universal pensions. The exclusion of Aboriginal people was dropped with these Acts. The OAS established a universal pension for those over 70, subject only to a 20-year residency requirement. The federal government funded and administered the program. The decision to institute a universal plan was made with some reluctance by the government, but any attempts to substitute a different design were resisted by seniors. The program remained universal until 1989. At the time, a special old age security tax was implemented to fund the program. The *Old Age Assistance Act*, on the other hand, was a provincially administered means-tested benefit with partial funding from the federal government.

The signing of the Dominion-Provincial Agreement on Old Age Pensions. Ottawa, May 18, 1928 (National Archives of Canada/C13233).

INCOME SECURITY FOR THE ELDERLY AND RETIRED

Canada's old age income security system balances public and private retirement benefits. It guarantees a minimum income for all seniors and allows Canadians to avoid serious disruptions in living standards upon retirement.

The two government-stated objectives of the retirement income system are: (1) to ensure that elderly people have sufficient income regardless of their pre-retirement income and (2) to maintain a reasonable relationship between working and retirement income to avoid drastic income reduction.

To accomplish these objectives, the government has devised a variety of income security measures that can be divided into three levels of income security for the retired and elderly:

- Level 1: Basic Minimum: Old Age Security, Guaranteed Income Supplement and Provincial/Territorial Supplements
- Level 2: Social Insurance: Public Pension Plans – Canada/Quebec Pension Plan (C/QPP)
- Level 3: Private Plans: Occupational Pensions and Private Savings

Total federal expenditures in 2002 for Canada's retirement income system were $25 billion for the OAS, GIS and SPA, up from $17 billion in 1990, and $26.4 billion for C/QPP, up from $14 billion in 1990, for a total federal cost of $51.4 billion (Health Canada 2002, 23). These programs account for the largest share of federal income security spending. Added to this are foregone tax revenues such as those diverted by RRSPs, which amounted to $16 billion in 2002. Given the changing demographics discussed above, this amount will increase in the future.

SENIORS CANADA ONLINE

A federal government web resource that provides single-window access to information and services that are relevant to seniors, their families, caregivers and supporting service organizations. Go to: http://www.seniors.gc.ca/index.jsp

"And if there's anything left over after we buy a coffee, we'll send him a thank-you note ..." (Yardley Jones/*Montreal Star*/National Archives/C145003).

WAR VETERANS PENSIONS AND ALLOWANCE

Veterans' Affairs Canada (VAC) administers the *Pension Act*. It provides pensions to those suffering from disabilities related to military service, either during peace or wartime. When a disability pensioner dies, the spouse/common-law partner will receive a Survivor's Pension. Surviving children may be eligible for Orphan's Benefits following a pensioner's death. In addition, an income-tested War Veterans Allowance is available for those in financial need. It is meant to increase a minimum income to meet basic needs. Eligibility is based on wartime service, age, health, income and residence.

- Level 1: Basic Minimum: Old Age Security, Guaranteed Income Supplement and Provincial/Territorial Supplements

The first level of income security for the retired and elderly comprises the following public programs:

- Old Age Security (OAS)
- Guaranteed Income Supplement (GIS)
- Allowance (previously the Spouse's Allowance)
- Provincial/Territorial Supplements

The **Old Age Security (OAS)** program provides a basic pension (adjusted for inflation) to virtually everyone over 65 years of age who has lived in Canada for a required length of time. It is a universal monetary benefit payable to Canadians over a specified age (some would argue that it is no longer universal due to the clawback for higher-income Canadians – see below). It is an income transfer program paid out of the general revenue of the federal government. The OAS program includes the income-tested **Guaranteed Income Supplement (GIS)**, which provides extra money to OAS recipients who have little or no other income, and the Allowance, which pays benefits to low-income spouses or partners of an OAS pensioner, or widows/widowers between the ages of 60 and 64. Annual OAS program expenditures were $25 billion in 2001-02 (Health Canada 2002, 23). This accounted for 2.3 percent of Gross Domestic Product (GDP).

As discussed above, the root of our public income security system for the elderly dates back to 1927 when the federal government introduced the *Old Age Pensions Act*. This early pension was a national means-tested program. In Canada, many of the elderly were not eligible for benefits

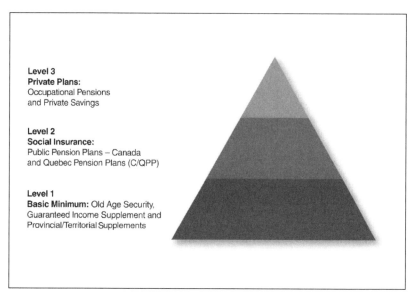

Figure 11.3: The three levels of income security for the retired and elderly. Level 1: Basic Minimum and Supplements; Level 2: Social Insurance; Level 3: Private Plans.

OLD-AGE INCOME SECURITY: 75 YEARS IN THE MAKING

- **1927:** The *Old Age Pensions Act* was enacted, permitting the federal government to give assistance to provinces that provided a pension to British subjects aged 70 and older.

- **1952:** The *Old Age Security Act* came into force, establishing a federally funded pension. It replaced the 1927 legislation that required the federal government to share the cost of provincially run, means-tested old age benefits.

- **1965:** Amendments to the *Old Age Security Act* lowered the eligible age for the OAS pension to 65, one year at a time, starting in 1966 at the age of 69.

- **1966**: The CPP and QPP came into force on January 1, 1966.

- **1967:** The Guaranteed Income Supplement was established under the Old Age Security program.

- **1972:** Full annual cost-of-living indexation was introduced for OAS.

- **1973:** Quarterly indexation was introduced for the Old Age Security program.

- **1974:** Full annual cost-of-living indexation was introduced for the CPP.

- **1975:** The Spouse's Allowance was established as part of the Old Age Security program.

- **1975:** The same Canada Pension Plan benefits became available to male and female contributors, as well as to their surviving spouses or common-law partners and dependent children.

- **1975:** The retirement and employment earnings test for Canada Pension Plan retirement pensions at the age of 65 was eliminated (a contributor can, upon application, receive his or her retirement pension the month following his or her 65th birthday, but can no longer contribute to the CPP).

- **1977:** The payment of partial Old Age Security pensions was permitted, based on years of residence in Canada.

- **1978:** Periods of zero or low earnings while caring for the contributor's child under the age of seven were excluded from the calculation of Canada Pension Plan benefits.

- **1978:** Canada Pension Plan pension credits could be split between spouses in the event of a marriage breakdown (CPP credit splitting).

- **1985:** Under OAS, the Spouse's Allowance was extended to all low-income widows and widowers aged 60 to 64.

- **1987:** Several new CPP provisions came into effect, including: flexible retirement benefits payable as early as the age of 60, increased disability benefits, continuation of survivor benefits if the survivor remarries, sharing of retirement pensions between spouses or common-law partners and expansion of credit splitting to cover the separation of married or common-law partners.

- **1989:** The repayment of OAS benefits or "clawback" was introduced.

- **1992:** Three major amendments to the CPP came into effect:

  - A new 25-year schedule for employer-employee contribution rates was established.

  - Children's benefits were increased.

  - Provision was made for individuals who were denied disability benefits because of late application.

  - 1995: The period of retroactivity for OAS benefits changed from five years to one year.

  - Individuals were permitted to request that their OAS benefits be cancelled.

  - 1998: The CPP moved from pay-as-you-go financing to fuller funding.

  - Contribution rates were increased.

  - A new investment policy was introduced.

- **2000:** All OAS and CPP benefits and obligations were extended to same-sex, common-law couples.

JUDY LAMARSH (1924-80)

Minister of National Health and Welfare Judy LaMarsh served from 1963 to 1965. She was instrumental in drafting Bill C-136, *An Act to Establish a Comprehensive Program of Old Age Pensions and Supplementary Benefits*, and in the implementation of the Canada Pension Plan in 1966. She also contributed to the creation of the Guaranteed Income Supplement, which was introduced in 1967.

MP Judy Lamarch laid the basis for the Canada Pension Plan (CP PHOTO).

due to the stringent eligibility rules of the 1927 program. Other problems with the program became apparent. It took nearly a decade for all provinces to participate in the program and, once they did, there were large discrepancies between them. Rising living costs led to public demand for increased benefits. These factors resulted in pressure from unions, some Members of Parliament and the public for changes.

In 1951, the Old Age Security program was created (it was implemented in 1952). It was the first major federal program without a cost-sharing arrangement with the provinces. Before it could be legislated, an amendment to the *British North America Act* was required to allow the federal government jurisdiction in the area of old age pensions. It was the second universal income transfer program in Canada, after the *Family Allowance Act* of 1944. It was financed from federal general revenues, and it was paid out to every person 65 years of age and older if they met certain residency requirements.

The OAS remained a universal program until 1989, when the Conservative government of Brian Mulroney introduced the "clawback" of benefits for people with higher incomes. At income tax time, it required upper-income earners to pay back the benefits they had received in the previous year. Now the benefit is deducted from their monthly payments before they are issued. Pensioners with an individual net income above $57,879 must repay part or the entire maximum Old Age Security pension amount. The repayment amounts are deducted from monthly payments before they are issued. The full OAS pension is eliminated when a pensioner's net income is $94,311 or above. Strictly speaking, the OAS is therefore no longer a universal program. The federal government argues that it is essentially still a universal program, as only about 5 percent of seniors receive reduced OAS benefits, and only 2 percent lose the entire benefit.

The Guaranteed Income Supplement (GIS) was implemented in 1966 as a selective, income-tested benefit paid to OAS recipients with no other income. The GIS was introduced in conjunction with the C/QPP in 1966. It was intended as a "guaranteed annual income" program. The program is an example of one of the few guaranteed income programs operating in industrialized countries, and the only such program in Canada. With this program, every Canadian over the age of 65, except for those who do not meet the residency requirement, have an income that is at least equal to OAS plus the maximum GIS. With this equation, the program guarantees a minimum income for elderly Canadians.

There has been some debate about whether or not the GIS, when taken together with the OAS, actually provides an adequate income. The National Council of Welfare report of 1999, entitled *A Pension Primer*, found that the maximum GIS for a single pensioner was $5,825 a year in 1998, and when this was combined with the OAS, a single person would have an annual income of $10,727 (National Council of Welfare 1999, 11). This was far below the LICO of $16,472 for a city with a population of 500,000 or more, and just below the $11,213 LICO for a rural area. Their analysis found a similar pattern for couples, thereby showing that a poverty gap still exists for the elderly in Canada.

The other basic minimum income program, the **Spouse's Allowance** (**SPA**), was created to deal with a hardship-creating anomaly in the OAS/GIS. In some cases, an elderly couple consisting of a woman under age 65 and an income-earning husband aged 65 would receive OAS and GIS intended for one person. When the woman reached age 65, their income would jump to the OAS/GIS amount intended for married couples. The 1975 SPA intended to correct the anomaly by providing an income-tested benefit to those between 60 and 65 years of age, when one spouse is over 65.

The SPA is now called the Allowance. The Allowance provides money for low-income seniors who meet the following conditions:

- His or her spouse or common-law partner (same sex or opposite sex) receives or is entitled to receive the Old Age Security pension and the Guaranteed Income Supplement.

- He or she is 60-64 years old.

- He or she is a Canadian citizen or a legal resident at the time the Allowance is approved or when he or she last lived here.

- He or she has lived in Canada after the age of 18 for at least 10 years.

In addition, the Allowance for the survivor provides benefits for those who are 60-64 years old and whose spouse or partner has died. The Allowance for the survivor stops when a recipient remarries or lives in a common-law relationship for at least one year.

Federal benefits are supplemented with provincial and territorial benefits in Ontario, Manitoba, Saskatchewan, Alberta, British Columbia, the Yukon, the Northwest Territories and Nunavut. The provincial programs are generally means- or income-tested and are administered by local Social Assistance or welfare departments. Finally, there are several benefits available to seniors through the tax system.

• Level 2: Social Insurance: Public Pensions — Canada/Quebec Pension Plan (C/QPP)

The earnings-based **Canada/Quebec Pension Plan** (**C/QPP**) makes up the second level. The plan provides a pension upon retirement to persons who have contributed to it. It is a social insurance type of income security program; it insures the contributor against loss of income due to retirement. All employed or self-employed Canadians over the age of 18 make compulsory contributions to the plan (matched by their employer) throughout their working careers. The plan also offers disability, survivor and death benefits, as well as inflation protection. The plan is fully portable from job to job. Annual C/QPP program expenditures in 2002 were $26.4 billion or 2.4 percent of GDP (Health Canada 2002, 23).

The Canada/Quebec Pension Plan began in 1966. The mandate was to provide all members of the labour force in Canada and their families with retirement income, death and disability benefits. Although we discuss the plans in tandem, the Quebec Pension Plan (QPP) is a separate

---

CANADA'S FIRST OLD AGE PENSIONS ACT

The 1927 *Old Age Pensions Act* was

- a maximum pension of $20 per month or $240 per year;

- available to British subjects aged 70 or over who had lived in Canada for 20 or more years;

- a means-tested provision of benefits, given only to the elderly whose income was less than $365 per year, including the pension benefits and

- a benefit from which Status Indians were excluded.

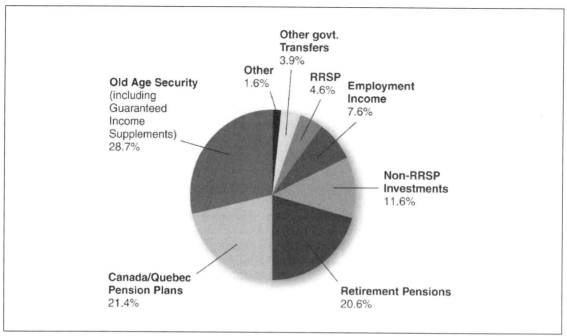

Figure 11.4: Income of seniors, by source, 1997.
Source: Colin Lindsay, *A Portrait of Seniors in Canada, 3rd ed.* (Ottawa: Statistics Canada, 1999), Catalogue No. 85-519 XPE, p.61.

QUEBEC PENSION PLAN

Although the option of having a separate, but highly linked pension plan is open to all provinces, Quebec is the only province to take the option. Information about the QPP is available at: http://www.rrq.gouv.qc.ca/an/accueil/00.htm

plan legislated by the province of Quebec – it has similar benefits and identical contribution rates to the Canadian Pension Plan (CPP). The QPP is closely associated with the CPP and is coordinated through a series of agreements between the federal government and Quebec. This ensures that Canadians who move in and out of Quebec carry all the pension benefits with them. The *Canada Pension Plan Act* allows any province to create its own program as Quebec has done.

Before the C/QPP was instituted, all pensions were administered by private insurance companies. A public contributory pension was a new way to provide income for retired persons. The level one programs (discussed above) addressed the income needs of the retired by transferring income to the retired from taxes collected every year. Within these programs, income is redistributed from those who are of working age to the retired person. Public contributory pensions, on the other hand, assist people to save from their earnings during their working years, and to use the accumulated funds to provide income during retirement.

As mentioned, all employed persons over the age of 18 must make compulsory contributions while employed. Therefore, all Canadians who have participated in the paid labour force are eligible for benefits, even a person with only one contribution. Benefits are payable at age 65 and are equal to 25 percent of a contributor's average earnings. Benefits are adjusted downward by 0.5 percent for each month for people who begin drawing benefits before 65 years of age. The plan is fully indexed annually to the cost of living as measured by the Consumers Price Index (CPI).

Table 11.1: Old Age Security Benefit Payment Rates, April-June 2003

Type of Benefit	Recipient	Average Monthly Benefit (January 2003)	Maximum Monthly Benefit	Maximum Annual Income
Old Age Security Pension	All recipients	$434.20	$456.08	See note
Guaranteed Income Supplement	Single person	$365.58	$542.03	$13,032
	Spouse of non-pensioner	$355.25	$542.03	$31,584
	Spouse of pensioner	$220.52	$353.06	$16,992
	Spouse of Allowance recipient	$278.26	$353.06	$31,584
Allowance	All recipients	$298.32	$809.14	$24,336
Allowance for the survivor	All recipients	$502.58	$893.31	$17,856

Note: Pensioners with an individual net income above $57,879 must repay part or the entire maximum Old Age Security pension amount. The repayment amounts are deducted from monthly payments before they are issued. The full OAS pension is eliminated when a pensioner's net income is $94,311 or above.

Source: Human Resources Development Canada, Old Age Security Payment Rates (Ottawa, 2003). Available at http://www.hrdc-drhc.gc.ca/isp/oas/rates1_e.shtml.

The C/QPP is used as a vehicle for other non-retirement based contingencies: disability benefits, death benefits and survivor benefits. The plan only provides disability benefits to contributors if they are unable to work due to a "severe" and "prolonged" disability – meaning that they are unable to regularly pursue any substantial gainful employment for an indefinite period. Survivor benefits are paid to the surviving spouse of deceased contributor. Finally, a death benefit or a lump-sum benefit equal to six times the contributor's monthly pension, up to a specified maximum, is paid upon the death of a contributor.

In 1998, Parliament amended the Canada Pension Plan through Bill C-2. The changes resulted in a larger reserve fund to help ensure that the future pensions of the growing retirement population can be funded. Contribution rates were increased from the 1998 5.85 percent of contributory earnings to 9.9 percent. These changes will increase the size of the fund of money that is put aside to pay for future retirement pensions. The aim is to avoid a situation where younger working age Canadians are left financing the pensions of their parents.

Members of the New Democratic Party, including Alexa McDonough (leader of the Party at the time), applaud their colleague Bill Blaikie as he takes the Liberal government to task over proposed changes to the Canada Pension Plan (CP PHOTO/1997/Fred Chartrand).

• Level 3: Private Plans: Occupational Pensions and Private Savings

The **private pension plans** component of the retirement income system consists of pensions from employers and publicly supported and regulated private savings plans such as Registered Retirement Savings Plans (RRSPs), Registered Pension Plans (RPPs) and Deferred Profit Sharing Plans (DPSPs). The federal government provides tax assistance on savings in RRSPs, RPPs and DPSPs. Taxes are deferred on the contributions and investment income in these plans until the savings are withdrawn or received as pension income. This tax assistance is intended to encourage Canadians to save privately for retirement. Private savings and assets also contribute to retirement incomes. As noted earlier, the tax-assisted private pension system accounts for an increasingly large share of retirement income system payments.

Private occupational pension plans were an outcome of the escalating economy after World War II, and the demand by labour unions for pension coverage within their collective agreements. Now private pension capital pools are the largest pools of capital in industrialized nations. RRSPs, RPPs and DPSPs allow for a tax deduction on the money placed into funds. Any interest or gains made in the fund also accumulate tax-free. More often, governments are relying on these private forms of savings, and are increasing the deductions allowed for contributors. Critics argue that a reliance on such plans is dangerous, as they only benefit those with high incomes.

Occupational pensions covered 46 percent of the labour force in 1986, but only one-third of the pensions are indexed to inflation. Most public sector employees are covered, but only 36 percent of private sector employees are covered. Many people with low-paying jobs do not have occupational pensions. People with irregular employment histories could also end up without a pension. Still, as Figure 11.4 indicates, in 1997, 20.6 percent of retirement income was derived from private retirement pensions. This almost equals the importance of the C/QPP (21.4 percent) as a source of retirement income.

Most of the gains in the overall average incomes of seniors, however, have come from work-related pensions. Between 1981 and 1997, for example, the proportion of the income of seniors coming from C/QPP more than doubled, rising from 10 to 21 percent, while the share coming from private employment pensions rose from 12 to 21 percent. In contrast, the share of income of seniors coming from the OAS program fell from 34 to 29 percent in the same period.

RETIREMENT INCOME SECURITY REFORM

Like other areas of income security, new reforms to the system for the retired and elderly have been widely discussed. In 1996, the federal government proposed the **Seniors Benefit.** This new program would combine the OAS, the GIS and the Allowance into one benefit that would be more targeted at seniors with low incomes. In short, the Seniors Benefit would slightly increase benefits for couples with incomes up to $30,000 and sharply reduce benefits for all others. The stated objective of the new program was to make the system more sustainable as the baby boom generation reaches retirement age. Due to extensive pressure from seniors and advocacy groups, the government announced in 1998 that the plans for the Seniors Benefit had been scrapped.

Efforts to reform Canada's old age income security system will probably not end with the Seniors Benefit. As mentioned, the OAS is not paid to those with incomes over $93,311, and is reduced on a sliding scale for those with incomes between $57,879 and $93,311. According to the exact definition of a universal program, the OAS does not qualify. But, according to the federal government, only a few Canadians actually lose the benefit. The concept of universality is being seriously challenged in Canada, and the OAS is the only remaining income security program with any aspect of universality (health care and education are universal but they are not income security programs). This will, no doubt, lead to further debate about the retirement system.

Another challenge to the retirement system stems from the demographic trends discussed earlier. Some refer to this as the demographic time bomb. As the baby boom generation retires, pension plan payouts will dramatically increase. Bill C-2 attempted to address this and ensure the sustainability of old age income security. Some say that the system will not be able to afford future pensions. Others point out that retirees have been paying contributions to the plan and that these invested contributions should finance the benefits. Unlike the OAS and GIS, which are paid out of general government revenues, the C/QPP payments are

Veteran New Democrat MP Stanley Knowles in a 1979 photo (CP PHOTO).

REFERENCES

* Bryden, Kenneth. 1974. *Old Age Pensions and Policy-making in Canada.* Montreal: McGill-Queen's University Press.

* Health Canada. 2002. *Canada's Aging Population* (prepared for the Second World Assembly on Ageing, a conference organized by the UN, held from April 8 to 12, 2002).

* National Council of Welfare. 1999. *A Pension Primer.* Ottawa: National Council of Welfare.

* Organization for Economic Co-operation and Development. 2001. *Ageing and Income: Financial Resources and Retirement in 9 OECD Countries.* Paris: OECD.

* Statistics Canada. 2002. CANSIM table 202-0802 and Catalogue no. 75-202-XIE.

* Statistics Canada. 2002. *Population Projections for 2001, 2006, 2011, 2016, 2021 and 2026, July 1.* Ottawa: Statistics Canada. Available at: http://www.statcan.ca/english/Pgdb/People/Population/demo23b.htm

covered by contributions made by those who are retiring. This is meant to avoid an inter-generational transfer of wealth, whereby the young who are working finance the pension of the old who are retired.

A problem arises, however, due to the commitment in law that the federal government loans the surplus CPP contributions to the nine provinces, at low interest rates. In most cases, the provinces are not in a hurry to pay back the low interest loans. When the funds are finally needed to pay pensions to the ageing population, the provinces will have to obtain the needed funds through current taxation. In this way, indirectly, the CPP becomes an inter-generational transfer, as the current working generation must pay the increased provincial taxes to enable the provinces to repay the loans to the CPP fund.

CONCLUSION

Canada should be applauded for the substantial gains it has made in the income security of seniors. Such gains were made largely as a result of public pressure for retirement programs by this large and vocal section of the population.

Federal and provincial governments have recognized that the ageing of Canadian society will put pressure on the Canada Pension Plan, and they have undertaken important reforms to ensure long-term sustainability. Their reforms include accelerating higher contribution rates, adopting a new investment strategy and benefit measures to reduce the growth in benefit expenditures. The changes must ensure that the system will be fair across generations and not place an unfair burden on contributors.

As further pressure mounts, Canada will have to make some choices. Do we break down a public system that has been recognized worldwide as exemplary, or do we make the necessary changes to maintain a viable and comprehensive public system? The workforce of tomorrow will also be significantly affected. Currently, Canadians lower their paid workforce participation between the ages of 55-65. Most stop working at the age of 65. The ageing of the population will eventually lead to a reduced growth of the labour force and a proportionally smaller workforce. The need for a workforce in the future may mean that fewer people have the option to retire, and the majority of older adults can still work productively. Therefore, it may become increasingly necessary that people who wish to work beyond the typical retirement age are given the opportunity to do so.

CHAPTER 11: THE ELDERLY AND RETIRED

Discussion Questions

1. What are the future trends regarding ageing and retirement in Canada?
2. How will these trends affect the old age income security system? What has the federal government done to try to ensure the sustainability of the pension system, for example?
3. List and describe the three levels of income security for old age and retirement.
4. Briefly describe the history of income security for the elderly, in particular the rise of the *Old Age Pensions Act* of 1927.
5. Calculate the total old age security benefits for an individual earning $58,000 per year. Explain.
6. Describe two key debates regarding old age income security reform.

Key Concepts

- Old Age Security (OAS)
- Guaranteed Income Supplement (GIS)
- Spouse's Allowance
- Canada/Quebec Pension Plan (C/QPP)
- Private pension plans
- Seniors Benefit

Websites

- **Human Resources and Development Canada**
  http://www.hrdc-drhc.gc.ca/isp/

  This link provides an overview of our retirement income system.

- **Caledon Institute of Social Policy**
  http://www.caledoninst.org

  The Caledon Institute of Social Policy does rigorous, high-quality research and analysis; seeks to inform and influence opinion and to foster public discussion on poverty and social policy; and develops and promotes concrete, practicable proposals for the reform of social programs at all levels of government.

- **Canadian Policy Research Network**
  http://www.cprn.org/cprn.html

  A network of policy researchers with an extensive collection of on-line reports about social policy.

- **Seniors Canada On-line**
  http://www.seniors.gc.ca

  Seniors Canada On-line provides single-window access to web-based information and services. Go to the "financial and legal" section for information on income security.

Canada Assistance Plan

R.S.C. 1985, C-1

[Note: This copy is for information only.]

An Act to authorize the making of contributions by Canada toward the cost of programs for the provision of assistance and welfare services to and in respect of persons in need

WHEREAS the Parliament of Canada, recognizing that the provision of adequate assistance to and in respect of persons in need and the prevention and removal of the causes of poverty and dependence on public assistance are the concern of all Canadians, is desirous of encouraging the further development and extension of assistance and welfare services programs throughout Canada by sharing more fully with the provinces in the cost thereof;

THEREFORE, Her Majesty, by and with the advice and consent of the Senate and House of Commons of Canada, enacts as follows:

SHORT TITLE

Short title

1. This Act may be cited as the Canada Assistance Plan.

R.S.C. c. C-1, s. 1.

INTERPRETATION

Definitions

2. In this Act,

"assistance"

"assistance" means aid in any form to or in respect of persons in need for the purpose of providing or providing for all or any of the following:

(a) food, shelter, clothing, fuel, utilities, household supplies and personal requirements (hereinafter referred to as "basic requirements"),

(b) prescribed items incidental to carrying on a trade or other employment and other prescribed special needs of any kind,

(c) care in a home for special care,

(d) travel and transportation,

(e) funerals and burials,

(f) health care services,

(g) prescribed welfare services purchased by or at the request of a provincially approved agency, and

(h) comfort allowances and other prescribed needs of residents or patients in hospitals or other prescribed institutions;

"child welfare authority"

"child welfare authority" means any provincially approved agency that has been designated by or under the provincial law or by the provincial authority for the purpose of administering or assisting in the administration of any law of the province relating to the protection and care of children;

"health care services"

"health care services" means medical, surgical, obstetrical, optical, dental and nursing services, and includes drugs, dressings, prosthetic appliances and any other items or health services necessary to or commonly associated with the provision of any such specified services, but does not include insured health services within the meaning of the Canada Health Act or any other prescribed hospital care services;

"home for special care"

"home for special care" means a residential welfare institution that is of a kind prescribed for the purposes of this Act as a home for special care and that is listed in a schedule to an agreement under section 4, but does not include a hospital, correctional institution or institution whose primary purpose is education, other than that part of a hospital that is used as a residential welfare institution and that is listed in a schedule to an agreement under section 4;

"Minister"

"Minister" means the Minister of Human Resources Development;

"municipality"

"municipality" means an incorporated city, metropolitan authority, town, village, township, district or rural municipality or other incorporated municipal body however designated, and includes any other local government body that is established by or under a law of a province and that is prescribed for the purposes of this Act as a municipality;

"person in need"

"person in need" means

(a) a person who, by reason of inability to obtain employment, loss of the principal family provider, illness, disability, age or other cause of any kind acceptable to the provincial authority, is found to be unable, on the basis of a test established by the provincial authority that takes into account the budgetary requirements of that person and the income and resources available to that person to meet those requirements, to provide adequately for himself, or for himself and his dependants or any of them, or

(b) a person under the age of twenty-one years who is in the care or custody or under the control or supervision of a child welfare authority, or a person who is a foster-child as defined by regulation,

and for the purposes of paragraph (e) of the definition "assistance" includes a deceased person who was a person described in paragraph (a) or (b) of this definition at the time of his death or who, although not such a person at the time of his death, would have been found to be such a person if an application for assistance to or in respect of him had been made immediately before his death;

"prescribed" means prescribed by regulation;

"provincial authority"

"provincial authority" means the provincial Minister or other official or body specified by the province in an agreement entered into under section 4 as being charged with the administration of the provincial law;

"provincial law"

"provincial law" means the Acts of the legislature of a province that provide for

(a) assistance, or

(b) welfare services in the province,

under conditions consistent with the provisions of this Act and the regulations, and includes any regulations made under those Acts;

"provincially approved agency"

"provincially approved agency" means any department of government, person or agency, including a private non-profit agency, that is authorized by or under the provincial law or by the provincial authority to accept applications for assistance, determine eligibility for assistance, provide or pay assistance or provide welfare services and that is listed in a schedule to an agreement under section 4;

"welfare services"

"welfare services" means services having as their object the lessening, removal or prevention of the causes and effects of poverty, child neglect or dependence on public assistance, and, without limiting the generality of the foregoing, includes

(a) rehabilitation services,

(b) casework, counselling, assessment and referral services,

(c) adoption services,

(d) homemaker, day-care and similar services,

(e) community development services,

(f) consulting, research and evaluation services with respect to welfare programs, and

(g) administrative, secretarial and clerical services, including staff training, relating to the provision of any of the foregoing services or to the provision of assistance,

but does not include any service relating wholly or mainly to education, correction or any other matter prescribed by regulation or, except for the purposes of the definition "assistance", any service provided by way of assistance;

"welfare services provided in the province"

"welfare services provided in the province" means welfare services provided in the province pursuant to the provincial law to or in respect of persons in need or persons who are likely to become persons in need unless those services are provided;

"year"

"year" means a twelve month period ending on March 31.

R.S.C. 1970, c. C-1, s. 2; 1984, c. 6, s. 24; R.S.C. 1985, c.C-1, s. 2; S.C. 1996, c. 11, s. 95.

PART I
GENERAL ASSISTANCE AND WELFARE SERVICES
INTERPRETATION

Definitions

3. In this Part,

"agreement"

"agreement" means an agreement made under section 4;

"contribution"

"contribution" means an amount payable by Canada under an agreement.

R.S.C. c. C-1, s. 3. Agreement Authorized

Agreement authorized

4. Subject to this Act, the Minister may, with the approval of the Governor in Council, enter into an agreement with any province to provide for the payment by Canada to the province of contributions in respect of the cost to the province and to municipalities in the province of

(a) assistance provided by or at the request of provincially approved agencies pursuant to the provincial law; and

(b) welfare services provided in the province by provincially approved agencies pursuant to the provincial law.

R.S.C. c. C-1, s. 4.

PART I
GENERAL ASSISTANCE AND WELFARE SERVICES
TERMINATION OF PAYMENTS LIMITATION ON
PAYMENTS

4.1 Notwithstanding any agreement made under this Act,

(a) no payment shall be made to a province under this Act in respect of any fiscal year commencing on or after April 1, 1996; and

(b) no payment shall be made to a province under this Act on or after April 1, 2000.

1995, c. 17, s. 31.

PART I
GENERAL ASSISTANCE AND WELFARE SERVICES

Final adjustment of contributions

4.2 Where, after March 1996, the Minister determines that contributions payable to a province under this Act in respect of a year ending before April 1996 differ from the total of payments made to the province under this Act in respect of the year,

(a) the amount, if any, by which those contributions exceed that total may be added to the amounts payable to the province under the Federal-Provincial Fiscal Arrangements Act; and

(b) the amount, if any, by which that total exceeds those contributions may be deducted from amounts payable to the province under the Federal-Provincial Fiscal Arrangements Act.

S.C. 1996, c. 18, s. 59. Contributions

Amount of contributions

5. (1) The contributions payable to a province under an agreement shall be paid in respect of each year and shall be the aggregate of

(a) fifty per cent of the cost to the province and to municipalities in the province in that year of assistance provided by or at the request of provincially approved agencies, and

(b) fifty per cent of either (i) the amount by which

(A) the cost to the province and to municipalities in the province in that year of welfare services provided in the province by provincially approved agencies

exceeds

(B) the total of

(I) the cost to the province, in the fiscal year of the province coinciding with or ending in the period commencing April 1, 1964 and ending March 31, 1965, of welfare services provided in the province, and

(II) the cost to municipalities in the province, in the fiscal years of those municipalities coinciding with or ending in the period commencing April 1, 1964 and ending March 31, 1965, of welfare services provided in the province,

or

(ii) the cost to the province and to municipalities in the province in that year of the employment by provincially approved agencies of persons employed by those agencies

(A) wholly or mainly in the performance of welfare services functions, and

(B) in positions filled after March 31, 1965,

at the election of the province made at such time or times and in such manner as may be prescribed.

Costs excluded

(2) In this section, "cost" does not include,

(a) with respect to assistance, any capital cost as defined by regulation for the purposes of this paragraph; (b) with respect to welfare services, any capital cost or any plant or equipment operating cost as defined by regulation for the purposes of this paragraph;

(c) any cost that Canada has shared or is required to share in any manner with the province, or that Canada has borne or is required to bear, pursuant to any other Part or pursuant to any Act of Parliament; or

(d) any cost of insurance premiums or of co-insurance or similar charges relating to the provision of

(i) insured health services within the meaning of the Canada Health Act, or

(ii) health or medical care services, if at the time the cost is incurred there is in force an Act of Parliament other than this Act, pursuant to which Canada is required to share in any manner with the province the cost of providing those services to the general public.

Cost of welfare services

(3) Notwithstanding paragraph (2)(c), the cost to the province and to municipalities in the province in a year of welfare services provided in the province as or as part of a project, other than a demonstration or research project as defined by regulation, approved by the Minister pursuant to the rules made by the Governor in Council for the purposes of the National Welfare Grants program shall be included for that year for the purposes of, and be deemed to be a cost within the meaning of, either clause (1)(b)(i)(A) or subparagraph (1)(b)(ii), depending on the election made by the province under paragraph (1)(b), if Canada has not previously made a payment to the province with respect to that cost.

Obligation to province satisfied

(4) Where any cost is included for the purposes of clause(1)(b)(I)(A) or subparagraph (1)(b)(ii) by virtue of subsection (3), Canada shall be deemed for the purposes of the rules made by the Governor in Council for the purposes of the National Welfare Grants program to have satisfied all of its obligations to the province with respect to that cost.

R.S.C. c. C-1, s. 5; 1984, c. 6, s. 24.

Limitation on certain contributions

5.1 (1) Notwithstanding sections 5 and 8 and any agreement, where no fiscal equalization payment is payable to a province pursuant to section 3 of the Federal-Provincial Fiscal Arrangements and Federal Post-Secondary Education and Health Contributions Act for a year ending on March 31, 1991, March 31, 1992, March 31, 1993, March 31, 1994 or March 31, 1995 (in this section referred to as the "current year"), the contributions to that province in respect of the current year shall not exceed the product obtained by multiplying

(a) the amount of the contributions payable to the province for assistance and welfare services provided in

(i) the year ending on March 31, 1990, or

(ii) where a fiscal equalization payment was payable to the province for the year ending on March 31, 1990, the last current year for which such a payment was payable,

whichever is the later year,

by

(b) if the later year referred to in paragraph (a) is

(i) the first year preceding the current year, 1.05,

(ii) the second year preceding the current year, 1.1025,

(iii) the third year preceding the current year, 1.157625,

(iv) the fourth year preceding the current year, 1.215506, or

(v) the fifth year preceding the current year, 1.276282.

Idem

(2) Notwithstanding sections 5 and 8 and any agreement, the contributions to each province in respect of a year ending after March 31, 1995 shall not exceed the contributions to that province in respect of the year ending on March 31, 1995.

1991, c. 9, s. 2; 1992, c. 9, s. 1; 1994, c. 18, s. 12. Terms of Agreement

Provisions to be included in agreements

6. (1) An agreement

(a) shall include schedules for the purposes of the definitions "home for special care" and "provincially approved agency" in section 2 and a schedule listing the Acts of the legislature of the province referred to in the definition "provincial law" in section 2;

(b) shall provide for the exchange between Canada and the province of statistical and other information relating to the administration and operation of this Act and the provincial law;

(c) may provide that any home for special care or any provincially approved agency that is listed in a schedule to the agreement shall be deemed to have been so listed as of any specified day before the agreement is made; and

(d) shall contain such other terms and conditions as the Minister and the province may agree on or as the regulations may require.

Undertakings by provinces

(2) An agreement shall provide that the province

(a) will provide financial aid or other assistance to or in respect of any person in the province who is a person in need described in paragraph (a) of the definition "person in need" in section 2, in an amount or manner that takes into account the basic requirements of that person;

(b) will, in determining whether a person is a person described in paragraph (a) and the assistance to be provided to that person, take into account the budgetary requirements of that person and the income and resources available to that person to meet those requirements;

(c) will continue, as may be necessary and expedient, the development and extension of welfare services in the province;

(d) will not require a period of residence in the province as a condition of eligibility for assistance or for the receipt or continued receipt thereof;

(e) will ensure the provision by law, not later than one year from the effective date of the agreement, of a procedure for appeals from decisions of provincially approved agencies with respect to applications for assistance or the granting or providing of assistance by persons directly affected by those decisions;

(f) will ensure the maintenance and availability, for examination and audit by the Minister or any person designated by the Minister, of such records and accounts respecting the provision of assistance and welfare services in the province as the agreement or the regulations may require; and

(g) will provide the Minister with copies of all Acts of the legislature of the province referred to in the definition "provincial law" in section 2 and of all regulations made under those Acts.

Undertakings by Canada

(3) An agreement shall provide that Canada

(a) will pay to the province the contributions or advances on account thereof that Canada is authorized to pay to the province under this Act and the regulations;

(b) will make available to the province, from time to time, statistical and other general reports and studies prepared by or under the direction of the Minister relating to assistance or welfare services programs or to related programs; and

(c) at the request of the provincial authority, will make available to the province where feasible, through the facilities of the Department of Human Resources Development, consultative services with respect to the development and operation of assistance and welfare services programs.

R.S.C. c. C-1, s. 6; R.S.C. 1985, c. C-1, s. 6; S.C. 1996, c.11, s. 97. Payment of Contributions

Payment of contributions

7. Contributions or advances on account thereof shall be paid, on the certificate of the Minister, out of the Consolidated Revenue Fund at such times and in such manner as may be prescribed, but all such payments are subject to the conditions specified in this Part and in the regulations and to the observance of the agreements and undertakings contained in an agreement.

R.S.C. c. C-1, s. 7. Operation of Agreements

Duration of agreements

8. (1) Every agreement shall continue in force so long as the provincial law remains in operation.

Amendments and termination

(2) Notwithstanding subsection (1),

(a) an agreement may, with the approval of the Governor in Council, be amended or terminated at any time by mutual consent of the Minister and the province,

(b) any schedule to an agreement may be amended at any time by mutual consent of the Minister and the province,

(c) the province may at any time give to Canada notice of intention to terminate an agreement, and

(d) Canada may, at any time, give to the province notice of intention to terminate an agreement, and, where notice of intention to terminate an agreement is given in accordance with paragraph (c) or (d), the agreement shall cease to be effective for any period after the day fixed in the notice or for any period after the expiration of one year from the day on which the notice is given, whichever is the later.

R.S.C. c. C-1, s. 8. Regulations

Regulations

9. (1) The Governor in Council may make regulations providing for any matters concerning which he deems regulations are necessary to carry out the purposes and provisions of this Part and, without limiting the generality of the foregoing, may make regulations

(a) for the administration of this Part and of agreements;

(b) prescribing or defining anything that by section 2 or this Part is to be prescribed or defined by regulation;

(c) defining the expressions "personal requirements", "budgetary requirements", "community development services", "wholly or mainly in the performance of welfare services functions" and "positions filled after March 31, 1965";

(d) for the purposes of section 5 or any of the provisions of that section, defining the expression "cost to the province and to municipalities in the province" and prescribing the manner in which that cost is to be determined;

(e) for the purposes of clause 5(1)(b)(i)(B), defining the expressions "cost to the province" and "cost to municipalities in the province" and prescribing the manner in which those costs are to be determined; (f) adapting, modifying or extending, for the purposes of clause 5(1)(b)(i)(B) and either generally or in respect of a particular province, the definitions "welfare services" and "welfare services provided in the province", respectively, as set out in section 2; and

(f) adapting, modifying or extending, for the purposes of clause 5(1)(b)(i)(B) and either generally or in respect of a particular province, the definitions "welfare services" and "welfare services provided in the province", respectively, as set out in section 2; and

(g) respecting the payment to a province of advances on account of any amount that may become payable to the province pursuant to this Part, the adjustment of other payments by reason of those advances and the recovery of overpayments.

Alteration of regulations

(2) No regulation that has the effect of altering any of the agreements or undertakings contained in an agreement entered into under this Part with a province, or that affects the method of payment or amount of payments thereunder, is effective in respect of that province unless the province has consented to the making of such regulation.

R.S.C. c. C-1, s. 9.

PART II
INDIAN WELFARE

Definitions

10. In this Part,

"band"

"band" means

(a) a band, as defined in the Indian Act,

(b) a band, as defined in the Cree-Naskapi (of Quebec) Act, chapter 18 of the Statutes of Canada, 1984,

(c) the Band, as defined in the Sechelt Indian Band Self-Government Act, chapter 27 of the Statutes of Canada, 1986, or (d) a first nation named in Schedule II to the Yukon First Nations Self-Government Act;

"council"

"council" means

(a) the "council of the band", as defined in the Indian Act,

(b) the "council", as defined in the Cree-Naskapi (of Quebec) Act, chapter 18 of the Statutes of Canada, 1984,

(c) the "Council", as defined in the Sechelt Indian Band Self-Government Act, chapter 27 of the Statutes of Canada, 1986, or

(d) a first nation named in Schedule II to the Yukon First Nations Self-Government Act;

"Indian"

"Indian" means an Indian, as defined in the Indian Act;

"Indian to whom this Part applies"

"Indian to whom this Part applies", in relation to any province, means an Indian

(a) who is resident on a reserve in the province,

(b) who is resident on land in the province the legal title to which is vested in Her Majesty or on land in any territory in the province that is without municipal organization, or

(c) who is resident in the province and is designated by the Minister charged with the administration of the Indian Act as an Indian to whom this Part applies,

but does not include an Indian who is designated in or under an agreement entered into with the province pursuant to section 11 as an Indian to whom this Part does not apply;

"provincial welfare program"

"provincial welfare program" means a welfare program administered by the province, by a municipality in the province or privately, to which public money of the province is or may be contributed and that is applicable or available generally to residents of the province.

"reserve"

"reserve" means

(a) a reserve, as defined in the Indian Act,

(b) Category IA land or Category IA-N land, as defined in the Cree-Naskapi (of Quebec) Act, chapter 18 of the Statutes of Canada, 1984,

(c) Sechelt lands, as defined in the Sechelt Indian Band Self-Government Act, chapter 27 of the Statutes of Canada, 1986, or

(d) settlement land, as defined in the Yukon First Nations Self-Government Act, and lands in which an interest is transferred or recognized under section 21 of that Act.

R.S.C. 1985, c. C-1, s. 10; R.S.C. 1985, c. 20 (2nd Supp.), s.1; 1994, c. 35, s. 33.

Agreements authorized

11. (1) The Minister and the Minister charged with the administration of the Indian Act may, with the approval of the Governor in Council, enter into an agreement with a province with respect to the extension of provincial welfare programs to Indians to whom this Part applies and for the payment by Canada to the province of any portion of the cost to the province of extending provincial welfare programs to those Indians.

Consent of council of Indian band required

(2) An agreement entered into under subsection (1) shall provide for the extension of a provincial welfare program to a member of an Indian band who ordinarily resides with that band, only with the consent of the council of that band signified in such manner as may be prescribed by the Governor in Council.

R.S.C. c. C-1, s. 11.

Payments to provinces

12. Where an agreement has been entered into with a province pursuant to section 11, the Minister of Finance shall, on the certificate of the Minister, cause to be paid to the province out of the Consolidated Revenue Fund, when and in the manner required by the agreement, such amounts as are required to fulfil the obligations of Canada to the province under the agreement, but all those payments are subject to the observance of the agreements and undertakings contained in the agreement.

R.S.C. c. C-1, s. 12.

Where no agreement in effect

13. Where, in the case of any province, no agreement is in effect pursuant to section 11, nothing in an agreement entered into with the province under Part I shall be construed to require the provision of assistance or welfare services to or in respect of any Indian to whom this Part applies.

R.S.C. c. C-1, s. 13.

PART III
WORK ACTIVITY PROJECTS

Definitions

14. In this Part,

"participant"

"participant" means any person described in the definition "work activity project" who takes part in such a work activity project;

"work activity project"

"work activity project" means a project the purpose of which is to prepare for entry or return to employment persons in need or likely to become persons in need who, because of environmental, personal or family reasons, have unusual difficulty in obtaining or holding employment or in improving, through participation in technical or vocational training programs or rehabilitation programs, their ability to obtain or hold employment.

R.S.C. c. C-1, s. 14.

Agreements authorized

15. (1) Subject to this Part, the Minister may, with the approval of the Governor in Council, enter into an agreement with any province with which an agreement under Part I is in effect, to provide for the payment by Canada to the province of an amount equal to fifty per cent of the cost of a work activity project undertaken in the province.

Definition of "cost of a work activity project"

(2) In this section, "cost of a work activity project" means the cost to the province and to municipalities in the province of

(a) salaries, wages or other remuneration paid to persons for services performed with respect to the operation or maintenance of the work activity project,

(b) travel and living expenses paid to persons performing services away from their ordinary places of residence with respect to the operation or maintenance of the work activity project,

(c) such equipment, materials and operational costs relating to the work activity project as may be prescribed by regulations made by the Governor in Council, and

(d) allowances paid to participants,

but does not include any cost that Canada has shared or is required to share in any manner with the province pursuant to Part II.

Provisions to be included in agreements

(3) Every agreement made pursuant to this section shall

(a) provide that no person shall be denied assistance because he refuses or has refused to take part in a work activity project;

(b) provide that welfare services shall be made available as required to participants;

(c) provide that allowances may be paid to participants;

(d) provide that a participant shall be eligible for assistance if, notwithstanding any allowance that he receives as a participant, he is a person in need;

(e) specify the agency that shall be responsible for the undertaking, operation or maintenance of any work activity project or of any part thereof; and

(f) contain such other terms and conditions as the regulations may require.

R.S.C. 1970, c. C-1, s. 15; 1972, c. 1, Sch. (NHW) vote 30b;1976-77, c. 54, s. 74; R.S.C. 1985, c. C-1, s. 15; S.C. 1996,c. 11, s. 47.

Payments to provinces

16. Where an agreement has been entered into with a province pursuant to section 15, the Minister of Finance shall, on the certificate of the Minister, cause to be paid to the province out of the Consolidated Revenue Fund, at such times and in such manner as may be prescribed by the regulations or the agreement, such amounts as are required to fulfil the obligations of Canada to the province under the agreement, but all such payments are subject to the conditions specified in this Part and in the regulations and to the observance of the agreements and undertakings contained in the agreement.

R.S.C. c. C-1, s. 16. Regulations

17. The Governor in Council may, on the recommendation of the Minister, make regulations providing for any matters concerning which the Governor in Council believes regulations are necessary to carry out the purposes and provisions of this Part.

R.S.C. 1970, c. C-1, s. 17; 1976-77, c. 54, s. 74; R.S.C. 1985,c. C-1, s. 17; S.C. 1996, c. 11, s. 48.

PART IV
REPORT TO PARLIAMENT

Annual report

18. The Minister shall, as soon as possible after the end of each year, prepare a report respecting the operation for that year of the agreements made under this Act and the payments made to the provinces under each of the agreements, and shall cause the report to be laid before Parliament forthwith on the completion thereof or, if Parliament is not then sitting, on any of the first fifteen days next thereafter that either House of Parliament is sitting.

R.S.C. c. C-1, s. 19.

Canada Health and Social Transfer Regulations

FEDERAL-PROVINCIAL FISCAL ARRANGEMENTS ACT, SOR/97-468

[Note: This copy is for information only.]

His Excellency the Governor General in Council, on the recommendation of the Minister of Finance, pursuant to section 40ᵃ of the *Federal-Provincial Fiscal Arrangements Act*ᵇ, hereby makes the annexed *Canada Health and Social Transfer Regulations*.

ᵃ S.C. 1997, c. 10, s. 264 ᵇ S.C. 1995, c. 17, s. 45(1)

CANADA HEALTH AND SOCIAL TRANSFER REGULATIONS

Interpretation

1. The definitions in this section apply in these Regulations.

"Act" means the *Federal-Provincial Fiscal Arrangements Act. (Loi)*

"population of a province for a fiscal year" means the population of a province for a fiscal year as determined in accordance with section 2. (*population d'une province pour un exercice*)

"taxation year" means a taxation year within the meaning of the *Income Tax Act.* (*année d'imposition*)

"Transfer" means the Canada Health and Social Transfer. (*Transfer*)

Determination of population of a province

2. Subject to subsection 5(7), the population of a province for a fiscal year shall be determined by the Chief Statistician of Canada on the basis of Statistics Canada's official estimate of the population of that province on the first day of June of that fiscal year.

Determination of gross domestic product

3. The gross domestic product of Canada for a calendar year shall be determined by the Chief Statistician of Canada on the basis of Statistics Canada's official estimate of the gross domestic product of Canada at market prices for that calendar year.

Calculation of equalized tax transfer

4. (1) For the purposes of clause 16(1)(b)(ii)(A) of the Act, the relevant revenue bases for a province for a fiscal year shall be determined as follows:

(a) with respect to personal income taxes, by aggregating

(i) 75% of the assessed federal individual income tax applicable to the province for the taxation year ending in the fiscal year, as determined by the Minister of National Revenue, and

(b) with respect to corporation income taxes, by aggregating

(i) 75% of the aggregate of taxable income earned in the taxation year in the province, as determined by the Minister of National Revenue under subsection 124(4) of the Income Tax Act, for all corporations having a taxation year ending in the calendar year that ends in the fiscal year, and

(ii) 25% of the aggregate of taxable income earned in the taxation year in the province, as determined by the Minister of National Revenue under subsection 124(4) of the Income Tax Act, for all corporations having a taxation year ending in the calendar year that begins in the fiscal year.

(2) For the purposes of clause 16(1)(b)(ii)(B) of the Act, the amount of equalization referred to in subparagraph 16(1)(b)(ii) of the Act shall be adjusted in the following manner:

(a) if subsection 4(6) of the Act applies in respect of a province for the fiscal year, the amount of equalization shall be increased by the amount determined by the formula

$$P \times [A \times C/B]$$

and

(b) if subsection 4(9) of the Act applies in respect of the fiscal year, the amount of equalization determined in accordance with subparagraph 16(1)(b)(ii) of the Act and increased in accordance with paragraph (a), if applicable, shall be reduced by the amount determined by the formula

$$P \times [A \times D/B]$$

where

P

is the population of a province for a fiscal year;

A

is the average per capita yield in the provinces of Ontario, Quebec, Manitoba, British Columbia and Saskatchewan for the revenue sources referred to in subsection 16(2) of the Act for the fiscal year;

B

is the average per capita yield in the provinces of Ontario, Quebec, Manitoba, British Columbia and Saskatchewan for all revenue sources for the fiscal year, under subsection 4(1) of the Act;

C

is the amount by which

(a) the equalization payment for the province determined in accordance with subsection 4(6) of the Act divided by the population of the province for that fiscal year

exceeds

(b) the equalization payment for the province, determined in accordance with subsection 4(1) of the Act, divided by the population of the province for that fiscal year; and

D

is the quotient determined under paragraph 4(9)(d) of the Act for the fiscal year.

Interim estimates

5. (1) In respect of each fiscal year,

(a) the Minister shall make an estimate of the amount, if any, of the Transfer that is payable pursuant to the Act to a province for the fiscal year

(i) before April 16 of that fiscal year,

(ii) during the period beginning on the first day of September and ending on the twelfth day of October of that fiscal year,

(iii) during the period beginning on the twelfth day of January and ending on the last day of February of that fiscal year,

(iv) during the period beginning on the first day of September and ending on the twelfth day of October of the first fiscal year following the end of that fiscal year,

(v) during the period beginning on the twelfth day of January and ending on the last day of February of the first fiscal year following the end of that fiscal year,

(vi) during the period beginning on the first day of September and ending on the twelfth day of October of the second fiscal year following the end of that fiscal year, and

(vii) during the period beginning on the twelfth day of January and ending on the last day of February of the second fiscal year following the end of that fiscal year; and

(b) where, in the opinion of the Minister, there is new information available that may have a significant effect on the amount of the Transfer that is payable pursuant to the Act to one or more provinces, the Minister may alter an estimate of the amount, if any, of the Transfer that is payable pursuant to the Act for the fiscal year to a province

(i) during the second quarter of that fiscal year,

(ii) during March of that fiscal year, and

(iii) during any period beginning on the first day of the final month of a quarter and ending on the twelfth day of the subsequent quarter, other than the periods specified in paragraph (a), following the end of the fiscal year, until such time as the final computation pursuant to subsection 6(2) is completed.

(2) Where an estimate made pursuant to subparagraph (1)(a)(i) shows that a Transfer is payable to a province for a fiscal year, the Minister shall pay to the province, on account of the final payment in respect of that fiscal year, an amount equal to one twenty-fourth of the amount so estimated on the first and third working days following the fifteenth calendar day of each month in that fiscal year.

(3) Where an estimate made pursuant to subparagraph (1)(a)(ii) or (iii) or (b)(i) establishes that the amounts payable to the province pursuant to

the immediately preceding estimate in respect of that fiscal year should be revised, the Minister shall

(a) if any amount remains payable to the province, adjust the remaining payments referred to in subsection (2) in respect of that fiscal year in accordance with the new estimate, beginning with the first payment in the month following the month during which that estimate was calculated; and

(b) if an overpayment has been made to the province, recover the amount of that overpayment before the end of the fiscal year.

(4) Where an estimate made pursuant to subparagraph (1)(a) (iv), (v), (vi) or (vii) or (b) (iii)

(a) establishes that an underpayment has been made to the province, the Minister shall pay the amount of the underpayment to the province within the four months following the month during which the estimate was made; and

(b) establishes that an overpayment has been made to the province, the Minister shall recover the amount of that overpayment within the four months following the month during which the estimate was made.

(5) Where an estimate made pursuant to subparagraph (1)(b)(ii) establishes that the amounts payable to the province pursuant to the immediately preceding estimate in respect of that fiscal year should be revised, the Minister shall

(a) if any amount remains payable to the province, pay to the province that amount in the month during which the estimate was made or, where the province so requests, pay the province that amount within the four months following the month during which the estimate was made; and

(b) if an overpayment has been made to the province, recover the amount of that overpayment in the month during which the estimate was made or, where the province so requests, recover the amount within the four months following that month.

(6) Where an estimate discloses an overpayment to a province in respect of a fiscal year, the Minister may, subject to paragraph (3)(b), (4)(b) or (5)(b), recover the amount of that overpayment

(a) from any amount payable to the province under the Act; or

(b) from the province as a debt due to Her Majesty in right of Canada.

(7) For the purpose of making an estimate under subsection (1), the population of a province for a fiscal year is the population of that province on the first day of June of that fiscal year as estimated by the Minister on the basis of population statistics made available to the Minister by the Chief Statistician of Canada. SOR/2000-59, s. 1.

Final computation

6. (1) The Chief Statistician of Canada shall, in respect of each fiscal year, prepare and submit to the Minister, not later than 30 months after the end of that fiscal year, a certificate in respect of that fiscal year based on the most recent information prepared by Statistics Canada for that fiscal year, setting out

(a) in respect of each province, the population of the province for each of the fiscal years required by the Act; and

(b) beginning with the fiscal year 2000-2001, the gross domestic product of Canada for a calendar year, determined in accordance with section 3, for the calendar years required by the Act.

(2) Within 30 days after the receipt by the Minister of the certificate submitted by the Chief Statistician of Canada pursuant to subsection (1) in respect of a fiscal year, the Minister shall make the final computation on the basis of the information contained in that certificate of the amount, if any, of the Transfer that is payable for that fiscal year pursuant to the Act to a province and the Minister shall subsequently furnish each province with tables setting out the details of that computation.

(3) Where, as a result of a final computation made pursuant to subsection (2), there remains an outstanding amount payable to a province in respect of a fiscal year, the Minister shall pay to the province the outstanding amount.

(4) Where a final computation made pursuant to subsection (2) discloses an overpayment to a province in respect of a fiscal year, the Minister shall recover the amount of that overpayment

(a) from any amount payable to the province under the Act; or

(b) from the province as a debt due to Her Majesty in right of Canada.

Coming into force

7. These Regulations come into force on October 9, 1997.

First Ministers' Meeting Ottawa, February 4, 1999

A Framework to Improve the Social Union for Canadians

[Note: This copy is for information only.]

An agreement between the Government of Canada and the Governments of the Provinces and Territories

February 4, 1999

The following agreement is based upon a mutual respect between orders of government and a willingness to work more closely together to meet the needs of Canadians.

1. PRINCIPLES

Canada's social union should reflect and give expression to the fundamental values of Canadians – equality, respect for diversity, fairness, individual dignity and responsibility, and mutual aid and our responsibilities for one another.

Within their respective constitutional jurisdictions and powers, governments commit to the following principles:

All Canadians are equal

- Treat all Canadians with fairness and equity
- Promote equality of opportunity for all Canadians
- Respect the equality, rights and dignity of all Canadian women and men and their diverse needs

Meeting the needs of Canadians

- Ensure access for all Canadians, wherever they live or move in Canada, to essential social programs and services of reasonably comparable quality
- Provide appropriate assistance to those in need
- Respect the principles of Medicare: comprehensiveness, universality, portability, public administration and accessibility
- Promote the full and active participation of all Canadians in Canada's social and economic life
- Work in partnership with individuals, families, communities, voluntary organizations, business and labour, and ensure appropriate

257

opportunities for Canadians to have meaningful input into social policies and programs

Sustaining social programs and services

- Ensure adequate, affordable, stable and sustainable funding for social programs

Aboriginal peoples of Canada

- For greater certainty, nothing in this agreement abrogates or derogates from any Aboriginal, treaty or other rights of Aboriginal peoples including self-government

2. MOBILITY WITHIN CANADA

All governments believe that the freedom of movement of Canadians to pursue opportunities anywhere in Canada is an essential element of Canadian citizenship.

Governments will ensure that no new barriers to mobility are created in new social policy initiatives.

Governments will eliminate, within three years, any residency-based policies or practices which constrain access to post-secondary education, training, health and social services and social assistance unless they can be demonstrated to be reasonable and consistent with the principles of the Social Union Framework.

Accordingly, sector Ministers will submit annual reports to the Ministerial Council identifying residency-based barriers to access and providing action plans to eliminate them.

Governments are also committed to ensure, by July 1, 2001, full compliance with the mobility provisions of the *Agreement on Internal Trade* by all entities subject to those provisions, including the requirements for mutual recognition of occupational qualifications and for eliminating residency requirements for access to employment opportunities.

3. INFORMING CANADIANS – PUBLIC ACCOUNTABILITY AND TRANSPARENCY

Canada's Social Union can be strengthened by enhancing each government's transparency and accountability to its constituents.
Each government therefore agrees to:

Achieving and Measuring Results

- Monitor and measure outcomes of its social programs and report regularly to its constituents on the performance of these programs
- Share information and best practices to support the development of outcome measures, and work with other governments to develop, over time, comparable indicators to measure progress on agreed objectives
- Publicly recognize and explain the respective roles and contributions of governments

- Use funds transferred from another order of government for the purposes agreed and pass on increases to its residents

- Use third parties, as appropriate, to assist in assessing progress on social priorities

Involvement of Canadians

- Ensure effective mechanisms for Canadians to participate in developing social priorities and reviewing outcomes

Ensuring fair and transparent practices

- Make eligibility criteria and service commitments for social programs publicly available

- Have in place appropriate mechanisms for citizens to appeal unfair administrative practices and bring complaints about access and service

- Report publicly on citizen's appeals and complaints, ensuring that confidentiality requirements are met

4. WORKING IN PARTNERSHIP FOR CANADIANS

Joint Planning and Collaboration

The Ministerial Council has demonstrated the benefits of joint planning and mutual help through which governments share knowledge and learn from each other.

Governments therefore agree to:

- Undertake joint planning to share information on social trends, problems and priorities and to work together to identify priorities for collaborative action

- Collaborate on implementation of joint priorities when this would result in more effective and efficient service to Canadians, including as appropriate joint development of objectives and principles, clarification of roles and responsibilities, and flexible implementation to respect diverse needs and circumstances, complement existing measures and avoid duplication

Reciprocal Notice and Consultation

The actions of one government or order of government often have significant effects on other governments. In a manner consistent with the principles of our system of parliamentary government and the budget-making process, governments therefore agree to:

- Give one another advance notice prior to implementation of a major change in a social policy or program which will likely substantially affect another government

- Offer to consult prior to implementing new social policies and programs that are likely to substantially affect other governments or the social union more generally. Governments participating in these consultations will have the opportunity to identify potential duplication and to propose alternative approaches to achieve flexible and effective implementation

Equitable Treatment

For any new Canada-wide social initiatives, arrangements made with one province/territory will be made available to all provinces/territories in a manner consistent with their diverse circumstances.

• Aboriginal Peoples

Governments will work with the Aboriginal peoples of Canada to find practical solutions to address their pressing needs.

5. THE FEDERAL SPENDING POWER – IMPROVING SOCIAL PROGRAMS FOR CANADIANS

Social Transfers to Provinces and Territories

The use of the federal spending power under the Constitution has been essential to the development of Canada's social union. An important use of the spending power by the Government of Canada has been to transfer money to the provincial and territorial governments. These transfers support the delivery of social programs and services by provinces and territories in order to promote equality of opportunity and mobility for all Canadians and to pursue Canada-wide objectives.

Conditional social transfers have enabled governments to introduce new and innovative social programs, such as Medicare, and to ensure that they are available to all Canadians. When the federal government uses such conditional transfers, whether cost-shared or block-funded, it should proceed in a cooperative manner that is respectful of the provincial and territorial governments and their priorities.

Funding Predictability

The Government of Canada will consult with provincial and territorial governments at least one year prior to renewal or significant funding changes in existing social transfers to provinces/territories, unless otherwise agreed, and will build due notice provisions into any new social transfers to provincial/territorial governments.

New Canada-wide Initiatives Supported by Transfers to Provinces and Territories

With respect to any new Canada-wide initiatives in health care, post-secondary education, social assistance and social services that are funded through intergovernmental transfers, whether block-funded or cost-shared, the Government of Canada will:

- Work collaboratively with all provincial and territorial governments to identify Canada-wide priorities and objectives
- Not introduce such new initiatives without the agreement of a majority of provincial governments

Each provincial and territorial government will determine the detailed program design and mix best suited to its own needs and circumstances to meet the agreed objectives.

A provincial/territorial government which, because of its existing programming, does not require the total transfer to fulfill the agreed objectives would be able to reinvest any funds not required for those objectives in the same or a related priority area.

The Government of Canada and the provincial/territorial governments will agree on an accountability framework for such new social initiatives and investments.

All provincial and territorial governments that meet or commit to meet the agreed Canada-wide objectives and agree to respect the accountability framework will receive their share of available funding.

Direct Federal Spending

Another use of the federal spending power is making transfers to individuals and to organizations in order to promote equality of opportunity, mobility, and other Canada-wide objectives.

When the federal government introduces new Canada-wide initiatives funded through direct transfers to individuals or organizations for health care, post-secondary education, social assistance and social services, it will, prior to implementation, give at least three months' notice and offer to consult. Governments participating in these consultations will have the opportunity to identify potential duplication and to propose alternative approaches to achieve flexible and effective implementation.

6. DISPUTE AVOIDANCE AND RESOLUTION

Governments are committed to working collaboratively to avoid and resolve intergovernmental disputes. Respecting existing legislative provisions, mechanisms to avoid and resolve disputes should:

- Be simple, timely, efficient, effective and transparent
- Allow maximum flexibility for governments to resolve disputes in a non-adversarial way
- Ensure that sectors design processes appropriate to their needs
- Provide for appropriate use of third parties for expert assistance and advice while ensuring democratic accountability by elected officials

Dispute avoidance and resolution will apply to commitments on mobility, intergovernmental transfers, interpretation of the *Canada Health Act* principles, and, as appropriate, on any new joint initiative.

Sector Ministers should be guided by the following process, as appropriate:

Dispute avoidance

- Governments are committed to working together and avoiding disputes through information-sharing, joint planning, collaboration, advance notice and early consultation, and flexibility in implementation

Sector negotiations

- Sector negotiations to resolve disputes will be based on joint fact-finding

- A written joint fact-finding report will be submitted to governments involved, who will have the opportunity to comment on the report before its completion

- Governments involved may seek assistance of a third party for fact-finding, advice, or mediation

- At the request of either party in a dispute, fact-finding or mediation reports will be made public

Review provisions

- Any government can require a review of a decision or action one year after it enters into effect or when changing circumstances justify

Each government involved in a dispute may consult and seek advice from third parties, including interested or knowledgeable persons or groups, at all stages of the process.

Governments will report publicly on an annual basis on the nature of intergovernmental disputes and their resolution.

Role of the Ministerial Council

The Ministerial Council will support sector Ministers by collecting information on effective ways of implementing the agreement and avoiding disputes and receiving reports from jurisdictions on progress on commitments under the Social Union Framework Agreement.

7. REVIEW OF THE SOCIAL UNION FRAMEWORK AGREEMENT

By the end of the third year of the Framework Agreement, governments will jointly undertake a full review of the Agreement and its implementation and make appropriate adjustments to the Framework as required. This review will ensure significant opportunities for input and feedback from Canadians and all interested parties, including social policy experts, private sector and voluntary organizations.

International Covenant on Economic, Social and Cultural Rights

G.A. res. 2200A (XXI), 21 U.N.GAOR Supp. (No. 16) at 49, U.N. Doc. A/6316 (1966), 993 U.N.T.S. 3, entered into force Jan. 3, 1976.

[Note: This copy is for information only.]

PREAMBLE

The States Parties to the present Covenant, considering that, in accordance with the principles proclaimed in the Charter of the United Nations, recognition of the inherent dignity and of the equal and inalienable rights of all members of the human family is the foundation of freedom, justice and peace in the world,

Recognizing that these rights derive from the inherent dignity of the human person,

Recognizing that, in accordance with the Universal Declaration of Human Rights, the ideal of free human beings enjoying freedom from fear and want can only be achieved if conditions are created whereby everyone may enjoy his economic, social and cultural rights, as well as his civil and political rights,

Considering the obligation of States under the Charter of the United Nations to promote universal respect for, and observance of, human rights and freedoms,

Realizing that the individual, having duties to other individuals and to the community to which he belongs, is under a responsibility to strive for the promotion and observance of the rights recognized in the present Covenant,

Agree upon the following articles:

PART I

Article 1

1. All peoples have the right of self-determination. By virtue of that right they freely determine their political status and freely pursue their economic, social and cultural development.

2. All peoples may, for their own ends, freely dispose of their natural wealth and resources without prejudice to any obligations arising out of international economic co-operation, based upon the principle of

mutual benefit, and international law. In no case may a people be deprived of its own means of subsistence.

3. The States Parties to the present Covenant, including those having responsibility for the administration of Non-Self-Governing and Trust Territories, shall promote the realization of the right of self-determination, and shall respect that right, in conformity with the provisions of the Charter of the United Nations.

PART II

Article 2

1. Each State Party to the present Covenant undertakes to take steps, individually and through international assistance and co-operation, especially economic and technical, to the maximum of its available resources, with a view to achieving progressively the full realization of the rights recognized in the present Covenant by all appropriate means, including particularly the adoption of legislative measures.

2. The States Parties to the present Covenant undertake to guarantee that the rights enunciated in the present Covenant will be exercised without discrimination of any kind as to race, colour, sex, language, religion, political or other opinion, national or social origin, property, birth or other status.

3. Developing countries, with due regard to human rights and their national economy, may determine to what extent they would guarantee the economic rights recognized in the present Covenant to non-nationals.

Article 3

The States Parties to the present Covenant undertake to ensure the equal right of men and women to the enjoyment of all economic, social and cultural rights set forth in the present Covenant.

Article 4

The States Parties to the present Covenant recognize that, in the enjoyment of those rights provided by the State in conformity with the present Covenant, the State may subject such rights only to such limitations as are determined by law only in so far as this may be compatible with the nature of these rights and solely for the purpose of promoting the general welfare in a democratic society.

Article 5

1. Nothing in the present Covenant may be interpreted as implying for any State, group or person any right to engage in any activity or to perform any act aimed at the destruction of any of the rights or freedoms recognized herein, or at their limitation to a greater extent than is provided for in the present Covenant.

2. No restriction upon or derogation from any of the fundamental human rights recognized or existing in any country in virtue of law, conventions, regulations or custom shall be admitted on the pretext that the present Covenant does not recognize such rights or that it recognizes them to a lesser extent.

PART III

Article 6

1. The States Parties to the present Covenant recognize the right to work, which includes the right of everyone to the opportunity to gain his living by work which he freely chooses or accepts, and will take appropriate steps to safeguard this right.

2. The steps to be taken by a State Party to the present Covenant to achieve the full realization of this right shall include technical and vocational guidance and training programmes, policies and techniques to achieve steady economic, social and cultural development and full and productive employment under conditions safeguarding fundamental political and economic freedoms to the individual.

Article 7

The States Parties to the present Covenant recognize the right of everyone to the enjoyment of just and favourable conditions of work which ensure, in particular:

(a) Remuneration which provides all workers, as a minimum, with:

(i) Fair wages and equal remuneration for work of equal value without distinction of any kind, in particular women being guaranteed conditions of work not inferior to those enjoyed by men, with equal pay for equal work;

(ii) A decent living for themselves and their families in accordance with the provisions of the present Covenant;

(b) Safe and healthy working conditions;

(c) Equal opportunity for everyone to be promoted in his employment to an appropriate higher level, subject to no considerations other than those of seniority and competence;

(d) Rest, leisure and reasonable limitation of working hours and periodic holidays with pay, as well as remuneration for public holidays.

Article 8

1. The States Parties to the present Covenant undertake to ensure:

(a) The right of everyone to form trade unions and join the trade union of his choice, subject only to the rules of the organization concerned, for the promotion and protection of his economic and social interests. No restrictions may be placed on the exercise of this right other than those prescribed by law and which are necessary in a democratic society in the interests of national security or public order or for the protection of the rights and freedoms of others;

(b) The right of trade unions to establish national federations or confederations and the right of the latter to form or join international trade-union organizations;

(c) The right of trade unions to function freely subject to no limitations other than those prescribed by law and which are necessary in a democratic society in the interests of national security or public order or for the protection of the rights and freedoms of others;

(d) The right to strike, provided that it is exercised in conformity with the laws of the particular country.

2. This article shall not prevent the imposition of lawful restrictions on the exercise of these rights by members of the armed forces or of the police or of the administration of the State.

3. Nothing in this article shall authorize States Parties to the International Labour Organisation Convention of 1948 concerning Freedom of Association and Protection of the Right to Organize to take legislative measures which would prejudice, or apply the law in such a manner as would prejudice, the guarantees provided for in that Convention.

Article 9

The States Parties to the present Covenant recognize the right of everyone to social security, including social insurance.

Article 10

The States Parties to the present Covenant recognize that:

1. The widest possible protection and assistance should be accorded to the family, which is the natural and fundamental group unit of society, particularly for its establishment and while it is responsible for the care and education of dependent children. Marriage must be entered into with the free consent of the intending spouses.

2. Special protection should be accorded to mothers during a reasonable period before and after childbirth. During such period working mothers should be accorded paid leave or leave with adequate social security benefits.

3. Special measures of protection and assistance should be taken on behalf of all children and young persons without any discrimination for reasons of parentage or other conditions. Children and young persons should be protected from economic and social exploitation. Their employment in work harmful to their morals or health or dangerous to life or likely to hamper their normal development should be punishable by law. States should also set age limits below which the paid employment of child labour should be prohibited and punishable by law.

Article 11

1. The States Parties to the present Covenant recognize the right of everyone to an adequate standard of living for himself and his family, including adequate food, clothing and housing, and to the continuous improvement of living conditions. The States Parties will take appropriate steps to ensure the realization of this right, recognizing to this effect the essential importance of international co-operation based on free consent.

2. The States Parties to the present Covenant, recognizing the fundamental right of everyone to be free from hunger, shall take, individually and through international co-operation, the measures, including specific programmes, which are needed:

(a) To improve methods of production, conservation and distribution of food by making full use of technical and scientific knowledge, by disseminating knowledge of the principles of nutrition and by developing or reforming agrarian systems in such a way as to achieve the most efficient development and utilization of natural resources;

(b) Taking into account the problems of both food-importing and food-exporting countries, to ensure an equitable distribution of world food supplies in relation to need.

Article 12

1. The States Parties to the present Covenant recognize the right of everyone to the enjoyment of the highest attainable standard of physical and mental health.

2. The steps to be taken by the States Parties to the present Covenant to achieve the full realization of this right shall include those necessary for:

(a) The provision for the reduction of the stillbirth-rate and of infant mortality and for the healthy development of the child;

(b) The improvement of all aspects of environmental and industrial hygiene;

(c) The prevention, treatment and control of epidemic, endemic, occupational and other diseases;

(d) The creation of conditions which would assure to all medical service and medical attention in the event of sickness.

Article 13

1. The States Parties to the present Covenant recognize the right of everyone to education. They agree that education shall be directed to the full development of the human personality and the sense of its dignity, and shall strengthen the respect for human rights and fundamental freedoms. They further agree that education shall enable all persons to participate effectively in a free society, promote understanding, tolerance and friendship among all nations and all racial, ethnic or religious groups, and further the activities of the United Nations for the maintenance of peace.

2. The States Parties to the present Covenant recognize that, with a view to achieving the full realization of this right:

(a) Primary education shall be compulsory and available free to all;

(b) Secondary education in its different forms, including technical and vocational secondary education, shall be made generally available and accessible to all by every appropriate means, and in particular by the progressive introduction of free education;

(c) Higher education shall be made equally accessible to all, on the basis of capacity, by every appropriate means, and in particular by the progressive introduction of free education;

(d) Fundamental education shall be encouraged or intensified as far as possible for those persons who have not received or completed the whole period of their primary education;

(e) The development of a system of schools at all levels shall be actively pursued, an adequate fellowship system shall be established, and the material conditions of teaching staff shall be continuously improved.

3. The States Parties to the present Covenant undertake to have respect for the liberty of parents and, when applicable, legal guardians to choose for their children schools, other than those established by the public authorities, which conform to such minimum educational standards as may be laid down or approved by the State and to ensure the religious and moral education of their children in conformity with their own convictions.

4. No part of this article shall be construed so as to interfere with the liberty of individuals and bodies to establish and direct educational institutions, subject always to the observance of the principles set forth in paragraph I of this article and to the requirement that the education given in such institutions shall conform to such minimum standards as may be laid down by the State.

Article 14

Each State Party to the present Covenant which, at the time of becoming a Party, has not been able to secure in its metropolitan territory or other territories under its jurisdiction compulsory primary education, free of charge, undertakes, within two years, to work out and adopt a detailed plan of action for the progressive implementation, within a reasonable number of years, to be fixed in the plan, of the principle of compulsory education free of charge for all.

Article 15

1. The States Parties to the present Covenant recognize the right of everyone:

(a) To take part in cultural life;

(b) To enjoy the benefits of scientific progress and its applications;

(c) To benefit from the protection of the moral and material interests resulting from any scientific, literary or artistic production of which he is the author.

2. The steps to be taken by the States Parties to the present Covenant to achieve the full realization of this right shall include those necessary for the conservation, the development and the diffusion of science and culture.

3. The States Parties to the present Covenant undertake to respect the freedom indispensable for scientific research and creative activity.

4. The States Parties to the present Covenant recognize the benefits to be derived from the encouragement and development of international contacts and co-operation in the scientific and cultural fields.

PART IV

Article 16

1. The States Parties to the present Covenant undertake to submit in conformity with this part of the Covenant reports on the measures which

they have adopted and the progress made in achieving the observance of the rights recognized herein.

2. (a) All reports shall be submitted to the Secretary-General of the United Nations, who shall transmit copies to the Economic and Social Council for consideration in accordance with the provisions of the present Covenant;

(b) The Secretary-General of the United Nations shall also transmit to the specialized agencies copies of the reports, or any relevant parts therefrom, from States Parties to the present Covenant which are also members of these specialized agencies in so far as these reports, or parts therefrom, relate to any matters which fall within the responsibilities of the said agencies in accordance with their constitutional instruments.

Article 17

1. The States Parties to the present Covenant shall furnish their reports in stages, in accordance with a programme to be established by the Economic and Social Council within one year of the entry into force of the present Covenant after consultation with the States Parties and the specialized agencies concerned.

2. Reports may indicate factors and difficulties affecting the degree of fulfilment of obligations under the present Covenant.

3. Where relevant information has previously been furnished to the United Nations or to any specialized agency by any State Party to the present Covenant, it will not be necessary to reproduce that information, but a precise reference to the information so furnished will suffice.

Article 18

Pursuant to its responsibilities under the Charter of the United Nations in the field of human rights and fundamental freedoms, the Economic and Social Council may make arrangements with the specialized agencies in respect of their reporting to it on the progress made in achieving the observance of the provisions of the present Covenant falling within the scope of their activities. These reports may include particulars of decisions and recommendations on such implementation adopted by their competent organs.

Article 19

The Economic and Social Council may transmit to the Commission on Human Rights for study and general recommendation or, as appropriate, for information the reports concerning human rights submitted by States in accordance with articles 16 and 17, and those concerning human rights submitted by the specialized agencies in accordance with article 18.

Article 20

The States Parties to the present Covenant and the specialized agencies concerned may submit comments to the Economic and Social Council on any general recommendation under article 19 or reference to such general recommendation in any report of the Commission on Human Rights or any documentation referred to therein.

Article 21

The Economic and Social Council may submit from time to time to the General Assembly reports with recommendations of a general nature and a summary of the information received from the States Parties to the present Covenant and the specialized agencies on the measures taken and the progress made in achieving general observance of the rights recognized in the present Covenant.

Article 22

The Economic and Social Council may bring to the attention of other organs of the United Nations, their subsidiary organs and specialized agencies concerned with furnishing technical assistance any matters arising out of the reports referred to in this part of the present Covenant which may assist such bodies in deciding, each within its field of competence, on the advisability of international measures likely to contribute to the effective progressive implementation of the present Covenant.

Article 23

The States Parties to the present Covenant agree that international action for the achievement of the rights recognized in the present Covenant includes such methods as the conclusion of conventions, the adoption of recommendations, the furnishing of technical assistance and the holding of regional meetings and technical meetings for the purpose of consultation and study organized in conjunction with the Governments concerned.

Article 24

Nothing in the present Covenant shall be interpreted as impairing the provisions of the Charter of the United Nations and of the constitutions of the specialized agencies which define the respective responsibilities of the various organs of the United Nations and of the specialized agencies in regard to the matters dealt with in the present Covenant.

Article 25

Nothing in the present Covenant shall be interpreted as impairing the inherent right of all peoples to enjoy and utilize fully and freely their natural wealth and resources.

PART V

Article 26

1. The present Covenant is open for signature by any State Member of the United Nations or member of any of its specialized agencies, by any State Party to the Statute of the International Court of Justice, and by any other State which has been invited by the General Assembly of the United Nations to become a party to the present Covenant.

2. The present Covenant is subject to ratification. Instruments of ratification shall be deposited with the Secretary-General of the United Nations.

3. The present Covenant shall be open to accession by any State referred to in paragraph 1 of this article.

4. Accession shall be effected by the deposit of an instrument of accession with the Secretary-General of the United Nations.

5. The Secretary-General of the United Nations shall inform all States which have signed the present Covenant or acceded to it of the deposit of each instrument of ratification or accession.

Article 27

1. The present Covenant shall enter into force three months after the date of the deposit with the Secretary-General of the United Nations of the thirty-fifth instrument of ratification or instrument of accession.

2. For each State ratifying the present Covenant or acceding to it after the deposit of the thirty-fifth instrument of ratification or instrument of accession, the present Covenant shall enter into force three months after the date of the deposit of its own instrument of ratification or instrument of accession.

Article 28

The provisions of the present Covenant shall extend to all parts of federal States without any limitations or exceptions.

Article 29

1. Any State Party to the present Covenant may propose an amendment and file it with the Secretary-General of the United Nations. The Secretary-General shall thereupon communicate any proposed amendments to the States Parties to the present Covenant with a request that they notify him whether they favour a conference of States Parties for the purpose of considering and voting upon the proposals. In the event that at least one third of the States Parties favours such a conference, the Secretary-General shall convene the conference under the auspices of the United Nations. Any amendment adopted by a majority of the States Parties present and voting at the conference shall be submitted to the General Assembly of the United Nations for approval.

2. Amendments shall come into force when they have been approved by the General Assembly of the United Nations and accepted by a two-thirds majority of the States Parties to the present Covenant in accordance with their respective constitutional processes.

3. When amendments come into force they shall be binding on those States Parties which have accepted them, other States Parties still being bound by the provisions of the present Covenant and any earlier amendment which they have accepted.

Article 30

Irrespective of the notifications made under article 26, paragraph 5, the Secretary-General of the United Nations shall inform all States referred to in paragraph I of the same article of the following particulars:

(a) Signatures, ratifications and accessions under article 26;

(b) The date of the entry into force of the present Covenant under article 27 and the date of the entry into force of any amendments under article 29.

Article 31

1. The present Covenant, of which the Chinese, English, French, Russian and Spanish texts are equally authentic, shall be deposited in the archives of the United Nations.

2. The Secretary-General of the United Nations shall transmit certified copies of the present Covenant to all States referred to in article 26.

Glossary

1970 White Paper on Unemployment Insurance. The 1970 White Paper on *Unemployment Insurance* recommended an extended and enhanced UI program, including universal coverage for all workers who could be considered employees, increased benefits that should be related to income and lower contributions rates. Sickness and pregnancy benefits were also recommended.

Absolute homelessness. Absolute homelessness is a situation in which an individual or family has no housing at all, or is staying in a temporary form of shelter.

Administrative eligibility. In order to qualify for Social Assistance, applicants are normally required to meet certain administrative criteria. In most provinces, this entails the completion of a formal application, providing evidence that they meet other eligibility criteria (e.g., bank books, pay stubs or doctors' notes), agreeing to meet with a worker in order to discuss his or her situation, etc.

B/U ratio. One way to measure the extent to which unemployed Canadians are covered by Employment Insurance is to calculate the proportion of unemployed who actually receive EI benefits. This is known as the B/U ratio – the ratio of unemployed EI beneficiaries to the unemployed without benefits.

Basic Needs Lines (BNL). In 1992, the Fraser Institute published the Basic Needs Lines (BNL) based on the basic subsistence requirements needed for survival (an absolute approach). They were widely criticized for being below most Canadian's survival expectations.

Beverage Report. The Beverage Report came out of Britain in 1943, the same year as the subsequent Canadian Marsh Report. These reports established the baseline for the rapid expansion of social welfare.

Bill C-12, The New Employment Insurance Act. On January 5, 1995, changes to the Employment Insurance system took effect with Bill C-12, *The New Employment Insurance Act.* The new system replaced the previous Unemployment Insurance system on July 1, 1996.

Bill C-21. The introduction of Bill C-21 in 1990 reversed several of the enhancements of Bill C-229. The Bill increased the number of weeks of work required to receive Unemployment Insurance benefits, reduced the maximum duration of benefits for most regions and reduced the replacement rate from 60 to 50 percent of insurable earnings for those who declined "suitable employment," quit "without just cause" or were fired.

Bill C-229. Bill C-229, introduced early in 1971, completed a revamped UI that followed many of the White Paper recommendations. This was part of Prime Minister Pierre Elliott Trudeau's "Just Society" initiative. Due to these changes, 80 percent of unemployed workers were covered by UI.

Campaign 2000. In 1989, the House of Commons declared its commitment to eliminate poverty among Canadian children by the year 2000. Campaign 2000, an across-Canada public education movement to build Canadian awareness and support for the 1989 all-party House of Commons resolution, reports yearly on the progress towards the goal of eliminating child poverty.

Canada Assistance Plan (CAP). In an effort to consolidate Social Assistance and other income security and social services programs, the federal government introduced a new cost-sharing arrangement with the provinces in 1966 – the Canada Assistance Plan (CAP). CAP brought together a range of cost-shared income security, social services, education and health programs into one system. It also included several national standards.

Canada Child Tax Benefit (CCTB). In 1998 a new initiative called the Canada Child Tax Benefit (CCTB) was introduced. The CCTB has two main elements: a Canada Child Tax Benefit (CCTB) basic benefit, and the National Child Benefit Supplement (NCBS). The NCBS is an additional tax credit that adds to the CCTB and is the federal contribution to the CCTB. It provides low-income families with additional child benefits on top of the basic benefit.

Canada Health and Social Transfer (CHST). Replacing Canada Assistance Plan (CAP) and Established Programs Financing (EPF), the 1996 CHST set the funding formula for Social Assistance, social services, health care services and post-secondary education.

Canada/Quebec Pension Plan (C/QPP). The earnings-based Canada/Quebec Pension Plan (C/QPP) provides a pension upon retirement to persons who have contributed to it. It is a social insurance type of income security program; it insures the contributor against loss of income due to retirement. All employed or self-employed Canadians over the age of 18 make compulsory contributions to the plan (matched by their employer) throughout their working careers. The plan also offers disability, survivor and death benefits, as well as inflation protection. The plan is fully portable from job to job.

Canadian Council for Social Development (CCSD) Income Lines. Canadian Council for Social Development (CCSD) Income Lines stress that poverty is a relative measure. One-half of the average family income constitutes the CCSD income line.

Capitalism. Capitalism is an economic and social system based on a monopoly of the ownership of capital rather than the ownership of land, as in the case of feudalism. Ownership of or access to capital (machinery and equipment, private property and money) provided industrialists with the basis for employing workers at a wage.

Categorical eligibility. Categorical eligibility refers to the different types of reasons why applicants might request Social Assistance. While all applicants are presumed to be in need, different criteria for needs are considered. Criteria can depend on whether the applicant is elderly, disabled, a single parent or otherwise employable.

Child Care Expense Deduction. The Child Care Expense Deduction was first introduced in 1971 and was originally intended for one-parent families. It was designed to offset the incremental costs of child rearing for parents in the labour force.

Child Tax Benefit (CTB). In 1993, the Government of Canada consolidated its child tax credits and the Family Allowance into a single Child Tax Benefit (CTB) that provided a monthly payment based on the number of children and the level of family income. It has now been changed to the CCTB and NCBS.

Child Tax Exemption. Income support to families with children began in 1918 with the introduction of the Child Tax Exemption in personal income tax. The exemption provided income tax savings that increased with taxable income. The after-tax benefit was of greatest absolute benefit to those in the highest tax brackets. The exemption provided no benefits to families that did not owe income tax.

Clawback rule. Programs such as EI, the NCBS and OAS take money back from certain beneficiaries. In the cases of EI and OAS, those with a certain income lose the benefit. With the NCBS, people on welfare have the benefit taken away.

Collective rights. The third category of human rights defines rights at a collective level. This type of rights generally has roots in anti-colonial struggles, environmental activism and the efforts for self-determination of indigenous peoples.

Conservative ideology. The basic values of the conservative ideology are freedom, individualism and social inequality. According to the conservative ideology, the role of government (including interference in the free market economy) should be limited and the role of private property and private enterprise should be paramount.

Conservative/Corporatist Continental Welfare States. Germany, Austria and France typify the conservative/corporatist continental welfare states model. Welfare states following this model provide income maintenance to uphold the status quo and maintain income difference between classes. They are not concerned with eradicating poverty or creating a more egalitarian society.

Consumer Price Index (CPI). The CPI is an indicator of the consumer prices in Canada. It is calculated, on a monthly basis, using the cost of a fixed "basket" of commodities purchased by a typical Canadian consumer during a given month. The CPI is a widely used indicator of inflation (or deflation) and indicates the changing purchasing power of money in Canada.

Contributory negligence. Contributory negligence states that, if the injured worker's own conduct contributed to the injury in even the slightest way, the employer completely escapes legal responsibility. This occurred up until the early 1900s when workers' compensation was introduced.]

Cyclical unemployment. Cyclical unemployment occurs due to a temporary downturn in the job market. The most common form of cyclical unemployment occurs when workers are temporarily laid off.

Deserving poor. A term, originating with the English Poor Laws, used to describe those not physically able to work – that is, the deserving poor or paupers. Many believe that this idea still informs much of social welfare policy towards the poor today.

Discouraged workers. Discouraged workers is the term used to refer to those individuals who are no longer looking for a job because they believe they will not find one. Discouraged workers are classified as not being in the labour force.

Dual-earner families. Currently, families that rely on the income of both partners predominate in Canada. This change has led to a complete revision of family obligations in a very short time and, hence, a great deal of uncertainty.

Economic costs of unemployment. The economic costs of unemployment include loss of output to the economy, loss of tax revenue, increase in government expenditures and loss of profits.

Economic efficiency. Economic efficiency refers to the existence of optimal and stable economic growth with a flexible and productive labour market.

Economic globalization. Economic globalization is the growing integration of international markets for goods, services and finance. It is the latest expression of market liberalism and the latest stage in the development of advanced capitalist economies. This globalization includes the expansion of free trade and investment, the expansion of trade in goods and services between countries, the geographical expansion and increase in power of transnational corporations (TNCs) and the use of agreements between nations and international bodies such as the World Trade Organization (WTO) to protect the rights of TNCs.

Economic theory approach. The economic theory approach, as its name implies, focuses on the influence of economic theories. Economists have differing theories about the root causes of unemployment and poverty that generally revolve around explanations derived from three economic theories: Keynesian economics, monetarism and political economy. Each economic theory has a different view of the role of government and the impacts of social spending on the economy.

Elizabethan Poor Laws. The famous Elizabethan Poor Laws provided the bedrock of the modern welfare states in England, the United States and Canada. In 1601, England passed the Elizabethan poor-relief act, mainly to suppress vagrancy and begging. The Act recognized the state's obligation to those in need, provided for compulsory local levies, and required work for the able-bodied poor. Institutional relief was provided by poorhouses and workhouses. The subsequent amendments of 1834 were based on the belief that pauperism was rooted in an unwillingness to work (rather than from inadequate employment opportunities), and the relief provided to the poor had to be set at a level below that of the poorest laborer.

Employment Insurance (EI). This social insurance type of income security program provides a level of income replacement to those workers who are temporarily out of work and meet strict eligibility conditions.

Employment population ratio. The employment population ratio is the ratio of employed to the working age population.

Employment. Employment includes any activity carried out for pay or profit. It also includes unpaid family work, when it is a direct contribution to the operation of a farm, business or professional practice owned or operated by a related member of the household. Some employed people are self-employed.

Export processing zone. An export processing zone (EPZ) is a particular area in a country from which benefits come in the form of preferential financial regulations and special investment incentives. There are export processing zones all over the world.

Family Allowance (FA). The *Family Allowance Act* of 1944 introduced the universal Family Allowance (FA), providing benefits to all Canadian families with dependent children. The FA was also popularly known as the "baby bonus." It was the first universal income security scheme (ended in 1993).

Family responsibility approach. According to the family responsibility approach, parents are solely responsible for making decisions and providing for their children's well-being. The role of income security and social services is to facilitate decision making and provide support when the family's ability to provide fails.

Family. This textbook uses the term "family" with some caution. Many definitions of families exclude common-law couples, most exclude lone-parent families and pretty well all still exclude same-sex relationships. In Canada today, the term family is defined according to either structural criteria (what they look like) or functional criteria (what they do).

Federalism. Federalism is a system of government in which a number of smaller states (in this case, provinces and territories) join to form a larger political entity while still retaining a measure of political power.

Fellow servant rule. The fellow servant rule maintained that, if a worker's injury was related to a co-worker's negligence, the employer was not responsible. The injured worker could sue the co-worker, but considering the income levels of workers at the time, this was an ineffective option. It also pitted worker against worker. This rule generally applied up until the early 1900s, when workers' compensation was introduced.

Feminization of poverty. Currently, almost 19 percent of adult women live below the Statistics Canada Low Income Cut-off, or LICO (Townson 2000, 1). Women are falling further and further into poverty. The term now commonly used to capture this social phenomenon is the feminization of poverty.

Feudalism. Prior to the fourteenth century, society was based largely on a system of obligations in a primarily agricultural society. This kind of social organization was known as feudalism. Feudalism was both an economic and a social system in which the owner of the property was responsible for the peasants working on the land.

Financial eligibility. To meet the financial eligibility requirement, an applicant must show the need for Social Assistance. A needs test compares the household's assets with its needs. When the cost of a household's needs is greater than its available income, Social Assistance may be granted.

Food banks and feeding programs. With cutbacks in many income security programs, Canadians are having to rely on food banks and feeding programs in order to survive. Food banks are charities that provide groceries, whereas feeding program provide cooked meals.

Fraser Institute Poverty Lines. The Fraser Institute Poverty Lines use an absolute approach. They calculate basic needs for physical survival.

Free trade. Free trade refers to the lowering and dismantling of the barriers and regulations that might impede the international flow of capital and products, or restrict marketplace demand. Free trade is embodied in the growing collection of free trade agreements and international trade organizations, including the General Agreement on Tariffs and Trade

(GATT), the Asia-Pacific Economic Cooperation (APEC) and the North American Free Trade Agreement (NAFTA).

Frictional unemployment. Frictional unemployment occurs when people move between jobs. This includes new labour force entrants, such as those returning to the labour force after completing school or raising children.

Full-time employment. Full-time employment refers to people who usually work 30 or more hours per week, or to people who work less than 30 hours per week but consider themselves to be employed full-time.

G8. The G8 (Group of 8) is a group of eight wealthy countries: Canada, France, Germany, Italy, Japan, Russia, the United Kingdom and the United States. Each year, G8 leaders and representatives from the European Union meet to discuss broad economic and foreign policies.

Gender-based approach. The gender-based approach to social welfare identifies two regime types based on an analysis of the family and unpaid labour: the male-breadwinner regime and the individual earner-carer regime.

Gini coefficient. The Gini coefficient measures the degree of inequality in income distribution. Values of the Gini coefficient can range from 0 to 1. A value of 0 indicates that income is equally divided among the population, with all units receiving exactly the same amount of income. At the opposite extreme, a Gini coefficient of 1 denotes a perfectly unequal distribution, where one unit possesses all of the income in the economy. A decrease in the value of the Gini coefficient can be interpreted as reflecting a decrease in inequality, and vice versa.

Global poverty. According to the World Bank, about one-quarter of the world's population lives on less than $1 per day and over half live on $2 per day. While some people can adequately survive on such meagre incomes given the cost of living in their home countries, many suffer with health problems, low life expectancies, high infant mortality rates, low levels of education and malnutrition.

Global social welfare. Given the new era of globalization, the traditional concerns of social welfare will need to be broadened to include a concern with the issue of global human rights. As noted earlier, global social welfare (a concern with justice, social regulation, social provision and redistribution between nations) is already a part of the activities of various supranational organizations or international governmental organizations of the United Nations.

Great Depression. The economic Depression of the late 1920s and early 1930s was an important event in the rise of income security and social services in Canada. Public perception of the poor began to shift. Massive numbers of people were unemployed, and Canadians began to see that this could not possibly be due to individual fault, but had more to do with the operation of the economy. The idea that help for the poor should be a local or family responsibility was replaced with the idea that the government should be responsible for providing relief to the unemployed.

Guaranteed Income Supplement (GIS). The Guaranteed Income Supplement (GIS) provides extra money to OAS recipients who have little or no other income.

Human Development Index. In 1992, Canada ranked first among all countries in the world on a composite Human Development Index (created by the United Nations Development Programme) that combined life expectancy, educational attainment and standard of living. Canada has recently dropped on this list, primarily due to child poverty and single-mother poverty levels.

Human rights approach to social welfare. The traditional needs-based model of welfare puts emphasis on the assessment of the individual's needs, and then on the process of addressing those needs. The human rights approach, by framing the issue as a person's right to an "adequate standard of living for his or her health and well-being," shifts income security away from a charity model towards the idea of social entitlements as a right of citizenship.

Income security. Income security provides monetary or other material benefits to supplement income or maintain minimum income levels (e.g., Employment Insurance, Social Assistance, Old Age Security and Workers' Compensation).

Indexation. Indexation is an arrangement in which periodic adjustments are made to benefits based on changes in an index of some kind, most often the Consumer Price Index (CPI). Non-indexation of benefits has the effect of reducing the benefit each year by the amount of any increases in the Consumer Price Index (CPI).

Individual earner-carer regimes. Individual earner-carer regimes are based on relations between men and women as shared roles leading to equal rights (Sainsbury 1999, 79). In this model, both sexes have equal rights to social entitlements as earners and caregivers. Paid work in the labour market and unpaid caregiving work have the same benefit entitlements, thereby neutralizing gender differentiation with respect to social rights. The state plays a central role in the provision of services and payments – whether it be caring for children, elderly relatives, the sick or people with disabilities.

Individual responsibility model of the family. The individual responsibility model of the family consists of three main elements: formal gender equality, gender-neutral policies, and equalized caregiving. Within this model, the family unit is still treated as the normal unit of administration, but the husband and wife are seen as equally responsible for the economic well-being of themselves, each other and any children.

Indoor relief. Indoor relief was provided to able-bodied men who were deemed employable. These recipients were obligated to live in a workhouse and undertake work duties in order to receive assistance. The objective was to limit relief and use work as a form of punishment.

Inequality. Inequality is linked to the differences between income groups. The way in which total income in a country is divided between households is a measure of inequality.

Institutional view. In the institutional view, social welfare is a necessary public response that helps people attain a reasonable standard of life and health. Within this view, it is accepted that people cannot always meet all of their needs through family and work. Therefore, in a complex industrial society, it is legitimate to help people through a set of publicly funded and organized systems of programs and institutions. The institutional model is based on the principle that all citizens are unconditionally entitled to a decent standard of living, and it is the role of the state to ensure this standard. The institutional model attempts to even out, rather than promote, economic stratification or status differences.

International Bill of Human Rights. This Bill is the primary basis of United Nations activities to promote, protect and monitor human rights and fundamental freedoms. The Bill comprises three texts: the *Universal Declaration of Human Rights* (1948); the *International Covenant on Economic, Social and Cultural Rights* (1966); and the *International Covenant on Civil and Political Rights* (1966) and its two optional protocols.

International Monetary Fund (IMF). Created in 1945, this international organization aims to promote international monetary cooperation, exchange stability and orderly exchange arrangements, to foster economic growth and high levels of employment, and to provide temporary financial assistance to countries to help ease balance of payments adjustment. Their structural adjustment programs have had many negative impacts on developing countries. At present they have $107 billion loaned out to 56 countries.

Investing in children approach. This approach entails building supports for families and households that enable them to attain positive outcomes for children. There is a recognition that the decisions open to families are increasingly limited and that the options for parents have narrowed insofar as most families need two incomes to adequately provide for themselves and their children.

Keynesians. Keynesians is the name given to the followers of the economic theory of the British economist John Maynard Keynes (1883-1946). His economic theories provided the intellectual rationale for the intervention of governments in economies and the transformation of social policy.

Labour force. The official definition of the labour force is the number of people in the country 15 years of age or over who either have a job or are actively looking for one. This excludes people living on Indian reserves, full-time members of the armed forces and institutional residents (e.g., prison inmates and patients in hospitals or in nursing homes who have resided there for more than six months). Retired people, students, people not actively seeking work and people not available for work for other reasons are also not considered part of the labour force, although they may be part of the working age population.

Labour force participation rate. The ratio of the labour force to the working age population (age 15+) is referred to as the labour force participation rate.

Liberal ideology. The primary values of a liberal ideology are pragmatism, liberty, individualism, social inequality and humanism. Pragmatism means that, as a government or an individual, you do what needs to be done. Liberals have often been described as less ideological conservative, which means they are willing to do things that suit the circumstances, but may not exactly follow "liberal" principles. Liberty, individualism and social inequality are tempered by a concern for justice for the poor. So, competition and markets are tempered by a concern for people and the need for a certain basic level of social security.

Liberal welfare regimes. Liberal welfare regimes include countries such as Canada, the United States, Australia, the United Kingdom and

Ireland. The term as used here refers to classical liberalism that is concerned with laissez-faire economics and minimal government interference.

Low Income Measure (LIM). A Statistics Canada relative poverty indicator that measures low-income rates as one-half of the median income of the country. Because it is a straightforward calculation and can be collected in all nations, it allows for simple comparisons between countries.

Male-breadwinner families. Over the past 30 years, male-breadwinner families have decreased drastically, and now constitute less than 25 percent of the total of all Canadian families.

Male-breadwinner regime. The male-breadwinner regime is characterized by an ideology of male privilege based on a division of labour between the sexes and resulting in unequal benefit entitlements. Men are seen as the family providers and thereby are entitled to benefits based on their labour force participation or their position as "head of the household."

Market Basket Measure (MBM). This new absolute measure of poverty calculates the amount of income needed by a given household to meet its needs based on "credible" community norms.

Market poverty. Market poverty refers to a situation in which a household remains below some measure of poverty, even though one or more members of the household earn a market income or are employed.

Marsh Report. The Report on Social Security for Canada by Leonard Marsh became commonly known as the Marsh Report and detailed the need for comprehensive and universal social welfare programs.

Meredith principle. The Meredith principle, also called the historic compromise, is a compromise in which workers give up the right to sue for work-related injuries, irrespective of fault, in return for guaranteed compensation for accepted claims.

Minimum wage. This is the lowest wage rate, by law, that an employer can pay employees to perform their work. Canada's provinces have all set a standard minimum wage.

Monetarists. The monetarists are a group of economists known for their preoccupation with the role and effects of money in the economy. Monetarist theory asserts that managing the money supply and interest rates (monetary policy) – rather than focusing on fiscal policy – is the key to managing the economy.

National Child Benefit Supplement (NCBS). The National Child Benefit Supplement is an additional tax credit that adds to the Canada Child Tax Benefit (CCTB). The NCBS is the federal contribution to the CCTB. It provides low-income families with additional child benefits on top of the basic benefit.

National Council of Welfare. The National Council of Welfare is a citizens' advisory body on matters of concern to low-income Canadians. It released a 1998 report entitled *Child Benefits: Kids Are Still Hungry.*

Natural unemployment. A combination of frictional and structural unemployment results in what is referred to as natural unemployment or NAIRU (non-accelerating inflation rate of unemployment). According to monetarist economists, attempts to lower unemployment below NAIRU will risk the acceleration or increase of inflation.

NCBS clawback. The distinctive feature of the National Child Benefit Supplement is that, by agreement with the provinces and territories, there is an NCBS clawback for Social Assistance recipients. Only Newfoundland and New Brunswick have increased Social Assistance benefits using NCBS funds. In all other provinces and territories, the supplement is clawed back from Social Assistance recipients in different ways.

Negative rights. The emphasis of negative rights is on protection. They are rights that need to be protected rather than realized through social security or provision. These rights call for inaction on the part of the person or institution fulfilling the rights. The right is met by merely refraining from acting in a way that would violate the right.

Non-profit and for-profit welfare agencies. With government cutbacks in recent years, more and more sources of income security protection are being provided by non-profit and for-profit welfare agencies. Food banks and emergency shelters are increasingly helping people with low incomes, while people with more material means are turning to private (for-profit) pensions and insurance programs to ensure their economic security in the future.

Old Age Security (OAS). The Old Age Security (OAS) program provides a basic pension (adjusted for inflation) to virtually everyone over 65 years of age who has lived in Canada for a required length of time. It is a universal monetary benefit payable to Canadians over a specified age. It is an income transfer program paid out of the general revenue of the federal government.

Outdoor relief. Outdoor relief was provided in place of residence to a select category of recipients: the sick, the aged, the disabled, the orphaned or the widowed – all groups that were seen as deserving of aid. The relief generally came in kind, meaning it was in the form of food, second-hand clothing or fuel.

Parental leave benefits. Important changes to the *Employment Insurance Act* in 2000 increased parental leave benefits from 10 weeks to 35 weeks, increasing the total maternity and parental paid leave time from six months to one year. In addition, the threshold for eligibility was lowered from 700 to 600 hours of insurable employment.

Part-time employment. Part-time employment refers to people who usually work less than 30 hours each week. The involuntary part-time worker prefers full-time work but can only find part-time employment.

Patriarchal model of the family. This model is based on perceptions that were dominant at the turn of the last century, whereby the husband was considered the undisputed master of the family, and the wife was economically and socially beneath her husband. Children were also treated as economic dependants of the husband/father. The wife/mother was seen as responsible for providing care and services to family members without pay. Finally, divorce did not exist (although there were separations not recognized by law).

Pay equity legislation. Refers to legislation (in Canada since the 1970s) that ensures people receive equal pay for work of equal value.

Political economy theorists. Political economy theorists believe that the operation of economic markets is tied to private concentrations of ownership and is essentially exploitative. Most adherents, while not opposed to providing support to those in need, would argue that social spending serves to prop up and justify an unjust economic system. The welfare state, in their view, is seen as one of the contradictions of capitalism: it increases well-being, but it also frustrates the pursuit of a just society. It reinforces the very institutions and values that the welfare state was established to do away with.

Political ideology approach. The political ideology approach situates social welfare in the context of economic, social and political theory – in Canada, this is normally distinguished according to conservative, liberal, social democratic and socialist beliefs.

Poor Law of 1834. The rather harsh Poor Law of 1834 had three main features: it forbade outdoor relief (relief outside the almshouse) for able-bodied persons and their families, it aimed to dramatically cut relief rates and it aimed to tighten administrative rules and clean up what it saw as abuses of the system.

Positive rights. Positive rights imply that the state plays a more positive and active role in ensuring that these rights are realized. A positive right requires action, rather than inaction, on the part of the duty-bearer or the person or institution fulfilling the right. They require the state to play an active role in providing income security and services.

Poverty duration. Poverty duration refers to the length of time that people experience low income. The Statistics Canada Survey of Labour and Income Dynamics (SLID) enables analysis of the duration of poverty. SLID follows the same set of people for six consecutive years and is designed to capture changes in the economic well-being of individuals and families over time.

Poverty gap. The poverty gap is a measurement of how much additional income would be required to raise an individual or household above the LICO or some other measure of poverty. It measures the depth of poverty.

Private welfare. Private welfare can be non-profit or for-profit, and provides "in-kind" benefits to those lacking income. In-kind benefits include such things as food, emergency shelter and other bare necessities. By law, organizations that provide these benefits are often registered, and rules and regulations govern their activities.

Public welfare. Public welfare takes place at the three levels of government: the federal or national government, the provincial and territorial governments and the regional and municipal governments. The various levels of government fund and deliver monetary benefit programs.

Rate of poverty. A variety of measures have been proposed for measuring the rate of poverty. In discussing how much poverty exists, three dimensions need to be considered: *how many* people are poor (the headcount measure), by *how much* they fall below the poverty line (the poverty gap measure) and for *how long* they are poor (the poverty duration measure).

Refundable Child Tax Credit. Beginning in 1978, Finance Minister Jean Chrétien announced a merging of social security programs and income tax provisions. The Liberal government introduced the Refundable Child Tax Credit as a way to target families in need of government assistance. The stated goal of the benefit was to help families meet the costs of raising children. It was income tested and varied according to the number of children in a family.

Relative homelessness. Relative homelessness is a situation in which people's homes do not meet the United Nation's basic housing standards, which are that a dwelling must have adequate protection from the elements, provide access to safe water and sanitation, provide secure tenure and personal safety and not cost more than 50 percent of total income.

Relative measure of poverty. The relative measure of poverty is based on how low one's income is relative to that of other people. This measure reflects the differences in income between the poor and the majority of society, rather than an abstract standard.

Residual view. In the residual view, social welfare is a limited and temporary response to human need, implemented only when all else fails. It is based on the premise that there are two natural ways through which an individual's needs are met: through the family and the market economy. The residual model is based on the idea that government should play a limited role in the distribution of social welfare.

Royal Commission on Aboriginal Peoples. The recent Royal Commission on Aboriginal Peoples issued a Final Report in 1996 that brought together six years of research and public consultation on First Nations issues, including an examination of the need for Aboriginal people to heal from the consequences of domination, displacement and assimilation. The foundation for a renewed relationship, according to the Report, involves recognition of Aboriginal nations as political entities.

Same-sex couples. The Government of Canada defines marriage as the "union of one man and one woman to the exclusion of all others." Same-sex couples are currently fighting for the right to be legally married with all the benefits and responsibilities that opposite-sex couples have.

Selective programs. Selective programs target benefits at those who are in need or eligible, based on a means test (sometimes called an income test) or a needs test.

Self-employment. Self-employed people rely on their own initiative and skills to generate income, and undertake the risks and uncertainties of starting their own businesses.

Seniors Benefit. In 1996, the federal government proposed the Seniors Benefit. This new program would combine the OAS, the GIS and the Spouse's Allowance into one benefit that would be more targeted at seniors with low incomes. Due to extensive pressure from seniors and advocacy groups, the government announced in 1998 that the plans for the Seniors Benefit had been scrapped.

Social Assistance (SA). When a person has no source of income, he or she is entitled to what is commonly known as Social Assistance (SA) (also known as welfare). SA is a province-based minimum income program for people defined as "in need." Strict eligibility criteria, known as a needs test, are applied to determine if people are in need. Social Assistance is a program of last resort with roots in early charity relief and the English Poor Laws.

Social democratic ideology. The key values of social democratic ideology are social equality, social justice, economic freedom and fellowship and cooperation. To the social democrat, social inequality wastes human ability and is inefficient in its distribution of resources. Freedom for social democrats is not only political, it is economic – the kind of freedom that results from government intervention in maintaining a stable economy and stable employment.

Social democratic welfare regimes. Social democratic welfare regimes include countries such as Sweden, Finland and Norway. This model emphasizes citizenship rights and the creation of a universal and comprehensive system of social benefits. The model is focused on optimum conditions for the citizen – as a right.

Social equity. Social equity refers to the existence of adequate levels of health and security for all people, and a reasonably equal distribution of income and wealth.

Social exclusion. Many scholars, particularly in Europe, are increasingly conceptualizing poverty in terms of social exclusion. The concept refers to marginalization – having limited opportunities or abilities to participate in the social, economic and cultural activities society. In short, social exclusion views poverty not as matter of a low degree of well-being, but as the inability to pursue well-being because of the lack of opportunities.

Social inclusion. This concept challenges social welfare scholars to consider the non-economic aspects of society that lead to social disadvantages or social exclusion, such as education, community life, health care access and political participation.

Social insurance scheme. The fundamental element of a modern welfare state is a social insurance scheme. You pay premiums and then have a right to benefits. Employment Insurance and Workers' Compensation are examples.

Social investment state. The social investment state focuses on social inclusion by strengthening civil society and providing equality of opportunity rather than equality of outcomes. Also known as the "third way," it claims that jobs that are *not* low-paying and dead-end are essential to attacking involuntary social exclusion. Nevertheless, an inclusive society must also provide for the basic needs of those who cannot work, and must recognize the wider diversity of goals that life has to offer (Giddens 1998, 31).

Social problem. A situation that is incompatible with some standard or norm held by a significant number of people in society, who agree that action is needed to alter the situation.

Social responsibility model of the family. The social responsibility model of the family directly addresses gender inequality, gender-sensitive policies and the social dimension of caregiving. The model contains minimal gender inequality or stratification. The goal with this model shifts from moving towards a society based on equality to one where inequality is minimized.

Social services. Social services (personal or community services) help people improve their well-being by providing non-monetary help to persons in need. Offered by social workers, services include probation, addiction treatment, youth drop-in centres, parent-child resource centres, child care facilities, child protection services, shelters for abused women and counselling.

Social Union Framework Agreement (SUFA). This 1999 government Act affecting income security and social services aims to smooth out federal-provincial/territorial relations after the fallout from the unilateral discontinuation of CAP and the implementation of the CHST. The SUFA refers to a range of programs such as Medicare, social services and education. It also addresses how these programs are funded, administered and delivered.

Social welfare system. The social welfare system consists of a combination of income security programs and social services.

Socialist ideology. Socialist ideology could be described as emphasizing freedom, collectivism and equality. Socialists believe in equality and a society that operates to meet people's needs. Marx's saying "From each according to their abilities, to each according to their needs" summarizes this view. In short, production should be organized according to social criteria and distributed according to need. Here, equality means the absence of special privilege.

Spouse's Allowance (SPA). The Spouse's Allowance (SPA) was created to deal with a hardship-creating anomaly in the OAS/GIS. In some cases, an elderly couple consisting of a woman under age 65 and an income-earning husband aged 65 would receive OAS and GIS intended for one person. When the woman reached age 65, their income would jump to the OAS/GIS amount intended for married couples. The 1975 SPA intended to correct the anomaly by providing an income-tested benefit to those between 60 and 65 years of age when one spouse is over 65.

Statute of Labourers. The Black Death ravaged Europe between 1347 and 1351 and brought about a serious labor shortage. English laborers took advantage of the situation and demanded higher wages. One response was the Statute of Labourers, which was issued by Edward III in 1351 and directed against the rise in prices and wages.

Structural adjustment. Structural adjustment policies (SAPs) have been imposed by the International Monetary Fund (IMF) on poor countries to ensure debt repayment and economic restructuring. With the stated goals of helping to reduce poverty and promoting economic health, SAPs have often had negative impacts.

Structural unemployment. Structural unemployment is due to mismatches between the skills of the unemployed and the skills necessary for available jobs.

Tax credit. A tax credit is an amount deducted directly from income tax otherwise payable. Examples of tax credits include the disability tax credit and the married credit for individuals, and the scientific research and experimental development investment tax credit for corporations.

Tax deduction. A tax deduction is an amount deducted from total income to arrive at taxable income. Child care expenses and capital cost allowances are tax deductions. Tax deductions are worth more to people with higher incomes as they are in a higher marginal tax bracket.

Tax expenditures. Tax expenditures are foregone tax revenues resulting from special exemptions, deductions, rate reductions, rebates, credits and deferrals that reduce the amount of tax that would otherwise be payable.

Toronto Social Planning Council Budget Guides. This measure combines an absolute shopping basket approach with a relative measure. It calculates an acceptable minimum expenditure for physical survival and social development.

Trade union movement. Trade unions are organizations that represent those individuals working in particular industries or industrial sectors, and they work to defend and advance the interests of these workers in terms of wages and working conditions as well as broader welfare concerns. One in three employees in Canada belongs to a union.

Transnational corporations. Transnational corporations (TNCs) are organizations that possess and control the means of production or services outside of the country in which they were established.

Types of Employment Insurance benefits. There are three main types of Employment Insurance benefits: (1) regular benefits, (2) maternity/parental and sickness benefits and (3) fishing benefits. Regular benefits are paid to people who have lost their job and want to return to work. In addition to regular benefits, Employment Insurance provides maternity/parental and sickness benefits to individuals who are pregnant, have recently given birth, are adopting a child, are caring for a newborn baby or are sick. Sickness benefits may be paid for up to 15 weeks to a person who is unable to work because of sickness, injury or quarantine.

Underemployment. Underemployment occurs when the education and training required for the job is less than the education and training of the worker who is doing the job. Evidence indicates that underemployment increases as higher quality jobs become relatively fewer in number.

Undeserving poor. In early English Poor Laws, those physically able to work were considered undeserving and were forced to work by law. Today, a similar concept persists.

Unemployment rate. The unemployment rate is the percentage of the labour force that is unemployed.

Universal benefits. Universal benefits are available to everyone in a specific category (such as people over age 65 and children), on the same terms and as a right of citizenship.

Universal Declaration of Human Rights (UDHR). The 1948 *Universal Declaration of Human Rights* (UDHR) defines the fundamental expectations for freedom and dignity in a free and just society. Accepted human rights include freedom of expression, freedom of association, freedom from fear and persecution and freedom of religion, as well as the right to shelter, education, health and work, among others.

Vanier Institute of the Family. The Vanier Institute of the Family is a national, charitable organization dedicated to promoting the well-being of Canadian families. It uses a functional definition of the family that emphasizes the activities of family members.

Visible minorities. Visible minorities are defined as being neither Caucasian nor Aboriginal. Members of visible minority groups now make up about 11 percent of the total Canadian population, compared to just 6 percent as recently as 1986.

Voluntary assumption of risk. One of the early principles used to define the relationship between employers and employees. The voluntary assumption of risk meant that the worker assumed the usual risks of the job, and the rate of pay for each job was assumed to reflect its level of risk. The principle is based on the assumption that contracts between workers and their employers are the same as commercial contracts between people of equal bargaining power.

Welfare fraud. Often exaggerated, fraud within the Social Assistance or welfare systems occurs when applicants are being deceptive in order to receive benefits. Almost half of the fraud cases in Ontario were instances of people collecting welfare while in prison. Many of the other reported frauds were overpayments and administrative errors, or cases where documents were missing.

Welfare state approach. The welfare state approach classifies welfare states according to how social welfare is provided in a given society.

Welfare wall. The term welfare wall refers to barriers that hinder the movement from reliance on Social Assistance to participation in the labour market.

Workers' Compensation. Workers' Compensation is a collection of provincial social insurance programs for employers and workers, established to replace the tort system (the courts) in determining compensation for workplace injuries and health-related risks. It provides no-fault compensation.

Workfare. Workfare takes many different forms – it could mean that a person must take a job to get their social assistance cheque or it could mean that people receive a smaller cheque if they refuse to do so. It could also involve mandatory community volunteer work or self-employment.

Workhouses. Erected as private enterprises, seventeenth-century workhouses were officially called almshouses. Able-bodied applicants for poor relief were forced to report to the workhouse to complete work tasks in order to obtain assistance.

Working Income Supplement (WIS). In addition to a basic benefit, the 1993 Child Tax Benefit included a Working Income Supplement (WIS) to supplement the earnings of working poor families.

Working poor. The low-wage earners or working poor are people who are participating in the labour force through paid employment, but do not earn enough income to lift them above the poverty line.

World Bank. The World Bank Group's mission is to fight poverty and improve the living standards of people in the developing world. It provides loans, policy advice, technical assistance and knowledge-sharing services to low- and middle-income countries to reduce poverty.

World Trade Organization (WTO). The WTO is a global international organization dealing with the rules of trade between nations. In this new era of globalization, the rules for the global economy that were once made by national governments are increasingly being made by international organizations such as the WTO (see: www.wto.org).

Youth unemployment. Youth unemployment refers to Canadians under of the 18 who are without a job, but want one.

Index